Y^r Affectionate Friend
J. C. Philpot

THROUGH

BACA'S VALE;

OR,

DAILY WORDS

FOR

ZION'S WAYFARERS.

SELECTED FROM THE WORKS OF

J. C. PHILPOT

BY HIS DAUGHTERS.

Blessed is the man whose strength is in thee; in whose heart are the ways of them. Who passing through the valley of Baca make it a well; the rain also filleth the pools. They go from strength to strength, every one of them in Zion appeareth before God.—PSALM lxxxiv. 5, 6, 7.

OXFORD:

GOSPEL STANDARD TRUST PUBLICATIONS

1992

7 Brackendale Grove, Harpenden, Herts AL5 3EL
England

First Edition 1893
Reprinted 1962, 1978, 1992

ISBN 0 903556 22 7

Printed and bound in Great Britain by
Biddles Ltd, Guildford and King's Lynn

PREFACE.

————••————

Some years ago, as is well known to most of our readers, we published a series of extracts in the form of Daily Portions from the works of our late dear Father, J. C. Philpot, which received a welcome far, far more cordial than we had ventured to hope or expect. Indeed, the numerous testimonies that have reached us again and again, from various quarters, of the blessing of God richly attending the perusal of these Portions have made our hearts burn within us, and the thought that He should condescend to put His seal of approbation upon our labours may well excite the deepest humility and gratitude.

Now, with mixed feelings of pleasure and regret, we find the edition is rapidly coming to an end, and as several friends have expressed a wish for another series of Portions culled from the same source, we thought, as there still remained sufficient material to draw upon, that we should prefer to bring out another book rather than merely reprint the former. That the present volume is larger and contains more matter will be seen at a glance : the fact is, all the suitable short pieces were selected for the earlier one, consequently, these in most cases are longer, which, under the circumstances, was unavoidable, but we trust that even the busiest may be able to spare a few minutes to read the portion for the day : if it is a little long, may it be found proportionately seasonable and weighty, refreshing to a weary spirit—a word of encouragement or exhortation to pilgrims journeying Zionwards.

As a frontispiece, a collotype portrait has been added, copied from the most pleasing photograph we possess of our dear Father. This we thought would be valued, not only by those who knew him personally, but by a new generation, who would doubtless like to have some idea of the outward form and features of one whom, though they never saw him in the flesh, they love and esteem for his works' sake.

It may be observed in this as in the former volume that some of the pieces begin and end rather abruptly, but it must be remembered that they were not written for the purpose to which they are now applied, as was the case with Mason's and Hawker's Portions, but are merely extracts gathered, as the title of the earlier work suggested, from those sheaves which have been garnered for the use and edification of the Household of Faith.

In conclusion, we can only express our earnest desire and prayer that the Lord God of Sabaoth may again be graciously pleased to smile upon our efforts, and continue to bless the words of His late dear servant, who "being dead, yet speaketh," to the souls of His living family, and His name shall have all the praise.

S. & D. M. PHILPOT.

Croydon, 1893.

THROUGH BACA'S VALE;

OR,

DAILY WORDS FOR ZION'S WAYFARERS.

January 1.

" Hold up my goings in thy paths, that my footsteps slip not."—Psalm xvii. 5.

WITHOUT scrupulously or superstitiously observing " days, and months, and times, and years," few of us altogether pass by so marked an epoch as the dawning of another year upon our path without some acknowledgment of it both to God and man. When we open our eyes on the first morning of the year, we almost instinctively say, " This is New-year's day." Nor is this, at least this should not be, all the notice we take, all the acknowledgment we make of that opening year of which we may not see the close. When we bend our knees before the throne of grace, we mingle with thankful acknowledgment for the mercies of the past year, both in providence and in grace, earnest petitions for similar mercies to be experienced and enjoyed through the present. Last evening witnessed our confessions of the many, many grievous sins, wanderings, backslidings, and departings from the living God during the year now gone ; this morning witnesses our supplications for grace to hold up our goings in his paths, that our footsteps slip not through the year just come. Tears are most suitable at the burial of the dead ; hopes and

desires at the birth of the living. The past year was the
departed sire, worn out with age and infirmity; the present
year the new-born babe in the arms of the smiling nurse. It
is still, however, mid-winter. To-day, the first of the present
year, differs little in outward appearance from yesterday, the
last of the past. But the thoughtful, prayerful mind takes
little notice of wintry skies. It feels that the old, worn-out
year has sunk into its grave, with all its trials and afflictions,
and that a new year has come in its place, with its new hopes
and new mercies; and if it bring new trials, yet that the
promise still stands, that new strength will be given to meet
and overcome them. Refreshed and strengthened at the
throne by such or similar communings with the God of all
our mercies, we go down to meet our families, and are at
once greeted on all sides with, "I wish you a happy new
year," a greeting which we as warmly and affectionately
return. Almost every friend, well-nigh every acquaintance
that we meet with in the course of the day, greets us with
the same kind wish. Now in all this there may be a great
deal of formality, lip-service, and traditional usage ; but there
may be also a good deal of sincerity, kindness, and affection.
We are not, surely, so shut up in miserable self as to have no
desire for the health and happiness, the temporal and spiritual
welfare, of our families, our friends, or even our acquaintances.
And if we desire their good, we need not be backward or unwilling to express it in a few words of friendly greeting. "Be
ye kind one to another, tender-hearted;" "Be pitiful, be
courteous;" "If it be possible, as much as lieth in you, live
peaceably with all men," are precepts imbued with all the
spirit of the gospel, and may be, indeed, should be, attended
to without the least sacrifice of that faithfulness which becomes those who would daily walk in the fear of the Lord.
There may be a form of kind words as well as " a form of
sound words;" and as we may use the latter in perfect har-

mony with the doctrines of the gospel, so we may use the former in perfect harmony with the spirit of the gospel.

January 2.

" But grow in grace, and in the knowledge of our Lord and Saviour Jesus Christ."—2 PETER iii. 18.

GROWTH is the sure mark of life. We see this in vegetation, in the animal creation, in the growth of our own bodies, and of every other thing in which there is life. Where, then, there is the life of God in the soul, there will be a growth in that life. Paul says to the Thessalonian Church : " We are bound to thank God always for you, brethren, as it is meet, because that your faith groweth exceedingly" (2 Thess. i. 3) ; and Peter says, " But grow in grace, and in the knowledge of our Lord and Saviour Jesus Christ." There is " an increasing in the knowledge of God " (Col. i. 10), and "a coming in the unity of the faith, and of the knowledge of the Son of God, unto a perfect man, unto the measure of the stature of the fulness of Christ " (Eph. iv. 13). It was for this increasing knowledge of the Son of God that Paul stretched every desire of his soul when he followed after, if that he might apprehend that for which also he was apprehended of Christ Jesus ; and thus reaching forth unto those things which were before, he pressed toward the mark, for the prize of the high calling of God in Christ Jesus (Phil. iii. 12–14). This is not what is called progressive sanctification, as if the flesh got holier and holier, for that is still ever " the old man, which is corrupt according to the deceitful lusts ; " but this is a growth of that " new man, which after God is created in righteousness and true holiness." After this growth in grace, this closer conformity to the image of Christ, should we ever be striving with all the powers of our soul ; not satisfied with a low and lean state before God, but with unceasing prayer and supplication, begging of the Lord

that we might be "filled with the knowledge of his will in all
wisdom and spiritual understanding, that we might walk
worthy of the Lord, unto all pleasing, being fruitful in every
good work, and increasing in the knowledge of God"
(Colossians i. 9, 10).

January 3.

"I will sing of the mercies of the Lord for ever."—Psalm
lxxxix. 1.

WE are surrounded with mercies; mercies for the body,
and mercies for the soul. There are indeed times and
seasons when all the mercies of God, both in providence
and grace, seem hidden from our eyes, when, what with the
workings of sin, rebellion, and unbelief, with a thorny path
in the world, and a rough, trying road in the soul, we see
little of the mercies of God, though surrounded by them.
Like Elisha's servant, though the mountain is surrounded by
the horses and chariots of fire, and the angels of God are
round about us, yet our eyes are holden, we cannot see
them; and at the very moment when God is already
showering mercies upon us, and preparing others in reserve,
through some trying dispensation, we are filled, perhaps, with
murmuring and rebellion, and cry, "Is his mercy clean gone
for ever, will he be favourable no more?" This is our
infirmity, our weakness; but it no more arrests the shower
of God's mercies than the parched field arrests the falling
rain. The mercies of God, like himself, are infinite, and he
showers them in rich profusion upon his Church and people.
They come freely as the beams of the sun shining in the
sky; as the breezes of the air we breathe; as the river that
never ceases to flow. Everything testifies of the mercy of
God to those whose eyes are anointed to see it, and are
interested in it. To them all things in nature, in providence,
and in grace, proclaim with one united harmonious voice,

" The mercy of the Lord endureth for ever." Now, as these mercies of God are sensibly felt in the soul, they soften, meeken, and subdue the spirit, melt it into the obedience of faith, and raise up in it the tenderness of love. By this we are prepared to enter into the beauty and blessedness of the precept as an integral part of the gospel. If I take a review of the mercies of God, and feel no interest in them ; if they are not personally and individually mine, I slight, perhaps even rebel, against the precept as too hard and severe. The yoke is too heavy for my neck to bear. My Jewish mind, my stiff-necked disposition, shrinks from obedience to God's word. But let my soul be favoured with a sweet discovery of the mercies of God ; let them reach my heart, soften and subdue my spirit, then there is no cross too heavy to be taken up, no trial too hard to be endured, no path of suffering and sorrow in which we cannot patiently, if not gladly, walk. The reason why the precepts are not obeyed is because the mercies of God are not felt. Love and obedience attend each other as the shadow waits upon the sun.

January 4.

" Confirming the souls of the disciples, and exhorting them to continue in the faith, and that we must through much tribulation enter into the kingdom of God."—ACTS xiv. 22.

THE very word " confirm " implies that the souls of Christ's disciples need strengthening. If there were no temptations to try, no sharp sorrows to grieve, no painful afflictions to distress them ; or if, on the other hand, there were no sensible weakness of soul, no sinking of heart, no despondency of spirit, no giving way of faith and hope, no doubt or fear in the mind, how could the souls of the disciples be strengthened ? The souls of God's people are not made of cast iron, against which arrow after arrow may

be discharged and leave no dent, make no impression. The
hearts of the Lord's people are in a measure conformed to
the heart of Christ. And what was his heart ? " My heart,"
he says, " is like wax; it is melted in the midst of my
bowels." And thus the Lord's people, who carry in their
bosom broken hearts and contrite spirits, made so by grace,
are often sinking, often shaken, often cast down through the
many trials they have to encounter. It is for this reason
that they need confirming, supporting, strengthening, and
that the Lord himself would lay his everlasting arms underneath them, lift them into his bosom, and make his strength
perfect in their weakness. And is not this the gospel way ?
Can I, by dint of creature exertion, brace up my soul to a
certain pitch ? If trouble come, am I like a patient sometimes under the keen knife of the surgeon to brace up my
nerves to bear the operation more unflinchingly ? This is
nature, flesh, reason; not grace. The Lord does not
require this of his people. He dealt not so with his beloved Apostle, according to the account which he gives in
2 Corinthians xii. What did the Lord speak into his heart,
under trial and temptation, that he might proclaim it upon
Zion's walls to the Church of the living God, " My grace is
sufficient for thee; for my strength is made perfect in weakness." Therefore, he adds, "Most gladly therefore will I
rather glory in my infirmities, that the power of Christ may
rest upon me." But it is very painful to the Lord's people
to find no strength when they want it most, no faith when
they have the greatest need of it, no help when most required.
To pass through this experience baffles and disconcerts many
of the living family; but when the Lord is pleased in a
mysterious way to communicate his own strength, and to
make it perfect in weakness; when he deals with them, as
with the worthies of old, who " out of weakness were made
strong," they can then bless the Lord for their very weak-

ness, and, like Paul, glory in their infirmities, because the power of Christ rests upon them.

January 5.

" Through the tender mercy of our God; whereby the day-spring from on high hath visited us, to give light to them that sit in darkness and in the shadow of death, to guide our feet into the way of peace."—LUKE i. 78, 79.

THERE is a way of peace, and that is the Lord Jesus Christ. For he is " our peace," and " the way," and therefore the way of peace. He has made peace through the blood of his cross (Col. i. 20), having slain the enmity thereby, and came and preached peace to them which were afar off, "sitting in darkness and the shadow of death," and to them that were nigh (Eph. ii. 16, 17). The dayspring, then, breaking in upon the soul, shines upon the way of peace, and guides the feet into it. The light shines upon the way lined with blood, the way of salvation through the finished work, atoning blood, and meritorious sufferings of the Son of God. As, then, the light shines upon the way, and it is seen as a way of peace, a way of pardon and reconciliation, a way of access and acceptance, a way of grace and glory, a way of life and happiness, the feet of faith move towards it, enter upon it, and walk in it. This is a peace that passeth all understanding, a peace which the world cannot give or take away, a holy calm, a gracious subduing of all rebellion; and that power which once said to the boiling waves and howling winds that chafed their whitened crests into a succession of billows, "Peace, be still!" does it all. How great the change! Instead of war with God, to be at peace; to see by the eye of faith that the whole way from earth to heaven, as revealed in the Person and work of the Son of God, is peace from first to last, and

that as long as the feet are moving in that path they are
walking in a way of peace here and hereafter. O to know,
feel, and enjoy more of this peace, the peace of which Jesus
said, " Peace I leave with you, my peace I give unto you!"
The only peace is peace in believing, peace through atoning
blood, peace by walking in sweet communion with Father,
Son, and Holy Ghost. Nor are we left ignorant how it is
to be attained and maintained : " Be careful for nothing ;
but in everything by prayer and supplication, with thanksgiving, let your requests be made known unto God. And
the peace of God, which passeth all understanding, shall
keep your hearts and minds through Christ Jesus" (Philippians iv. 6, 7).

January 6.

" O God, thou art my God ; early will I seek thee."—
PSALM lxiii. 1.

DAVID here speaks of seeking God for what *he is in himself* as distinct from what he has to give. His gifts are one
thing, himself is another. Therefore he says, " O God, thou
art my God ; early will I seek *thee ;*" thee as distinct from
thy gifts. The bride may value her bridegroom's costly
gifts ; but what are his gifts apart from himself? So the
Church highly prizes her royal Husband's gifts and blessings ;
but what are these compared to Him who, in her admiring
eyes, is the chiefest among ten thousand and altogether
lovely ? Thus, as seen by the eye of faith, there is that in
his most blessed Majesty which alone can satisfy the soul
taught by his Spirit and influenced by his grace. The soul
was made *for* him ; it was gifted with immortality *by* him.
Powers and faculties were given to it that might be expanded
into an infinite capacity to know and to enjoy him. So that
being created for God, nothing but God can really satisfy its

cravings and desires. But there is that in him, as revealed to a believing heart, which can satisfy. His favour is life; his presence heaven begun; his love a foretaste of eternal bliss. Thus in seeking the blessings he has to bestow, we do not seek them independent of the Giver. We love the gift, but we prize the Giver more. Without the Giver, the gift would be worthless. The bridal ring is the pledge of union. But what would be the ring without the bridegroom? Mockery. So all the favours and blessings which the Lord has to bestow, if he gave all and withheld himself, would be but to mock us. But in giving them, he gives himself. As when the bridegroom puts the ring on the finger of his betrothed he gives himself with the gift; so when the Lord seals a sense of his espousal upon the heart of his beloved one, in giving his love he gives himself. Nor can anything else satisfy the desires of an awakened soul. "It is Jesus," it says, "that I want; without him, heaven itself would be hell; without him, life would not be life, nor glory be glory, nor immortality be immortality!" As without the sun, the earth could not exist; so the Church could not exist without Jesus. And as in the absence of the sun, no tapers could take the place of heaven's own glorious light; so no sparks, however bright, of fires kindled by human hands, could make up to the Church for the absence of the Sun of righteousness. He must be, as he is, our all; having him, we have everything; not having him, we have nothing. The Lord the Spirit write that truth deeply upon your heart that you may take it wherever you go, and make it ever your bosom companion. If you have Jesus, you have everything; if you have not him, you have nothing. This continual feeling of happiness in and with him, and of misery out of and without him, as maintained in your breast by the power of the blessed Spirit, will be leading you to seek him perpetually. This made David say, "Early will I seek thee."

January 7.

" Let us lift up our heart with our hands unto God in the heavens."—LAMENTATIONS iii. 41.

WHEN the Lord lays judgment to the line, and righteousness to the plummet, when he makes the living man complain on account of deserved chastisement for his sins, and thus brings him to search and try his ways, he raises up an earnest cry in his soul. " Let us lift up our heart with our hands," and not the hands without the heart ; not the mere bended knee ; not the mere grave and solemn countenance, that easiest and most frequent cover of hypocrisy; not the mere form of prayer, that increasing idol of the day, but the lifting up of the heart with the hand. This is the only true prayer, when the heart is poured out before the throne of grace, the Spirit interceding for us and within us with groanings that cannot be uttered. " God is a Spirit; and they that worship him must worship him in spirit and in truth." The contrite heart and broken spirit, the inward panting of the soul after his manifested presence, the heaving sigh and penitential tear will be regarded by him, when he will turn away from lip-service and bodily exercise.

But there is much also implied in the words, "*God in the heavens.*" This expression represents him as seated far above all heavens, enthroned in light, majesty, and glory unspeakable ; and yet sitting on his throne of mercy and grace to bless the soul that waits upon him, full of love and compassion for the poor and needy one that lifts up his heart together with the hand, that he may receive pardon and peace out of Jesu's fulness, and pants with unutterable longings that the Lord himself would graciously smile and beam love and favour into his soul. This lifting up of the heart—the only true and acceptable prayer—no man can create in himself. God, who works all things after the counsel of his own will, can alone work in us thus "to will and to do of his own good pleasure." Nature cannot, with all her efforts, and all her counterfeit imitations of vital godliness, accomplish this spiritual sacrifice. She may cut her flesh with lancets, and cry, "Baal, hear us," from morning till evening, but she cannot bring down the holy fire from heaven. She can lift the hand, but she cannot lift up the heart. Depend upon it that in this spiritual intercourse with the living God, out of the sight and out of the reach of the most refined hypocrite and self-deceiver, much of the power of vital godliness lies. This lifting up of the heart when no eye sees and no ear hears, in the daily and often hourly transactions of life, in the lonely chamber, and on the midnight bed, surrounded perhaps by the world, and yet in spirit separate from it, is a secret known only to the living family of God.

January 8.

"*And I will pray the Father, and he shall give you another Comforter, that he may abide with you for ever; even the Spirit of truth; whom the world cannot receive, because it seeth him not, neither knoweth him: but ye know him; for he dwelleth with you, and shall be in you.*"—JOHN xiv. 16, 17.

THE holy Comforter and most gracious Spirit does not take up a temporary abode in the heart of the Lord's people. Where he once takes up his dwelling, there he for ever dwells and lives. "He shall give you another Comforter, that *he may abide with you for ever*." Oh, the blessing! Where once that holy Dove has lighted, there that Dove abides. He does not visit the soul with his grace, and then leave it to perish under the wrath of God, or allow his work to wither, droop, and die. But where he has once come into the soul with power, there he fixes his continual habitation, for he makes the bodies of the saints his temple. He consecrates them to the service of God. He takes up his dwelling in their hearts; there he lives, there he moves, there he works, and sanctifies body and soul to the honour and glory of the Lord God Almighty.

And oh, what a blessing it is to have received the same gracious and heavenly Teacher as *the Spirit of truth!* If this be your happy case, you know the truth for yourself, and the truth is dear to your soul; it has been ingrafted by a divine witness in your heart, and inlaid by the power of God in your conscience. The truth as it is in Jesus is very, very precious to you. You cannot part with it; it is your very life. Sooner than part with God's truth and your interest therein, you would be willing in favoured moments to lay down your life itself. But what makes you love God's truth? What has given you a heart to embrace and delight in it; and when you have come to the house of prayer, it may be with a fainting body and a troubled mind, has yet supported your weary steps and brought you on; or when you have gone home from hearing the word, has cheered your heart in the dark and gloomy night as you have lain upon your bed, and drawn your affections up to the Lord Jesus Christ? The Comforter, the Spirit of truth. He, and he alone, could give it so firm and enduring a place in your heart, conscience, and affections.

Then live that truth as well as love it, and proclaim its power and efficacy in your life and conversation. If the Spirit has written his truth upon your heart, he will bring forth that truth in your lips and in your life. He will make it manifest that you are "children that cannot lie." You will shew forth the power of truth, in the sincerity of your speech, in the uprightness of your movements, in your family, in the Church, in your business, in your general character and deportment, and in everything which stamps the reality of religion and the power of vital godliness.

January 9.

" Knowing this first, that no prophecy of the scripture is of any private interpretation. For the prophecy came not in old time by the will of man : but holy men of God spake as they were moved by the Holy Ghost."—2 PETER i. 20, 21.

THE Bible is put into our hands as a revelation from God. As such we have received it from our fathers. As such, and as such only, does it claim our attention and our obedience. If it is not the word of God—we speak with reverence— it is an imposture. Now, if we can but firmly establish the *necessity* of a revelation from God, we have laid a strong foundation for a belief that the Bible is that revelation; for no other is worth a moment's examination. This argument from necessity, then, is very strong, stronger, perhaps, than it at first appears, and as extensive in application as firm in strength. To feel the force of this argument, cast your eyes for a few moments over creation, and see what a provision has been made everywhere by its All-wise and All-powerful Creator for necessity. From man, at the head of creation, down to the lowest organised structure, there is not a neces- sity for which provision has not been made, and that in exact proportion to its wants. You yourself came into this world a poor, naked, helpless infant, full of necessities, and must have perished from the womb unless provision had been made for them. Who filled for you your mother's breast with milk and your mother's heart with love? But you have a soul as well as a body—no less naked, no less necessitous. Shall, then, the body have its necessities, and these be pro- vided for, and shall the soul have its necessities too, and for these there be no provision made? Is there no milk for the soul as well as for the body? no "sincere milk of the word that it may grow thereby?" The craving after God felt by every new-born soul, the eagerness with which it flies at

once to get comfort and instruction from the word, the holy
joy with which it hails every ray of heavenly light that shines
on its dark path, evidently shew how deep the necessity of
a divine revelation is laid in the relationship between man
and his Maker.

January 10.

*"Bless the Lord, O my soul: and all that is within me,
bless his holy name."*—PSALM ciii. 1.

As the Son has glorified the Father and the Father has
glorified the Son, so there is a people in whom both the
Father and the Son will be glorified. He therefore said,
"And the glory which thou gavest me I have given them;
that they may be one, even as we are one" (John xvii. 22);
and again, "And all mine are thine, and thine are mine;
and I am glorified in them." When, then, God's goodness
and mercy in the face of Jesus Christ are manifested to this
people whom he has formed for himself that they might shew
forth his praise, then they give him back his glory. But how
is this done? By praising and blessing his holy name for
the manifestation of his goodness and mercy to their soul.
We thus see in what a blessed circle this glory runs. The
Father glorifies the Son; the Son glorifies the Father; both
unite in glorifying his chosen and redeemed people; and
they glorify Father and Son by giving them the glory due to
their name. We therefore read that "the Gentiles glorify
God for his mercy." But how? "Rejoice, ye Gentiles,
with his people. Praise the Lord, all ye Gentiles; and laud
him, all ye people" (Romans xv. 9-11). This is beautifully
developed in Psalm ciii. It begins with blessing and praising
God. "Bless the Lord, O my soul: and all that is within
me, bless his holy name. Bless the Lord, O my soul, and
forget not all his benefits." Why was it that David called
upon his soul to bless the Lord—yea, appealed to every

faculty within him to unite in blessing his holy name?
Why did he charge it upon his soul not to forget all God's
benefits, but bear them in perpetual remembrance? For
this reason, that he might render unto God a tribute of
thankful praise. Now by this God is glorified, for whoso
offereth praise glorifieth him. We cannot add to his glory;
for his glory is above the heavens. It is infinite, eternal,
ineffable. No creature therefore can add to it or take from
it; but he does permit poor worms of earth to glorify him by
giving him a tribute of thankful praise. But this we can
only do by believing in his dear Son, receiving of his fulness
grace for grace, and blessing and praising his holy name for
the manifestation of his goodness, mercy, and love, as brought
into our soul by his own divine power.

January 11.

" Preserved in Jesus Christ, and called."—JUDE 1.

WHAT a mercy it is for God's people that before they have
a vital union with Christ, before they are grafted into him
experimentally, they have an eternal, immanent union with
him before all worlds. It is this eternal union that brings
them into time existence. It is by virtue of this eternal
union that they come into the world at such a time, at such
a place, from such parents, under such circumstances, as
God has appointed. It is by virtue of this eternal union
that the circumstances of their time-state are ordained. By
virtue of this eternal union they are preserved in Christ
before they are called; they cannot die till God has brought
about a vital union with Christ. Whatever sickness they
may pass through, whatever injuries they may be exposed
to, whatever perils assault them on sea or land, fall they
will not, fall they cannot, till God's purposes are executed in
bringing them into a vital union with the Son of his love.
Thus, this eternal union watched over every circumstance of

their birth, watched over their childhood, watched over their manhood, watched over them till the appointed time and spot, when "the God of all grace," according to his eternal purpose, was pleased to quicken their souls, and thus bring about an experimental union with the Lord of life and glory.

January 12.

" But we are bound to give thanks alway to God for you, brethren beloved of the Lord, because God hath from the beginning chosen you to salvation through sanctification of the Spirit and belief of the truth."—2 THESSALONIANS ii. 13.

THERE is the impartation of righteousness, as well as the imputation of it ; and the impartation of it is the communication of a divine nature to the soul. Have I one grain of holiness in myself ? Not one. Can all the men in the world, by all their united exertions, raise up a grain of spiritual holiness in their hearts ? Not an atom, with all their efforts. If all the preachers in the world were to unite together for the purpose of working a grain of holiness in one man's soul, they might strive to all eternity : they could no more by their preaching create holiness, than by their preaching they could create a lump of gold. But because, by a gracious act of God the Father, Jesus is made unto his people sanctification, he imparts a measure of his own holiness to them. He works in them to will and to do of his own good pleasure ; he sends the Holy Spirit, to raise up holy desires : in a word, he communicates a nature perfectly holy, which therefore loves holiness, and has communion with a holy God ; a heavenly, spiritual, and divine nature, which bathes in eternal things as its element, and enjoys spiritual things as sweet and precious. It may indeed be small in measure ; and he that has it is often exercised and troubled because he has so little of it ; yet he has enough just to know what it is. Has not your soul, though you feel

to be a defiled wretch, though every iniquity is at times
working in your heart, though every worm of obscenity and
corruption is too often trailing its filthy slime upon your
carnal mind—has it not felt, does it not sometimes feel, a
measure of holiness Godward? Do you never feel a breathing forth of your soul into the bosom of a holy God?
Heavenly desires, pure affections, singleness of eye, simplicity of purpose, a heart that longs to have the mind,
image, and likeness of Jesus stamped upon it—this is a holiness such as the Lord of life and glory imparts out of his
fulness to his poor and needy family.

January 13.

" The Lord bless thee."—NUMBERS vi. 24.

THE key to the words, "The Lord bless thee," is, I
believe, to be found in Ephesians i. 3: "Blessed be the God
and Father of our Lord Jesus Christ, who hath blessed
us with *all spiritual blessings* in heavenly places in Christ;"
for the blessings prayed for in our text would seem to
be chiefly spiritual blessings. Not that we are to think
lightly of temporal favours. They are left-hand blessings, if
not right-hand mercies; they are gifts to be thankful for on
earth, if not graces that take to heaven; provision for the
perishing body, if not food for the immortal soul. Health,
strength, such a measure of worldly goods as shall keep the
wolf from the door, and enable us to owe no man anything
but love; children growing up to be a comfort to their
parents; a kind and affectionate partner; warm and faithful
friends; an untarnished name; and a little provision for
those dear and near to us, that their tears over our body may
not be doubly embittered by poverty and dependence; who
shall say that these are not blessings for which God is to be
praised? Viewed by the eye of faith, blessings in providence
come down from heaven steeped in mercy. And yet how

short, oh, how infinitely short do these temporal blessings, which perish in the using, fall of spiritual blessings, which endure for evermore! A striking proof of this is that when we are privileged to draw near to a throne of grace with some measure of faith and feeling, the heart's desire is wholly towards spiritual blessings; and the eye of the soul is so wholly and solely fixed upon them, that there is scarcely left place either in the heart or lips to ask for any other.

But look at the personality of the blessing asked : " The Lord bless thee;" not "you." And yet when the high priest pronounced the blessing he did not fix his eye upon, nor did he address his speech to, any one individual. It was spoken to the whole assembly of the congregation of Israel; and yet the words were so framed as though the blessing were for each individual. Such are God's blessings—personal, individual. Gracious souls, sometimes, when they have heard the word with any particular sweetness or power, say, " It was all for me." Well, it was all for thee ; but art thou the only " me " in the place ? Might not some one sitting by thy side say, " It was all for me ?" Don't think that one alone is to be blessed, and all others excluded. There is enough for each, and there is enough for all. But there is something so singularly appropriating in the mercy of God when brought into the heart, that it seems as though it were for me, and for me alone. But here is the blessedness of the mercies of God, of the riches of his grace and glory— that one having a part does not exclude the other. It is not like a natural family, where each successive child seems to withdraw a portion of the inheritance from the others ; so that, if they had the covetous feelings of grown-up people, the elder might well say to the new-born babe, " We don't want thee, thou little robber! Why art thou come to cry halves with us ? " It does not narrow the heavenly inheritance that there are so many to enjoy it ; if it did, it would narrow God himself, for God is their inheritance, and in God is enough to satisfy myriads of elect angels as well as myriads of ransomed men. There need be no envy in the things of God; it is excluded by the freeness, fulness, and richness of God's love.

January 14.

" The Lord keep thee."—NUMBERS vi. 24.

How we need the Lord to keep us! We stand upon slippery places. Snares and traps are laid for us in every direction. Every employment, every profession in life, from the highest to the lowest, has its special temptations. Snares are spread for the feet of the most illiterate as well as the most highly cultivated minds ; nor is there any one, whatever his position in life may be, who has not a snare laid for him, and such a snare as will surely prove his downfall if God keep him not. When Elisha sat upon the mountain and his servant was distressed lest his master should be taken away by violence, the prophet prayed the Lord to open his servant's eyes. What then saw he? Chariots and horses of fire all round about the mountain guarding the prophet. Perhaps if the Lord were to open our eyes as he opened the eyes of Elisha's servant, we might see devils where he saw angels, see ourselves surrounded by Beelzebub and his legions, as the eyes of the servant saw Michael with the flaming hosts of heaven. Well, then, may it be the desire of our soul, "The Lord keep me"—keep me in his providence, keep me by his grace ; keep me by planting his fear deep in my soul, and maintaining that fear alive and effectual in my heart ; keep me waking, keep me sleeping ; keep me by night, keep me by day ; keep me at home, keep me abroad; keep me with my family, and keep me with my friends ; keep me in the world, and keep me in the Church; the Lord keep me, according to his promise, every moment ; keep me by his

Spirit and grace with all the tenderness implied in his words,
" O keep me as the apple of thine eye!" My friends, you
can know little of your own heart, little of Satan's devices,
little of the snares spread for your feet, unless you feel how
deeply you need an interest in this blessing: "The Lord
keep thee." And he will, for we read of the righteous, that
they are kept "by the power of God through faith unto
salvation ; " and that "He will keep the feet of his saints."

January 15.

" The Lord make his face shine upon thee."—NUMBERS vi. 25.

THE allusion here seems, to my mind, to be to the sun.
Sometimes the natural sun has not risen ; and the world
must needs be dark if the sun be still beneath the horizon.
So with many gracious souls; it is darkness with them, midnight darkness, Egyptian darkness, darkness to be felt,
because at present neither the Day-star has appeared nor the
Sun of righteousness risen upon them with healing in his
wings. It will and must be dark with them till the Sun rise.
But sometimes after the sun has risen we see not his face ;
clouds, deep, dark clouds, may obscure the face of that
bright luminary throughout the whole day, and we may not
get a single ray from him through the whole period that he
is above the visible horizon. So, many of the Lord's family,
after the Sun has risen upon them in the morning of their
spiritual life, may pass, perhaps, much of their subsequent
time in the dark shadow, till perhaps at evening tide there is
light, and a departing ray gilds the dying pillow. But again,
there are sometimes days when mists drive rapidly across
the face of the bright orb of day, and yet occasionally he
peeps through the breaking clouds. And is not this, in
some measure, an emblem of the way in which the Sun of
righteousness is continually obscured by the mists and fogs
which spring up out of our unbelieving heart, hidden from

view by the doubts and fears that, like the vapours of the valley, spread themselves, to our view, over his beauteous face? Yet there are times when he gleams through the clouds and disperses the mists. When the Lord is pleased to bless the soul and shine upon it with any sweet manifestation, then he breaks in through the dark clouds, but they gather again. It is not in Christian experience one bright summer day. We do not live in Australia or Peru, where clouds and mists rarely obscure the face of the sun. Our spiritual climate is humid, our inward latitude northern.

"The Lord make his face shine upon thee." Is the Lord, then, sovereign in these matters? Can we not lift up our hand and remove the cloud? We have as much power to stretch forth our hand and sweep away the mists that obscure the Sun of righteousness, as we have power with the same hand to sweep away a London fog. How this puts the creature into his right place! And the creature is only in his right place when he is nothing, and God is all in all. How blessed to see the face of the Father, and to see it shine! not covered with lowering clouds of justly-merited displeasure, as sometimes we see in the natural sky an obscured sun looking angrily down, presaging wind and storm. It is indeed true that, when we have brought guilt into our consciences, the face of God is seen to lower with anger. We have brought his just displeasure upon our heads; though not angry with the persons of his people, yet is he justly angry with their sins; and a sense of this in the soul covers his face with clouds: "Thou hast covered thyself with a cloud, that our prayer should not pass through" (Lam. iii. 44).

"The Lord make his face shine upon thee." And if he make his face shine upon thee, he will make thy face shine too. It was so with Moses, when he was in the mount and was holding sweet communion with God. When he came down amongst the people, the skin of his face shone; the glory of God was reflected upon it. And if the Lord make his face shine upon thee, it will make thy face not unlike the face of Moses when thou goest among the people of God.

January 16.

"And be gracious unto thee."—NUMBERS vi. 25.

How sweet the gospel is! But what makes the gospel sweet? That one word which sheds a perfume through the whole—*grace*. Take grace out of the gospel and you destroy the gospel; you nullify and overthrow it; it is the gospel no more. Grace pervades every part and every branch of the blessed gospel; it is the life of the gospel; in a word, it is the gospel itself. "Be *gracious* unto thee." In what, then, is God gracious? In a broken law? What does that know of grace? In resolutions of amendment, creature performances, and human righteousness? Can the Lord, will the Lord shew himself gracious in these? I have read of a project for extracting sunbeams out of cucumbers. We might as well expect to make sunbeams out of cucumbers as to make grace out of the law; it is cold as cucumbers; there is no sun in it. Grace, to be grace, must come out of the gospel. It is *in* the gospel, and *out* of the gospel must it come; and it does come, excluding all creature righteousness, putting an extinguisher upon all human merit. As the Apostle argues: "And if by grace, then is it no more of works; otherwise grace is no more grace. But if it be of works, then is it no more grace; otherwise work is no more work" (Rom. xi. 6). "The Lord be gracious unto thee."

But *how* is the Lord gracious? Perhaps you have had occasion, at some time of your life, to go into the presence of some one in worldly rank far your superior, and you

went timid, nervous, and trembling; but you experienced
what is called a "gracious reception." Did not that
enable you to speak and open your petition? So it is in
the things of God. A sense of our meanness and unworthiness may and does make us tremble and feel timid
before the face of the Most High; but when he draws us
into his presence, and receives us graciously, as king
Ahasuerus received the trembling Esther, extending to her
the sceptre of his grace, it emboldens the soul to lay its
petition at his feet. Nothing will do it but this. But you
feel and say often, "I am so unworthy." Will you ever
be anything else? When do you hope to be worthy?
When do you mean to be worthy? If you could be
worthy to-morrow, where is your worthiness to-day? Is
the old score yet paid? If you venture upon the ground
of worthiness you must have the old score rubbed off
before you come to the new. *Worthiness!* where is it?
In man? Never since the day that Adam fell. Righteousness fell in Paradise; when Adam's hand touched the
apple, worthiness fell to the ground, and never since has
been able to raise its head. I must not, then, go to God
upon the ground of worthiness. But may I go on the
ground of unworthiness? I read of one who did, and met
with a very gracious reception. "Lord," said one, "I am
not worthy that thou shouldest come under my roof; but
speak the word only and my servant shall be healed."
What did the Lord say of this man? That he had not
found so great faith, no, not in Israel. What, too, was
the confession of the returning prodigal? "I am no more
worthy to be called thy son." But this brought oùt the
best robe, the ring for the hand, and the shoes for the
feet. Why? Faith dwells with a sense of unworthiness;
they are bosom companions; it dwells in no other but
unworthy breasts. Feel spiritually unworthy and you are

spiritually believing, for it is faith that gives a sense of unworthiness. You believe you are unworthy; by the same faith that you believe your unworthiness you believe God's grace. "Be gracious unto thee." That melts the heart; law and terrors do but harden. It is grace that softens, grace that melts, grace that constrains, grace that produces godly obedience.

January 17.

"The Lord lift up his countenance upon thee, and give thee peace."—NUMBERS vi. 26.

WHEN we offend a person, his face is not toward us as at other times. It was so with Laban towards Jacob; and if we have in any way incurred a friend's or superior's displeasure, we watch instinctively his countenance. Is it down or up? Does it wear a frown or a smile? Is it looking upon us with the eye of affection, or are the eyes averted? We can tell in a moment if we know the countenance. Thus is the blessing asked, "The Lord lift up his countenance upon thee," as a kind and affectionate parent upon an obedient child, as a fond husband upon a loving, devoted wife; for such is God to his children— Father and Husband. And do we not, as children, often provoke him to look upon us with frowning brow, or rather, not to look upon us at all, to "hide his face," as we read, "that we cannot see him?" The prayer then is, "The Lord lift up his countenance upon thee," with a smile upon it; free, open, forgiving, merciful, and mild, that thou mayest advance therein. When a disobedient child comes home and sees its father's face not towards it as before, it shrinks away; there is no pressing forward to get upon the knee, no throwing the little arms round the neck and snatching a kiss, but a shrinking away through guilt and shame. So it is in the things of God.

When conscience tells us how in this and that instance we
have disobeyed, been inconsistent, transgressed, and done
amiss, when we go into God's presence there is a hanging
back, a shrinking away, through fear of an ill reception.
But oh, the change in the child when the frown disappears
and the smile succeeds; when the little one is taken once
more into the arms and the tears are kissed away! How
much more so in the things of God when he kisses away
the tears of the disobedient child, as in the case of the
returning prodigal! There are no kisses like those kisses
of forgiveness, of mercy, and of restoring grace.

" And give thee peace." Oh, what a blessing! As Hart
says,

> " I'll lay me down and sweetly sleep,
> For I have peace with God."

It is this that makes the pillow easy in life, and will alone
make that pillow easy in death—peace with God through
Jesus Christ, peace through the reconciliation, peace through
the blood of sprinkling, "the peace of God which passeth
all understanding." Many covet great things, high things.
But what said the Lord to Baruch? "Seekest thou great
things for thyself? seek them not." Ministers often seek
great gifts, great eloquence, great knowledge of mysteries,
great congregations, great popularity and influence. They
are wrong in seeking these so-called great things. Let them
rather seek *real* things, gracious things, things that will make
their souls blessed here and hereafter. The blessing that the
gracious soul most earnestly covets is peace ; for this is
the sweetest honey-drop in God's cup. It is true that it does
not make the heart overflow like joy, nor to dance with
exultation like the first beaming in of the rays of hope, nor
melt it down like the visits of love; but it is in some respects
sweeter than all, because it so settles down the soul into
sweet assurance ; it is the realisation of the Saviour himself,

for " he is our peace," and may thus be called the crowning
blessing.

January 18.

" *From all your idols will I cleanse you.*"—EZEKIEL xxxvi. 25.

WHEN there are no crosses, temptations, or exercises, a
man is sure to go out after and cleave to idols. It matters
not what experience he has had, whether of trouble or consolation, distress or enjoyment ; if once he cease to be
plagued and exercised, he will be setting up his household
gods in the secret chambers of imagery. Profit or pleasure,
self-indulgence or self-gratification will surely, in one form or
another, engross his thoughts, and steal away his heart.
Nor is there anything too trifling or insignificant to become
an idol. Whatever is meditated on preferably to God, whatever is desired more than he, whatever more interests us,
pleases us, occupies our waking hours, or is more constantly
in our mind, becomes an idol and a source of sin. It is not
the magnitude of the idol, but its existence as an object of
worship, that constitutes idolatry. I have seen some Burmese
idols not much larger than my hand, and I have seen some
Egyptian idols weighing many tons. But both were equally
idols, and the comparative size had nothing to do with the
question. So spiritually, the idol is not to be measured by
its size, its relative importance or non-importance. An
auricula may be as much an idol to one man as a chest full
of gold to another. If you watch your heart, you will see
idols rising and setting all day long, nearly as thickly as the
stars by night. Now exercises, difficulties, temptations, be-
setments, losses, trials, afflictions, are all sent to pull down
these idols, or rather to pull away our hearts from them.
They pull us out of fleshly ease, and prevent us from sitting
down contented with a name to live whilst dead. They
make us cry for mercy, pull down all rotten props, hunt us

out of false refuges, and strip us of vain hopes and delusive expectations.

We do not learn that we are sinners merely by reading it in the Bible. It must be wrought, I might say, *burnt* into us. Nor will any one sincerely and spiritually cry for mercy, a sense of pardon and reconciliation by the application of atoning blood, until sin in its misery, in its dominion, in its guilt, in its entanglements, in its wiles and allurements, in its filth and pollution, and in its condemnation, is spiritually felt and known. Where the Holy Ghost works, he kindles sighs, groans, supplications, wrestlings, and pleadings to know Christ, feel his love, taste the efficacy of his atoning blood, and embrace him as all our salvation and all our desire. And though there may, and doubtless will be, much barrenness, hardness, deadness, and apparent carelessness often felt, still that heavenly Teacher will revive his work, though often by painful methods ; nor will he let the quickened soul rest short of a personal and experimental enjoyment of Christ and his glorious salvation.

January 19.

" For the Lord God is a sun and shield."—Psalm lxxxiv. 11.

Is not the sun made to shine? It is his office to do so. So it is with the Sun of righteousness ; he is made to shine. And does the natural sun lose any of his light by shining? Why, the more he shines, the more light he seems to have. For ages he has shone as brightly as now. His beams were as glorious before we had birth or being, and will be as glorious when the eyes which now see him are mouldering in the dust. Thousands of harvests has he ripened, millions and thousands of millions has he fed; but he shews no sign of exhaustion or decay. And does Jesus lose anything by communicating his light, life, love, and grace? He is all the

more glorified thereby; and the more you look to him as the
Sun, that as such he might shine into and upon your soul,
the more you glorify him as the Sun of righteousness.
When in the morning we throw the shutters back, or draw
up the blinds, it is to receive the sun into the dark room. So
the more we are enabled by divine grace to throw back the
shutters of doubt and fear, and draw up the blinds of unbelief
which hang down over the mind, the more we glorify the
Lord Jesus by receiving out of his fulness, and grace for
grace. Oh! it is good to be sometimes enabled to look
beyond and above doubts, fears, misgivings, and the many
things that try the mind. You may pore over your sins and
miseries till you fall well-nigh into despair; you may look
back upon your wanderings, inconsistencies, and want of
fruitfulness, till you are almost ready to sink down without
hope and die. To do this is to resemble a person wandering in a dark room, tumbling over the furniture, and at
last sitting down and saying, "There is no light." If he
can but throw back the shutters, the sun will shine into
the room. So we sometimes may sit pondering over our
many inconsistencies till we say, "There is no light in my
soul; there never was, and there never will be." O to be
enabled (when I speak thus, I know well, from soul experience, that it is only God who can do it in us and for us) to
throw back the shutters, and look away from those things
that so weigh down the mind! Look up, O sinking soul,
and see the blessed Sun still shining in the firmament of
heaven! Why, the very power to do this, the very act of
doing so, brings with it a felt blessedness.

How good, also, to be enabled to make use of Christ as a
shield! Oh, how often we go to battle without this shield
upon our arm! But depend upon it, the Lord would not
have provided such a shield for you unless he knew that
your enemies were too many for you. Doubt, fear, dark-

ness, despair, the law, the accusations of a guilty conscience, the fiery darts of the devil—how can you fight against these enemies without a shield? Why, you would be like a soldier going out against the foe without either sword or musket, and laying his bosom bare to every weapon, without Minié or bayonet in his hand to defend himself. So, to go into combat against the law; the accusations of a guilty conscience, and a desponding heart, and have no blessed Jesus to hold up as a shield against these deadly foes, would be enough to sink a man into despair. But if he be enabled to make use of the shield that God has provided, and to hold Christ up against a condemning law, a guilty conscience, an accusing devil, and a desponding mind, and say to them all, " Christ hath died, and died for me," then he receives into the shield those darts which would otherwise sink into his soul, and then they all fall harmless, because they all fell on the Lord Jesus.

January 20.

"*All scripture is given by inspiration of God, and is profitable for doctrine, for reproof, for correction, for instruction in righteousness; that the man of God may be perfect, throughly furnished unto all good works.*"—2 Timothy iii. 16, 17.

On all subjects connected with our most holy faith, it is most desirable to have clear views. Every point of divine truth is laid down with the greatest clearness and precision in the word of God. The darkness, the ignorance, the confusion which prevent us from seeing it are all in us. But as we search the Scriptures, as we meditate upon them, as we by prayer and supplication draw light, life, and wisdom out of Him " in whom are hid all the treasures of wisdom and knowledge ; " and, above all, as we mix faith with what we read, there is often, if not usually, a gradual breaking-in of light ; and as we follow up its heavenly rays, it shines more clearly and broadly, and the truth stands out more fully and prominently before our eyes. This is the only way in which we can be " filled with the knowledge of God's will in all wisdom and spiritual understanding," and thus be established in the faith, abounding therein with thanksgiving. To understand the scripture, to see in it the mind of the Holy Spirit, to be deeply penetrated with, and inwardly possessed of the heavenly wisdom, holy instruction, and gracious revelation of the counsels and will of God unfolded therein, demands much and continual patient and prayerful study. As in business, diligence and industry lead on to prosperity and success, and sloth and idleness are the sure road to ruin ; so in the greatest, most serious, and important of all business, the concerns of the soul, there is a holy diligence, a heavenly industry, whereby it thrives and grows, and there is a slothful indolence whereby it becomes clothed with rags (Proverbs xxiii. 21).

January 21.

"A thousand shall fall at thy side, and ten thousand at thy right hand; but it shall not come nigh thee."—PSALM xci. 7.

WHEN Noah was shut up in the ark, Noah and the favoured few, you know how they were tossed about, the rains coming down from heaven, the waters rushing and dashing below. The windows of heaven were opened and the fountains of the great deep were broken up, and while they were thus dashed upon the waters, not a drop came in unto them that were within. " It shall not come nigh thee." So you see the believer may be surrounded with troubles, and yet " it shall not come nigh him." And there is something more in the expression used in reference to the making of the ark : " And shalt pitch it within and without with pitch" (Gen. vi. 14). Now, it is a most remarkable fact that the word pitch in Hebrew (the word is Gopher) signifies also *atonement*. Now see, the slime or pitch with which the ark was daubed within and without kept every drop of water out. This very expression for slime or pitch in the Hebrew signifies also atonement; and is it not the atonement that keeps out the water? Can anything but the atonement keep the soul from the waters of God's wrath and from the floods of vengeance that shall sweep away the world with the ungodly? There is nothing but the atonement, and that bears up the soul, and keeps out every drop of rain. "It shall not come nigh thee." "Many sorrows shall be to the wicked, but he that trusteth in the Lord, mercy shall compass him about." "And not only so, but we also joy in God through our Lord Jesus Christ, by whom we have now received the atonement." "Received the atonement." This is it, to have the "atonement." God cannot twice exact payment for the debt. He is satisfied; he has declared that he is well pleased with the righteousness of his beloved Son. He exacts no more; his justice demands no more, and, therefore, fury is not in him.

January 22.

"For in him dwelleth all the fulness of the Godhead bodily."— Colossians ii. 9.

THE temple erected by Solomon in Jerusalem, and the tabernacle set up by Moses in the wilderness were but types of the true temple, the Lord of life and glory. The Lord himself said, "Destroy this temple, and in three days I will raise it up," speaking of his own body. All the beauty and glory of the temple were, therefore, figurative; they typified and shadowed forth the glory of Immanuel, for " in him dwelleth all the fulness of the Godhead bodily." God the Son has taken to himself a body, according to those words in the fortieth Psalm, as quoted by Paul (Hebrews x. 5): " a body hast thou prepared me ; " a holy body, a sinless, spot-

less body. According to those words: "Therefore that
holy thing which shall be born of thee shall be called the Son
of God;" and not only a holy body, but united to it a holy,
spotless soul. "He shall see of the travail of *his soul*, and
be satisfied." "*My soul* is exceeding sorrowful, even unto
death" (Matthew xxvi. 38). This holy body, as united with
a holy soul, the two forming his spotless human nature, the
Son of God took into union with himself, and thus became
the God-man, Immanuel, God with us. It is this glorious
mystery of godliness that a living soul pants to know. We
cannot approach pure Godhead; we cannot understand it;
it is a mystery too high and too deep for us; for who, "by
searching, can find out God? It is as high as heaven;
what canst thou do? deeper than hell; what canst thou know?"
(Job xi. 7, 8.) But when God would make himself known
to the children of men, he made himself known by his only
begotten Son, the second Person in the glorious Godhead,
taking into union with himself the flesh and blood of the
children; and thus we can, so far as the Lord gives us faith,
approach to an invisible God through the visible God-man;
as John says, "We beheld his glory, the glory as of the only
begotten of the Father, full of grace and truth." "No man
hath seen God at any time: the only begotten Son which is
in the bosom of the Father, he hath declared him." And,
therefore, when Philip said to him (John xiv. 8), "Lord,
shew us the Father, and it sufficeth us;" Jesus said, "Have
I been so long time with you, and yet hast thou not known
me, Philip? he that hath seen me hath seen the Father;
and how sayest thou then, Shew us the Father?" And why,
but because as he says in another place, "I and my Father
are one."

The desire, then, of every living soul (I am sure it is my
desire when the Lord is pleased to work it in my heart) is to
be led by the Spirit of God into an acquaintance with the

God-man; to behold the glory of God in Jesus Christ; to see the Godhead shining through the manhood, and yet to see the manhood veiling and yet deriving glory from the Godhead; and thus to come to Jesus as a high priest that is able to save to the uttermost all that come unto God by him; to feel nearness of access to the Father by approaching him through the Son of his love; and thus to enjoy sweet communion with Immanuel, God with us, God in our nature, God making himself known by taking our flesh and blood into union with himself.

January 23.

" So that we ourselves glory in you in the churches of God for your patience and faith in all your persecutions and tribulations that ye endure; which is a manifest token of the righteous judgment of God, that ye may be counted worthy of the kingdom of God, for which ye also suffer."—2 THESSALONIANS i. 4, 5.

THE Lord has chosen that his people should pass through deep and cutting afflictions, for it is through much, or *many* tribulations, as the word really signifies, "through many tribulations" they are to enter the kingdom of God above, and into the sweetness and power of the kingdom of God below (Acts xiv. 22). But every man will resent this doctrine, except God has led him experimentally into it. It is such a rough and rugged path; it is so contrary to flesh and blood; it is so inexplicable to nature and reason, that man, proud, rebellious man, whether he be in a profession or whether he be out of a profession, will never believe that he must through much tribulation enter into the kingdom. And this is the reason why so many find, or seek to find, a smoother way to glory than the Lord has appointed his saints to walk in. But shall the Head travel in one path, and the members in another? Shall the Bridegroom walk and wade through seas of sorrow, and the bride never so much as wet her feet with the water? Shall the Bridegroom be crucified in weakness and suffering, and there be no inward crucifixion for the dearly-beloved of his heart? Shall the Head suffer, grieve, agonise, groan, and die, and the members dance down a flowery road, without inward sorrow or outward suffering?

> " Bastards may escape the rod,
> Sunk in earthly, vain delight;
> But the true-born child of God
> Must not, would not, if he might."

But, perhaps, there are some who say in their heart, " I am well convinced of this; but my coward flesh shrinks from it. I know if I am to reach the Canaan above, I must pass through the appointed portion of tribulation. But my coward flesh shrinks back." It does! it does! Who would willingly bring trials upon himself? Therefore the Lord does not leave these trials in our hands; but he himself appoints a certain measure of tribulation for each of his people to pass through. They will come soon enough; you need not anticipate them; you need not wish for them. God will bring them, in his own time and in his own way; and what is more, God will not merely bring you into them, but God will bring you through them, and God will bring you out of them; for the third part was not merely brought into the fire, but through the fire, to cause them to call upon his name. What, then, will be our mercy? It will be our mercy if enabled to ask the Lord to bless us with faith and patience under tribulation; to ask the Lord to give us strength to bear the storm; to lie as clay in his hands, and ask the Lord to conform us to the image of his Son, to guide us through this vale of tears below, and eventually to take us to be with him above.

January 24.

"Always bearing about in the body the dying of the Lord Jesus."—2 CORINTHIANS iv. 10.

THE two aspects, if I may use the expression, of our gracious Lord, in which are wrapped up all our faith, and hope, and love, are a dying Jesus and a risen Jesus; Christ in his sufferings and death, Christ in his resurrection and life. This is the Christ of God, this is the Son of God in whom we believe unto life eternal, as he is presented to our view in the Scriptures of truth, and by the inward teaching and testimony of the Holy Ghost. If, then, you do not believe in a dying Christ and in a risen Christ, your faith is not the faith of a Christian. Now just see how this bears upon our text. Why do we bear about the *dying* of the Lord Jesus? It is that the *life* of Jesus might be made manifest in our body. As then we bear about in the body the dying of the Lord Jesus; as we suffer with Christ, die with Christ, and enter by faith into the mystery of his crucifixion so as to be mystically and spiritually crucified with him, we rise, so to speak, out of this death into union with the risen, living Christ, so as to derive life and strength, grace and power out of his glorious fulness. For he is risen from the dead : he is no more in the tomb, into which he sank in all the weakness of death; but is risen again, and was thus "declared to be the Son of God with power." Yes, he has gone up on high, and now sits at the right hand of God in the highest heavens. He is gone within the veil, to be the High Priest over the house of God; there, too, he rules and reigns as King in Zion; and there he ever lives as our glorified and risen Head. As, then, we bear about in the body the dying of the Lord Jesus, as crucified with him and conformed to his death, so as "risen with him," there is even now in our body a manifestation of his risen life.

January 25.

" That the life also of Jesus might be made manifest in our body."—2 CORINTHIANS iv. 10.

IT is in this earthen vessel, our poor mortal body, that both the death of Jesus and the life of Jesus are manifested. In the trouble, the perplexity, the being cast down, is the dying of Jesus; in not being distressed, in not being in despair, in not being forsaken, in not being destroyed, is the life of Jesus. Thus in the same body there is a dying Christ and a living Christ, Christ in his cross in his weakness, and Christ at the right hand of God in his power. To know these two things is to know the power of Christ's resurrection, and the fellowship of his sufferings, those two divine blessings which the soul of Paul so longed to realise and experience. In the knowledge then, the experimental knowledge, I mean, for all other is of no avail, of Christ crucified and Christ risen, consists the spiritual life of a child of God. So to live is to live a life of faith in the Son of God. So to live is to be baptised with that Spirit wherewith Paul was baptised when he said, "I am crucified with Christ: nevertheless I live; yet not I, but Christ liveth in me: and the life which I now live in the flesh I live by the faith of the Son of God, who loved me, and gave himself for me." The present life of Christ at the right hand of God the Father, is the source and foundation of all our present life. "Because I live, ye shall live also," was his gracious promise when here below; and he is gone up on high, to fulfil that promise and make it effectual. He is "our life," and this life must be made manifest in our mortal flesh, manifest to ourselves, and manifest to others; manifest to ourselves by the communication of light, life, liberty, and love, manifest to others by the fruits of a life and conversation adorning the gospel, and by walking in all holy obedience to its precepts.

January 26.

" For there is one God, and one Mediator between God and men, the man Christ Jesus."—1 TIMOTHY ii. 5.

No sooner has living faith embraced the Person of Jesus (and that is the first object which faith lays hold of), than it embraces him as the divinely-appointed Mediator. And how sweet and suitable is such a Mediator to a poor, sinful, crawling reptile, a wretch defiled, morning, noon, and night, with everything foul and filthy, who has broken the law of God a million times, and cannot keep it a single moment! " How can I," argues the soul, " so full of sin and depravity, how can I approach with acceptance the great, glorious, and holy Jehovah? I cannot, I dare not!" But when it sees, by the eye of faith, a divinely-appointed Mediator, a glorious Intercessor, a great High Priest over the house of God: One that has shed his blood to put away sin; One who has righteousness to justify, and has a fulness of grace and glory to give to the poor, needy, and naked: as faith sees, as hope embraces, as love enjoys this, there is a coming to God through this divine Mediator; as the Apostle saith, " Through him we both have access by one Spirit unto the Father." " Who by him do believe in God, that raised him up from the dead, and gave him glory; that your faith and hope might be in God." Our only access to God is through the Mediator whom he hath appointed. All your prayers, tears, sighs, and groans; all your religious thoughts, acts, and words are worthless, utterly worthless, unless perfumed by the intercession of the only-begotten Son of God. See to this point; and I would, in all affection, charge it upon your conscience, that you look well how you approach the Father. Do you approach him through the Son of his love? Is there a solemn feeling in your heart, when you draw near to the throne, that you approach only through Jesus? Is there

a believing reception of his atoning blood into your conscience as the only sacrifice that purges away sin, and of his
justifying righteousness as the only robe of acceptance before
God? See to it well, examine your conscience well upon
the matter, for it is vital ground. See that you approach the
Father through the Son of his love, and through him alone;
for depend upon it, if you approach in any other way, you
are but a presumptuous professor; there is no holy fire burning on the altar of your soul; nor will any answer come
down but through this divinely-appointed way.

January 27.

*" The eyes of all wait upon thee; and thou givest them their
meat in due season."*—Psalm cxlv. 15.

The Lord will bring all his children sooner or later, each
in their measure, to " wait upon him." Whatever trouble
they are in, " the eyes of all wait upon thee;" whatever
temptations they have to pass through, " the eyes of all wait
upon thee;" whatever difficulty in temporal things, whatever
conflict in spiritual things, whatever strait in providence,
whatever exercise in grace be their lot, the Lord will bring
all his children at one time or another into this experience,
" the eyes of all wait upon thee." " Wait upon thee" for
deliverance; " wait upon thee" for a manifestation; " wait
upon thee" for the lifting up the light of thy countenance;
" wait upon thee" for one soft word spoken by thy mouth to
the soul; " wait upon thee" for one smile of thine approving countenance; " wait upon thee" for one testimony of
thine everlasting favour. And he that knows not what it is
to " wait upon God" in this manner, wait upon him by night
and by day as the Lord works it in him, wait upon him on
his bed, wait upon him behind his counter, wait upon him in
the solitary fields, wait upon him in the crowded streets—he

lacks that evidence, he wants that divine feature, which the
Holy Ghost has stamped here upon all the living family.

"And thou givest them their meat in due season." There
is "meat," then, that they are waiting upon God for, to
receive at his hands. And it is called "*their* meat." It
belongs to them. All the elect of God have provision laid
up for them in Christ; for "it hath pleased the Father, that
in him should all fulness dwell." "I will abundantly bless
her provision" (Psalm cxxxii. 15). Though none of God's
quickened family ever dare to *claim* the blessing at God's
hands, yet the Lord has so stored up blessings in Christ, that
they are actually and eternally theirs; for, as the Apostle says,
"all things are yours." It is "*their* meat" then; that is,
the meat peculiar to the elect. Blood shed for their sins,
and for their sins only; righteousness brought in for them,
and for them only; love bestowed upon them, and upon
them only; promises revealed for their comfort, and for
their comfort only; an eternal inheritance, "incorruptible
and undefiled, and that fadeth not away, reserved in heaven
for them," and for them only. It is "their meat," because it
is theirs in Christ, being lodged in Christ for their benefit.
But it is theirs in another sense; and that is, they are the
only people who hunger after it, who have an appetite for
it, who have a mouth to feed upon it, who have a stomach
to digest it. They are the only people whose eyes are
really open to see what "meat" is. Others feed upon
shadows; they know nothing of the savoury food of the
gospel. As the Lord said to his disciples, "I have meat
to eat which ye know not of." His meat was the hidden
communications of God's love, the visitations of his Father's
presence, the divine communion that he enjoyed with his
Father while the disciples were gone away, "to do the will
of him that sent him, and to finish his work." So, for the
children of God, there is meat in Christ; and this meat the

Lord gives them a hunger after. He not only sets before
their eyes what the meat is, but he kindles inexpressible
longings in their soul to be fed therewith. God's people cannot feed upon husks, nor upon ashes, nor upon chaff, nor
upon the east wind, nor upon grapes of gall and the bitter
clusters of Gomorrah (Deuteronomy xxxii. 32). They must
have "meat," "savoury meat such as their soul loveth," that
which God himself communicates, and which his hand alone
can bring down, and give unto them, so that they may receive it from him as their soul-satisfying portion.

January 28.

"The fire shall try every man's work of what sort it is."—
1 CORINTHIANS iii. 13.

How careful and anxious we should be to have two points
well secured in our hearts. First, to be right as concerns
the foundation. "Do I believe in the Son of God? Have
I clear views of the Sonship, the Deity, and the pure
humanity of the Christ of God? Have I drunk in no secret
error? Am I hiding in my bosom no corrupt doctrine? Is
my creed sound? Is the word of God received by me, as
God has revealed it, into a believing heart?" How many
are wrong as to the foundation itself. Then comes, "Am I
upon the foundation? Did God himself put me there? Did
I see its suitability to my lost and undone soul? Did the
blessed Spirit take of the things of Christ and reveal them to
me in the hour of need? Was the Son of God made
precious to my soul by an act of faith? Am I looking to
him, cleaving to him, longing for him, hanging upon him,
and trusting wholly to his Person and work? How stands
the foundation? Am I on it?"

The next important question is, "How stands the superstructure? Has the Holy Ghost wrought anything with a

divine power in my soul? The faith I profess, is it of God? The hope I enjoy, do I believe it came from the Lord himself to support my soul in the trying storm? My repentance, is it genuine? My profession, is it sincere? My walk, is it consistent? My conscience, is it tender? My desires, are they spiritual? My prayers, are they fervent? My heart, is it honest? My soul, is it right before God? What am I looking to as the foundation, and what am I looking to as the superstructure? Do I hang all my hopes upon Christ as the Rock, and all my religion upon the work of the Holy Ghost in my heart?"

If you can answer these questions as in the sight of God, "Yes, yes, ten times yes;" then you are right, you are right. If you stand upon the foundation that God has laid in Zion, you are right; you are right if God the Spirit has wrought a living faith in your heart. But you are wrong, you are wrong if you stand not upon God's foundation; you are wrong, you are wrong, and that for eternity, unless the Holy Ghost is at work upon your conscience.

January 29.

"Lay hold on eternal life."—1 TIMOTHY vi. 12.

THE main office of the hand is to *take hold of and grasp an object.* The human hand is the master-piece of anatomy, the fingers and the strong opposing thumb being expressly constructed by their Divine Artificer to seize and retain objects; and therefore every muscle, artery, vein, and nerve conspire together to fulfil this destined office. Is there not in the office of faith something analogous to and corresponding with this? What says the Lord? "Let him take hold of my strength that he may make peace with me, and he shall make peace with me." There is a taking hold, then, of God's strength. Is not this by faith? Is there any other grace of the Spirit which takes hold of the

Lord, as Jacob took hold of the 'wrestling angel, or as sinking Peter laid hold of the hand of Jesus? "Lay hold on eternal life," is Paul's charge to Timothy. But how is eternal life, and especially Jesus, "the Life," laid hold of, except by faith? "He that believeth on me," says Jesus, "hath everlasting life." He has it by laying hold of it.

So we read also of "fleeing for refuge to lay hold upon the hope set before us" (Heb. vi. 18). As the manslayer fled for refuge to the appointed city, and when his hand grasped the gates was safe, so guilty sinners flee for refuge to the Lord Jesus, and by faith lay hold upon the hope set before them in the gospel of the grace of God.

January 30.

" Let us run with patience the race that is set before us."— HEBREWS xii. 1.

NONE can run this race but the saints of God, for the ground itself is holy ground, of which we read that " no unclean beast is to be found therein." None but the redeemed walk there; and none have ever won the prize but those who have run this heavenly race as redeemed by precious blood.

Now no sooner do we see by faith the race set before us than we begin to run; and, like Christian in the " Pilgrim's Progress," we run from the City of Destruction, our steps being winged with fear and apprehension. All this, especially in the outset, implies energy, movement, activity, pressing forward; running, as it were, for our life; escaping, as Lot, to the mountain; fleeing, as the prophet speaks, " like as ye fled from before the earthquake in the days of Uzziah " (Zech. xiv. 5); or as the manslayer fled to the city of refuge from the avenger of blood. As, then, the runner stretches forward hands, and feet, and head, intent only on being first to reach the goal, so in the spiritual race there is a stretching forth of the faculties of the new-born soul to win the heavenly prize. There is a stretching forth of the spiritual *understanding* to become possessed of clear views of heavenly truth. There is a stretching forth of the *desires* of the heart to experience the love of God ; to feel acceptance with him through the blood of sprinkling ; to know the way of salvation for ourselves, and to have clear evidences that our feet are in it; to receive tokens for good, and manifestations of the pardoning love of God; to walk in his fear, live to his praise, and enjoy union and communion with the blessed Lord. And there is a stretching forth of the *affections* of the heart after Jesus and the truth as it is in Jesus, with many longings, breathings, earnest cries, and fervent wrestlings at the throne of grace, that we may know the truth and by the truth be sanctified and made free. So that when you look at the word " race " as emblematic of a Christian's path, you see that it is not any movement of the body, what the Apostle calls " bodily exercise," that is intended, but an inward movement of the soul, or rather of the grace that God has lodged in your bosom, and to which are communicated spiritual faculties, whereby it moves forward in the ways of God, under the influences of the blessed Spirit.

January 31.

" *Howbeit when he, the Spirit of truth, is come, he will guide you into all truth; for he shall not speak of himself; but whatsoever he shall hear, that shall he speak ; and he will shew you things to come.*"—JOHN xvi. 13.

" HE shall not speak of himself." There is something peculiarly gracious in this feature of the Holy Spirit, that, if we may use the expression, he does not glorify himself by speaking of himself in the same direct, personal manner as the Father and the Son speak of themselves. Thus the

Father speaks of himself all through the word; and the Son
speaks of himself in Scripture after Scripture; but the Holy
Ghost, though he speaks in the Scripture, for by his divine
inspiration the whole was written, yet does not speak of himself in a positive, direct manner, nor call upon us in a clear,
personal way to believe in, worship, and adore him. But his
office and work are to testify to our conscience and bear witness to our spirit of both the Father and the Son. Thus as
a Spirit of adoption he enables the soul to cry, "Abba,
Father," and so testifies of the Father. As a Spirit of revelation he manifests to the soul the glorious Person of Christ,
and thus testifies of the Son. But he does not in a personal
manner manifest himself, or testify of himself. How, then,
do we know him? By his operations, his influences, his
teachings, his consolations, his sealings, his softenings, meltings, humblings, waterings, enlargings, openings, liberatings,
strengthenings, and enablings. The Lord therefore said to
his disciples, "But ye know him, for he dwelleth with you,
and shall be in you." Thus we know his indwelling by
the light he gives to see our evidences clear and bright;
by the life which he diffuses into the soul, to renew and
revive our drooping graces; by the submission which he
imparts in affliction and tribulation to the sovereign will
of God; by the meekness which he bestows under the
chastening rod; by the gracious confidence which he will
not suffer us to cast away; by the holy boldness which
he grants before the enemies of truth; by the zeal which
he kindles in the heart for the truth as it is in Jesus, and
for the glory of God; by the suitable words which he
brings to the mind in defence of the gospel; and by the
power which he gives to speak them forth with an authority
which silences, if it does not convince, the adversary.
Thus, though the blessed Spirit does not speak of himself, he makes himself effectually known by his indwelling

power and grace. O blessed Teacher, holy Comforter, gracious Intercessor, and heavenly Witness, come and take up thine abode in our heart; there reveal and form Jesus, the hope of glory; there shed abroad the love of God; there bear thy divine testimony to our sonship; there cry, "Abba, Father;" there teach and sanctify and bless, that we and all in whom thou hast wrought thy work of grace may be "filled with all joy and peace in believing, that we may abound in hope, through the power of the Holy Ghost."

February 1.

"And if children, then heirs; heirs of God, and joint-heirs with Christ."—ROMANS viii. 17.

THIS is the peculiar blessedness of being a child of God, that death, which puts a final extinguisher on all the hopes and happiness of the children of men, gives him the fulfilment of all his hopes and the consummation of all his happiness; for it places him in possession of " an inheritance incorruptible and undefiled, and that fadeth not away, reserved in heaven for those who are kept by the power of God through faith unto salvation." In this life we have sometimes sips and tastes of sonship, feeble indeed and interrupted, so that it is with us as Mr. Hart speaks :

"Though thou here receive but little,
Scarce enough
For the proof
Of thy proper title;"

yet are they so far pledges of an inheritance to come. But this life is only an introduction to a better. In this life we are but children, heirs indeed, but heirs in their minority; but in the life to come, if indeed we are what we profess to be, sons and daughters of the Lord Almighty, we shall be put into full possession of the eternal inheritance. And what is

this ? Nothing less than God himself. " Heirs of God," says
the Apostle. For as the Lord said to Abraham, " I am thy
shield and exceeding great reward ; " as he said to the Levites,
" I am their inheritance," so God himself is the inheritance of
his people ; yes, he himself in all his glorious perfections.
All the love of God, the goodness of God, the holiness of
God, all his happiness, bliss, and blessedness, all his might,
majesty, and glory, as shining forth in the Person of his dear
Son in all the blaze of one eternal, unclouded day—this is
the saint's inheritance. Let us not then be weary in well-
doing; nor faint and tire in running the race set before us,
with this prize in view; but press on by faith and prayer
to win this eternal and glorious crown.

February 2.

" *They shall ask their way to Zion with their faces thither-
ward.*"—JEREMIAH l. 5.

ZION is the seat of all gospel blessings. In it is laid "the
precious corner-stone" (Isaiah xxviii. 16); in it is " placed
salvation for Israel" (Isaiah xlvi. 13); the Lamb of God
stands upon it (Rev. xiv. 1) ; mercy, redemption, pardon,
comfort, strength, deliverance, and glory come out of it. In
turning the face then Zionwards, is implied the seeking of
gospel blessings. The redeemed are therefore said " to seek
the Lord their God," who is only to be found in Zion, his
dwelling-place, and where praise waiteth for him (Psalm
lxv. 1). But they ask the way to Zion with their faces thither-
ward in no light and trifling spirit, and in no positive certainty
that they shall ever arrive there. They have to ask the way
step by step, often doubting and fearing whether they be in
the way. Having been so often deceived and deluded, they
dare no more trust their own hearts ; but have to beg of the
Lord to shew them every inch of the road. They can no

longer blindly follow every presumptuous guide, but have to cry to the Lord himself to teach and lead and quicken them in the way. And as they go, they weep. They mourn over their base backslidings, over the many evils they have committed, over the levity of mind which they have indulged, over the worldliness of spirit, the pride, presumption, hypocrisy, carnality, carelessness, and obstinacy of their heart. They go and weep with a broken heart and softened spirit; not resting in their tears as evidences, but seeking the Lord their God; seeking the secret manifestations of his mercy, the visitations of his favour, the "lifting up of the light of his countenance;" seeking after a revelation of the love of Jesus; to know him by a spiritual discovery of himself. Being thus minded, they seek not to establish their own righteousness; they seek not the applause of the world; they seek not the good opinion of professors; they seek not the smiles of saints; they seek not to make themselves Christians by their own exertions. But "they seek the Lord their God," seek his face day and night, seek his favour, seek his mercy, seek his grace, seek his love, seek his glory, seek the sweet visitations of his presence and power, seek him wrestling with him till they find him to be their covenant God, who heals all their backslidings.

February 3.

" The sacrifices of God are a broken spirit: a broken and a contrite heart, O God, thou wilt not despise."—Psalm li. 17.

The heart that feels the burden of sin, that suffers under temptation, that groans beneath Satan's fiery assaults, that bleeds under the wounds inflicted by committed evil, is broken and contrite. This brokenness of heart and contrition of spirit is a thing which a child of God alone can feel. However hard his heart at times may seem to be, there will be seasons of spiritual reviving; however he may seem steeled against any sense of love and mercy, or even of misery and guilt, from time to time when he is least expecting and looking for it, there will be a breaking down of his soul before the Lord; there will be a bewailing of himself, a turning from the world to seek the Lord's favour, and a casting himself as a sinner once more on undeserved mercy, tears will flow down his cheeks, sighs burst from his bosom, and he will lie humble at the Saviour's feet. If your soul has ever felt this, you have a better thing than any gift; for this brokenness of spirit is a thing that accompanies salvation, and is a sacrifice that God will not despise.

February 4.

"Woe to them that are at ease in Zion."—AMOS vi. 1.

BUNYAN says, in his plain, homely language:

> "A Christian man is never long at ease,
> When one fright's gone, another doth him seize."

Sin will never let him rest long, nor Satan let him rest long, nor God let him rest long, nor his own fears let him rest long. He cannot be at ease till his conscience is purged with the blood of sprinkling; till his soul has been blest with a feeling sense and enjoyment of the love of God; till he has sweet manifestations of pardoning mercy, blessed revelations of Christ to his soul, with the voice and witness of the Spirit in his breast. This is not the ease of Moab (Jer. xlviii. 11), but the ease of which the Psalmist speaks when he says, "His soul shall dwell at ease" (Psalm xxv. 13). All ease but this is the sleep of the sluggard; carnal ease as opposed to spiritual. If then he drop into carnal ease, and for a time sin do not seem to plague, nor Satan tempt, nor the world persecute, the Christian man feels that he is getting wrong; he has lost a burden, but not in the right way, and would rather have the burden back than be left to have his portion amongst those who are at ease in Zion.

February 5.

"For my people have committed two evils; they have forsaken me the fountain of living waters, and hewed them out cisterns, broken cisterns, that can hold no water."—JEREMIAH ii. 13.

THERE is nothing so cutting as the remembrance of back-sliding against a good and holy God. There is nothing so wounding to a tender conscience as having sinned against manifested mercy and revealed salvation. It seems almost like doing despite to the Spirit of grace; almost like trampling under foot the blood of the covenant whereby we were sanctified, and treating our best Friend worse than his very enemies treated him. And as these things are brought to mind, and laid upon the conscience with weight and power, they will sometimes sink us very low into despondency and gloom so as almost to take away our very hope.

But the Lord is very merciful and compassionate to those who fear his name. He regards the prayer of the destitute, and will not despise their cry. He listens to the sighs and confessions of the penitent heart, and broken, contrite spirit; and thus, though he will ever abase him that is high, he will exalt him that is low. He will never give up his rightful claim to his people. If he has bought us with his precious blood, he will never suffer that purchase to be annulled by the malice of Satan or by the wickedness of our own nature. How striking are those words, "Thou hast played the harlot with many lovers; yet return again to me, saith the Lord." And again, "Turn, O backsliding children, saith the Lord, for I am married unto you." "Return, ye backsliding children, and I will heal your backslidings." And shall we not answer, "Behold, we come unto thee, for thou art the Lord our God? Truly in vain is salvation hoped for from the hills, and from the multitude of mountains: truly in the Lord our God is the salvation of Israel" (Jer. iii. 23).

February 6.

" And the Lord will create upon every dwelling-place of mount Zion, and upon her assemblies, a cloud and smoke by day, and the shining of a flaming fire by night."—ISAIAH iv. 5.

THERE is an allusion here to the cloudy pillar which rested upon the tabernacle. It was as a cloud by day, but as a pillar of fire by night. The reason of this is evident. By day, the cloud and the smoke were sufficiently visible; but not so in the night season. In the night, therefore, it was a pillar of fire, that the presence of the Lord might be distinctly seen. Spiritually viewed, this night may signify dark seasons in the soul; for there is night as well as day in the experience of God's saints. Now when they are in these dark seasons, they want clearer and brighter manifestations of the Lord's presence than when they are walking in the light of day. Thus this "shining of a flaming fire by night" may represent the shining in of the Lord's clearer, fuller, and more manifested presence, the livelier and more powerful application of his word to the heart; the brighter evidences and clearer marks that he gives of his favour, which, compared with the cloud, are as the shining of a flaming fire. It is the same presence of God, and the same glory, as was the case with the cloudy pillar; but that presence and that glory are seen in a more conspicuous manner as giving light in seasons of darkness.

The shining of a flaming fire by night may also represent the shining light of the word of truth which is spoken of as "a light that shineth in a dark place" (2 Peter i. 19). How often when the mind is dark, and evidences obscured, there is little else seen but the clear shining of the word of truth to which the soul turns its eyes as its only guiding light. "Thy word," says David, "is a lamp unto my feet, and a light unto my path." We often get into spots where

we have to look out of ourselves to the clear shining of truth
in the word of God; for there is darkness everywhere else;
and to that light we have to look and wait, and sometimes at
a great distance and for a long season, until that word comes
near and begins to shine into the heart. But with that
shining light, as it draws near and gives forth its comforting
rays and beams, comes in due time the presence and glory of
God. So to fix our heart upon the word of promise, and
wait for its fulfilment, is to walk by faith and not by sight.
Thus to Abraham the word of promise was by day a cloud;
but when "a horror of great darkness fell upon him," the
same word of promise, as the word of a covenant God, was as
a burning lamp that passed between the pieces of the offered
sacrifices (Gen. xv. 17).

February 7.

"For upon all the glory shall be a defence."—ISAIAH iv. 5.

THE glory of the Lord is his presence in the soul, for that
is represented by the cloud, as it was when his glory filled the
house of God, which Solomon built. Now this glory of the
Lord in the cloud and smoke by day, and in the shining
of a flaming fire by night, is to be a defence, both upon
every dwelling-place of mount Zion and upon her assemblies.
A defence against what? Chiefly against four things.

1. First, it is a defence against *error*. No person can
embrace error who knows anything of the presence and
power of God in his soul, or has ever seen anything of
the glory of God in the face of Jesus Christ; for all error
is opposed not only to God's truth, as revealed in the word,
but to God's presence, as revealed in the heart. And this
is true both as regards individuals and churches. God will
never sanction error as held by either. He will never bless
with his manifested presence any erroneous man, be he
minister or private individual, for he never honours or blesses

anything but his own truth, and those only who believe and
hold it. " Them that honour me I will honour." This is
a very important point, for you will often hear erroneous
men speak as if they knew spiritual things by divine teaching
and by divine testimony, and will often boast confidently of
their comforts and enjoyments, as if they had got their views
from God himself, though they turn the truth of God into
a lie. But be not deceived by these men or their false
pretensions. They have only kindled a fire to compass
themselves about with sparks, that they may walk in the
light of their fire, and in the sparks which they have kindled.
The Spirit of truth guides into all truth, and cannot and
will not countenance or bless error. The Lord's own prayer
to his heavenly Father for his disciples was, " Sanctify them
through thy truth: thy word is truth." The soul never was
divinely sanctified by a lie, nor the heart truly comforted by
error.

2. But this glory will also be a defence against all *evil;*
for nothing makes sin so to be seen and abhorred as sin as
the presence of the Lord. He is known and felt at such
moments to be infinitely pure and holy, and a holy God
must needs hate sin. If, then, his presence be felt in the
soul as a cloud in which he manifests his glory in the face of
Jesus Christ, it will be a defence against all the sins in which
you might be entangled, when there is no such sensible
presence to make you revere and adore his great and glorious
Majesty.

3. It is, therefore, also a defence against all *temptations*,
which would lead us into anything contrary to God and
godliness.

4. And it will be a defence too against all *enemies.* You
may have many enemies, both without and within; but
all their attempts to injure you will be unsuccessful if you
have the cloud of the Lord's presence in your soul, and his

glory in your midst. No enemy can hurt you if the Lord be your defence. He will watch very jealously over what he himself has communicated by his Spirit and grace to your heart, and his presence will be your best defence against every foe and against every fear.

February 8.

" And for their sakes I sanctify myself, that they also might be sanctified through the truth."—JOHN xvii. 19.

CHRIST is made to his people sanctification (1 Cor. i. 30). What am I? What are you? Filthy, polluted, defiled; are we not? Do not some of us, more or less, daily feel altogether as an unclean thing? Is not every thought of our heart altogether vile? Does any holiness, any spirituality, any heavenly-mindedness, any purity, any resemblance to the divine image dwell in our hearts by nature? Not a grain, not an atom. How then can I, a polluted sinner, ever see the face of a holy God? How can I, a worm of earth, corrupted within and without by indwelling and committed sin, ever hope to see a holy God without shrinking into destruction? I cannot see him, except so far as the Lord of life and glory is made sanctification to me. Why should men start so at "imputed sanctification?" Why should not Christ's holiness be imputed to his people as well as Christ's righteousness? Why should they not stand sanctified in him, as well as justified? Why not? Is there anything in Jesus, as God-man Mediator, which he has not for his people? Has he any perfection, any attribute, any gift, any blessing, which is not for their use? Did he not sanctify himself that they might be sanctified by the truth? Is he not the holy Lamb of God, that they might be "holy, and without blame before him in love?" What is my holiness, even such as God may be pleased to impart to me? Is it not, to say the least, scanty? Is it not, to say the least, but little in measure? But when we view the pure and spotless holiness of Jesus imputed to his people, and view them holy in him, pure in him, without spot in him, how it does away with all the wrinkles of the creature, and makes them stand holy and spotless before God.

February 9.

" Look unto me, and be ye saved, all the ends of the earth: for I am God, and there is none else."—ISAIAH xlv. 22.

How often we seem not to have any real religion, or enjoy any solid comfort! How often are our evidences obscured and beclouded, and our minds covered with deep darkness! How often does the Lord hide himself, so that we cannot behold him, nor get near to him; and how often the ground on which we thought we stood is cut from under our feet, and we have no firm standing! What a painful path is this to walk in, but how profitable! When we are reduced to poverty and beggary, we learn to value Christ's glorious riches; the worse opinion we have of our own heart, and the more deceitful and desperately wicked that we find it, the more we put our trust in his faithfulness; and the more black we are in our own esteem, the more beautiful and comely does he appear in our eyes. As we sink, Jesus rises; as we become feeble, he puts torth his strength; as we come into danger, he brings deliverance; as we get into temptation, he breaks the snare; and as we are shut up in darkness and obscurity, he causes the light of his countenance to shine. Now it is by being led in this way, and walking in these paths, that we come rightly to know who Jesus is, and to see and feel how suitable and precious such a Saviour is to our undone souls. We are needy, he has in himself all riches; we are hungry, he is the bread of life; we are thirsty, he says, "If any man thirst, let him come unto me, and drink;" we are naked, and he has clothing to bestow; we are fools, and he has wisdom to grant; we are lost, and he speaks, "Look unto me, and be ye saved." Thus, so far from our misery shutting us out from God's mercy, it is the only requisite for it; so far from our guilt excluding his pardon, it is the only thing needful for it; so far from our helplessness ruining our souls, it is the needful preparation for the manifestation of his power in our weakness; we cannot heal our own wounds and sores; that is the very reason why he should stretch forth his arm. It is because there is no salvation in ourselves, or in any other creature, that he says, "Look unto *me, for I am God,* and there is none else."

February 10.

"For the word of God is quick and powerful."—HEBREWS iv. 12.

WHAT is meant by the word of God being "quick?" That it moves with swiftness and velocity? It is certainly said of God's word (Psalm cxlvii. 15) that "it runneth very swiftly;" but that is not the meaning of the word "*quick*" in the text. It there means "living," and corresponds with the expression (Acts vii. 38) "lively (or living) oracles." It is an old English word signifying "living;" as in the expression, "who shall judge the quick and the dead" (2 Timothy iv. 1), that is, the living and the dead. So we read of Korah, Dathan, and Abiram "going down quick (that is, alive) into the pit" (Numbers xvi. 30). So the Lord is said to have "quickened (that is, made spiritually alive) those who were previously dead in trespasses and sins" (Eph. ii. 1). The word "quick," then, means not moving with velocity, but living, or rather communicating life, and thus distinguished from the dead letter. Truth, as it stands in the naked word of God, is lifeless and dead; and as such, has no power to communicate what it has not in itself, that is, life and power to the hearts of God's people. It stands there in so many letters and syllables, as lifeless as the types by which they were printed. But when the incarnate Word takes of the written word, and speaks it home into the heart and conscience of a vessel of mercy, whether in letter or substance, then he endues it with divine life, and it enters into the soul, communicating to it a life that can never die. As James speaks, "Of his own will begat he us with the word of truth." And also Peter, "Being born again, not of corruptible seed, but of incorruptible, by the word of God, which *liveth* and abideth for ever" (1 Peter i. 23). Eternal realities are brought into the soul, fixed and fastened by an Almighty hand. The conscience is made alive in the fear of God; and the soul is raised up from a death in sin, or a death in profession, to a life heavenly, new, and supernatural.

February 11.

" Not as though I had already attained, either were already perfect: but I follow after, if that I may apprehend that for which also I am apprehended of Christ Jesus." — PHILIPPIANS iii. 12.

THE Apostle Paul, perhaps the greatest saint that ever lived upon earth, had to confess that even he had not attained. There was that in Christ more than he had ever seen, ever known, ever felt, ever tasted, ever handled, ever realised. There were heights in his glory, depths in his love, in his sufferings, in his bitter agonies in the garden and on the cross, which passed all apprehension and comprehension. Therefore he says, "Not as though I had already attained." I am a child still, a learner still, as weak as ever, as helpless

as ever to obtain what I want. Though I follow on; though
I forget the things which are behind and reach forward to
the things before; though I know what I am aiming at, what
I am seeking; though my eye is single, my heart earnest, yet
it is not with me as if I had already attained. Now just put
yourself in that scale; and to measure yourself aright, look
at these things. Are you following after? Do you see that
there is something which is to be tasted, handled, felt, and
realised of the precious things of God? Have you ever had
any sips, tastes, drops, foretastes? Has your heart ever been
melted, softened, warmed by the goodness and mercy of God,
by the love of Christ? Did you ever feel that there was
a sweetness, blessedness, and happiness in the things of God
to which nothing else could be compared? Has your heart
ever been opened and enlarged by the love of God, so that
you felt that spirituality of mind which is life and peace; and
could you have continued in that spot it would have been to
you all that you wanted to make you look death calmly in the
face? Now it is these sips, tastes, and drops, these sweet
discoveries of what the Lord is to believing souls, which draw
forth the desires of the heart and enable it to follow after.
But darkness supervenes; the Lord withdraws himself, sin
works, Satan tempts, trials perplex your mind, unbelief rises
up and begins to question everything. Then there is no
following on. Everything looks so dark, so gloomy; divine
things are so out of sight; doubts and fears so possess the
mind; and it seems as if we came so short, so very short,
that the question arises whether we may not come short
at last; whether we may not have deceived ourselves;
whether all we have felt may not have been an awful
delusion. And yet see how this works. How it stirs the
mind up; how it makes us seek again and again to possess
realities; how it seems to open the eyes afresh to see what
true religion is, and that it consists in the teachings and

operations of the Holy Ghost upon the heart. Thus our very short-comings, deficiencies, and complaints are blessedly overruled and made to work graciously to stir us up to run again the race set before us. But depend upon it, the most highly-favoured saint upon earth will have reason to say with Paul, "Not as though I had already attained, either were already perfect," that is, matured and ripe. Not perfect in understanding, nor perfect in heart, nor perfect in lip, nor perfect in life. Every saint of God will have to confess imperfection, imperfection stamped upon all that he has and is; imperfection, imperfection upon everything but the work of the Son of God upon the cross and the work of God the Holy Ghost in the soul.

February 12.

" I drew them with cords of a man, with bands of love."— Hosea xi. 4.

When God draws his people near unto himself, it is not done in a mechanical way. They are drawn, not with cords of iron, but with the cords of a man; the idea being of something feeling, human, tender, touching; not as if God laid an iron arm upon his people to drag them to his breast, whether they wished to come or not. This would not be grace nor the work of the Spirit upon the heart. God does not so act in a way of mechanical force. We therefore read, "Thy people shall be willing in the day of thy power" (Psalm cx. 3). He touches their heart with his gracious finger, like the band of men whom he thus inclined to follow Saul (1 Sam. x. 26); he communicates to their soul both faith and feeling; he melts, softens, and humbles their heart by a sense of his goodness and mercy; for it is his goodness, as experimentally felt and realised, which leads to repentance. If you have ever felt any secret and sacred drawing of your soul upward to heaven, it was not compulsion, not violence,

not a mechanical constraint, but an arm of pity and compassion let down into your very heart, which, touching your
inmost spirit, drew it up into the bosom of God. It was
some such gracious touch as that spoken of in the Song
of Solomon, " My beloved put in his hand by the hole of the
door, and my bowels were moved for him." It was some
view of his goodness, mercy, and love in the face of a
Mediator, with some dropping into your spirit of his pity and
compassion towards you, which softened, broke, and melted
your heart. You were not driven onward by being flogged
and scourged, but blessedly drawn with the cords of a man,
which seemed to touch every tender feeling and enter into
the very depths of your spirit. And why is this? Because it
is as *man* that our blessed Lord is the Mediator; it is the
man Christ Jesus, the man who groaned and sighed in the
garden, the man that hung upon the cross, the man who lay
in the sepulchre, who is now the man at the right hand of the
Father, and yet God-man; for it is through his humanity that
we draw near unto God. As his blood, which was the blood
of humanity; and as his sufferings, which were the sufferings
of humanity; and as his sacrifice, which was the sacrifice of
the humanity; and as his death, which was the death of the
humanity; as these are opened up with divine power, they
form, so to speak, a medium whereby we may draw near
unto God, without terror, without alarm, because God in
Christ manifests himself as altogether love.

February 13.

" *Who gave himself for us, that he might redeem us from all
iniquity, and purify unto himself a peculiar people, zealous of
good works.*"—TITUS ii. 14.

How can any one who knows anything of the blessedness
of atoning blood and redeeming love and the sanctifying

influences of the Holy Spirit continue in sin that grace
may abound? Doctrinal professors may do these things,
for a mere letter knowledge of the truth brings with it no
deliverance from the power of sin; but the living soul, in
whom the God of all grace is carrying on his gracious work,
can it trample under foot the cross of the suffering Son of
God? It is impossible that a man who knows for himself
the redeeming efficacy of Christ's atoning blood, and whose
conscience is made tender in the fear of God, can, under
the sweet influence of his love, deliberately crucify him again.
Not but what there is a falling under the power of sin and
temptation, as David and Peter fell; but there will not be
a wilful sinning against him, when the blessed Spirit is
bringing near his blood and grace and love. May we never
forget that the suffering Son of God gave himself to purify
unto himself a peculiar people—a people whose *thoughts* are
peculiar, for their thoughts are the thoughts of God, as
having the mind of Christ; a people whose *affections* are
peculiar, for they are fixed on things above; whose *prayers*
are peculiar, for they are wrought in their heart by the Spirit
of grace and supplication; whose *sorrows* are peculiar, because they spring from a spiritual source; whose *joys* are
peculiar, for they are joys which the stranger intermeddleth
not with; whose *hopes* are peculiar, as anchoring within the
veil; and whose *expectations* are peculiar, as not expecting to
reap a crop of happiness in this marred world, but looking
for happiness in the kingdom of rest and peace in the
bosom of God. And if they are peculiar *inwardly*, they
should be peculiar *outwardly*. They should make it manifest that they are a peculiar people by walking in the
footsteps of the Lord the Lamb, taking up the cross, denying themselves, and living to the honour, praise, and glory
of God.

February 14.

"Jesus answered and said unto her, If thou knewest the gift of God, and who it is that saith to thee, Give me to drink; thou wouldest have asked of him, and he would have given thee living water."—JOHN iv. 10.

How blessed a thing is vital godliness! That is the thing I always wish to contend for. Not for forms and ceremonies, or doctrines floating in the brain, but for the life of God in the soul; the only thing worth knowing; the only thing to live by, and I am sure the only thing to die by. How different is vital godliness received into the heart and conscience, by the operation of God the Spirit, out of the fulness of Christ, how different is this fountain of living water from the stagnant, dead water of lip-service, formality, and hypocrisy! And sure I am, if our souls have ever been baptised into a spiritual knowledge of this heavenly secret; if ever we have tasted the sweetness, felt the power, and experienced a measure of the enjoyment of vital godliness in the heart and conscience, we shall want no other but living water. Nay, in all that we do for the Lord, or for those that fear his name, in every prayer, in every ordinance, we shall be, more or less, looking out for living water.

Are we, who profess to be in the wilderness, like the thirsty traveller in the deserts of Arabia, panting after the wells and the palm trees? Do we know what it is, after long seasons of drought, when the living water has sunk well-nigh out of sight, to find its streams again springing up in the conscience? How living souls thirst after these revivings! We cannot now be satisfied with lip religion, pharisaical religion, doctrinal religion, a name to live while dead, the form of godliness without the power. A living soul can no more satisfy his thirst with mere forms and ceremonies, than a man naturally thirsty can drink out of a horse pond. He must

have living water, something given by the Lord himself,
springing up in his soul. But, does not the Lord say, that
he will give it to those that ask it? Shall we not ask, then,
and seek for it? And will he deny us? Has he denied
us in time past? Will he deny us in time to come? Has he
not the same loving and compassionate heart now, as beat in
his bosom towards this poor sinner at the well of Samaria?
He still emboldens us to ask. He is now seated upon
the throne of grace and mercy as the Mediator between God
and man. And if, through mercy, we know something of
the gift of God; and if, through divine teaching, we know
something of the glorious Person of Jesus, and have enjoyed
a measure of its sweetness in our heart, sure I am, we
shall ask, and our souls will receive the testimony of God
in our conscience, that he will not deny us, but give unto us
" living water."

February 15.

" *And I heard a loud voice saying in heaven, Now is come
salvation.*"—REVELATION xii. 10.

" SALVATION." What " salvation?" Salvation by grace,
full and free ; salvation without any intermixture of creature
righteousness ; salvation gushing from the bosom of God ;
salvation flowing wholly and solely through the blood of
the Lamb. But salvation can never be tasted without a previous foretaste of condemnation. Heaven can never be
looked up into before there has been a looking down into
the wicket-gate of hell. There must have been an experience of guilt, before there can be the enjoyment of pardon.
" Now is come salvation." *From what ?* From the accusations of Satan, the curses of the law, the fear of death, the
terrors of hell, and sentence of damnation. And *how* does
salvation come? Whilst the battle is going on, whilst the
issue is doubtful, whilst hand to hand, foot to foot, and

shoulder to shoulder, Satan and the soul are engaged in deadly strife, there is no felt experience of salvation. There may be hope, enabling the soldier to stand his ground; there is no shout of victory till the enemy is put to flight. But when Satan is defeated, his accusations silenced, and the soul liberated, then "is come salvation." The sweetest song that heaven ever proclaimed, the most blessed note that ever melted the soul, is "salvation." To be saved—saved from death and hell; saved from "the worm which dieth not, and the fire which is not quenched;" saved from the sulphurous flames of the bottomless pit; saved from the companionship of tormenting fiends, and of all the foul wretches under which earth has groaned; saved from blaspheming God in unutterable woe; saved from an eternity of misery without hope; and saved into heaven—the sight of Jesus as he is, perfect holiness and happiness, the blissful company of holy angels and glorified saints! And all this during the countless ages of a blessed eternity! What tongue of men or angels can describe the millionth part of what is contained in the word "*salvation!*"

February 16.

"*Shew me thy ways, O Lord; teach me thy paths.*"—PSALM XXV. 4.

To lie with a broken heart and contrite spirit at the footstool of mercy beseeching God to teach us is indeed a blessed spot to be in. It is the evidence of a childlike spirit, and shews such simplicity, reality, and genuineness that it bears stamped upon it the indubitable marks of true discipleship. Wherever we see such a coming out of self, with a renunciation of our own wisdom, strength, and righteousness, such a putting aside of all creature religion, and such a real spirit of humility before God, we must receive it as something beyond and above nature. Nothing but the

power of God seems able to bring a soul so completely out
of the shell and crust of self-righteousness, and so to lay open
its spiritual nakedness before him. Naturally there is something very sweet in seeing a docile, teachable disposition.
And on the other hand, few things are more offensive than
the pride of ignorance, the abominable conceit of people who
think they know everything when really they know nothing,
but are too proud to be taught. The only road to knowledge is to possess a meek, teachable, inquiring spirit, a
willingness to learn springing out of a consciousness of
ignorance. This spirit is what we see sometimes in children,
nor is there a more pleasant sight for parent or instructor
than to see a child docile, earnestly seeking information, and
glad to receive instruction. If anything can open the mouth
to teach, it is finding such a disposition to learn. So in
grace; where there is a humble, quiet, docile spirit, it seems
to draw forth out of the Lord's heart and mouth these secrets
of heavenly wisdom which he hides from others; as he
spake in the days of his flesh, "I thank thee, O Father, Lord
of heaven and earth, because thou hast hid these things from
the wise and prudent, and hast revealed them unto babes."
The babes are those who are teachable and childlike, and to
whom as such God reveals the treasures of his heavenly
wisdom.

February 17.

*" And there I will meet with thee, and I will commune with
thee from above the mercy seat."*—Exodus xxv. 22.

After a child of God has enjoyed something of the goodness and mercy of God revealed in the face of his dear Son,
he may wander from his mercies, stray away from these
choice gospel pastures, and get into a waste-howling wilderness, where there is neither food nor water; and yet, though
half-starved for want, has in himself no power to return. But

what has brought him for the most part into this state? Forgetfulness of the mercy seat; and as the Lord meets his people only there, a gradual estrangement from him. But in due time the Lord seeks out this wandering sheep, and the first place he brings him to is the mercy seat, confessing his sins and seeking mercy. Faithful to his own word, once more the Lord meets him there; and O what a meeting! A penitent backslider and a forgiving God! O what a meeting! A guilty wretch drowned in tears, and a loving Father falling upon his neck and kissing him! O what a meeting for a poor, self-condemned wretch, who can never mourn too deeply over his sins, and yet finds grace superabounding over all its aboundings, and the love of God bursting through the cloud, like the sun upon an April day, and melting his heart into contrition and love!

But this is not all. The Lord is pleased sometimes to shew his dear people the evils of their heart, to remove by his Spirit and grace that veil of pride and self-righteousness which hides so much of lost self from our eyes, and to discover what is really in us, the deep corruptions which lurk in our depraved nature, the filth and folly which is part and parcel of ourselves, the unutterable baseness and vileness so involved in our very being. Now this in itself would drive us from the throne of grace. " Can God dwell here?" is the sinner's feeling. "Can I be possessed of the fear of God when such thoughts and feelings overflow my mind, and seem to fill me as if with the very dregs of hell?" Yet still he is drawn from time to time to the throne of grace to con-fess these sins before the mercy seat, for he cannot, dare not, stay away from it; and again God is true to his word: " There will I meet with thee." There once more he re-veals a sense of his mercy and goodness, and once more shews that, whatever the sinner be in himself, he is faithful to his own promise.

February 18.

" But speaking the truth (margin, *being sincere*) *in love."*-— EPHESIANS iv. 15.

SINCERITY lies at the root of all gracious profession. If a man be not sincere he is nothing. God makes a man sincere by planting his truth in his heart; and whenever God does make a man sincere, the truth which he has implanted will grow. Truth does not lie in a man's soul dead and motionless, like a stone in the street; it is a living, active, expansive principle. If the truth be in the soul it will be ever pushing out error, because the two principles cannot exist together; and as Isaac thrust out Ishmael, and Jacob proved stronger than Esau, so will simplicity and godly sincerity be ever mightier than craft and deception. The truth of God in the heart will not wither and die, but will be shined upon by the Sun of righteousness, and sunned into fruitfulness by the smiles of God; and as truth becomes day by day more and more precious, so will error and evil become day by day more and more hateful. A sincere soul stands " girt about with truth;" and truth forms its shield and buckler.

But how does this Christian sincerity prove the soul's safeguard from error? By putting it ever on the watch tower, looking out and looking up for the teaching of God and the light of his countenance. A soul made spiritually sincere takes nothing upon trust; it requires the seal of God on all it receives, and the witness of the Spirit to all that it feels. He who is sincere sees the rocks ahead on which others concerning faith make shipwreck; and being well ballasted with temptations, afflictions, and trials, he is not easily tossed to and fro with every wind of doctrine. His desire to be right keeps him right; his fear to be wrong preserves him from wrong. The light of God in his soul makes him see; the

life of God in his heart makes him feel ; the fear of God in
his conscience makes him honest; the love of God in his
affections makes him love; and all this gives truth such a
firm place in him that there is no room for error. The
Apostle adds, therefore, " in love." It is not enough to be
" sincere ; " we must be " sincere in love." Mark that. It
is not receiving God's truth as a certain orderly system ; it is
not furnishing our heads with a sound doctrinal creed and
compact Calvinistic scheme which will avail us in the trying
hour ; but it is to have the truth of God brought into our soul
by a divine power, and realising such unutterable sweetness
in it as communicates a firm abiding love, both to the truth
itself, and to Him of whom it testifies and from whom it
comes. It is thus we are made " sincere in love." The
fear of God creates the sincerity, the application of the truth
with power creates the love to it. And when we are thus
made " sincere in love " we are brought out of the childish
state in which we are carried about with every wind of
doctrine, and in danger of being entrapped by the cunning
craft of every deceiver. We know the truth, love the truth,
and become established in the truth.

February 19.

" *Thou openest thine hand, and satisfiest the desire of every
living thing.*"—Psalm cxlv. 16.

THAT word has been sweet to me sometimes, " Every
living thing." How comprehensive it is ! And how low it
descends ! How it comes down to the weakest and meanest
and least of God's family, if he is only " *a thing*," only " a
living thing ! " if he cannot see himself " a man in Christ ; "
no, nor see himself a child of God; no, nor see himself
a new-born babe ! If he cannot see in himself the features
of a child even, yet to be " a living thing ! " Now, perhaps,
if you cannot trace the features of a grown-up man as

stamped upon you, and are exercised with distressing doubts whether your experience even amounts to the new-born babe, you may yet come in here, as being " a living thing," a *non-descript;* a sort of person that cannot make yourself out, having an experience which you think nobody can fathom, having exercises which nobody else seems to be harassed with, and walking in a path where no other child of God seems ever to have walked before you. Did not one say of old, (and have not you and I echoed his words?) he was "as a beast before thee;" not a man, for "surely I am more brutish than any man, and have not the understanding of a man " (Proverbs xxx. 2), but possessed of life still, breathing after God still, with that in the soul which cannot rest satisfied short of the manifestation and the presence of God.

But here is the mark of the " living thing "—*the desire:* " Thou satisfiest *the desire* of every living thing : " not natural desires ; not " the desire of the sluggard, which hath nothing," that is, nothing spiritual in the want, or in the answer ; but the spiritual desires that the Holy Ghost himself has kindled, desires after God, "as the hart panteth after the water brooks," desires to know Christ by some sweet revelation of his glory, desires to be brought to the foot of the cross, and to have his image stamped upon our soul, desires to be led into the length and breadth and depth and height of that love of his which passeth knowledge, desires to walk before God accepted in the Beloved, desires to feel that in our souls which shall sweetly satisfy us that we are eternally His. This " living thing," though a nondescript in his own feelings, has that which marks the existence of life in him ; and that is, living desires towards the living God, breathing affections after Jesus, a restless, dissatisfied heart, discontented with the things of time and sense, feeling no pleasure in what the world presents, and sighing to the Lord for the discoveries of his grace and his love.

February 20.

"Where the Spirit of the Lord is, there is liberty."—
2 CORINTHIANS iii. 17.

THE gospel is "the perfect law of liberty," therefore the
very perfection of liberty, and thus thoroughly and entirely
free from the least taint of bondage, the slightest tincture of
servitude.   It is this perfect freedom which distinguishes it
from the law which "worketh wrath" and "gendereth to
bondage."   It is, therefore, a freedom *from* sin; from its
guilt, as having "the heart sprinkled from an evil conscience;" from its *filth*, by "the washing of regeneration and
renewing of the Holy Ghost;" from its *love*, through "the
love of God, shed abroad in the heart by the Holy Ghost;"
from its *dominion*, as "not being under the law but under
grace;" and from its *practice*, by becoming "servants to
God, so as to have our fruit unto holiness, and the end everlasting life."   How, then, can this pure, holy, and precious
gospel be condemned as leading to licentiousness?   It is
because its power, its preciousness, its happy, holy, heavenly
liberty have never been experimentally known by some who,
like the Galatians, do all they can to "frustrate the grace of
God," by "turning again to the weak and beggarly elements
whereunto they desire to be in bondage;" whilst others, like
those monsters of wickedness whom Jude and Peter denounce
with such burning words, pervert and abuse the liberty of the
gospel unto licentiousness, "sporting themselves with their
own deceivings," and, "while they promise others liberty,
are themselves the servants of corruption."   Now the liberty
of the gospel, as revealed in the Scriptures, and made experimentally known to the soul, steers, so to speak, between these
two extremes, and is as perfectly free from the least intermixture of legal bondage as from the least taint of Antinomian licentiousness.   It is, indeed, this holy liberty,

heavenly power, and gracious influence of the precious
gospel, under the teaching and testimony of the Holy Ghost,
which makes it so suitable to our case and state when first
convinced of sin, and cast into prison under guilt and condemnation. What release but a perfect release would suit
our deplorable case as prisoners in the pit where there is no
water, shut up under wrath and guilty fear through a condemning law and an accusing conscience ? This pure and
precious gospel, therefore, comes down to our pitiable
state and condition as a message of pure mercy, revealing pardon and peace through a Saviour's blood; and
when, by grace, we can receive, embrace, and entertain it
as a word from God to us, proclaiming liberty as with a
jubilee trumpet through every court and ward of the soul.
What were we before this precious gospel reached our ears
and hearts ? Were we not bondslaves to sin, serving divers
lusts and pleasures, taken and led captive by Satan at his
will, and while we talked about enjoying life, were, through
fear of death, subject to bondage ? When we saw the saints
of God not daring to do what we did greedily, we thought
that *they* were the slaves, and *we* the free men, not knowing
that " to whom we yield ourselves servants to obey, his servants we are, whether of sin unto death, or of obedience
unto righteousness;" not knowing that " whosoever com-
mitteth sin is the servant of sin," and that our boasted
freedom was real servitude, whilst their apparent bondage
was real freedom ; for they had an interest in that precious
declaration : " If the Son, therefore, shall make you free, ye
shall be free indeed."

February 21.

" *I kill, and I make alive ; I wound, and I heal.*"—
Deuteronomy xxxii. 39.

The work of grace in the soul, in its very beginnings,

penetrates deeply into its inmost substance. It wounds and
lays open the conscience to the eye of infinite Purity and
Holiness.   " The entrance of thy words (that is, the very
first entrance) giveth light."   " The word of God is quick
and powerful, and sharper than any two-edged sword,
piercing even to the dividing asunder of soul and spirit,
and of the joints and marrow, and is a discerner of the
thoughts and intents of the heart."   All conviction to be
true conviction must be thorough.   The field must be
ploughed, broken up, and furrowed, before the seed can
find a tilth, a seed-bed for the seed to fall in so as to
germinate and grow.   There is much to be done in a
sinner's heart before Christ can dwell in him by faith, or be
formed in him the hope of glory.   The heart is naturally
very hard ; thorns, thistles, and briars overspread its surface;
the rank weeds of pride and lust have taken deep root ;
much grubbing up of these bosom sins, as well as of our
inbred self-righteousness and fleshly holiness, creature
strength and sufficiency, is needed to prepare us to receive
a free grace salvation, separate us from the world and false
professors, embitter to us the loved things of time and
sense, and lay us suing for mercy at the foot of the cross.
The first work, therefore, of conviction must be deep, or at
least thorough, in order to make room for Christ and his
salvation.   And so it is with any manifestation 'or discovery
of the Lord Jesus Christ, any application of his blood, any
visitation of his presence, or shedding abroad of his love ;
these divine realities do not float upon the surface, but sink
deep, and penetrate into his heart of hearts, into a man's
inmost and deepest soul.   How soon is all lost and forgotten, but what the blessed Spirit writes himself in the
heart !   People say, " How well we have heard ! " but all is
lost and dropped before they get home from the house of
prayer.   They read a chapter, close the Bible, and with it

all they have read is closed too. Many have passing pangs
of conviction, and passing desires, who give little proof
of living under the Spirit's anointings. That divine Spirit
does not let the saints of God off so easily. He holds them
fast and firm to the work of conviction till he has slain them
outright; and when he blesses he heals as deep as he
wounds, and reveals the gospel as powerfully as he applies
the law.

February 22.

*" But when the Comforter is come, whom I will send unto
you from the Father, even the Spirit of truth, which proceedeth
from the Father, he shall testify of me."*—JOHN xv. 26.

THE special work and office of the Holy Ghost is to
testify of Jesus, to glorify him, to take of the things that are
his, and to shew them to the soul; and therefore without
these teachings and testimonies of the Holy Ghost we have
no true, no saving knowledge of him, no living faith in him,
no sweet communion with him, no tender and affectionate
love toward him. And are not these the marks which
peculiarly distinguish the living family of God from the
dead in sin and the dead in profession? A bare knowledge
of the letter of truth can communicate no such gracious
affections as warm, soften, melt, and animate the soul of
a child of God, under the felt power and influence of the
Holy Ghost; can create no such faith as gives him manifest
union with Jesus; can inspire no such hope as carries every
desire of his heart within the veil; can produce no such
godly sorrow for sin as makes him loathe and abhor himself
in dust and ashes; can shed abroad no such love as makes
him love the Lord with a pure heart fervently. But the
same blessed and holy Teacher who takes of the things that
are Christ's and reveals them to the soul, thus raising up
faith, hope, and love, and bringing into living exercise every

other spiritual gift and grace, first prepares the heart to receive him in all his gracious characters and covenant relationships by deeply and powerfully convincing us of our need of him as our all in all. Is he a Priest? We need his atoning blood and his all-prevailing intercession that we may have peace with God, and that our prayers and supplications may rise up with acceptance into his ears. Is he a Prophet? We need his heavenly instruction, that we may sit at his feet and hear his word, so as to believe his promises and obey his precepts. Is he a King? We need his powerful and peaceful sceptre to subdue every foe, calm every fear, subdue every lust, crucify the whole body of sin, and bring into captivity every thought to the obedience of Christ.

February 23.

" Forasmuch then as the children are partakers of flesh and blood, he also himself likewise took part of the same ; that through death he might destroy him that had the power of death, that is, the devil."—HEBREWS ii. 14.

By his sufferings, bloodshedding, and death our gracious Lord not only made a complete atonement for sin, fulfilled every demand of the law, washed his people from all their iniquities in the fountain of his precious blood, and wrought out and brought in a perfect and everlasting righteousness for their justification, but *" through death destroyed* him that had the power of death, that is, *the devil."* It was by the death of the cross that the gracious Lord "spoiled principalities and powers, and made a show of them openly, triumphing over them in it." It is a point little considered, though one of much importance, that the Lord Jesus had, as if personally, to grapple with and overcome the prince of the power of the air, to hurl Satan from his usurped throne, to destroy his works, and overthrow his kingdom; and this

not by an act of omnipotent power, but by an act of the
lowest weakness, for " he was crucified through weakness."
According to our simple views, we might think that all that
was needed to overthrow Satan was an act of omnipotent
power.   But this was not God's way.   The king over all
the children of pride, in the depths of infinite wisdom, was
to be dethroned by an act of the deepest humility, of the
most meek and submissive obedience, of the intensest
suffering of God's own beloved Son, as standing in the
place of those over whom Satan and death had triumphed
through sin.   We read that " the Son of God was manifested
that he might destroy (literally, ' loosen ' or ' untie ') the
works of the devil."   Thus he came, not only to untie and
undo all that Satan had fastened and done by traversing, as
it were, the whole ground, from the first entrance of sin and
death, and, by a course of holy and meritorious obedience,
repair the wreck and ruin produced by the primary author of
all disobedience, but, as the final stroke, to destroy and put
down the disobedient and rebellious prince of darkness
himself.

February 24.

" *Thus saith the Lord; I remember thee, the kindness of
thy youth, the love of thine espousals, when thou wentest after
me in the wilderness, in a land that was not sown.*"—
JEREMIAH ii. 2.

SALVATION is a gift, the choicest and richest gift which the
hands of a Triune God, whose name is Love, can bestow.
It is a portion, an inheritance, an estate, a treasure, an
eternal reality.   The full possession, the entire enjoyment,
the complete acquisition of this predestinated weight of
glory, is indeed reserved until a future state ; but the
earnests, the firstfruits, the early ripe clusters, the first
dew-drops of this eternal inheritance, are given to the

elect whilst upon earth. The everlasting enjoyment of the presence and glory of Christ is often compared in Scripture to a wedding. Thus we read (Rev. xix. 7) of "the Lamb's wife," and of "the marriage of the Lamb." So the Church is said to be "brought unto the King in raiment of needle-work," as the bride, in Eastern countries, was brought by the father to the bridegroom. But we read of "espousals" also, which always preceded the celebration of the marriage. "I remember thee, the kindness of thy youth, the love of thine *espousals*." "I have *espoused* you to one husband, that I may present you as a chaste virgin to Christ." So Joseph was "espoused to the virgin Mary, before they came together," that is, before they became man and wife. Now this espousal was a necessary prelude to marriage, though it was not the same thing. And, therefore, a betrothed virgin was punished as an adulteress by the Levitical law, if she was unfaithful to her espoused husband. To be betrothed had the nature of marriage in it, though it was not the same thing as marriage. The parties did not live together, and were not put in possession of each other. Thus, it is *in this life* that the spiritual betrothment takes place, and the spiritual marriage in the life to come. "I will betroth thee unto me in righteousness and in judgment, and in loving-kindness and in mercies; I will even betroth thee unto me in faithfulness, and thou shalt know the Lord" (Hosea ii. 19, 20).

February 25.

"*It is a faithful saying: For if we be dead with him, we shall also live with him: if we suffer, we shall also reign with him.*"—2 TIMOTHY ii. 11, 12.

To be partakers of Christ's crown, we must be partakers of Christ's cross. Union with him in suffering must precede union with him in glory. This is the express testimony of the Holy

Ghost: "If so be that we suffer with him, that we may be also glorified together." The flesh and the world are to be crucified to us, and we to them; and this can only be by virtue of a living union with a crucified Lord. This made the Apostle say, "I am crucified with Christ: nevertheless I live; yet not I, but Christ liveth in me: and the life which I now live in the flesh, I live by the faith of the Son of God, who loved me and gave himself for me." And again, "But God forbid that I should glory save in the cross of our Lord Jesus Christ, by whom the world is crucified unto me and I unto the world." An experimental knowledge of crucifixion with his crucified Lord made Paul preach the cross, not only in its power to save, but in its power to sanctify. Through the cross, that is, through union and communion with him who suffered upon it, not only is there a·fountain opened for all sin, but for all uncleanness (Zech. xiii. 1). Blood and water gushed from the side of Jesus when pierced by the Roman spear.

> "This fountain so dear, he'll freely impart;
> Unlock'd by the spear, it gushed from his heart,
> With blood and with water; the first to atone,
> To cleanse us the latter; the fountain's but one."

"All my springs are in thee," said the man after God's own heart ; and well may we re-echo his words. All our springs, not only of pardon and peace, acceptance and justification, but of happiness and holiness, of wisdom and strength, of victory over the world, of mortification of a body of sin and death; of every fresh revival and renewal of hope and confidence; of all prayer and praise; of every new budding forth of the soul, as of Aaron's rod, in blossom and fruit; of every gracious feeling, spiritual desire, warm supplication, honest confession, melting contrition, and godly sorrow for sin—all these springs of that life which is hid with Christ in God are in a crucified Lord. Thus Christ

crucified is, "to them who are saved, the power of God."
And as he "of God is made unto us wisdom, righteousness,
sanctification, and redemption," at the cross alone can we
be made wise unto salvation, become righteous by a free
justification, receive of his Spirit to make us holy, and be
redeemed and delivered by blood and power from sin, Satan,
death, and hell.

February 26.

" The dead are raised up."—MATTHEW xi. 5.

" THE dead are raised up." The "dead" are those who
by nature are dead in sin. These dead are raised up when
life from God visits their souls. They are raised up to faith
in Jesus, raised up to hope in his name, raised up to a sense
of his dying love to their souls, raised up from doubt and
fear, raised up from the depths of despondency, to look unto
him and be saved. What a mercy it is that the Lord of life
and glory still puts forth the same power in the hearts of his
people, that he once put forth in their bodies, and that he
raises them up from their state of death and deadness! Do
we not often feel so dead, as though we had not a particle of
the grace of God? So dead, that it seems scarcely possible
to have a sensation of spiritual life again? So dead, that we
almost fear whether the power of God was ever felt in our
hearts? Now, the Lord raises up life and feeling in our
souls, by putting forth the same power that called Lazarus
out of the tomb. And every lifting up of the heart towards
him, every panting desire to know him, and the power of his
resurrection, every breathing of tender affection, every sigh,
cry, and groan, yea, every feeling, however short, however
transient, Godward, is a proof that the Lord of life and
glory is still putting forth his power in the hearts of his
people.

February 27.

" O that thou wouldest bless me indeed !"—1 Chronicles
iv. 10.

An "indeed" blessing is what the soul is seeking after
which has ever felt the misery and bitterness of sin, and ever
tasted the sweetness of God's salvation.   And these "indeed"
blessings are seen to be spiritual and eternal.   Compared
with such blessings as these, it sees how vain and empty are
all earthly things, what vain toys, what idle dreams, what
passing shadows.   It wonders at the folly of men in hunting
after such vain shows, and spending time, health, money,.life
itself, in a pursuit of nothing but misery and destruction.
Every passing bell that it hears, every corpse borne slowly
along to the grave that it sees, impresses it with solemn
feelings as to the state of those who live and die in their sins.
Thus it learns more and more to contrast time with eternity,
earth with heaven, sinners with saints, and professors with
possessors.   By these things it is taught, with Baruch, not
" to seek great things" for itself, but real things ; things
which will outlast time, and fit it for eternity.   It is thus
brought to care little for the opinion of men as to what is
good or great, but much for what God has stamped his own
approbation upon, such as a tender conscience, a broken
heart, a contrite spirit, a humble mind, a separation from the
world and everything worldly, a submission to his holy will,
a meek endurance of the cross, a conformity to Christ's
suffering image, and a living to God's glory.   As, then, the
gracious Lord is pleased to indulge it with some discovery of
himself, shedding abroad a sweet sense of his goodness and
mercy, atoning blood, and dying love, it is made to long
more and more for the manifestation of those blessings
which alone are to be found in him.   For his blessings are
not like the mere temporal mercies which we enjoy at his

hands, all of which perish in the using, but are for ever and ever; and when once given are never taken away. They thus become earnests and foretastes of eternal joys, for they are absolutely irreversible. When Isaac had once blessed Jacob in God's name, though the blessing had been obtained by guile, yet having been once given, it could not be recalled. He said, therefore, to Esau, "I have blessed him, and he shall be blessed." So when the Lord has blessed his people with any of those spiritual blessings which are stored up in his inexhaustible fulness, these blessings are like himself, unchanging and unchangeable; for "he is in one mind and none can turn him;" "The same yesterday, to-day, and for ever."

February 28.

"And enlarge my coast."—1 CHRONICLES iv. 10.

A coast means a boundary line such as divides one territory from another, or terminates a country, as the sea coast is the boundary of our island. Every quickened soul has a coast; that is, a territory of inward experience, which is limited and bounded by the line that the Holy Spirit has drawn in his conscience. As the Lord divided the tribes, to cast their inheritance by line (Psalm lxxviii. 55), so hath he cast the lot for every vessel of mercy, and his hand hath divided it unto them by line (Isaiah xxxiv. 17). This is as it were the tether which fastens down every quickened soul to his own appointed portion of inward experience. Within this tether he may walk, feed, and lie down. It is "the food convenient for him," the strip of pasture allotted him. He cannot, he dare not break this tether, which is fastened round a tender conscience, and every stretching forth beyond his measure to boast in another man's line of things, cuts into and galls this tender conscience. But the living soul cannot but earnestly desire to have his coast enlarged. He wants more light, more life, more feeling, more liberty, more

knowledge of God in Christ, more faith, hope, and love, and
to have his narrow, contracted, shut-up heart enlarged in
prayer, in meditation, in communion, in affection to the
people of God.   He is not satisfied with the scanty pasture
allotted him, but wants a larger measure of heavenly teaching, to be indulged with more filial confidence in, and access
unto God, and be more delivered from that fear which hath
torment.   " God shall *enlarge* Japheth, and he shall dwell in
the tents of Shem" (Gen. ix. 27).   " I will run the way of
thy commandments, when thou shalt *enlarge* my heart"
(Psalm cxix. 32).   This enlargement of their border the
Lord had sworn to Israel, and to give them all the land
which he had promised unto their fathers ; and therefore
when he had said, " Sing, O barren, thou that didst not
bear," he adds, " enlarge the place of thy tent, and let them
stretch forth the curtains of thy habitations ; spare not,
lengthen thy cords, and strengthen thy stakes" (Isaiah
liv. 1, 2).   Have you any of these fervent desires after
light, love, and liberty, that the world, pride, lust, unbelief,
covetousness, and carnality may not shut up your heart, but
that you may know the love of Christ that passeth knowledge,
so as to be filled with all the fulness of God ?   These are
good desires, and very different from rushing presumptuously
forward, and chattering about liberty whilst you are slaves of
corruption.   It is one thing to look through the park palings,
and another to enjoy the estate ; but it is far better to look
through the palings with wishful desires, than to break down
the fence as a trespasser.   To look upon the coffer is not to
be put into possession of the writings, but it is better to wait
and cry for the key of David than break it open, and steal
the deeds.   And he that is kept in the narrow, narrow path
between sloth and presumption will be at solemn seasons
crying out with Jabez, " O that thou wouldest enlarge my
coast ! "

February 29.

"Let my soul live, and it shall praise thee ; and let thy judgments help me."—PSALM cxix. 175.

WHEN we "live," we live by faith ; as the Apostle says, " The life which I now live in the flesh, I live by the faith of the Son of God." We live by faith when the Lord is pleased to communicate true faith, the precious gift of faith to the heart. Then indeed we believe. We then believe in Jesus, believe in his blood, believe in his righteousness, believe in his Person, believe in his dying love ; and as faith begins to lift up its drooping head in the soul, we begin to live a life of faith in the Son of God. And as we begin to live, we also begin to love. When we are in darkness, coldness, and barrenness there is neither love to God nor man ; the very ways of God are a perfect misery to us ; the Bible is neglected, and prayer is little attended to; under preaching we are cold, dead, and listless ; the company of God's people is forsaken, and the things of eternity seem to fade from our view. But let the Lord revive his work upon the heart, let him bestow a gracious renewing, let him drop the unction of his Spirit, let the rain and dew of his grace fall, let him manifest himself with life and power; then the whole scene changes. It is like spring after a dreary winter ; it is like the outpouring of the rain from heaven after a long season of drought, "Thou renewest the face of the earth." There is a blessed change when the Lord himself is pleased to appear in the soul. Then it begins to live. And this life will manifest itself in various ways. Whilst we are dead, prayer is a burden ; when we have life, prayer is our very breath. When we are dead, the very thoughts of God are grievous; when we are alive, the thoughts of God are sweet and pleasant. When we are dead, our affections cleave to the things of time and sense ; when we are alive, our affections mount upward. When we are dead, the world is our home, though it is but a miserable one; when we are alive, we are looking upward to heaven as the home of the soul when time shall be no more.

March 1.

"The church of God, which he hath purchased with his own blood."—ACTS xx. 28.

ATONEMENT for sin stands or falls with the Deity of Christ. If we deny his Deity, we must deny the atonement, for what value or merit can there be in the blood of a mere man that God, for its sake, should pardon millions of sins? This the Socinians clearly see, and therefore deny the atonement altogether. But if there be no atonement, no sacrifice, no propitiation for sin, where can we look for pardon and peace? Whichever way we turn our eyes there is despair, and we might well take up the language of the fallen angel:

> " Me miserable! which way shall I fly
> Infinite wrath, and infinite despair?
> Which way I fly is hell; myself am hell;
> And, in the lowest deep, a lower deep
> Still threatening to devour me opens wide,
> To which the hell I suffer seems a heaven."

But when by the eye of faith we see the Son of God obeying the law, rendering, by doing and dying, acting and suffering, a satisfaction to the violated justice of the Most High and offering a sacrifice for sin, then we see such a glory and such a value breathing through every thought, word, and action of his suffering humanity, that we embrace him and all that he is and has, with every desire and affection of our regenerated soul. All our religion lies here; all our faith, hope, and love flow unto, and are, as it were, fixed and concentrated in Jesus Christ, and him crucified; and without a measure of this in our heart and conscience, we have

no religion worth the name, nothing that either saves or
sanctifies, nothing that delivers from the guilt, filth, love,
power, and practice of sin, nothing that supports in life, comforts in death, or fits for eternity. The way, then, whereby
we come to a knowledge of, and a faith in, the Deity of
Christ is first by feeling a need of all that he is as a Saviour,
and a great one, and then having a manifestation of him by
the blessed Spirit to our soul. When he is thus revealed and
brought near, we see, by the eye of faith, his pure and perfect humanity and his eternal Deity; and these two distinct
natures we see combined, but not intermingled, in one
glorious Person, Immanuel, God with us. Till thus favoured
we may see the Deity of Christ in the Scriptures, and have
so far a belief in it, but we have not that personal appropriating faith whereby, with Thomas, we can say, "My Lord
and my God."

March 2.

*" There are many devices in a man's heart; nevertheless the
counsel of the Lord, that shall stand."*—Proverbs xix. 21.

A man in his fleshly mind is generally devising some
method or other whereby he may escape a practical subjection to the gospel; some way or other whereby he may
escape walking in the path of self-denial and mortification of
the flesh, and the crucifixion of " the old man with the affections and lusts." He is generally seeking some way or other
to indulge the flesh, and yet, at the same time, to stand in
gospel liberty, to have everything that can gratify his carnal
mind, and, at the same time, have a well-grounded hope of
eternal life. But the Lord says, " No, these two things are
not compatible; he that shall live with Christ must die with
Christ; he that shall reign with Christ must suffer with
Christ; he that shall wear the crown must carry the cross."
So, that whatever devices there be in a man's heart, or what-

ever ways and plans he shall undertake to bring his devices
to pass, "the counsel of the Lord still shall stand." Divine
sovereignty shall fulfil that which divine sovereignty has appointed, and the purposes of God shall stand upon the ruins
of the purposes of the creature. And it is our mercy (so far
as we are children of the living God), it is our mercy, that it
should be so. Where should we have been this moment, if
the devices in our hearts had succeeded? We should have
been in hell. Where should we have been, since the Lord
has been pleased, as we trust, to quicken our souls into
spiritual life, if all our devices had succeeded? Our "eyes
would have stood out with fatness," and we should have
"had more than heart could wish." We should have been
now, if the Lord had left us to our own devices, indulging in
some awful temptation, or already have disgraced our name
before the Church of God; or, if we had escaped that, we
should have a name to live, whilst our hearts were secretly
dead before God; have had "a form of godliness, whilst we
inwardly or outwardly denied the power thereof." And
therefore it is our mercy that the devices of our hearts should
not stand, but that "the counsel of the Lord" should prevail
over all the purposes of our base nature. When a man is
brought to the right spot, and is in a right mind to trace out
the Lord's dealings with him from the first, he sees it was a
kind hand which "blasted his gourds and laid them low;" it
was a kind hand that swept away his worldly prospects,
which reduced him to natural as well as to spiritual poverty,
which led him into exercises, trials, sorrows, griefs, and tribulations; because, in those trials he has found the Lord, more
or less, experimentally precious. Jacob found it so; he
blessed the Lord for the path he had led him in. Though
his days had been few and evil, he could see how the Lord
had "fed him all his life long unto that day," amid all the
changing vicissitudes through which he had passed in body

and soul; and he blessed that hand which had guided him through that difficult way, and yet brought him to a " city of habitation."

March 3.

"*For we which live are alway delivered unto death for Jesus' sake, that the life also of Jesus might be made manifest in our mortal flesh.*"—2 CORINTHIANS iv. 11.

WHAT is meant by the expression, "*our mortal flesh?*" It does not mean the carnal mind, but our earthly tabernacle; and the expression is similar to another in this chapter, " We have this treasure in *earthen vessels,* that the excellency of the power may be of God, and not of us." It is, then, in this poor body, compassed with infirmities, that the life of Jesus is made manifest. This divine life will often spring up in fervent breathings after God, in the actings of living faith, in the sweet intercourse the people of God have with one another, in reading the Scriptures, in the application of precious promises, and under the preached word. From time to time it bubbles up like a spring from its source. Sometimes indeed it runs underground, buried as it were under the load of " our mortal flesh ; " but again and again it reappears, drawn up by the Sun of righteousness. "Spring up, O well." But its risings are ever proportionate to its sinkings. Thus in proportion as we cease to pray naturally, do we pray spiritually ; as we cease to hope in the flesh, do we hope in the Lord ; as we cease to believe with the head, do we believe with the heart; when we see an end of all perfection in self, then we begin to find perfection in Christ; and when we see nothing in our hearts but sin, misery, and wretchedness, then we begin to taste spiritual consolation. Thus in proportion as nature sinks, the life of Jesus rises, and is made manifest in our mortal flesh.

Is the soul, then, longing to have sweet manifestations

of the life of Jesus? Where must it go to get them?
What does the word of God say? "Whence cometh wisdom? and where is the place of understanding? Seeing it is
hid from the eyes of all living, and kept close from the fowls
of the air. Destruction and death say, We have heard the
fame thereof with our ears" (Job xxviii. 20–22). Till,
then, we get to "destruction and death," the destruction of
fleshly hopes and the death of creature religion, we do not so
much as ever hear the fame of true wisdom with our ears.
Thus, when we get into darkness, then light springs up;
when we get into despondency, hope arises; when we are
tempted with unbelief and infidelity, faith appears. Thus
those are the wisest in whom creature wisdom has most
ceased; those are the strongest who have learned most experimentally their own weakness; those are the holiest who
have known most of their own filthiness; those are the most
religious in a true sense who have least religion of their own.
So that just in proportion as we are delivered unto death,
and execution takes place on what the creature loves, so
does the life of Jesus begin to rise and make itself blessedly
manifest.

March 4.

"*Bind the sacrifice with cords, even unto the horns of the
altar.*"—PSALM cxviii. 27.

ARE you a poor broken-hearted child of the living God?
Is there any measure of the Spirit of Christ in you? Is
there any faint resemblance of his meekness and holy image
stamped upon you? Then you feel yourself bound with
cords to the horns of the altar. You feel the strong ties of
necessity, and you feel the strong ties of affection binding
you there. But with this, you feel also that you are a
struggling victim; that you would gladly escape the troubles
and trials that being bound to the horns of the altar brings

upon you; you would gladly get into an easier path if you could; or if you dared, would willingly set up some altar yourself, made after the pattern of Damascus (2 Kings xvi. 10); and would gladly, like the Roman Catholic, worship with your body a material cross, instead of worshipping in your soul the adorable God-man who hung and bled there. You would gladly, if you could, step out of a self-loathing, exercised, tried, harassed, and tempted path, to get into the flowery meadow of doctrine and speculation, and there walk at ease without one pang in your conscience, or one trial in your soul. But the Lord has said, "Bind the sacrifice with cords, even unto the horns of the altar." You are bound to the horns of the altar. From those horns you cannot escape. You may fume, fret, and rebel against all or any of these cords, but you cannot break them. Aye, you may, in your strugglings, stretch to their utmost extent these cords; but they are too firmly fastened round your tender conscience, and too strongly wreathed round your broken heart, for you to burst them. They would sooner cut your heart in two, than you should break them, or escape from them. And in your right mind, you would not be otherwise than bound with cords to the horns of the altar. In your right mind, you want the cords tightened, and so to be drawn nearer and nearer unto it; and to have the blood that was shed upon it sprinkled upon your conscience. In your right mind, you want to see with the eye of faith the Victim that once lay bleeding and writhing there; and as you look upon him, to drink into his image, and to feel the melting power and softening efficacy of that sight. But, then, connected with it, there are such trials, such temptations, and such sacrifices, that you, in your fits of rebellion or flesh-pleasing ease, would at times as gladly get away, as at others you would gladly get near. Vile wretches that we are, who would often prefer to serve the flesh and the world, and take our

chance, as men speak, for eternity, than suffer trials and
temptations as the followers of Christ! But it is our mercy
that we can neither make nor unmake, do nor undo, bind
nor break any one cord of eternal love, but that, in spite of
the creature, God will "fulfil all the good pleasure of his
goodness, and the work of faith with power."

March 5.

*"And what is the exceeding greatness of his power to us-
ward who believe, according to the working of his mighty
power, which he wrought in Christ, when he raised him from
the dead."*—EPHESIANS i. 19, 20.

MAN needs to be roused by a mighty and effectual power
out of his state of sleep and death. It is not a little pull, a
gentle snatch at his coat, a slight tug of his sleeve, which will
pull him out of his sins. He must be snatched from them
as a person would be snatched out of bed when the house
is on fire, or pulled out of a river when sinking for the
last time. Let us never think that the work of grace
upon the heart is a slight or superficial one. Indeed, there
needs a mighty work of grace upon a sinner's heart to
deliver him from his destructions. We always, therefore,
find the work of grace to begin by a spiritual sight and
sense of our ruined condition before God. But this alone
will not suffice to make us true-hearted disciples of Jesus.
It is a preparation, a most needful preparation for a sight
of the King in his beauty, but it is not the same thing as
to see and believe in the Son of God unto eternal life. We
must have something far beyond any convictions of sin or
any sense of our lost and ruined condition. We must have
by faith a view of the blessed Lord more or less manifested
to our souls by that Holy Spirit whose office it is to take of
the things of Christ and to reveal them to the heart so as to

see his suitability, his grace, his glory, his work, his blood, his obedience; and to so see these divine and blessed realities by the eye of faith, as to know and feel for ourselves that they are exactly adapted to our case and state; that they are the very things we require to save us from the wrath to come; and that so far as we have an interest in them we are saved from the floods of destruction. Wherever this believing sight of Christ is given to the soul, it creates and maintains a faith that works by love. Thus wherever there is a view of Jesus by the eye of faith, wherever he manifests and makes himself in any measure precious to the soul, love is the certain fruit of it; for we love him because he first loved us, and, when we begin to love the Lord, love gives us a binding tie which creates union and communion with him. As, then, he unveils his lovely face, and discovers more and more of his beauty and blessedness, it gives him a firm place in the heart's warmest, tenderest affections, and then he comes and takes up his abode in the soul and rules there as its rightful Lord. The following things therefore are indispensably necessary to true discipleship; first, a spiritual sense of our lost, ruined condition; then a knowledge of Christ by a gracious discovery of his suitability, beauty, and blessedness; and thirdly, a faith in him that works by love and purifies the heart, overcomes the world, and delivers from death and hell.

March 6.

" Therefore it is of faith, that it might be by grace." — Romans iv. 16.

Of faith we read expressly that "it is the gift of God." This is the grand master-grace of the soul; it is the grand wheel which moves every other wheel in the heart; it is the eye, the ear, the hand of the new man of grace. Only so far as we have faith, and the Lord draws out this faith in exercise, have we any true spiritual feeling. But what makes me prize the gift of faith? It is knowing so much and so painfully the inbeing and inworking of unbelief. Is not this the case naturally? What makes me prize health? It is having a poor, weakly tabernacle. What makes me prize rest? Fatigue. What makes me prize ease? It is pain. What makes me prize food? It is hunger. What makes me prize the cup of cold water? It is thirst. By these feelings, I not only know the reality by the want of it, but also enjoy the blessing when communicated. It is just so spiritually, as naturally. What can I know of faith, except I am exercised (and exercised I am more or less daily) by the workings of unbelief, infidelity, questionings of the reasoning mind, and all the spawn of an unbelieving heart? As the soul is tossed up and down, (and often, it is tossed up and down on this sea of unbelief,) it learns to prize the harbour of faith. And when the Lord mercifully communicates a little faith to the soul, and faith begins to realise, feel, experience, and feed upon the truth as it is in Jesus, then we know what faith is by the possession of it.

What a mercy it is that the Lord has the gift of faith to bestow! Here are poor souls toiling, troubling, labouring, groaning, sighing, oppressed with unbelief, that great giant in the heart, who has slain his thousands and tens of thousands. How our souls sometimes sink down under this wretched unbelief! But how we prize the faith all the more when it comes! How all the sinkings make the risings higher, and all the sadness makes the change more blessed! As the tossings to and fro of the sailor upon the sea, with all the perils and sufferings of the voyage, make the calm harbour so pleasant; so all the tossing up and down of unbelief endears the holy calm of living faith to the soul.

March 7.

" *Beautiful for situation, the joy of the whole earth, is mount Zion, on the sides of the north, the city of the great King.*"— PSALM xlviii. 2.

WE have sometimes thought that the reason why Zion typically represents the royal throne of Jesus is by many not well understood. Mount Zion literally was a steep hill of Jerusalem, so steep and inaccessible that for generations after the children of Israel had gained possession of the land, it still remained, like a little Gibraltar, in the hands of the Jebusites, the original inhabitants of the place. "As for the Jebusites, the inhabitants of Jerusalem, the children of Judah could not drive them out; but the Jebusites dwell with the children of Judah at Jerusalem unto this day" (Jos. xv. 63). But when David was anointed king over Israel, and had reigned at Hebron seven years and six months, he cast his eyes toward Jerusalem, as a preferable metropolis, and a more suitable seat of his extended empire. But as long as the hill of Zion was occupied by the warlike Jebusites, they would retain their command of the lower city. His first step, therefore, was, with the help of God, to dispossess the Jebusites of this their stronghold. But so strong was this hill-fort by nature and art, that the Jebusites ridiculed all his attempts to capture it, putting on the ramparts "the blind and the lame" soldiers of the garrison, what we should call the worn-out invalids of the army, as if these Chelsea pensioners, who could neither see nor walk, were amply sufficient to baffle all David's attempts at its capture (2 Sam. v. 6–8). Joab, however, as a prize set before him, for which he was to be David's chief captain, mounted the hill, smote the lame and the blind on the wall, and the Jebusites behind the wall, and won possession of the coveted spot (1 Chron. xi. 6). There David henceforward dwelt, as its conqueror, as in a castle ; there he fixed his royal abode, and thence he swayed his sceptre over the whole land of Israel, from Dan to Beer-sheba. Its very name was typical, for it signifies literally, " sunny," or " shine upon," as facing the south, and ever basking in the rays of the warm sun. Thus the sunny hill of Zion, as a hill of conquest, and as the royal seat of David, became a suitable type of the throne of Jesus in the courts above, won by lawful conquest (Rev. iii. 21), where is now his royal palace, and where he rules and reigns as the anointed King of heaven and earth. Thus mount Zion typically represents not the cross, but the crown; not the law, but the gospel ; not the battle, but the victory.

March 8.

" O Lord, be gracious unto us ; we have waited for thee : be thou their arm every morning, our salvation also in the time of trouble."—ISAIAH xxxiii. 2.

ISRAEL has often to pass through times of sorrow and trouble. Deep temporal and deep spiritual trouble is the allotted portion of many, if not of most of the people of God. But having found that the Lord is a Saviour, and the only Saviour who can support in trouble and deliver out of trouble, there is this conviction deeply implanted and firmly written upon their heart, that he is a Saviour in the time of trouble. It is the purpose of God to hunt us out of all lying refuges, that we may believe in Jesus to the saving of our soul ; that we may prove that he is able to save to the uttermost all who come unto God by him ; that we may learn what salvation is, and that we may know it for ourselves as a divine and blessed reality. Thus though he is always a Saviour, yet he is not experimentally a Saviour in times of worldly ease, carnal prosperity, and seasons of carelessness. But in times of trouble, when none can do us any good or stretch forth a healing hand but the Lord alone, then to come to his

gracious Majesty and find there and then how he can and
does save in trouble and out of trouble, this is that which
endears such a Saviour to believing hearts. And observe the
expression, " *time* of trouble," and how it includes not only
every trouble which may befall us temporally or spiritually,
but clearly intimates that there is not a single season or
time when trouble comes that the Lord is not able and
willing to save us out of it. How well this corresponds with
those gracious words and that sweet promise, " Call upon
me in the day of trouble; I will deliver thee, and thou
shalt glorify me."

March 9.

" *But God be thanked, that ye were the servants of sin, but ye
have obeyed from the heart that form of doctrine which was
delivered you.*"—Romans vi. 17.

What reason have we to bless God that he so instructed
his Apostle to set forth how a sinner is justified ! For how
could we have attained to the knowledge of this mystery
without divine revelation ? How could we know in what way
God could be just, and yet the justifier of the ungodly? How
could we see all the perfections of God harmonizing in the
Person and work of Jesus ? his law maintained in all its rigid
purity and strictest justice, and yet mercy, grace, and love to
have full play in a sinner's salvation? But the Spirit of God
led Paul deeply into this blessed subject; and especially in
the Epistle to the Romans does he trace out this grand
foundation truth with such clearness, weight, and power, that
the Church of God can never be sufficiently thankful for this
portion of divine revelation. His grand object is, to shew
how God justifies the ungodly by the blood and obedience of
his dear Son; so that " as by one man's disobedience many
were made sinners, so by the obedience of one shall many
be made righteous." He declares that " the righteousness of

God is unto and upon all them that believe;" and that
" through the redemption that is in Christ Jesus, whom God
hath set forth to be a propitiation through faith in his blood,"
he pardons the sinner, justifies the ungodly, and views him as
righteous in the Son of his love. In opening up this subject,
the Apostle (Romans v) traces up this justification to the
union of the Church with her covenant Head; shews us her
standing in Christ as well as in Adam; and that all the
miseries which she derives from her standing in the latter are
overbalanced by the mercies that flow from her standing in
the former; winding up with that heart-reviving truth, that
" where sin abounded, grace did much more abound; that
as sin hath reigned unto death, even so might grace reign
through righteousness unto eternal life." This then is a
" form of doctrine," or mould of teaching, into which the soul
is delivered when it is brought into a heart-felt reception of,
and a feeling acquaintance with it; and by being led more
or less into the experimental enjoyment of it, is favoured with
a solemn acquiescence in, and a filial submission to it, as all
its salvation and all its desire. And as the mould impresses
its image upon the moist plaster or melted metal poured into
it, so the heart, softened and melted by the blessed Spirit's
teaching, receives the impress of this glorious truth with filial
confidence, feels its sweetness and power, and is filled with a
holy admiration of it as the only way in which God can justify
an ungodly wretch, not only without sacrificing any one attribute of his holy character, but rather magnifying thereby the
purity of his nature, and the demands of his unbending justice.

March 10.

" *For I am not ashamed of the gospel of Christ: for it is the
power of God unto salvation to every one that believeth.*"—
Romans i. 16.

WHAT is meant by the word "*power?*" It is a term much

used in the New Testament. "The kingdom of God," it is declared, "is not in word, but in power;" and true faith is said to "stand not in the wisdom of men, but in the power of God." What, then, is power? It is a divine operation that God himself puts forth in the soul. It cannot be described by words, nor explained so as to be understood by our mental capacity. It must be felt to be known; and must be realised in a man's own soul before he can have any spiritual conception of it. But "thy people," we read, "shall be willing in the day of thy power." And when the gospel does come to the soul by the application of the blessed Spirit, and a divine power accompanies it, though the power itself cannot be described even by the person himself, it is made known by the effects which follow it. For instance, here is a poor wretch condemned by the law, and in his apprehensions lying for ever under its fearful curse. He may, perhaps, see there is salvation in Christ, and know in his judgment there is salvation in no other; but he cannot lay hold of Christ, nor get from under the condemnation he feels. Why? Because the gospel is not made the power of God unto salvation to his soul. But how he begs, cries, prays, and supplicates God to have mercy on him. Continually he is endeavouring to seek God, and beseech him to have mercy on his soul. But he cannot get peace to his conscience; he is still in trouble and distress, bowed down with bondage, guilt, and fear. Here is a man longing for "power." Now, when the Lord is pleased to apply some portion of his blessed word to his soul, or to speak home some particular promise, the power which accompanies this raises up a special faith, whereby that portion of God's holy word, which speaks of Christ, or that particular promise is laid hold of. Here, then, is "power" communicated with the gospel. The gospel has now come to him, "not in word only," as it might often have done before, leaving him all the while in guilt and fear, but with "power ;" and, by the faith thus raised up, he believes in Jesus to the saving of his soul. He could not believe in him before, for his faith, such as it was, being devoid of power, left him where it found him, as forlorn and helpless as the man who fell among thieves. No. He might as well attempt to create a world, as to believe in the Son of God unto deliverance ; but no sooner does he believe what the Holy Spirit applies, than a sweet and sacred power comes into his soul, which takes away his doubts and fears; dispels guilt from his conscience; banishes the mists and fogs that for months have hung over his soul ; reveals in him a precious Jesus ; makes the promises of the gospel to glitter before his eyes like dew-drops in autumn ; and gives him an unspeakable nearness to God, through the Person, blood, and righteousness of Christ, such as he never knew until the gospel came with power, and faith was raised up in his soul.

March 11.

" Let thy mercies come also unto me, O Lord, even thy salvation, according to thy word. So shall I have wherewith to answer him that reproacheth me: for I trust in thy word." — PSALM cxix. 41, 42.

A living soul wants to return an answer to him that reproaches it. But he cannot do it of himself, for he has not a word to speak in self-justification ; that is utterly cut off; and therefore he wants to have that which shall furnish him with an answer to these reproaches. And what alone can furnish him with an answer? The mercies of God in his soul. " Let thy mercies come also unto me, O Lord, even thy salvation, according to thy word. So shall I have where-with to answer him that reproacheth me." The coming in of " mercies " into the soul, and the manifestation of " salva-tion " to the heart afford an answer " to him that reproacheth us." If you will observe, the word " mercies " is in the plural number, there being many mercies; but "salvation" is in the singular number, there being only one salvation. In what way, then, did the Psalmist want these mercies? Merely as standing in the letter of the word? Only as recorded in the inspired word of truth? As things to look at, as objects hung up, as it were, in a picture, merely for the eye to gaze upon? No; he wanted them in his heart, to "come to him," to visit him, to be breathed into him, to be made part and parcel of him, to be the life-blood that should circulate in his veins, to be the very kingdom of God set up with power in his soul. And why did he want internal mercies? Because he had internal reproaches. Why did he need mercies in his soul? Because condemnation was in his soul. It was there the sentence of death was written; it was there the sentence of acquittal was to be recorded. It was there that reproach was felt; it was there the answer to the reproach was to be given. If the reproach were merely outward, the answer might be outward also; but the reproof being inward, in the heart, in the conscience, in the feelings, it was needed that the answer should be in the same place, written in the same spot, engraved in the same tablets, and brought home with the same or far greater power, so as to be a sufficient answer to the reproaches of him that reproached him.

March 12.

"*Such as sit in darkness and in the shadow of death.*"— Psalm cvii. 10.

What a blessed thing is light, the light of life, the light of God's countenance, of the glorious gospel, of Jesus' face! "Truly light is sweet, and a pleasant thing it is for the eyes to behold the sun." But to whom? To those who sit in darkness and the shadow of death. How such hail the first rays of light! If you were shipwrecked, cast by night upon a desert rock, how you would hail the first beams of the morning light to shew you where you were, and what hopes there were of final escape. So, similarly, how a sense of danger, magnified by the darkness, makes the shipwrecked soul hail the first beam of light, that it may see the way of escape from hell to heaven. How sweet to such it is to have any divine light dawn upon the mind, to have any breaking in of the goodness and mercy, grace and glory, of the blessed Jesus. The more we sit in darkness, the more we prize light. Many high professors despise all this, and run out against it as a building upon frames and feelings, and making a Christ of our experience. Poor things! Their light is not worth having; and their religion, it is to be feared, is but a fire of their own kindling, the light of which will never light them to heaven. But why do they despise it? Because they never sit in darkness and the shadow of death. Therefore, really and truly, what is their light? An ignis fatuus, a will-o'-the-wisp, a gas-lamp, a meteor, a falling star, anything, everything but the dayspring from on high, or the Sun of righteousness. But the Lord's people cannot be put off with a gas-lamp, an ignis fatuus, a will-o'-the-wisp. They must have Jesus. They must have his blood upon their consciences, his grace in their hearts, his presence in their souls; sweet discoveries of his Person and work, the whispers of his love, the touch of his finger, the smiles of his face. They must have Jesus for themselves.

"Give me Christ, or else I die,"

is their feeling. But what makes them break forth with these earnest sighs and cries? They are in darkness and in the shadow of death. Were they otherwise, they would be content to remain as they naturally are; dark and dead. But feeling their state, it makes them long for the beams of light; and when it breaks in upon their soul, they can bless it because it comes from and leads to God.

March 13.

" But he knoweth the way that I take: when he hath tried me, I shall come forth as gold."—Job xxiii. 10.

What a purifying effect experience of temptation produces; what a separation it makes of the dross from the ore ! If a man has a grain of faith in his soul, temptation will discover it; if he has a particle of living hope, temptation will bring it to light; if he has a grain of love, temptation will extract it from the ore ; if he has any patience, any humility, any fear of God, any desire to be right, any dread to be wrong, any honesty, any sincerity, any integrity, in a word, if he has any vital power in his soul, anything of the grace of God in his heart, temptation will make it manifest, as the hot flame of the furnace, acting upon the crucible, manifests the gold by breaking up its alliance with the dross. You scarcely know whether you are a believer or an unbeliever until you pass through temptation. You do not know what the nature of faith is as a divine gift and a spiritual grace, unless you have passed through this fiery trial. You do not know the worthlessness of creature religion, the emptiness of everything in self, until you have been put into the furnace of temptation. We are tempted sometimes, perhaps, to doubt the truth of the Scriptures, the Deity of Christ, the efficacy of his atonement, and many things which I will not even hint at in your ears lest I unwittingly sow infidel seeds in your heart. Now when we are thus exercised, temptation as a fire burns up everything that stands in the wisdom and strength of the creature, and brings us to this point, that nothing but that which is of God in the soul can live in the flame. If, then, we find there is that in our heart which lives in the flame, that there is a faith which temptation cannot burn up, a hope it cannot destroy, a love it cannot consume, a fear of God which it cannot conquer, then we see there is that in our heart which is like pure gold in the midst of the dross, and can say in some measure with Job, " When he hath tried me, I shall come forth as gold."

March 14.

" Is there no balm in Gilead ? is there no physician there?" — JEREMIAH viii. 22.

THERE is balm in Gilead, and there is a physician there. This is, and must ever be, our only hope. If there were no balm in Gilead, what could we do but lie down in despair and die? For our sins are so great, our backslidings so repeated, our minds so dark, our hearts so hard, our affections so cold, our souls so wavering and wandering, that if there were no balm in Gilead, no precious blood, no sweet promises, no sovereign grace, and if there were no physician there, no risen Jesus, no great High Priest over the house of God, what well-grounded hope could we entertain? Not a ray. Our own obedience and consistency! These are a bed too short and a covering too narrow. But when there is some application of the balm in Gilead, it softens, melts, humbles, and at the same time thoroughly heals. Nay, this balm strengthens every nerve and sinew, heals blindness, remedies deafness, cures paralysis, makes the lame man leap as a hart and the tongue of the dumb to sing, and thus produces gospel sight, gospel hearing, gospel strength, and a gospel walk. When the spirit is melted, and the heart touched by a sense of God's goodness, mercy, and love to such base, undeserving wretches, it produces gospel obedience, aye, a humble obedience ; not that proud obedience which those .manifest who are trusting to their own goodness and seeking to scale the battlements of heaven by the ladder of self-righteousness, but an obedience of gratitude, love, and submission, willingly, cheerfully rendered, and therefore acceptable to God, because flowing from his own Spirit and grace. It is the application of this divine balm which purifies the heart, makes sin hateful, and Jesus precious, and not only dissolves the soul in sweet gratitude, but fills it with earnest desires to live to God's honour and glory. This is the mysterious way the Lord takes to get honour to himself. As he opens up the depth of the fall, makes the burden of sin felt, and shews the sinner how his iniquities have abounded, he brings the proud heart down, and lays the head low in the dust; and as he makes him sigh and cry, grieve and groan, he applies his sovereign balm to the soul, brings the blood of sprinkling into the conscience, sheds abroad his mercy and love, and thus constrains the feet to walk in cheerful and willing obedience. This is obeying the precept from right motives, right views, right influences, under right feelings, and to right ends. This is the true Christian obedience, obedience " in the spirit and not in the letter," an obedience which glorifies God, and is attended by every fruit and grace of the Spirit.

March 15.

" *Foolishness is bound in the heart of a child; but the rod of correction shall drive it far from him.*"—PROVERBS xxii. 15.

WE profess to believe in an Almighty, All-present, All-seeing God; and we should be highly offended if a person said to us, " You do not believe that God sees everything, that he is everywhere present, that he is an Almighty Jehovah:" we should almost think that he was taking us for an atheist. And yet practical atheists we daily prove ourselves to be. For instance, we profess to believe that God sees everything, and yet we are plotting and planning as though he saw nothing; we profess to know that God can do everything, and yet we are always cutting out schemes, and carving out contrivances, as though he were like the gods

of the heathen, looking on and taking no notice; we profess
to believe that God is everywhere present to relieve every
difficulty and bring his people out of every trial, and yet
when we get into the difficulty and into the trial, we speak,
think, and act as though there were no such omnipresent
God, who knows the circumstances of the case, and can
stretch forth his hand to bring us out of it. Thus the Lord
is obliged, (to speak with all reverence,) to thrust us into
trials and afflictions, because we are such blind fools, that we
cannot learn what a God we have to deal with, until we come
experimentally into those spots of difficulty and trial, out of
which none but such a God can deliver us. This, then, is
one reason why the Lord often plunges his people so deeply
into a sense of sin; it is to shew them what a wonderful
salvation from the guilt, filth, and power of sin there is in the
Person, blood, and righteousness of the Lord Jesus Christ.
For the same reason, too, they walk in such scenes of
temptation; it is in order to shew them what a wonder-
working God he is in bringing them out. This, too, is the
reason why many of them are so harassed and plagued;
it is that they may not live and act as though there were no
God to go to, no Almighty Friend to consult, no kind Jesus
to rest their weary heads upon; it is in order to teach them
experimentally and inwardly those lessons of grace and truth
which they never would know till the Lord, as it were, thus
compels them to learn, and actually forces them to believe
what they profess to believe. Such pains is he obliged to
take with us; such poor scholars, such dull creatures we are.
In order, then, to teach us what a God he is, what a merciful
and compassionate High Priest; in order to open up the
heights, and depths, and lengths, and breadths of his love,
he is compelled to treat, at times, his people very roughly,
and handle them very sharply; he is obliged to make very
great use of his rod, because he sees that " foolishness is so

bound up in the hearts" of his children that nothing but the repeated "rod of correction will ever drive it far from them."

March 16.

"Now therefore ye are no more strangers and foreigners, but fellow-citizens with the saints, and of the household of God."—EPHESIANS ii. 19.

IF grace has touched your heart ; if the love of God has come into your soul, it has placed you among the saints of the Most High, and given you every privilege which God ever did or could give to them. And what are their privileges? To be washed in the atoning blood of the suffering Son of God, to be clothed in the justifying righteousness of his perfect and meritorious obedience, to be consecrated by the indwelling of the Holy Ghost, the Comforter, to have the love of God as their enduring portion, peace in believing, supplies of grace as needed, support and strength as they pass through this vale of tears, comforts abounding in proportion to the abundance of afflictions, everlasting arms beneath in death, a mansion of eternal bliss for the soul when the body drops into the grave, and a glorious resurrection of the body at the appearance of Christ in glory. All that the love of God can give ; all that the blood of Christ has been a channel for communicating ; and all that the Spirit of God can reveal to any heart, or has ever brought with power into the soul of any saint,—all these things become ours when we become fellow-citizens with the saints of God ; not indeed always or often by vital enjoyment, though we get sips and tastes, drops and crumbs; but as Abraham was given possession of Canaan when he had not so much as to set his foot on, yet was it his as much by promise as it became his children's by strength of hand. Does not the Apostle declare this, in the broadest and clearest language,

where he says, "All things are yours; whether Paul, or
Apollos, or Cephas, or the world, or life, or death, or things
present, or things to come; *all are yours?*" and why all
yours? "for ye are Christ's; and Christ is God's."

March 17.

"I and my Father are one."—JOHN x. 30.

THERE is a great deal of cavilling in some men's minds
about the expression, "the blood of God." "How," say
they, "could the Godhead bleed? How could the Godhead
suffer?" But if it is not the blood of Him who was God, I
might just as well rely for salvation on the blood of one of
the thieves that were crucified with him. What is Christ's
human nature? That is the rock on which many gallant
ships have struck. It is not a *person,* having a distinct
existence apart from the Deity of Christ; but it is a *nature:*
what the Holy Ghost calls a "Holy Thing" (Luke i. 35);
"a body that God had prepared for him" (Heb. x. 5), taken
into intimate, mysterious, and inexplicable union with the
Person of the Son of God. So that, whatever that human
nature did and suffered, from its intimacy and union with the
Son of God, the Son of God did and suffered. Did that
nature bleed? It bled as having union with Deity; it being,
so to speak, the instrument that Deity made use of. To use
an illustration: as my soul touches an object through my
hand, or speaks its thoughts by my tongue; so Deity not
being itself able to bleed, bled through the humanity. Did
that nature suffer? It was not the mere suffering of a
human person, as a man might suffer; but it was the
suffering of a holy nature in intimate union with the Person
of the Son of God. And did that nature obey? The Son
of God obeyed through and with that nature. So that, to
cavil at the expression, "the blood of God" is nothing less
than to strike a blow at a great fundamental truth. We

might object, on the same ground, to the expression, " God
our righteousness," as the Prophet speaks, " And this is the
name whereby he shall be called, The Lord our righteousness," that is, " Jehovah our righteousness " (Jer. xxiii. 6).
Who is our righteousness but the Son of God? And what
was that righteousness but the obedience of his human nature,
for Godhead could no more obey than suffer and bleed;
and yet Jehovah is our righteousness. And if we do not
object to the expression, " the righteousness of God," why
should we cavil at the expression, " the blood of God?"

Now this is the grand mystery which faith embraces, and
which is dear to the heart of every God-taught soul. What
a power and efficacy, as the veil is taken off the heart, does
faith see in that sacrifice! What a propitiation does it see
made for sin by the blood of the Son of God! Faith does
not view it as the blood of man! Can the blood of man put
away sin? But when we see it as the blood of the Son of
God, oh, what value, efficacy, power, and glory shine forth
in it! But till the veil is taken off the heart we cannot see
it; nor can we, till the Spirit makes it experimentally known,
learn what a divine reality there is in this blood to purge the
guilty conscience.

March 18.

" *We have also a more sure word of prophecy; whereunto
ye do well that ye take heed, as unto a light that shineth in a
dark place, until the day dawn, and the day star arise in your
hearts.*"—2 PETER i. 19.

THE "sure word of prophecy" is the mind of God revealed
in the Scripture of truth. This is compared to "a light
shining in a dark place." This "dark place" is the heart
of man, and a dark place it is; and the light shining in the
dark place is when the Spirit of God pours his own heavenly
light into the dark heart. The Spirit of God works by the

word of God. He makes use of the Scriptures of truth, by
means of these blessed Scriptures to communicate light.
There is no light in the Scriptures themselves ; they cannot
teach a man to profit, that being God's prerogative. They
are a dead letter, nothing but a collection of words and
syllables; there is no light in them, no, not a particle, but
what the Spirit of God throws upon them when he shines
through them. I might compare the Scriptures to the moon :
the moon has no light in herself, but she borrows all her
light from the sun : blot out the sun from the sky, and the
moon would cease to shine. Or I might compare the
Scriptures to what James compares them : " If any be a
hearer of the word, and not a doer, he is like unto a man
beholding his natural face in a glass." Here the Scriptures
are compared to a mirror, or looking-glass. But light must
shine upon the glass. Of what use is a looking-glass in a
dark night ? It reflects no image; it presents to you no
likeness ; you discern not your features therein ; it might be
nothing else but a naked board, as far as any reflection it
gives of your face. But let light come into the room, or let
the sun rise and shine upon it, and your countenance is
reflected therein. So with the word of God ; it is utterly
ineffectual until the Spirit shines upon it ; and when he
shines upon it, he casts at the same time a ray of light into
your heart ; and as he shines with this twofold ray, first
upon the word, and then into your soul, he reflects from
the word your very image, and you see yourself just as you
are, clearly portrayed. Now this is the light shining in a
dark place ; the light of God's truth shining into your dark
heart. This becomes " a sure word " to you ; faith is raised
up in your heart to credit what God has revealed ; the
shining in of this light into the dark place causes you to
believe ; and you, believing in the light which is thus come into
your dark heart, receive the word of prophecy as a sure word.

March 19.

"That which is born of the flesh is flesh; and that which is born of the Spirit is spirit."—JOHN iii. 6.

THERE is no promise made that we shall be set free in this life from the in-being and the in-working of sin. Many think that they are to become progressively holier and holier, that sin after sin is to be removed gradually out of the heart, until at last they are almost made perfect in the flesh. But this is an idle dream, and one which, sooner or later in the case of God's people, will be rudely and roughly broken to pieces. Nature will ever remain the same; and we shall ever find that the flesh will lust against the spirit. Our Adam nature is corrupt to the very core. It cannot be mended, it cannot be sanctified, it is at the last what it was at the first, inherently evil, and as such will never cease to be corrupt till we put off mortality, and with it the body of sin and death. All we can hope for, long after, expect and pray for, is, that this evil nature may be subdued, kept down, mortified, crucified, and held in subjection under the power of grace ; but as to any such change passing upon it or taking place in it as to make it holy, it is but a pharisaic delusion, which, promising a holiness in the flesh, leaves us still under the power of sin, whilst it opposes with deadly enmity that true sanctification of the new man of grace, which is wrought by a divine power, and is utterly distinct from any fancied holiness in the flesh, or any vain dream of its progressive sanctification.

March 20.

" For whom he did foreknow, he also did predestinate to be conformed to the image of his Son, that he might be the first-born among many brethren."—ROMANS viii. 29.

THE risen body of Christ is the type to which the risen

bodies of the saints are to be conformed, for "as we have borne the image of the earthy, we shall also bear the image of the heavenly." This is that glorious image to which the saints are to be all conformed. But though fully retaining all the essential characteristics of humanity, for otherwise it would cease to be manhood in conjunction with Godhead, yet so unspeakably glorious is this risen body of the blessed Lord, to the image of which the risen saints will be conformed, that in this time-state we can not only form no conception of its surpassing glory, but not even of that inferior degree of glory which will clothe the bodies of the saints at the resurrection. "Beloved, now are we the sons of God, and it doth not yet appear what we shall be: but we know that, when he shall appear, we shall be like him, for we shall see him as he is" (1 John iii. 2). But of this we may be sure, that there will always be an essential and unapproachable distinction between the glory of Christ's humanity and theirs. His humanity, being in eternal union with his Deity, derives thence a glory which is distinct from all other, and to which there can be no approach, and with which there can be no comparison. The glory of the moon never can be the glory of the sun, though she shines with his reflected light. "He will change our vile body that it may be fashioned like unto his glorious body;" but though like, it will not be the same. It will be the saints' eternal happiness to see him as he is, and to be made like unto him; but it will be their everlasting joy that he should ever have that pre-eminence of glory which is his birthright, and to adore which will ever be their supreme delight. To have a body free from all sin, sickness, and sorrow, filled to its utmost capacity of holiness and happiness, able to see him as he is without dying under the sight, and to be re-united to its once suffering but now equally glorified companion, an immortal soul, expanded to its fullest powers of joy and bliss—if this be not sufficient, what more can God give?

March 21.

"The light of the glorious gospel of Christ, who is the image of God."—2 CORINTHIANS iv. 4.

OH! what beauty and blessedness shine forth in the gospel, when we view it connected with the Person and work of the Son of God! Take the doctrines of grace isolated from the Person of Christ; they are scattered limbs; there is no beauty in them; but view the truths of the gospel, in connection with the Person and work of the Son of God, what a heavenly light, what a divine glory is cast upon every truth connected with his sacred Person, atoning blood, finished work, and dying love! This is the way to receive the gospel: not as a thing of shreds and patches, a mere collection or scheme of certain doctrines floating up and down God's word, as waifs and strays from a stranded ship; but as one harmonious gospel, full of grace, mercy, and truth, impregnated with divine blessedness, and all connected with, all springing out of, the Person of the God-man. How it seems to lift us up for a time, whilst the feeling lasts, above sin, misery, and wretchedness, to view our completeness in Christ, to see our interest in his finished work, to behold ourselves members of his mystical body, to triumph in his holy triumphs, to rejoice in his victories, and to ascend with him above the smoke and stir of this dim spot that men call earth. As one might rise out of a London fog into a pure atmosphere, and bask on some mountain-top in the bright beams of the sun, so the dear saint of God, when he is privileged to read his title clear, see his name in the book of life, feel the love of God in his heart, and rejoice in Christ, is lifted up above the fog and smoke of this dim spot, and sitting with Christ in heavenly places, he feels a sweet victory over every foe internal, external, and infernal. And there is no other way whereby we can get out of it. Like a man in the London fog, struggling on with fog in the east, west, north, south, fog and smoke all around ; so it is whilst we are struggling onward with sin and self, north, south, east, and west, there is nothing but fog, fog, deep and dense. We must be raised out of it to the mountain-top, and this only can be by being lifted up by a sweet testimony of interest in the blood and love of the Son of God. This lifts up, this lifts out ; this gives strength, and this alone will give victory ; and so far as we fall short of realising these precious things, we grope for the wall like the blind, and stumble in desolate places like dead men. It is true that for the most part the saints of God only have a little of these blessed things, from time to time, just brought in and taken away, but sufficient to taste their sweetness, to know their beauty, to see their glory, and therefore sufficient, whilst they last, to help them onward in their course, and keep them struggling on, till they reach that eternal glory.

March 22.

" Elect according to the foreknowledge of God the Father."— 1 Peter i. 2.

Foreknowledge of the persons of the elect in the divine economy precedes election. " Whom he did foreknow he also did predestinate ; " and this foreknowledge was not any eternal foreview of their faith or love in time, as if *that* were the ground of God's choice of them ; but it implies, first, that thorough knowledge which God had of them, and of all that should concern them, of all the depths of sin and rebellion, disobedience and ungodliness, of which they might be guilty before called by grace, and of all their grievous backslidings, slips, and falls, with all the base returns that they should make for his goodness and mercy toward them after he had touched their hearts by his finger. And secondly and chiefly, it signifies the good will and pleasure, with that everlasting love of God the Father, whereby he foreknew them with a holy approbation of them, a divine affection toward them, and a holy and unalterable delight in them as viewed in his dear Son, chosen in him and accepted in the Beloved. And thus election is not, if we may use the expression without irreverence, a dry choice of them in Christ, but a choice of them as foreknowing, with a holy approbation, each of his elect family, personally and individually, and however they might differ among themselves in the infinite variety whereby one man varies both naturally and spiritually from another, yet that his approving knowledge of each and all of them in Christ Jesus was in sweet harmony with his determinate choice. To realise this in soul feeling is very sweet and precious. We do not know ourselves. We may have seen a little into our fallen state by nature, and may know something of the awful evils that lurk and work within; we may have had some passing skirmishes, or even some hôt battles with our proud, rebellious, unbelieving, infidel, and desperately wicked heart, but we do not know ourselves as God knows us. And though we may cry, " Search me, O God, and know my heart; try me, and know my thoughts," yet how shallow for the most part and superficial is that knowledge and experience of ourselves! How little do we measure our sinfulness by the holiness of God, or look down into the depths of our nature as they lie naked and open before the eyes of him with whom we have to do! When, then, we think that he who knew from the beginning all that we ever should be in the depths of the Adam fall, yet chose us by determinate decree in his dear Son unto eternal life, what a blessed lift does it give to the soul out of all those sinkings into which a sight and sense of sin is continually casting it.

March 23.

"The Lord will give grace and glory."—Psalm lxxxiv. 11.

Wherever the Lord gives grace, he in and with that grace gives glory. We, therefore, read, "Moreover whom he did predestinate, them he also called; and whom he called, them he also justified; and whom he justified, them he also glorified." Thus he has already made them, even while on earth, partakers of his glory; and this by making them partakers of his grace; for as in the bud is the bloom, and in the bloom the fruit, so in budding grace is blooming glory—grace being but glory begun, and glory being but grace finished.

But what is *"glory?"* Viewed as future, in its full consummation, it is to be with Jesus in realms of eternal bliss, where tears are wiped from off all faces; it is to see him as he is; to be conformed to his glorious likeness; to be delivered from all sin and sorrow; to be perfectly free from all temptations, trials, burdens, and exercises, and to dwell for ever in that happy land, "the inhabitants of which shall not say, I am sick;" where a weary body, a burdened conscience, a troubled heart, a faint and weary mind, are utterly and for ever unknown. In a word, it is to have a glorified body re-united to a glorified soul, and for both to be as full of happiness and holiness, bliss and blessedness, as an immortal spirit can hold, and an immortal frame can endure, drinking in to the full, with unutterable satisfaction but without satiety, the pleasures that are at God's right hand for evermore. But no human heart can conceive, nor human tongue unfold in what the nature and fulness of this glory consist; for "eye hath not seen, nor ear heard, neither have entered into the heart of man, the things which God hath prepared for them that love him." Yet all this glory will the Lord give to those upon whom he has already bestowed his

grace. He gives them grace now, to bring them through
this wilderness world, this vale of tears, this scene of temptation, sin, and sorrow; and when he lands them on that
happy shore, he gives them there the fulness of his glory.
Then will be fully accomplished the Redeemer's prayer and
will: "Father, I will that they also, whom thou hast given
me, be with me where I am; that they may behold my glory,
which thou hast given me; for thou lovedst me before the
foundation of the world" (John xvii. 24). Their right and
title to the enjoyment of this predestinated inheritance are
securely lodged in the hands of their covenant Head; and he
living at God's right hand to save them to the uttermost, all
their temptations, enemies, sins, and sorrows can never
hinder them from reaching the shore on which God has
decreed they shall safely land. Satan may spread a thousand
snares to entangle their feet; not a day or scarcely an hour
may pass that they are not burdened with indwelling sin; a
myriad of lusts may start up in arms from the depths of their
carnal mind; and many a pang of guilt and thrill of despair
may seem at times wholly to cut them off from eternal life.
But yet, where the Lord has given grace he will give glory;
for when he gives grace with the left hand, he gives glory
with the right; yea, we may say that with both hands he
gives at once both grace and glory; for as grace and glory
flow out of the same loving heart, and are given by the same
loving God, they may be said to be given by both hands at
one and the same time. A portion or foretaste of this glory
is given on earth in every discovery of the glory of Christ;
as the Lord speaks, "And the glory which thou gavest me
I have given them"—already given them; and this he did
when "he manifested forth his glory, and his disciples
believed on him" (John xvii. 22; ii. 11).

March 24.

" *And he led them forth by the right way, that they might
go to a city of habitation.*"—Psalm cvii. 7.

When the Lord leads, we can follow.   The path may be
rough, but if the Lord upholds, we can walk in it without
stumbling.   Whatever the Lord bids, we can do if we have
but his presence ; whatever he calls upon us to suffer, we
can bear if we have but the approbation of a good conscience
and his approving smile. Oh, the wonders of sovereign grace !
The cross is no cross if the Lord give strength to bear it ;
affliction is no affliction if the Lord support under it ; trial is
no trial sweetened by his smile, and sorrow no grief if
lightened by his love.   It is our fretfulness, unbelief, carnal
reasoning, rebellion, and self-pity which make a rough way
a wrong way ; but grace in its all-conquering power, not
only subdues every difficulty without, but what is its greater
triumph, subdues every difficulty within.

It is, and ever must be, one of the strongest principles of
our faith, that every way must, in the end, be a right way if
it be God's way.   And is it not, according to the verdict of
our own conscience, a right way to lead us forth out of the
world, out of sin, out of self, out of pride and self-righteousness, out of evil in every form, into everything which is good,
holy, gracious, acceptable, saving, and sanctifying ; everything that can conform us to the image of Christ, who was a
man of sorrows and acquainted with grief, and make us meet
for the inheritance of the saints in light ?

And what is the end of all this leading and guiding ?
" *That they might go to a city of habitation*"—the new Jerusalem, the glorious city which hath foundations, whose builder
and maker is God.   There, some of our friends have gone
before ; there they dwell as citizens of that blessed city which
is all of pure gold, like unto clear glass ; a city which has no

need of the sun, neither of the moon to shine in it, for the glory of the Lord lightens it, and the Lamb is the light thereof. This is the city of habitation where the saints will for ever dwell; and the Lord is leading forth each and all of his wilderness wanderers by the right way, that he may bring them in the same way into his eternal presence, and to the enjoyment of those pleasures which are at his right hand for evermore.

March 25.

" Who in the days of his flesh, when he had offered up prayers and supplications with strong crying and tears unto him that was able to save him from death."—Hebrews v. 7.

THE Apostle says that Christ was "crucified through weakness" (2 Cor. xiii. 4). We must remember, however, that weakness was not imperfection in him, though it is imperfection in us; for when we speak of the weakness of Christ's human nature, we mean its weakness as compared with the strength and power of his divine nature. Our Lord felt the weakness of his humanity, for though in union with his eternal Deity, though most blessedly upheld and supported by the power and strength and consolation of the Holy Ghost, yet it was inherently weak, and an experience of its weakness was a part of the sufferings that he endured. Having, then, to bear as laid upon this weakness the whole weight of imputed sin, the whole curse of the law, the whole indignation of the Almighty, our Lord was brought to a spot where he needed special support. To be brought through that work safely, honourably, successfully, agreeably to the will of God and in the fullest harmony with the eternal purposes—to this point were the prayers and supplications of our suffering Lord directed; this was the solemn conflict which our gracious Lord had to endure in the garden in its beginning and upon the cross in its finishing. We know

what he felt—at least the Holy Ghost has given us an
account of that solemn agony in the garden, when he said,
as in a moment of weakness, " Let this cup pass from me."
It was so bitter in contemplation ; it was so full of unmitigated wrath ; the ingredients were so mingled with the anger
of the Almighty against sin and the manifestation of his
displeasure against every one who was chargeable with it,
that as he stood there and then as our substitute, in our
place, to endure what we must have endured without him,
and to bear the whole weight of eternal wrath and indignation,
which must have sunk us and all with us, were we millions,
to a deserved hell, that he needed the special interposition of
the help of God to hold him up as he drank it to the very
dregs.   It was to obtain this help that he offered up prayers
and supplications, with strong crying and tears ; .and it was
the vehemency of the conflict which made the blood fall from
his brow and tears drop from his eyes, and his whole soul
engaged in an agony of mingled grief and horror, fear and
supplication, each increasing and stimulating the other, and
the whole poured forth with prayers, cries, weeping, and supplications unto him that was able to save him from death ;
not from the death that he came to die, but to save him from
everything connected with the original sentence of death, as
involving in it the wrath of God and its consequences.

March 26.

" And was heard in that he feared."—HEBREWS v. 7.

THERE is something in my mind extremely mysterious
and yet divinely blessed in the expression, " in that he
feared," and it is right to mention that there is some little
difficulty as to the right rendering of the expression.   The
word means in the original not so much fear, as indicating
dread or apprehension, as a holy reverence and tender
cautiousness.   It means literally the great care with which

we handle brittle vessels, and, as used in the New Testament,
signifies a reverential fear of God.   It is used, for instance,
of Noah, where he is said to be "moved with fear" (Heb.
xi. 7), and is translated "godly fear" in those words, "whereby
we may serve God acceptably with reverence and godly
fear" (Heb. xii. 28).   It does not, therefore, mean fear in
any such sense of the word as would imply a servile dread.
It does not mean that our gracious Lord was possessed with
that servile dread of the Almighty which reprobates feel and
those who never were partakers of the grace of God.   But
our Lord, as an exemplar of every grace of the Spirit, was
possessed of that holy reverence and godly fear in its abundant measure of which we have but a small portion.   Now
just in proportion to the depth of the grace that was in him,
the power of God that rested upon him, and the operations
and influence of the Holy Ghost in his soul, so was the
measure of holy reverence and godly fear which dwelt in his
sacred humanity.   Contemplating, therefore, the greatness of
the work ; having before his eyes not so much the bodily
sufferings of the cross as all the mental agonies—the distress of soul, the conflict with the law in its load and curse,
the indignation of the Almighty against sin in the Person of
the Surety, the hidings of his Father's face, and the with-
drawal of the light of his countenance,—foreseeing all these
dolorous sufferings of the cross, and tasting the first drops of
that shower which was so soon to fall upon his sacred head,
it seemed as if his holy soul was filled with the most solemn
reverence and deep apprehension of the majesty of God.
This is the fear of which our text speaks.   It is in the margin
"his piety."   But reverence, godly fear, holy apprehension,
and tender awe convey the meaning of the word much better
than the expression "piety."   It was prophesied of him that
"the Spirit of the Lord should rest upon him, the spirit of
knowledge and of the fear of the Lord, and should make

him of quick understanding in the fear of the Lord" (Isaiah
xi. 1, 2). Thus his prayers, his cries, his supplications, and
his tears rose up with sweet acceptance into the ears of his
Father, because they came out of a heart filled with reverence
and godly fear under the promptings and influences of that
eternal Spirit who wrought in him every grace both in its
possession and its exercise, and through whom he offered
himself without spot to God.

March 27.

"*Is anything too hard for the Lord?*"—Genesis xviii. 14.

THE Lord will make us feel that though his arm is not
shortened that it cannot save, nor his ear heavy that it
cannot hear, yet he is to be enquired of. He is indeed a
God that worketh wonders ; apparent impossibilities are
nothing with him ; he has but to speak and it is done. But
he will make us know his power by making us feel our
weakness. He will often keep at a great distance, and for
a long time, in order to make us value his presence. He
will make us sink very low that he may lift us very high.
He will make us taste the bitterness of the gall and wormwood of sin that we may know the sweetness of manifested
pardon. He will teach us to abhor ourselves in our own
sight, and loathe ourselves for our abominations, before we
shall see and know ourselves washed in his blood, clothed
in his righteousness, and to stand before him without spot
or wrinkle or any such thing. The Lord in one sense is
easy of access upon his throne of grace, but in another very
hard to be got at. He invites his dear people to come and
spread their wants before him ; he encourages them with a
thousand promises ; he says in our text, " Is anything too
hard for the Lord ? " But he will make us set a due value
upon his visitations ; they shall not be given to us very easily
or very frequently that we may not hold them cheap. It is

not "ask and have" immediately. We have to learn what
sin cost our dear Redeemer; we have to see the holiness
and majesty of God; we have to learn that though mercy is
free, and grace superabounds over the aboundings of sin,
yet it must be got at after many a struggle, many a cry,
many a sigh and groan, and many a fervent petition; that
though all fulness dwells in the Lord the Lamb, and he
invites us to come and take of the water of life freely, yet it
is guarded on every side by many things that would drive us
back. And thus he teaches us to put due value upon his
grace, upon the visitations of his countenance and the words
of his lips. They cost the dear Redeemer the deepest
agonies of body and soul, and sufferings of which no finite
mind can form a conception; and, therefore, are not to be
given out without teaching us to know through what channel
they came, nor what it cost the blessed Son of God to give
out of his fulness those supplies of grace by which he
enriches our need.

March 28.

*" For thou wilt not leave my soul in hell; neither wilt thou
suffer thine Holy One to see corruption."*—Psalm xvi. 10.

When the adorable Lord by a voluntary act laid down his
life, the last words that he spoke were, "Father, into thy
hands I commend my spirit." By his "spirit" we are to
understand his human soul which at once went into paradise,
into the immediate presence of God, as he intimated in the
words, "And now come I to thee" (John xvii. 13). Nor
did he go thither that day alone. A trophy was soon to
follow him; the soul of that repenting, believing malefactor,
who, a partner with him in suffering, had become by his
sovereign grace a partner with him in glory.

There was, then, an actual separation of the Redeemer's
body and soul; but this did not destroy or affect the union

of his Deity with his humanity. That union remained
entire, as his holy soul went into paradise in union with his
Deity, and thus he was still God-man as much in paradise as
he was at the tomb of Lazarus, or at the Last Supper. But
his sacred body, though by the act of death life was gone out
of it, still remained as before, " that holy thing." Death did
not taint that sacred body any more than sin did not taint it
in the womb of the Virgin. The promise was, therefore,
" Thou wilt not leave my soul in hell [rather, in Hades, or
that paradise in which it was after death], nor suffer thy
Holy One to see corruption." This holy body was essentially
incorruptible, as being begotten of the Holy Ghost, by special
and supernatural generation, of the flesh of the Virgin ; but
as in all other acts of the sacred Trinity, Father, Son, and
Holy Ghost were all engaged that no taint of corruption
should in death assail it. The Father promised, and as a
God that cannot lie, performed by his almighty, superintend-
ing power; the Son, by the same innate, active, divine
energy by which he assumed that body in the womb of the
Virgin, preserved it untainted, uncorrupted in the grave ; and
the Holy Ghost who formed that body in its first conception,
breathed over it his holy influence to maintain it, in spite of
death and the tomb, as pure and as incorruptible as when he
first created it. These things are indeed difficult to understand or indeed conceive ; but they are heavenly mysteries,
which faith receives and holds fast in spite of sense, reason,
and unbelief. For see the tremendous consequences of
allowing any taint of corruption to assail that blessed body.
Could a tainted body be resumed at the resurrection ?
Corruption would have marred it as it will mar ours ; and
how could a corrupt body have been again the habitation of
the Son of God ? We are often instrumentally preserved
from error not only by knowing and feeling the sweetness
and power of truth, but by seeing, as at a glance, the

tremendous consequences which a denial of vital, fundamental truths involves.

March 29.

*" For by one offering he hath perfected for ever them that
are sanctified."*—HEBREWS X. 14.

To be "sanctified" is to be made a partaker of that
holiness, without which no man shall see the Lord; to be
made a new creature; to "put on the new man, which after
God is created in righteousness and true holiness;" in a
word, to be "made a partaker of the divine nature," and
thus have the holiness of God breathed into and communicated to the soul. Without this inward sanctification, none
can enter the gates of heaven. To be made meet, therefore,
for the heavenly inheritance, you must have a heavenly heart
and a praising, adoring, loving spirit ; you must delight
yourself in the Lord as being so holy and yet so gracious, so
pure and yet so loving, so bright and glorious and yet so
condescending and sympathising. Now this meetness for
the holiness, happiness, and employments of heaven is
communicated at regeneration, in which the new man of
grace, though weak, is still perfect. Look at the thief upon
the cross : what an instance is he how the Spirit of God can
in a moment make a man meet for heaven! Here was a
vile malefactor, whose life had been spent in robbery and
murder, brought at last to suffer the just punishment of his
crimes ; and as we are told that " they which were crucified
with him reviled him," we have reason to believe that at
first he joined his brother malefactor in blaspheming the
Redeemer. But sovereign grace, and what but sovereign
grace ? touched his heart, brought him to see and feel what
he was as a ruined sinner, opened his eyes to view the Son
of God bleeding before him, raised up faith in his soul to
believe in his name, and created a spirit of prayer that the

Lord of heaven and earth would remember him when he
came into his kingdom—perhaps the greatest act of faith we
have recorded in all Scripture, almost equal if not superior
to the faith of Abraham when he offered up Isaac on the
altar.   The dying Redeemer heard and answered his cry,
and said to him, " To-day shalt thou be with me in paradise."
Spirit and life accompanied the words, and raised up at once
in his soul a meetness for the inheritance, and before the
shades of night fell his happy spirit passed into paradise,
where he is now singing the praises of God and of the Lamb.
Many a poor child of God has gone on almost to his last
hours on earth without a manifestation of pardoning love
and the application of atoning blood; but he has not been
suffered to die without the Holy Ghost revealing salvation to
his soul, and attuning his heart to sing the immortal anthem
of the glorified spirits before the throne.

March 30.

" The eternal God is thy refuge."—DEUTERONOMY xxxiii. 27.

WHO is this eternal God ?   He is the great and glorious
Jehovah, eternal in his Trinity of Persons and in the Unity
of his Essence.   And what a depth of blessedness there is in
this God being an eternal God; and that in and of this
eternity, each Person of the Godhead has an equal share.
Look at the *love* of the eternal God.   How eternal was that
—not a thing of time, not fixed upon us when first brought
into being, not issuing out of his bosom first when we were
quickened into divine life; but a love from all eternity, as
being the love of an eternal God.   "I have loved thee with
an everlasting love; therefore with lovingkindness have I
drawn thee."   And how eternal are the *thoughts* of God ;
those thoughts which were of good, not of evil.   They were
eternal thoughts of peace to the Church ; eternal thoughts of

mercy to his beloved family; eternal thoughts of manifesting his grace in the Person and work of his dear Son; eternal flowings forth of goodness and love to those whom he had chosen in Christ, that they might be one with him, members of that glorious body of which his dear Son should be the Head. And eternal *purposes* also that nothing could defeat, that all the waves of time could not break through ; eternal *wisdom* also to devise, and eternal *power* to accomplish. Oh, this eternal God ! We look back into eternity; we see what a God he was from all eternity; and then we look forward to what he will be to all eternity. And we see him unchanging and unchangeable, resting in his love without variableness or the shadow of a turn, whether in eternity past, or in eternity to come. We think of the spirits of just men made perfect ; we follow in faith and hope the souls of our dear departed friends ; we view them drinking the· pleasures which are at his right hand for ever; and so they will be there to all eternity, ever basking in the smiles of an eternal God, ever living in his favour, ever conformed to the glorious image of his eternal Son, and ever drinking fresh draughts of love and bliss in his eternal presence. Oh, this eternal Father in the depths of his fatherly love in the gift of his dear Son ! Oh, the love, condescension, and tenderness of this eternal Son in the depths of his mercy and grace in suffering, bleeding, and dying for poor, guilty sinners ! Oh, the wisdom, the power, the grace, and the blessedness of this eternal Spirit, in taking of the things of Christ, unfolding the Person of Jesus, bringing him near, revealing him to the soul, sprinkling the conscience with his blood, and making him known and precious ! What a depth of gratitude is everlastingly due from the redeemed Church of God, to all the three sacred Persons of the glorious and undivided Trinity, and that both in his Trinity of Persons and his Unity of Essence the eternal God should be their refuge !

March 31.

" Yet doth he devise means that his banished be not expelled from him."—2 Samuel xiv. 14.

The promise runs, " I will bring again that which was driven away " (Ezekiel xxxiv. 16). Guilt, temptation, Satan, doubts, and fears had driven them away from the shelter of the tabernacle. Yet the Lord has respect unto these also. He says, " I will bring again." But how? By nothing but a sense of mercy. It is not by frowns, but by smiles. " I drew them," says the Lord, " with cords of a man " (that is, the tender feelings that are bound up in the human heart), " with bands of love." You may thunder, you may lighten, you may take the whip and flog a poor backslider; you can never flog him home. He must be drawn by mercy, by the goodness of God, which leads to repentance. How was Peter brought back? By that look which Jesus gave him, as he stood in the hall of the high priest; that look of mingled love and reproach. It was this that made Peter go out and weep bitterly. A frown would have driven him into despair, and made him hang himself by the side of Judas; but that look of mingled reproof and love wounded and healed, filled heart and eyes with the deepest grief and sorrow; and yet poured such a healing balm into his mourning soul that when Jesus was risen from the dead, and by his angel sent him a special message that he would see him again in Galilee, he leaped into the sea to meet him, when he stood on the shore of the lake Tiberias. But for that look and for that message, he would rather have leaped to the bottom with self-reproach, than leaped to the shore with love and affection. Thus was brought again poor driven-away Peter. And thus too, by the voice of pardon, was brought again poor driven-away David. For the Lord deviseth means that his banished be not expelled from him.

April 1.

" O Israel, thou hast destroyed thyself; but in me is thine help."—Hosea xiii. 9.

God is all-wise, and therefore takes no rash, precipitate steps. As the original plan of salvation was devised by infinite wisdom, so all the successive steps of the execution of that plan are directed by the same boundless wisdom also. "Wherein he hath abounded towards us," says Paul (Eph. i. 8), "in all wisdom and prudence." Thus, in his dealings with his people, God does not put them at once into possession of all the blessings which he has laid up for them. He has pardoned, for instance, their sins; but he does not immediately, when he calls them by his grace, put them into possession of this blessing. He has first to teach them their need of it. He has to prepare their heart for the right reception of it. It is no common gift, and he has to teach them how to value it. They are saved from wrath and eternal misery, from his dreadful displeasure and ever-burning indignation against sin. They have need to be shewn, and made deeply to feel, *from* what they are saved, as well as *to* what they are saved. And as the oak does not grow to its full stature in a day, but needs years of sunshine and storm, of beating winds and howling tempests, to give it strength and consistency, a deep and wide root, as well as a lofty and branching stem, so do God's children need months and years of trial and temptation, that they may push a deep root downwards, and shoot up healthy and vigorous upwards. Thus, before the soul can know anything about salvation, it must learn deeply and experimentally the nature of sin, and of itself, as stained and polluted thereby. It is proud, and needs to be humbled; careless, and needs to be awakened; alive, and needs to be killed; full, and requires to be emptied; whole, and needs to be wounded; clothed, and

requires to be stripped. It is, by nature, self-righteous and
self-seeking; is buried deep in worldliness and carnality; is
utterly blind and ignorant; is filled with presumption, arro-
gance, conceit, and enmity, and hates all that is heavenly
and spiritual. Sin, in all its various forms, is its natural
element. " The Ethiopian cannot change his skin, nor
the leopard his spots." To make man the direct contrary
of what he originally is; to make him love God instead of
hating him; fear, instead of mocking him; obey, instead of
rebelling against him; and to tremble at his terrible majesty,
instead of running upon the thick bosses of his buckler;—to
do this mighty work, and to effect this wonderful change,
requires the implantation of a new nature by the immediate
hand of God himself.

April 2.

" *That your faith should not stand in the wisdom of men,
but in the power of God.*"—1 Corinthians ii. 5.

True faith I may call the *grand tidal wave* of the soul.
I will endeavour to explain the expression. We see the river
Thames day by day ebbing and flowing. What causes this
change? You answer, " It is produced by the sea in the
Channel alternately coming up and retiring." It is a true
explanation. But what makes the sea of the Channel alternately come up and retire? There is what is called " a
grand tidal wave" that comes across the Atlantic Ocean,
which, as it ebbs and flows, affects all the minor tides of the
neighbouring seas; and thus the tide of the Channel, and
that of the river Thames, ebb and flow in unison with this
huge Atlantic wave. In the same way faith is the tidal wave
of the soul; and all the graces and fruits of the Spirit ebb
and flow just as faith rises, or just as faith sinks. If faith
rises in the soul, all the graces and fruits of the Spirit rise

with it; light increases, life is deepened, the fear of God
strengthened, hope brightened, and love augmented. And
when this great tidal wave of faith falls in the soul, all the
minor tides of the Spirit's graces fall in unison with it.
Thus when faith recedes and becomes low in the soul,
all the other graces of the Spirit sink with it; consolation
ebbs out altogether, hope recedes to a narrow streamlet, life
dwindles to a scanty current, and love is reduced to a
shallow channel. And as in the Thames we see, at low tide,
the muddy banks which the stream has forsaken, so as faith
sinks to a low ebb in the soul, there seems little else left but
the mud and mire of corruption. But what makes the grand
tidal wave itself move? There is a cause for that also. It is
drawn up by, and obeys the attraction of the sun. And is
not this true spiritually of the grand tidal wave of faith in the
soul? Is it not drawn up by the Sun of righteousness, as
the natural sun draws up the wave of the ocean, and makes
it ebb and flow? And when that glorious Sun ceases to
draw up faith, does it not ebb and sensibly sink in the soul,
as the natural sea sinks when the sun recedes from it?

April 3.

"*In the house of the righteous is much treasure: but in the
revenues of the wicked is trouble.*"—Proverbs xv. 6.

How different is the estimate that faith makes of riches,
honours, and comforts from that made by the world and the
flesh! The world has no idea of riches but such as consist
in gold and silver, in houses, lands, or other tangible property; no thought of honour, but such as man has to
bestow; and no notion of comfort, except in "fulfilling the
desires of the flesh and of the mind." But the soul that is
anointed by an "unction from the Holy One," takes a different estimate of these matters, and feels that the only true

riches are those of God's grace in the heart, that the only
real honour is that which cometh from God, and that the
only solid comfort is that which is imparted by the Holy
Ghost to a broken and contrite spirit. Now, just in proportion as we have the Spirit of God, shall we take faith's
estimate of riches, honour, and comfort; and just so much
as we are imbued with the spirit of the world, shall we take
the world's estimate of these things.

When the eye of the world looked on the Apostles, it
viewed them as a company of poor ignorant men, a set of
wild enthusiasts, that travelled about the country preaching
concerning one Jesus, who, they said, had been crucified,
and was risen from the dead. The natural eye saw no
beauty, no power, no glory in the truths they brought forth;
nor did it see that the poor perishing tabernacles of these
outcast men contained in them a heavenly treasure; and
that they would one day shine as the stars for ever and ever,
whilst those who despised their word would sink into endless
woe. The spirit of the world, and the views that the flesh
takes are not altered now. Nature ever remains the same,
and can never understand or love the things of eternity; it
can only look to, and can only rest upon, the poor perishing
things of time and sense. By this test, therefore, we may in
a measure try our state. What, for instance, are our daily
and hourly feelings about the things of time and sense, and
what about the things of eternity? Which of the two press
with more power on our minds, which occupy more of our
thoughts, which are laid up more warmly in our affections?
And just in proportion as the solemn things of eternity,
or the things of time and sense, occupy our mind; just so
much as our hearts are fixed upon heaven or earth; just so
much as we are living to God, or to ourselves, in the same
degree is the strength of our faith, and the depth of the work
of grace upon our conscience.

April 4.

" But we see Jesus, who was made a little lower than the angels for the suffering of death, crowned with glory and honour ; that he by the grace of God should taste death for every man."—HEBREWS ii. 9.

How wondrous that he who, as the Son of God, made angels (Colossians i. 16), should be made inferior to them, and even need and receive their ministering aid and succour (Matthew iv. 11). O the depths of humiliation to which the blessed Redeemer stooped, carrying down into their lowest point that pure, spotless, holy humanity which he had assumed into union with his divine Person as the Son of God ! And let us ever bear carefully in mind that humiliation is not degradation. Our blessed Lord "humbled himself" by a voluntary act of surpassing grace ; and it was no more in the power of men or circumstances to debase him of his glory than of lying witnesses to strip him of his innocency. The spotless purity of his sacred humanity, as in union with his divine nature, and as filled with and upheld by the Holy Ghost, preserved it from degradation in its lowest humiliation. The crown of thorns and the purple robe, the mocking knee of the Roman soldier and the taunting scoff of the Jewish priest, though they called forth the grace, did not tarnish the glory of our suffering Lord. His holy obedience to his Father's will in drinking the bitter cup, his meek dignity amidst the worst of insults, and his calm resignation to all the weight of suffering which God or man laid upon him, all shone forth the more conspicuously under every attempt to dishonour him. It is most sweet and blessed to look down, as it were, into some of those depths of humiliation into which the Redeemer sank, and to see that in the lowest depths of his soul travail, when he was poured out like water, and his heart, broken with grief and sorrow, was

melted within him like wax, he was, in the midst of all, the
glorious Son of God, though then the suffering Son of man;
and that he was the same Jesus yesterday when hanging on
the cross, as he is to-day at the right hand of his Father, and
will be for ever in the realms of heavenly bliss.

April 5.

"*And the servant abideth not in the house for ever: but the
son abideth ever.*"—JOHN viii. 35.

IT is the irreversible blessing of a son, that he is never to
be turned out of the house, that the union between the Parent
and the child can never be broken, but that he is to reign with
Christ through the ages of one everlasting day. This is a
sweet consolation to God's family that "the son abideth
ever." How often is a child of God exercised, whether he
shall abide for ever, whether he may not draw back to perdition, whether some temptation may not overtake him
whereby it shall be made manifest that he is nothing but
a deceiver and deceived! But the Lord himself says, "the
son abideth ever;" let him be but a babe, let him have but
the first beginning of spiritual life in his soul, he "abideth
ever;" he has the same interest in the affections of the
Father, is a fellow-heir with Christ, and has a title to the
same inheritance as those who are of longer standing, and
those who are his elders in age.

But sometimes the son may get tired of the restraint of his
Father's house. God is a wise Parent as well as a kind one.
He will treat his children with the most tender kindness and
intimacy, but he will never allow them to be guilty of dis-
respect towards him. Sometimes, then, the sons get weary of
their Father's house; they are like the younger son in the
parable, when he asked his father to give him his portion,
and when he had got it he went away into a far country,

away from his father's house, from under his father's roof, and wasted it in riotous living. This is where many of God's children get. There is a restraint in God's house, where the soul is not really blessed with the personal and present enjoyment of gospel truth, and restraint being ever irksome, the vain, idolatrous heart thinks it can derive some pleasure from the world which is not to be found under the roof of the Father. And, therefore, he gradually withdraws his steps from his Father's house, seeks to derive some pleasure from the things of time and sense, erects some idol, and falls down to worship it. But notwithstanding all this, "the son abideth ever." The Father of all his people in Christ does not disinherit his dear children; and though earthly parents may disinherit theirs, God's family are never cast out of the inheritance. The true-born Israelite who had waxed poor and sold himself unto the stranger was to obtain his freedom in the year of jubilee (Leviticus xxv. 47, 54), and to return to his own house and his own estate. So the son who has departed from his Father's house, and sold himself under sin, and become a slave to that cruel taskmaster, when the year of jubilee comes, the year of restoration, and the silver trumpet is blown, shakes off his shackles and fetters, casts aside the livery of servitude, returns to his Father's house, and is received with joy beneath his Father's roof. O what a meeting! The forgiving Parent, and the disobedient child! The Father dissolved in tears of affection; the child dissolved in tears of contrition! Whatever, then, be our wanderings of heart, alienation of affection, and backsliding of soul; however we may depart from God, so far as we are sons, we shall "abide in the house for ever," and possess an "inheritance incorruptible and undefiled, and that fadeth not away, reserved in heaven for those that are kept by the power of God through faith unto salvation." And it will be our mercy to abide in the house below as members of the family, without departing from it, until re-united to the family above, "the general assembly and church of the firstborn, whose names are written in heaven."

April 6.

"And shall not God avenge his own elect, which cry day and night unto him?"—LUKE xviii. 7.

"BEHOLD, he prayeth," was the word of the Lord to Ananias to convince him that that dreaded persecutor, Saul of Tarsus, had been quickened by the Spirit. And what a mercy it is for the quickened soul that the blessed Spirit thus helps his sinking, trembling spirit, puts life and energy into his cries and sighs, holds him up and keeps him steadfast at the throne, and thus enables him to persevere with his earnest suings for mercy, mingles faith with his petitions, and himself most graciously and kindly intercedes within him and for him with groanings which cannot be uttered. This is "praying with the spirit" (1 Cor. xiv. 15) and "in the Holy Ghost" (Jude 20). This is pouring out the heart before God (Psalm lxii. 8), pouring out the soul before the Lord (1 Sam. i. 15); and by this free discharge of the contents of an almost bursting heart, sensible relief is given to the burdened spirit. By this special mark, the convictions of a quickened soul are distinguished from the pangs of guilt and remorse which are sometimes aroused in the natural conscience. Cain said, "My punishment is greater than I can bear," but there was neither repentance nor prayer in his heart; for "he went out from the presence of the Lord"—the very presence which the living soul is seeking to reach and be found in, and into which the Spirit brings him (Eph. ii. 18). Saul was "sore distressed," when God answered him, "neither by dreams, nor by Urim, nor by prophets," but he goes to the witch of Endor, and in the end falls upon his own sword. Judas repented himself of his accursed treachery, but went and hanged himself. No prayer, no supplication was in either of their hearts. So it is prophesied that men shall gnaw their tongues for pain, and yet shall blaspheme the God of heaven because of their pains and their sores, and not repent of their deeds (Rev. xvi. 10, 11). But the elect cry day and night unto God; and their prayers, perfumed with the incense of their all-prevailing Intercessor at the right hand of the Father, enter into the ears of the Lord of Sabaoth.

April 7.

" But we all, with open face beholding as in a glass the glory of the Lord, are changed into the same image from glory to glory, even as by the Spirit of the Lord."—2 CORINTHIANS iii. 18.

A view of Christ's glory and a foretaste of the bliss and blessedness it communicates has a transforming effect upon the soul. We are naturally proud, covetous, and worldly, often led aside by, and grievously entangled in various lusts and passions, prone to evil, averse to good, easily elated by prosperity, soon dejected by adversity, peevish under trials, rebellious under heavy strokes, unthankful for daily mercies of food and raiment, and in other ways ever manifesting our base original. To be brought from under the power of these abounding evils, and be made " meet for the inheritance of the saints in light," we need to be " transformed by the renewing of our mind," and conformed to the image of Christ. Now this can only be by beholding his glory by faith, as the Apostle speaks, " But we all, with open face beholding as in a glass the glory of the Lord, are changed into the same image from glory to glory, even as by the Spirit of the Lord." It is this believing view of the glory of Christ which supports under heavy trials, producing meekness

and resignation to the will of God. We are, therefore, bidden
to "consider him that endured such contradiction of sinners
against himself, lest we be wearied and faint in our minds;"
and to "run with patience the race that is set before us,
looking unto Jesus." Sicknesses, too, sometimes befall us,
when we need special support; the sands of our time are
fast running out, and there is no turning the glass; our
"days are passing away as the swift ships, as the eagle that
hasteth to the prey;" and death and eternity are fast hasten-
ing on. When the body sinks under a load of pain and
disease, and all sources of happiness and enjoyment from
health and strength are cut off; when flesh and heart fail,
and the eye-strings are breaking in death, what can support
the soul or bear it safe through Jordan's swelling flood, but
those discoveries of the glory of Christ that shall make it
sick of earth, sin and self, and willing to lay the poor body
in the grave, that it may be for ever ravished with his glory
and his love? Thus we see how the glory of Christ is not
only in heaven the unspeakable delight of the saints, whose
glorified souls and bodies will then bear "an exceeding and
eternal weight of glory;" but here on earth, in their days of
tribulation and sorrow, this same glory, as revealed to their
hearts, supports and upholds their steps, draws them out of
the world, delivers them from the power of sin, gives them
union and communion with Christ, conforms them to his
image, comforts them in death, and lands them in glory.
We thus see Christ, like the sun, not only illuminating all
heaven with his glory, the delight of the Father, the joy of
the spirits of just men made perfect, and the adoration of all
the angelic host, but irradiating also the path of the just on
earth, casting his blessed beams on all their troubles and
sorrows, and lighting up the way wherein they follow their
Lord from the suffering cross to the triumphant crown.

April 8.

"*Praying always with all prayer and supplication in the Spirit, and watching thereunto with all perseverance and supplication for all saints.*"—EPHESIANS vi. 18.

IF we do not continually " pray in the Spirit," our limbs will, so to speak, shrink, and our armour drop off. The knights of old exercised themselves every day in their full armour, or they could not have borne it, nor used their weapons with dexterity and strength. So must the Christian warrior, by prayer and supplication, " exercise himself unto godliness." To this must be added, "*watching thereunto.*" To watch for the answer; to wait for the appearing of the Lord "more than they that watch for the morning." And this, "*with all perseverance,*" never giving it up, taking no denial, begging of the Lord again and again, and wrestling with him till he appear to bless, visit, and shine upon the soul. O how this heavenly recipe keeps every part of the armour bright, and the soldier active and expert in its use ! The armour indeed of itself, as being from heaven, gets neither dull nor rusty. It is *we* who get sluggish in its use. But, to our apprehension, faith and prayer make it glitter more brightly. How, for instance, " the prayer of faith " brightens up the girdle of truth, and makes it glitter and shine ! How it burnishes the breast-plate, and makes it fit tightly round the bosom ! How it makes the helmet glitter in the sun, and its noble plumes to wave in all their native lustre ! How it beats out every dint the shield may have received from the fiery darts, and fits it for fresh encounters ! And how it sharpens " the sword of the Spirit," gives it a brighter polish, and nerves the arm to wield it with renewed activity and vigour ! Oh, this is the secret of all true victory ! All is, all must be well, when we are in a prayerful, meditative, watching state ; and all is ill, when this heavenly recipe is neglected; when the hands droop, and the knees faint, and prayer seems dead and motionless in the breast. Let there be in the soul an abiding spirit of prayer, and victory is sure. Satan has little power against the soul that has an abiding spirit of prayer, and is "watching thereunto with all perseverance." But without this spirit of prayer, we are a prey to all his temptations, and can neither take, wear, nor use the only armour against them.

April 9.

"Let your light so shine before men, that they may see your good works, and glorify your Father which is in heaven."—MATTHEW v. 16.

To glorify God is the highest ambition of angels. The brightest seraph before the throne has no higher aim, no greater happiness, than to bring glory to his name. And yet a poor sinner on earth may glorify God as much, and in some way more, than the brightest angel in the courts of eternal bliss. What different views the eyes of God and the eyes of men take of events passing on the earth. What glory is brought to God by all the victories gained by one country over another? I have thought sometimes that a poor old man, or feeble, decrepit woman, lying on a workhouse pallet, fighting with sin, self and Satan, yet enabled amidst all to look to the Lord Jesus, and by a word from his lips overcoming death and hell, though when dead thrust into an elm coffin, to rot in a pauper's grave, brings more glory to God than all the exploits of Nelson or Wellington, and that such victories are more glorious than those of Waterloo or Trafalgar. It is true that the parish officers will not proclaim such a victory; nor will bells ring or cannons roar at such exploits; but the God of heaven and earth may get more glory from such a despised creature, than from all the generals and admirals who have ever drawn up armies in battle, or sunk hostile fleets beneath the wave. Truly does the Lord say, " My thoughts are not your thoughts, neither are your ways my ways." It is indeed marvellous that glory should be brought to his great name by what his people do and suffer upon earth; that their feeble attempts to believe, to love, and to hope in him; to speak well of his name ; and to adorn his doctrine in their life and conversation, should redound to his honour and praise. Wondrous indeed is it that a poor, insignificant worm, whom perhaps his fellow-mortal will scarcely deign to look at, or passes by with a shrug of contempt, should add glory to the great God that inhabiteth eternity, before whom the highest angels and brightest seraphs bow with holy adoration ! Well may we say, " What are all the glorious exploits that men are so proud of, compared with the tribute of glory rendered to God by his suffering saints ? " You may feel yourself one of the poorest, vilest, neediest worms of earth; and yet if you believe in the Lord Jesus Christ with a living faith, hope in his mercy, love his dear name, and in your vocation adorn his doctrine by a godly, consistent life, you are privileged above princes and nobles, yes, even above crowned heads, and all the glory of man, because you are bringing glory to God. It matters not what may be your station in life. You may be a servant, master, wife, husband, child ; your rank and station may be high or low ; but whatever it be, still in it you may bring glory to God. If a servant, by obedience, cleanliness, industry, and attention to the directions of your master or mistress. If a master or mistress, by kindness and liberality to your dependents, and doing all that you can to render the yoke of servitude light. There is not a single Christian who may not glorify God, though in worldly circumstances he be, or seem to be, totally insignificant. Glory is brought to God by those who live and walk in his fear, and more sometimes by the poor than by the rich. Only adorn the doctrine of God in all things, and you will bring glory to God in all things.

April 10.

" *Verily, verily, I say unto you, He that entereth not by the door into the sheepfold, but climbeth up some other way, the same is a thief and a robber.*"—JOHN X. 1.

HERE are three marks whereby you may know whether you have entered by faith into the sheepfold. First, have you any evidence of being saved in the Lord Jesus Christ with an everlasting salvation? Secondly, have you felt any blessed and holy freedom and liberty of going in and coming out of the heavenly sheepfold? Thirdly, have you found pasture? Sometimes finding pasture in the ordinances of God's house; sometimes in the sacred truths of the gospel, as you read or hear the word of truth; and especially in partaking by faith of the flesh and blood of the Lamb.

But there may be those who are in *this* spot. They see plainly that Christ is the door, and are fully convinced there is no other way of entrance into the fold but by him ; and yet they do not seem to have entered personally and ex-perimentally in, so as to enjoy for themselves its privileges and blessings. But have you never entered in by hope and expectation ? And how could you enter in by expectation unless something in you, which you could not give yourself, were expecting a blessing from God ; unless you possessed a principle of living faith, whereby, though at present weak and feeble, you yet seem to realise the sweetness of the blessings held forth in the gospel? How different is this state of soul experience from climbing daringly and pre-sumptuously over the wall, or taking the ladder of self-righteousness, and thus helping yourself in by some other way than the door. How much better to be lying in humility at the gate, looking to Jesus and longing to enter in, begging of him to open the door and give you admission, than to make yourself a daring and rash intruder. How different is this humble, dependent, and self-abased state of soul from self-righteousness on the one hand, and bold presumption on the other. There is everything to encourage the weak and feeble part of the flock who long to enter into the fold. To them Jesus opens his arms wide, and says in their heart and ears, " 'I am the door : ' enter through me, and by no other way. There is access to God by me, for ' I am the way, the truth, and the life.' If ye enter in by me, ye shall be saved from all you justly dread and fear, both as regards this life and the life to come. Ye shall go freely in and freely out, and find pasture; lying down and feeding on my divine Person, flesh, and blood on earth, as the prelude and foretaste of enjoying me for ever in the blissful courts of heaven above."

April 11.

" *Behold, a virgin shall conceive, and bear a son, and shall call his name Immanuel.*"—Isaiah vii. 14.

The Deity of the Son of God shines all through the sacred page. It is the grand cardinal point, on which all the doctrines of grace turn; and he that is unsound there, is unsound everywhere. The Godhead of Christ does not rest upon a few texts of Scripture, but it shines all through the Scripture; it is the light of the Scripture, and it is the life of the Scripture. Take away the Deity of Jesus out of the Scripture, and you would do the same thing spiritually as though you blotted the sun out of the sky naturally; the sacred page would be one black darkness. But the Person of Jesus is not Deity only. No man can see God and live ; we could not bear to look upon pure Deity. And therefore the Son of God has taken into union with himself our nature; he has "taken upon him the seed of Abraham"— that " holy thing " which was begotten by the Holy Ghost in

the womb of the Virgin Mary, and there united to the second
Person of the glorious Trinity, that Godhead and manhood
might form one glorious Person, Immanuel, God with us.
Now to the eye of faith there is the greatest beauty and glory
in Christ's humanity. The enlightened soul views Deity
shining through the manhood; and when it sees Jesus
"going about, doing good," when it hears the words that
dropped from his gracious lips, when it views him by the eye
of faith, bleeding, suffering, agonising, and dying, it sees the
Godhead in all these acts, upholding and shining through the
manhood. And it is this union of the two natures in one
glorious Person, that fills the heart that receives it in the
faith of it and in the love of it with a measure of pure
affection.

Here, then, the Church has a view of the glorious Person
of Jesus ; and she falls in love with him. There is something in supernatural beauty which kindles spiritual affection,
as there is something in natural beauty which kindles natural
affection. When the quickened soul sees supernatural
beauty, it immediately falls in love with it. The spiritual
affections centre in spiritual beauty. And thus, when the
redeemed and regenerated soul sees the glorious Person of
Christ, God-man, Immanuel, God with us, and has a taste
and sense of his love, the blessed Spirit thereby kindles in
it spiritual affection, and attracts it with these " cords of love
and bands of a man."

April 12.

" As the truth is in Jesus."—EPHESIANS iv. 21.

WITHOUT truth there is no *regeneration ;* for it is by " the
word of truth " that we are begotten and born again (James
i. 18; 1 Peter i. 23). Without truth there is no *justification ;*
for we are justified by faith, which faith consists in crediting
God's truth, and so gives peace with God. Without the
truth there is no *sanctification ;* for the Lord himself says,

" Sanctify them through thy truth : thy word is truth." And
without the truth there is no *salvation;* for " God hath chosen
us to salvation through sanctification of the Spirit and belief
of the truth."

And as the truth is the instrumental cause of all these
blessings, the divinely-appointed means whereby they become
manifested mercies, so truth enters into and is received by all
the *graces* of the Spirit as they come forth into living exercise.
Thus, without the truth, there is no *faith;* for the work
of faith is to believe the truth. What is all the difference
between faith and delusion? That faith believes God's
truth, and delusion credits Satan's lies. " And for this
cause God shall send them strong delusion, that they should
believe a lie, that they all might be damned who believed not
the truth, but had pleasure in unrighteousness." Without
truth there is no *hope;* for the province of hope is to anchor
in the truth. " That by two immutable things in which
it was impossible for God to lie, we might have a strong
consolation, who have fled for refuge to lay hold upon the
hope set before us; which hope we have as an anchor of the
soul, both sure and steadfast, and which entereth into that
within the veil." The two immutable things in which hope
anchors are God's word and God's truth ; in other words,
the pledged veracity and faithfulness of him who cannot lie.
This made holy David say, " I have hoped in thy word."
" They that go down to the pit," said good king Hezekiah,
" cannot hope for thy truth." No ; it is " the living, the
living who praise thee as I do this day." And it is " through
patience and comfort of the Scriptures," that is, the consolation which the truth of God revealed in the Scriptures affords,
" that we have hope." Without truth there is no *love,* for it
is by " the love of the truth " that the saved are distinguished
from the lost. " And with all deceivableness of unrighteousness in them that perish ; because they received not the love

of the truth that they might be saved." And it is only as we
speak " the truth in love that we grow up into him in all
things, which is the head, even Christ." Thus "the fruit of
the Spirit is in all goodness, and righteousness, and truth; "
and this in the Person of the Son of God, for " grace and
truth came by Jesus Christ."

April 13.

" Fools die for want of wisdom."—Proverbs x. 21.

There is such a connection between true wisdom, which
is " a knowledge of the holy " (Prov. xxx. 3), and the fear of
the Lord, and such a connection between ignorance of the
Lord and sin, that saved saints are called " wise," and lost
sinners are called " fools," not only in the Old Testament, as
continually in the Proverbs, but in the New. Many of the
Lord's people look with suspicion upon knowledge, from not
seeing clearly the vast distinction between the spiritual,
experimental knowledge for which we are now contending,
and what is called " head knowledge." They see that a
man may have a well-furnished head and a graceless heart,
that he may understand " all mysteries and all knowledge,"
and yet be " nothing " (1 Cor. xiii. 2); and as some of these
all-knowing professors are the basest characters that can
infest the churches of truth, those who really fear the Lord
stand not only in doubt of them, but of all the knowledge
possessed by them. But put it in a different form; ask the
people of God whether there is not such a divine reality,
such a heavenly blessing, as being " taught of God " (John
vi. 45); having " an unction from the Holy One, whereby we
know all things " (1 John ii. 20) : knowing the truth for oneself, and finding it maketh free (John viii. 32); whether
there is not a " counting of all things but loss for the excellency of the knowledge of Christ Jesus our Lord," and a
stretching forth of the desires of the soul to "know him,

and the power of his resurrection, and the fellowship of his sufferings;" whether there is not "a knowledge of salvation by the remission of sins" (Luke i. 77); "a knowledge of the glory of God in the face of Jesus Christ" (2 Cor. iv. 6); a being "filled with the knowledge of his will" (Col. i. 9); an "increasing in the knowledge of God" (Col. i. 10); "a growing in grace and in the knowledge of the Lord and Saviour Jesus Christ" (2 Pet. iii. 18);—ask the living family of God whether there be not such a knowledge as this, and if this knowledge is not the very pith and marrow, the very sum and substance of vital godliness, and they will with one voice say, "It is."

April 14.

"Now ye are clean through the word which I have spoken unto you."—JOHN xv. 3.

WHAT God does, he does by the word of his grace and the influences which accompany that word; for ever bear in mind that God does nothing but by his word. The sanctifying, cleansing effects therefore which attend the word of his grace under the operations of the Spirit are spoken of as "the washing of water by the word" (Eph. v. 26). "The word" is the written Scripture; the "water" is the power of the Holy Ghost; the "washing" is the cleansing effect of the application of the word. Let me ask you this question, if you doubt my words, How are we to get the burden and guilt of our sins off our conscience, the defilement of mind which sin produces, the bondage of spirit which sin creates, the fears and alarm of the soul which sin works? You will say, "By believing in Jesus Christ, for being justified by faith we have peace with God." That is true; but how can we believe in Jesus Christ, so as to find this peace? By the word of his grace, accompanied by the special influence, unction, and dew of the Holy Ghost revealing and making known pardon and acceptance with God, which is therefore spoken of as "the washing of water by the word." For as water washes the body, so the word of truth washes the soul, by washing away the guilt and filth and defilement of sin. As the blessed Lord said, " Ye shall know the truth, and the truth shall make you free." And again, "He that is washed needeth not save to wash his feet, but is clean every whit." Thus as water when applied cleanses the body from natural filth, so does the word of promise, the word of truth, the word of salvation revealing and making known the Saviour's precious blood, cleanse the conscience from the guilt, filth, and defilement of sin.

April 15.

" But all things that are reproved are made manifest by the light; for whatsoever doth make manifest is light."— EPHESIANS v. 13.

FEELING is the first evidence of supernatural life; a feeling compounded of two distinct sensations, one referring to God, and the other referring to self. The same ray of light has manifested two opposite things, " for that which maketh manifest is light;" and the sinner sees at one and the same moment God and self, justice and guilt, power and helplessness, a holy law and a broken commandment, eternity and time, the purity of the Creator and the filthiness of the creature. And these things he sees, not merely as declared in the Bible, but as revealed in himself as personal realities, involving all his happiness or all his misery in time and in eternity. Thus it is with him as though a new existence had been communicated, and as if for the first time he had found there was a God. One ray of supernatural light, penetrating through the veil spread over the heart, has revealed that terrible secret—a just God, who will by no means clear the guilty. This piercing ray has torn away the bed too short, and stripped off the covering too narrow. A sudden, peculiar conviction has rushed into the soul. One absorbing feeling has seized fast hold of it, and well-nigh banished every other. "There is a God, and I am a sinner before him," is written upon the heart by the same divine finger that traced those fatal letters on the palace wall of the king of Babylon, which made the joints of his loins to be loosed, and his knees to smite one against another (Dan. v. 5, 6). "What shall I do? Where shall I go? What will become of me? Mercy, O God! Mercy, mercy! I am lost, ruined, undone! Fool, madman, wretch, monster that I have been! I have ruined my soul. O my sins, my sins! O eternity, eternity!" Such and similar cries and groans, though differing in depth and intensity, go up out of the new-born soul well-nigh day and night at the first discovery of God and of itself. These feelings have taken such complete possession of the heart that it can find no rest except in calling upon God. This is the first pushing of the young bud through the bark, the first formation of the green shoot, wrapped up as yet in its leaves, and not opened to view. These are the first pangs and throes of the new birth, before the tidings are brought, "A manchild is born." "What shall I do to be saved?" cried the jailer. "God be merciful to me a sinner!" exclaimed the publican. "Woe is me, for I am undone!" burst forth from the lips of Isaiah.

April 16.

"Shall iron break the northern iron and the steel?"— JEREMIAH XV. 12.

You see that the Lord, when he is pointing out the trials his people are passing through, compares them to "iron." He does not diminish their weight; he does not at all lower their oppressive tendency. But, then, in order to administer

a suitable remedy to Jeremiah's soul, he brings forward
something much stronger. "Shall iron," he says, "break
the northern iron and the steel?" No surely; the "northern
iron and the steel" shall break through that. The common
iron never can break through the northern iron, which is a
metal of such a far superior nature; still less prevail against
that keen well-tempered steel which can cut through everything it touches.

Now if your hearts are exercised with iron sorrows, temptations, trials, and perplexities, I am sure you will want the
almighty power of God in your souls to cut them asunder.
And God can do it. Are you a poor persecuted believer?
God can cut down in a moment that enemy who is persecut-
ing you. Are you tempted of Satan? He in a moment can
cut his fiery darts asunder. Are you passing through a
severe trial? By the application of some precious promise
the Lord can in a moment cut the trial asunder. Are you
entangled in some grievous snare that you feel and cry out
under night and day, and yet are unable to extricate yourself?
The Lord can in a moment, by the application of his
precious word to your soul, cut that snare asunder. He has
but to bring against it "the northern iron and the steel,"
and it is done in a moment. How was it with Jeremiah?
Did not he say, "Thy words were found, and I did eat
them; and thy word was unto me the joy and rejoicing
of my heart?" Why? Because keen persecutions, sharp
trials, severe temptations had given him an appetite; *that*
was the reason why the "word was found." He fell upon it
as a hungry man upon a crust. It was sweet to his soul,
because it brought with it a precious deliverance from the
temptations and the sorrows his soul was groaning under.

Thus, we see that in proportion as we feel the iron nature
of trials and sorrows, shall we experience "the northern
iron and the steel" of God's almighty power and grace to

deliver. Happy are the people that are in such a case !
Happy the people that have this Lord for their manifested
God !

April 17.

" Lead me in thy truth, and teach me."—Psalm xxv. 5.

By what steps do we usually embrace the truth as it is in
Jesus? First of all, for the most part, we receive it *as a
doctrine;* the judgment being more or less informed, the eyes
of the understanding being enlightened to see it in the
word. The doctrine for some time may be floating in our
mind; but after a time, as the Lord leads us more into
a knowledge of our own hearts, and into a deeper feeling of
our necessities, he lets down the truth from our head into the
heart, and it then becomes *a truth.* It is very sweet to have
a doctrine turned into a truth. But after a time, we want
something more than a truth ; we want it *as a blessing.*
When we are brought into pressing straits and severe trials,
we need the doctrines which we first received into our minds
as truths, now to be blessed by a divine application to our
souls. Thus, what we first knew in our judgments as
a doctrine, is afterwards received in our conscience as *a truth,*
and then is applied to our very heart of hearts as *a blessing;*
and so we find God's word, and eat it, to the joy and
rejoicing of our souls.

Thus it is with respect to Christ's ascension. We receive
it first as *a doctrine,* as a great and glorious part of the
scheme of salvation ; then we begin to see, as we are led
more and more into a knowledge of it, what a wonderful
truth it is, to have a Mediator at the right hand of God; to
have an Intercessor pleading by the efficacy of his atoning
blood and justifying righteousness, for poor, needy, guilty
souls. This draws out the faith, hope, and love of the heart
to this ascended and interceding Mediator; and then, as the

Lord the Spirit reveals the virtue and efficacy of this glorious Mediator in the guilty conscience, the truth becomes a rich, unctuous, and savoury *blessing*. So that so far from experience casting out the doctrines of grace, it only leads the soul into a vital acquaintance with them; and we might as well think of saving our lives by drawing the bones out of our body, as of blessing our souls by casting out the doctrines of grace; yea, we daily feel more deeply the need of the doctrines being brought into our heart by divine power; we feel them more to be the stay and support of our soul, as my arm when raised is stayed and supported by the bones which God has placed there.

April 18.

" Of his own will begat he us with the word of truth, that we should be a kind of firstfruits of his creatures."— JAMES i. 18.

IF we look at the work of the Spirit on the heart, we shall see how, in all his sacred dealings and gracious movements, he invariably employs truth as his grand instrument. Does he pierce and wound? It is by the truth; for the " sword of the Spirit is the word of God," and that we know is " the word of truth." If he mercifully heal, if he kindly bless, it is still by means of truth; for the promise is, " Howbeit, when he, the Spirit of truth is come, he will guide you into all truth." And when he thus comes, it is as a Comforter, according to those gracious words, " But when the Comforter is come, whom I will send unto you from the Father, even the Spirit of truth, which proceedeth from the Father, he shall testify of me."

In fact, if we look at the new man of grace that the blessed Spirit begets and brings forth in the heart, we shall see that all his *members* and *faculties* are formed and adapted to a living reception of the truth. As the eye is adapted to light; as the ear to sound; as the lungs to the pure air that fills them with every breath; as the heart to the vital blood which it propels through every bounding artery, so is the new man of grace fitted and adapted to the truth of God. And as these vital organs perform their peculiar functions only as they receive the impressions which these external agents produce upon them, so the organs of the new man of grace only act as truth is impressed upon them by the power of the blessed Spirit. Has, then, the new man of grace *eyes?* It is to see the truth (Eph. i. 18, 19). Has he *ears?* It is to hear the truth (Isa. lv. 3; Luke ix. 44). Has he *hands?* It is to lay hold of and embrace the truth (Prov. iv. 13; Isa. xxvii. 5; Heb. vi. 18). Has he *feet?* It is that he may walk in the truth (Psa. cxix. 45; Luke i. 6; 3 John 4). Has he a *mouth?* " Open thy mouth wide, and I will fill it." It is that he may feed upon the truth, the living truth, yea, upon His flesh who is truth itself (John vi. 35, xiv. 6).

April 19.

" I have poured out my soul before the Lord."—1 SAMUEL i. 15.

How much there is in that expression pouring out the soul before the Lord! Shall I use a familiar figure to illustrate it, as sometimes familiar figures are best adapted to that purpose? Look at a sack of corn; you know, when the mouth of the sack is tied up, there is no pouring out its contents; but let the sack be opened and thrown down, and then its contents are immediately poured out, and the rich grain falls upon the floor. Our hearts are sometimes like the sack with the mouth tied; there are desires, pantings, and longings; there are wants, and these urgently felt; but we cannot give them utterance. As we read, " I opened my mouth and panted." But the Lord in mercy, at times, opens the mouth; and then when the mouth is opened, the heart can pour out its desires, just as the rich grain is poured out of a sack when the mouth is untied. But must not the sack be full before the grain is poured out? If there are but a few grains at the bottom, or only half-a-pint of wheat in one corner of the sack, though you open the mouth, there is no pouring out of the rich grain. So with our hearts. If the heart be not full; if there be no vehement desires struggling for utterance, we may open the mouth, but there is no pouring it out in pantings and longings. If you want a scriptural instance of what it is to pour out the soul before the Lord, read the first chapter of the first book of Samuel, where you will find that gracious woman Hannah, so agitated, and so discovering the state of her mind by the convulsive movements of her frame, that the high priest charged her with being drunken; but though her heart was so full that her lips quivered, and her very features betrayed what was passing within, yet she meekly replied to his chiding speech, when he bade her to put away her wine, "No, my Lord; I am a woman of a sorrowful spirit; I have drunk neither wine nor strong drink, but *have poured out my soul before the Lord.*" That was something like prayer. And we know what a blessed answer the Lord gave her, and how the Holy Ghost has recorded her triumphal song.

April 20.

"O our God, wilt thou not judge them? for we have no might against this great company that cometh against us; neither know we what to do; but our eyes are upon thee."— 2 CHRONICLES XX. 12.

JEHOSHAPHAT did not know what to do; he was altogether at his wit's end; and yet he took the wisest course a man could take. This is the beauty of it; that when we are fools, then we are wise; when we are weak, then we are strong;

when we know not what to do, then we do the only right thing. O had Jehoshaphat taken any other course; had he collected an army, sent through Judah, raised troops and forged swords and spears he would certainly have been defeated! But not knowing what to do, he did the very thing he should do. *"Our eyes are upon thee."* "Thou must fight our battles; thou must take the matter into thy own hands. Our eyes are upon thee, waiting upon thee, looking up, and hoping in thee; believing in thy holy name, expecting help from thee, from whom alone help can come." But this is painful work to be brought to this point, "Our eyes are upon thee," implying there is no use looking to any other quarter. It assumes that the soul has looked, and looked, and looked elsewhere in vain, and then fixed its eyes upon God as knowing that from him alone all help must come. This I believe to be the distinctive mark of a Christian, that his eyes are upon God. On his bed by night; in his room by day; in business or at market, when his soul is in trouble, cast down, and perplexed, his eyes are upon God. From him alone all help must come; none else can reach his case. All other but the help of God is ineffectual; it leaves him where it found him; it does him no good. We are never safe except our eyes are upon God. Let our eyes be upon him, we can walk safely; let our eyes be upon the creature, we are pretty sure to slip and stumble.

April 21.

"*But of him are ye in Christ Jesus, who of God is made unto us wisdom, and righteousness, and sanctification, and redemption: that, according as it is written, He that glorieth, let him glory in the Lord.*"—1 CORINTHIANS i. 30, 31.

WISDOM, righteousness, sanctification, and redemption. God has made Christ all these to his people. He has set him up as their eternal Head, made him the Bridegroom of their souls, that out of his fulness they may all receive. Then, just in proportion as they learn these two lessons—what *they* are, and what *he* is—they receive him into their hearts actually what he is to them in the purpose of God. Am I a fool? Do I feel it and know it? Have I had painful experience of it, so that all my creature wisdom is turned into one mass of foolishness? Do I catch by the eye of faith a view of the risen Mediator, "Immanuel, God with us," and see what he is made of God to us? The moment my eye sees him as "wisdom," that moment a measure of divine wisdom flows into my conscience. Am I polluted and defiled throughout? Have I no righteousness of my own? Is all my obedience imperfect? Am I unable to fulfil the requirements of God's holy law? If once I catch by the eye of faith this glorious truth, through him who is the truth, that Jesus Christ is of God made unto me "righteousness"—the moment I see *that* by the eye of faith, that moment a measure of imparted righteousness flows into my heart. Am I an unholy, depraved, filthy wretch? Does corruption work in my heart? The moment I catch by the eye of faith Jesus made unto me of God "sanctification," that moment a measure of sanctification comes into my heart, drawing up holy affections, casting out the love of the world, curbing my reigning lusts, and bringing my soul into submission at his footstool. Am I a poor captive, entangled by Satan, by the world, and my own evil heart? The moment that I catch this glorious view, that Jesus Christ at the right hand of the Father is made unto me "redemption"—if I can believe that he is made such for me, that I have a standing in him, and a union with him, so that he is my redemption—that moment a measure of deliverance comes into my soul, and redemption imputed becomes redemption imparted; the soul receives then internally what Christ has done externally. In a word, when Christ is received as "wisdom, righteousness, sanctification, and redemption," he becomes all these in vital manifestation.

April 22.

"Beloved, now are we the sons of God, and it doth not yet appear what we shall be: but we know that, when he shall appear, we shall be like him; for we shall see him as he is."— 1 JOHN iii. 2.

WHAT Christ is to the Church, what the Church is to Christ, can never be really known till time gives place to eternity, faith to sight, and hope to enjoyment. Nor even *then*, however beyond all present conception the powers and faculties of the glorified souls and bodies of the saints may be expanded, however conformed to the glorious image of Christ, or however ravished with the discoveries of his glory and the sight of him as he is in one unclouded day,—no, not even then, will the utmost stretch of creature love, or highest refinement of creature intellect, wholly embrace or fully comprehend that love of Christ, which, as in time so in eternity, "passeth knowledge," as being in itself essentially incomprehensible, because infinite and divine. Who can calculate the amount of light and heat that dwell in, and are given forth by the sun that shines so gloriously in the noon-day sky? We see, we feel, we enjoy its bright beams; but who can number the millions of millions of rays that it casts forth upon all the surface of the earth, diffusing light, heat, and fertility to every part? If the creature be so great, glorious and incomprehensible, how much more great, glorious and incomprehensible must be its divine Creator! The Scripture testimony of the saints in glory is that "when Christ shall appear, they shall be like him, for they shall see him as he is;" that they shall then see the Lord "face to face, and know even as also they are known;" that their "vile body shall be fashioned like unto his glorious body;" that they shall be "conformed to his image," and "be satisfied when they awake with his likeness;" that they shall be "before the throne of God, and serve him day and night in his temple;" that "their sun shall no more go down, for the Lord shall be their everlasting light;" that they shall have "an exceeding and eternal weight of glory;" and shall "shine as the brightness of the firmament, and as the stars for ever and ever." But, with all this unspeakable bliss and glory, there must be in infinite Deity unfathomable depths which no creature, however highly exalted, can ever sound; heights which no finite, dependent being can ever scan. God became man, but man never can become God. He fully knows us, but we never can fully know him, for even in eternity, as in time, it may be said to the creature, "Canst thou by searching find out God? canst thou find out the Almighty unto perfection? It is as high as heaven; what canst thou do? deeper than hell, what canst thou know? The measure thereof is longer than the earth, and broader than the sea." But if, as we believe, eternity itself can never fully or entirely reveal the heights and depths of the love of a Triune God, how little can be known of it in a time state! and yet that little is the only balm for all sorrow, the only foundation of solid rest and peace.

April 23.

"A friend loveth at all times, and a brother is born for adversity."—Proverbs xvii. 17.

If I may use the expression, we want not a dead but a living, not an absent but a present, not a once but a now Jesus; we want a friend at the right hand of God at the present moment; an omniscient, omnipresent, omnipotent and yet pitiful and loving Mediator between God and us; an

interceding High Priest, Surety, and Representative in our
nature in the courts of heaven, who can shew mercy and
compassion to us now upon earth:

> "Whose heart is made of tenderness,
> Whose bowels melt with love."

Our wants make us feel this. Our sins and sorrows give us
perpetual errands to the throne. This vale of tears is ever
before our eyes, and thorns and briars are perpetually
springing up in it that rend and tear our flesh. We want a
real friend. Have you not sometimes tossed to and fro upon
your weary couch, and almost cried aloud, "O that I had a
friend!" You may have received cruel blows from one whom
you regarded as a real friend; but you have been cruelly
deceived. You feel now you have no one to take care of you
or love you, and whom you can love again; and your heart
sighs for a friend who shall be a friend indeed. The widow,
the orphan, the friendless, the deserted one, all keenly and
deeply feel this. But if grace has touched your heart, you
feel that though all men forsake you, there is the Friend of
sinners, a Brother born for adversity, a Friend who loveth at
all times, who will never leave or forsake you. But we want
this friend to be almighty, for no other can suit our case: he
must be a divine Friend. For who but God can see us
wherever we are? What but a divine eye can read our
thoughts? What but a divine ear can hear our petitions?
And what but a divine hand can stretch itself forth and
deliver? Thus the Deity of Christ is no dry, barren
speculation, no mere Bible truth, but an experience wrought
powerfully into a believer's inmost soul. Happy soul! happy
season! when you can say with the Church, "This is my
beloved, and this is my friend, O daughters of Jerusalem"
(Song Sol. v. 16). Thus the very wants of the soul instinctively teach us that a friend, to be a friend, must be a heavenly
friend; that his heart and hand must be divine, or they are

not the heart and hand for us.   This Friend, whose bitterest reproach on earth that he "was the Friend of sinners," is his highest glory in heaven, is the blessed Jesus, our great High Priest in the courts above.   We find him at times to be very merciful, very pitiful, and very compassionate.   And I am sure that we need all the compassion of his loving breast; for we are continually in states of mind when nothing but his pure mercy can suit, when nothing but his rich and boundless compassion is adapted to our case.

April 24.

"Yet a little while, and the world seeth me no more; but ye see me: because I live, ye shall live also."—JOHN xiv. 19.

COMMUNION with Christ rests on three things—seeing him by faith, living upon his life, and experiencing his manifested presence.   But all these three things depend on his resurrection and a knowledge of its power.   As risen from the dead, the saints see him; as risen from the dead, they live a life of faith upon him; as risen from the dead, he manifests himself unto them; and as life and feeling spring up in their souls from sweet communion with him, the power of his resurrection becomes manifest in them.

This communion, therefore, with the Lord Jesus as a risen Head all the reconciled and justified saints of God are pressing forward after, according to the measure of their grace and the life and power of God in their soul.   It is indeed often sadly interrupted and grievously broken through by the sin that dwelleth in us.   But the principle is there, for that principle is life; and life is the privilege, the possession, and the distinction of the children of God.   You need none to assure you that Jesus is risen from the dead if he manifests himself to your soul.   You want no evidence that you are a sheep if you have heard and know his voice.   So you may say, "Jesus is risen, for I have seen him; Jesus is risen, for I have heard him; Jesus is risen, for I live upon him." Communion with Jesus is the life of religion, and indeed without it religion is but an empty name. If without him we can do nothing; if he is our life, our risen covenant Head, our Advocate with the Father, our Husband, our Friend, our Brother, how are we to draw sap out of his fulness, as the branch from the vine, or to know him personally and experimentally in any one of his endearing relationships, unless by continual communion with him on his throne of grace? In fact, this is the grand distinguishing point between the living and the dead, between the true child of God and the mere professor, that the one has real union and communion with a risen Jesus, and the other is satisfied with a form of godliness. Every quickened soul is made to feel after the power of God, after communion from above, after pardon and peace, after visitations of mercy and grace; and when he has had a view of Christ by faith, and some revelation of his Person and work, grace and glory, nothing afterwards can ever really satisfy him but that inward communion of spirit with Jesus whereby the Lord and he become one; "for he that is joined to the Lord is one spirit."

April 25.

"*Then said I, Woe is me! for I am undone; because I am a man of unclean lips, and I dwell in the midst of a people of unclean lips: for mine eyes have seen the King, the Lord of hosts.*"—Isaiah vi. 5.

God has described his Zion as "full of wounds, and bruises, and putrifying sores." When the Church of God fell in Adam, she fell with a crash which broke every bone and bruised her flesh with wounds which are ulcerated from top to toe. Her understanding, her conscience, and her affections were all fearfully maimed. The first was blinded, the second stupified, and the third alienated. Every mental

faculty thus became perverted and distorted. As in a shipwrecked vessel the water runs in through every leak, so
when Adam fell upon the lee-shore of sin and temptation,
and made shipwreck of the image of God in which he was
created, sin rushed into every faculty of body and soul, and
penetrated into the inmost recesses of his being. Or to use
another figure; as when a man is bitten by a poisonous
serpent, the venom courses through every artery and vein,
and he dies a corrupted mass from head to foot, so did the
poison fang of sin penetrate into Adam's inmost soul and
body, and infect him with its venom from the sole to the
crown. But the fearful havoc which sin has made is never
seen nor felt till the soul is quickened into spiritual life. Oh,
what work does sin then make in the conscience, when it is
opened up by the Spirit of God! Whatever superficial or
shallow views we may have had of sin before, it is only as its
desperate and malignant character is opened up by the Holy
Spirit that it is really seen, felt, grieved under, and mourned
over as indeed a most dreadful and fearful reality. It is this
sword of the Spirit which cuts and wounds; it is this
entrance of life and light that gashes the conscience; it is
this divine work which lacerates the heart and inflicts those
deep wounds which nothing but the "balm in Gilead" can
heal. And not only is a poor convinced sinner cut in his
conscience, inwardly lacerated and gashed by sin as thus
opened up by the Spirit of God, but, as the prophet speaks,
" the whole head is sick, and the whole heart faint." He is
thus labouring under a complication of diseases. Every
thought, word, and action is polluted by sin. Every mental
faculty is depraved. The will chooses evil; the affections
cleave to earthly things; the memory, like a broken sieve,
retains the bad and lets fall the good; the judgment, like a
bribed or drunken juryman, pronounces heedless or wrong
decisions; and the conscience, like an opium-eater, lies

asleep and drugged in stupified silence. This miserable
state, brought upon us and into us by the fall, all the people
of God must in some measure feel. It is of no use mincing
the matter and saying that a person can be saved by the
grace of God and the blood of Christ, without knowing
anything of the depth of misery and wretchedness into
which he is sunk as the fallen child of a fallen sire. We
must go down into the depths of the fall to know what our
hearts are and what they are capable of; we must have the
keen knife of God to cut deep gashes in our conscience and
lay bare the evil that lies so deeply imbedded in our carnal
mind, before we can enter into and experience the beauty
and blessedness of salvation by grace.

April 26.

" *We having the same spirit of faith, according as it is
written, I believed, and therefore have I spoken; we also believe,
and therefore speak.*"—2 CORINTHIANS iv. 13.

THERE is a distinction to be made between faith and the
spirit of faith. The spirit of faith is faith in exercise. Faith
sometimes is like a day in which there is no wind blowing.
It is so calm, that there scarcely appears to be any air
stirring to move a leaf. But after a time a gentle breeze
comes and blows over the earth. Thus it is with faith and
the spirit of faith. Faith in repose is like the calm air of a
summer's day, when there is nothing moving or stirring;
faith acting, faith in exercise, is like the same air in the
gentle breeze which makes itself sensibly felt. If God has
given me faith, that faith is never lost out of my breast. If
once a believer, I always am a believer; for if I could cease
to believe, I should cease to be a child of God; I should
lose salvation out of my heart, for I am saved by grace
through faith. And yet there may be many times and
seasons when I may not have much of the spirit of faith.

Faith may be very inactive, I will not say stagnant, for that would almost imply death, but still, quiet, calm, sleeping like a bird with its head under its wing. But in due time there is a stirring, a movement, a gracious blowing of the Spirit: "Awake, O north wind, and come, O south; blow upon my garden" (Song Sol. iv. 16). "Come from the four winds, O breath" (Ezek. xxxvii. 9). This heavenly breath of the Holy Spirit acts upon faith, awakens it, revives and reanimates it, and draws it forth into lively operation. It thus becomes a spirit of faith, acting spiritually and energetically according to its measure. John was "in the Spirit on the Lord's day" (Rev. i. 10). He was not always in the Spirit by lively action, though he was never out of the Spirit by his extinction. So faith is sometimes, so to speak, in the Spirit; and then its eyes are open, like the eyes of John, to see spiritually what he saw visibly, the Person of Christ, and its ear open to hear inwardly what he heard outwardly, the words of Christ.

April 27.

" For there are three that bear record in heaven, the Father, the Word, and the Holy Ghost: and these three are one."— 1 JOHN v. 7.

ALL God's people are led into a knowledge of the Trinity; not indeed by metaphysical reasoning or subtle arguments addressed to the understanding. The Spirit teaches them, not by reasoning addressed to the head, but by the power and dew of divine truth resting upon the heart. All God's people learn the doctrine of the Trinity in their souls. They learn, under divine teaching, the authority, justice, majesty, holiness, and in due time feel the love of God the Father. They learn the Godhead of Christ in their souls, by seeing and feeling the power of his blood, as the blood of God (Acts xx. 28), and his righteousness as the "righteous-

ness of God." And they learn the Deity and Personality of
the Holy Ghost by feeling the divine power of his operations
on their hearts. They learn also that he is God, by
perceiving how he scrutinizes all their actions, brings to light
every secret thought, and applies passages of Scripture to
their souls, which none but God could produce, or so
suitably apply. And when they are thus led by divine
teaching, into the Three Persons of the Godhead, they are
brought to know and feel in the depths of conscience, that
there are Three Persons, equal in power, will, essence, and
glory, and but one Jehovah. Now these truths no man can
learn in a saving manner, except by this special teaching.
He may know all this, and much more than this, in his
understanding and judgment; but a sensible realisation of
the power of these things in the conscience, a divine melting
of the heart under them, with an enlargement of soul, and
an experimental enjoyment of them, is the alone fruit of
God's teaching resting on him, so as to make him "a new
creature" in Christ.

April 28.

" *That by two immutable things, in which it was impossible
for God to lie, we might have a strong consolation, who have
fled for refuge to lay hold upon the hope set before us.*"—
HEBREWS vi. 18.

No: it is utterly impossible for God to lie. The earth
may be dissolved, and all creation reduced to chaos before
God could lie. He would cease to be God if the faintest
breath of a change, or the shadow of a turn should pass
over the glorious Godhead. But it is impossible for God to
lie. Therefore this holds out strong consolation for those that
have fled for refuge to lay hold of the hope set before them.

And what is the ground of this strong consolation? This
is the ground, that God has eternally determined and sworn

by himself—that he will save and bless those that have " fled for refuge to the hope set before them in the gospel." This is the foundation of their consolation, this is the ground of their hope, that God has made such and such promises, and confirmed such and such promises by his solemn oath—that those who flee for refuge, and lay hold upon this hope, have an interest in and title to them, and have a manifest assurance of being " heirs of promise."

Now, did you ever in your life feel spiritual consolation ? If ever you did, it was by laying hold of the hope set before you in the gospel. There was no consolation ever got by looking at fallen self. If ever there was any true consolation, any hope raised up in the heart, any solid comfort, it came out of the actings of living faith, embracing the blood and righteousness of Christ, tasting a measure of his precious-ness, seeing his glory and beauty, and feeling the heart in some measure dissolved into nothingness at his footstool. Not looking at ourselves, but receiving as empty sinners out of his fulness ; not trusting to ourselves, or our own attain-ments, but going to Jesus, and receiving something into our hearts out of him. Nothing but this can give us consolation ; and the more this is felt, the more this will give us " strong consolation."

April 29.

" The God of all grace."—1 PETER v. 10.

ALL we have and are, everything we know and feel, comes from " the God of all grace." We have nothing spiritually good in ourselves ; all therefore that we have is the free gift of his hand, and comes from the ever-flowing Fountain of mercy and truth. It will be our mercy, then, as the Lord may enable us, to be ever looking to him, not looking to books, not looking to ministers ; these are only instruments, and in themselves but poor instruments. The soul must look through all and above all to " the God of all grace."

The Lord enable you to examine every truth as it is brought
before you by the light of God's Spirit in your heart, to
"prove all things, and hold fast that which is good." And
however deeply you may feel the vileness of your heart,
remember this, there is "the God of all grace" to go to. If
you feel yourself the vilest of sinners, he suits you the more
as "the God of *all* grace." If you feel dark, stupid, and
barren, it is the greater reason that you should call on "the
God of all grace" to revive your drooping soul. If any
have lost past enjoyments, and are now "walking in darkness" that may be felt, it is the more reason they should
seek "the God of all grace," that he may supply their wants
out of Christ's fulness, as the covenant Head. Yea, whatever trials, perplexities, and temptations may harass your
soul, it is only to open the way for "the God of all grace"
to appear. In whatever affliction you may be, it will be
your wisdom, as it will be your mercy, to be looking up unto
him, that he may comfort your soul; and, turning from man,
as Hezekiah turned his face to the wall, commit your case
to him.

April 30.

*" For I was alive without the law once: but when the com-
mandment came, sin revived, and I died."*—ROMANS vii. 9.

THE Apostle describes in his own case how men are
affected toward the law before it enters as a condemning
sentence into their heart. "I was alive without the law
once." The law was hanging over him as a condemning
sentence, as a minister of death, as a messenger of wrath, as
a consuming fire, but he felt it not. As with a thunderstorm
in the remote distance, he might hear the low mutterings of
the thunder which once rolled over Sinai's fiery mount, or
might see from far the play of those lightnings which
scorched its top. But at present the storm was in the
distance. He went about without thinking, or feeling, or

fearing, or caring whether the law was his friend or enemy. In fact he rather viewed it as his friend, for he was using it as a friendly help to build up his own righteousness. He had gone to it, but it had not come to him; he knew its letter, but not its spirit; its outward commands, but not its inward demands. He therefore speaks of himself as being "alive without the law," that is, without any knowledge of what it was as a ministration of condemnation and death. But in God's own appointed time and way, "the commandment came;" that is, it came with power into his conscience. He found that he could keep every one of the commandments but the tenth; for according to his apprehension and his interpretation of them, they did not extend beyond an external obedience. But the tenth commandment, "Thou shalt not covet," struck into the very depth of his conscience, for it was a prohibition from the mouth of God of the inward lusts of the heart, and that prohibition attended with an awful curse. Under this stroke sin, which before lay seemingly dead in his breast, revived like a sleeping serpent; and what was the consequence? It stung him to death, for he says, "And I died;" for the commandment which was ordained unto life he found to be unto death! Sin could not brook to be thwarted or opposed; it therefore rose up in enmity against God, took advantage of the commandment to rebel against the authority of Jehovah, and its guilt in consequence falling upon his conscience, made tender in the fear of God, slew him. It would not have done so had there been no life in his soul; but there being light to see and life to feel the anger of God revealed in the commandment, when the law came into his conscience as a sentence from a just and holy Jehovah, the effect was to produce a sentence of death in himself. And this experience which the Apostle describes as his own is what the law does and ever must do when applied to the conscience by the power of God. It kills, it slays the condemned sinner; it is a sentence of death in a man's own conscience, which only awaits the hour of death and the day of judgment to be carried into execution.

May 1.

"Wherefore in all things it behoved him to be made like unto his brethren, that he might be a merciful and faithful high priest in things pertaining to God, to make reconciliation for the sins of the people."—Hebrews ii. 17.

God gave the persons of the elect into the hands of his dear Son, as Jacob committed Benjamin into the hands of Judah; and as Judah accepted Benjamin, so Christ accepted the Church and undertook to bring it unto God, or he himself would bear the blame for ever. But how this faithfulness was tried! Men tried it; devils tried it; God tried it; but it came gloriously through all. Yet what loads were laid upon it! How the very knees of Jesus, so to speak, staggered beneath it! How, as Hart says, he had

"Strength enough, and none to spare!"

How he had to sustain the curse of the law and the load of imputed sin! How he had to drink up a very hell of inward torment! How he had to be agonised in body and more than agonised in soul! What bloody sweat in the garden, what tears, what sore amazement, what heaviness of spirit, what sorrowfulness even unto death; what pangs of body upon the cross, what grief of mind, what distress of soul, did the Holy Lamb endure in being faithful unto God! How he might have prayed, and his Father would have sent him twelve legions of angels! He had but to speak, and he might have soared to heaven and left the cross and all its shame and suffering behind. But he was faithful to God and to the work which he had undertaken. Six weary hours he hung upon the cross. Six weary hours he endured the

wrath of God, and that most cutting stroke of all, reserved
to the last as the bitterest drop in the whole cup, the hiding
of his Father's countenance, which wrung from his bosom
that cry, such as neither earth nor heaven had heard before
—" My God, my God, why hast thou forsaken me?" And
yet not until he had finished the work did he give up the
ghost. So he was faithful " in all things pertaining to God."
And he is faithful, too, in all things pertaining to man. He
could say to the Father, " Of all which thou hast given me "
—save the son of perdition, Judas; he had no charge to
save him from death and hell; but of all the others whom he
had received as his Father's gift, he could say, " I have lost
none." Thus he was faithful while he was on earth. And
how faithful he is now ! The high priest under the law had
two offices to execute; he had to offer sacrifice for the
people, and to offer prayer and intercession for them.
Upon earth Jesus fulfilled the first; in heaven he fulfils the
second, as there making by virtue of his presence continual
intercession for us.

May 2.

" Watch and pray, that ye enter not into temptation."—
MATTHEW xxvi. 41.

THE entering into temptation is a different thing from
temptation itself. "Watch and pray, that ye *enter not into*
temptation." A temptation presents itself, draws near to us,
or we draw near to it. If conscience sound an alarm, and
we keep, so to speak, to the windward of temptation, we are
for the present safe. Temptation is a lee shore on which
the wind fiercely blows; it is a coast strewed with a thousand
wrecks, and with the bleached bones of innumerable drowned
mariners. Keep the ship's head to windward, and she may
weather the point; neglect sail and helm, and she will
go ashore. David and Joseph were exposed to a similar
temptation. David entered into it, and fell; Joseph was

kept from entering into it, and stood. In the country you often see a footpath across a field; if we keep in it we are safe. But we may be tempted by various objects to diverge a little, to gather a flower, or saunter upon the banks of the river, or make a short cut across the fields. Whilst we are in the footpath, temptation may be very near, but we have not yet entered into it; we are upon the borders of it, but we have not yet entered into its territory. Few, if any, enter into temptation without falling by it. The fly hovers round the spider's web; to touch it is to enter into it. The bird flies around the fowler's snare; to peck at the bait is to enter the trap. The moth flutters round the candle; to enter the flame is to burn its wings. The Lord's words were not, "watch and pray *against* temptation," but "that ye *enter not into* temptation." Few come out of temptation as they entered into it. How clearly James has described the difference between enduring temptation and falling by temptation. He does not say, "Blessed is the man who is *free from* temptation," but "who *endureth* temptation." Blessed is the man who is kept in the footpath, who sees temptation on every side, but endures it, is not drawn out of the path by it, for "when he is tried, he shall receive a crown of life." He has fought the good fight, won the battle, and shall receive the crown. But he adds, "Let no man say when he is tempted, I am tempted of God." He must not say that the Lord presents temptation to him, and is therefore chargeable with it if he falls. "No," says James, "let that thought be abhorred. God cannot be tempted with evil, neither tempteth he any man. But every man is tempted when he is drawn away of his own lust and enticed." There is no sin in temptation, for the Lord Jesus was "tempted in all points like as we are, yet without sin." Nor in lust is there practical, though there is speculative sin. It is when the two meet and embrace, and the will consents to the union, silencing the voice of God and conscience, that sin is produced. And thirdly, follows the fearful and fatal *fruit,* " Sin, when it is finished, bringeth forth *death;* " that is, as I understand it, death in the conscience, guilt, condemnation, and misery, and the deadening of all the fruits and graces of the blessed Spirit.

May 3.

" In that day shall the Branch of the Lord be beautiful and glorious."—Isaiah iv. 2.

Where in heaven or on earth can there be found such a lovely Object as the Son of God? " What is thy beloved more than another beloved?" ask the companions of the Bride. But she answers, " My beloved is white and ruddy, the chiefest among ten thousand." If, then, you have never seen any beauty in Jesus, you have never seen Jesus; he has never revealed himself to you ; you never had a glimpse of his lovely face, nor a sense of his presence, nor a word from his lips, nor a touch from his hand. But if you have seen him by the eye of faith, and he has revealed himself to you even in a small measure, you have seen a beauty in him beyond all other beauties, for it is a holy beauty, a divine beauty, the beauty of his heavenly grace, the beauty of his uncreated and eternal glory, such as no earthly countenance can wear, nor man or woman, no, not Adam, in all his unfallen innocency, nor his fair partner Eve, with all her virtue, grace, and dignity, ever could shew, for it is the beauty of the glorious Son of God, which he for ever wears as the Son of the Father in truth and love.

And as he is " beautiful," so is he "*glorious.*" Oh, what a glory does faith see sometimes in his eternal Deity, in his divine Sonship, in what he is in himself as the brightness of the Father's glory and the express image of his Person, and in what he is as made unto us wisdom and righteousness, sanctification and redemption! How glorious does he shew himself to be in his atoning blood and dying love. Even as sweating great drops of blood in Gethsemane's gloomy garden, and as hanging in torture and agony upon Calvary's cross, faith can see a beauty in the glorious Redeemer, even in the lowest depths of ignominy and shame. Was there not a glory in his meek obedience, in his suffering patience, in his submission to his Father's holy will, in his uncomplaining resignation to the heaviest strokes of vindictive justice, in bearing our sins in his own body on the tree, and thus putting away sin by the sacrifice of himself? But more especially does faith see him glorious as rising from the dead and going up on high, and sitting down at the right hand of the Father, crowned with glory and honour, and all things put under his feet.

May 4.

" And the fruit of the earth shall be excellent and comely for them that are escaped of Israel."—Isaiah iv. 2.

By "the fruit of the earth" we may understand that gracious and holy fruit which grew upon the Branch : and it seems to be called "the fruit of the earth," because it appeared on earth when our Lord was there. Thus not only all his words, works, and ways, all the parables, doctrines, precepts, and promises uttered by the mouth of the Son of God in the days of his flesh, but all the benefits and blessings that spring in the way of redemption out of his complex Person, and grow as it were a holy fruit out of him as the Branch, such as his atoning blood, his glorious righteousness, his dying love, his resurrection and ascension, and his power to save to the uttermost all that come unto God by him, may all be considered as "the fruit of the earth," because wrought by him in and upon the earth, and done in the days of his flesh when his gracious feet were upon this earthly ball. This fruit is "excellent" to the escaped of Israel. There is seen in it to be a divine excellency. Therefore, there is not a shadow of a fault to be found with it. It is perfect in all its parts; complete to the very centre, and therefore seen to be excellent, as so glorifying to God, and so adapted to every want and woe of those that are left in Zion and remain in Jerusalem.

And "comely" too. In his sufferings, in his blood-shedding, obedience, holy life and expiatory death, there is a surpassing comeliness, because in them shine forth a divine glory and a heavenly beauty. It is indeed the same word as is translated " beauty " in the holy garments made for Aaron by Moses (Exod. xxviii. 2), and clothed in which he minis-tered before the Lord when he went into the holy place. So our great High Priest now ministers within the veil in the holiness and beauty of his glorified humanity; and as this is seen and apprehended by faith, the Church sings, " I sat under his shadow with great delight, and his fruit was sweet to my taste." " His glory is great in thy salvation : honour and majesty hast thou laid upon him."

May 5.

" Then shall we know, if we follow on to know the Lord."—
Hosea vi. 3.

We gather from these words that there is such a thing in soul experience as "a following on to know the Lord ;" and indeed there is no obtaining the blessings which are laid up for the righteous, unless there is this following on. " To know the Lord " is the desire of every living soul ; that is, to know him by his own divine manifestations, by the gracious revelation of his grace, his love, his presence, and his glory.

But the expression, "follow on," implies that there are many difficulties, obstacles, and hindrances in a man's way, which keep him back from " knowing the Lord." Now the work of the Spirit in his soul is to carry him on in spite of all these obstacles. Nature, and all the work of nature, and all the power of Satan working on nature, is to draw the man back ; but the work of the Spirit on the soul is to lead him forward, to keep alive in him the fear of God, to strengthen him from time to time with strength in his inner man, to give him those enlargements, to drop in those hopes, to com- municate that inward grace, and to gird up the loins of his mind, so that in spite of sense, reason, and nature, he is compelled to follow on. Sometimes he seems driven, and sometimes drawn, sometimes led, and sometimes carried, but in one way or another the Spirit of God so works upon him that, though he scarce knows how, he still " follows on." His very burdens make him groan for deliverance ; his very temptations cause him to cry for help ; the very difficulty and ruggedness of the road make him want to be carried every step ; the very intricacy of the path compels him to cry out for a guide ; so that the Lord the Spirit working in the midst of, and under, and through every difficulty and dis- couragement, still bears him through, and carries him on ; and thus brings him through every trial and trouble and temptation and obstacle, till he sets him before the Lord in glory. It is astonishing to me how our souls are kept alive. I believe a living man is a marvel to himself. Carried on, and yet so secretly ; worked upon, and yet so myste- riously ; and yet led on, guided, and supported through so many difficulties and obstacles, that he is a miracle of mercy, and, as the Apostle says, " a spectacle unto the world, and to angels, and to men ; " the world wondering, the angels admiring, and men standing astonished, how the quickened soul is carried on amidst all its difficulties, obstacles, trials, and temptations ; and yet in spite of all " following on."

But " following on " for what ? " To know the Lord," as

the sum and substance of all religion, as the very marrow of vital godliness; to know Jesus, so as by faith to enter into his beauty and loveliness, and feel ourselves one spirit with him, according to those words, "He that is joined to the Lord is one spirit."

May 6.

"Brethren, I count not myself to have apprehended: but this one thing I do, forgetting those things which are behind, and reaching forth unto those things which are before, I press toward the mark for the prize of the high calling of God in Christ Jesus."—PHILIPPIANS iii. 13, 14.

THE faith that rests short of believing in, laying hold of, and resting upon the Son of God in his finished work, will not be the work of faith that God will own and crown with his approbation; the love that never labours for an entrance into the mysteries of his dying love, will be found to be a love more in lip and tongue than in heart and life; and the hope that anchors in anything short of the finished work of the Son of God, will be a brittle cable which will snap asunder, or a rotten piece of iron which will break in the first heavy storm. Do not rest in the knowledge of a few doctrines in the letter of truth. Do not take up with a few passing thoughts and feelings; do not be satisfied with a few fleeting convictions or a few transient desires. Press on to know the blessed mysteries of the gospel as the food of your soul; press on to know the Son of God, not only as a crucified man, not only as sweating blood in Gethsemane's garden, and agonising on Calvary's tree; but press on to know him as the exalted God-man Mediator at the right hand of the Father, ever living to make intercession, able to save to the uttermost all that come unto God by him; and press on to enjoy him as your living Head, distilling into you as a living member of his mystical body, what the

Psalmist calls, " the dew of his youth;" that is, the fruits of his resurrection, ascension and glorification, as manifested by the gifts and graces of the Holy Ghost. Press onward to know the power of the precious gospel you profess, to enjoy it more in your soul, and to manifest its reality more in your conduct, your conversation, and your life.

May 7.

" *For to be carnally-minded is death ; but to be spiritually-minded is life and peace.*"—ROMANS viii. 6.

ONE of the most blessed marks of regenerating grace and the sure fruit of the love of God shed abroad in the heart, is that spiritual-mindedness of which Paul declares, it is " life and peace." " To be spiritually-minded," to live and walk under the blessed power and influence of the Holy Spirit, to have the heart and affections drawn up from this poor, vain scene to where Jesus sits at the right hand of God, this is " *life,*" the life of God in the soul, with all its present blessed-ness and all its future glory, and "*peace,*" for peace and rest are alone to be found in this path of union and communion with a glorified Redeemer. In this sweet spirituality of mind, in these heavenly affections, and in this intercourse with the Lord at his own throne of grace, the life and power of godli-ness much consist. We trust we know, from what we have felt in our own bosom, what this sweet spiritual-mindedness is, and what are its blessed effects. It is a key to unlock the Scriptures, for then we read them under the same sacred influence, and by the same divine teaching by which they were written ; it is a door of prayer, for under these calm and peaceful emotions the soul, as if instinctively and necessarily, seeks holy communion with God ; it is the fruitful parent of sweet meditation, for the truth of God is then thought over, fed upon, and is found to be bread from heaven; it is the secret of all life and power in preaching, for unless the heart be engaged in, and melted and softened by the truth delivered, there will be a hardness in its delivery which will make itself sensibly felt by the living hearer ; and it is the power of all spiritual conversation, for how can we talk with any unction or profit unless we are spiritually-minded, and in that frame of soul wherein the things of God are our chief element, the language of our lips, because the delight of our soul? But to be otherwise—to be carnally-minded on our knees, with the Bible open before our eyes, in the house of prayer, at the Lord's table, in the company of the family of God—what a burden to our spirit, what a condemnation to our conscience, what a parent of doubt and fear whether matters can be right between God and our own soul, when there is such a distance between him and us !

It is true that the most eminent saints and servants of God have their dead and dark seasons, when the life of God seems sunk to so low an ebb as to be hardly visible, so hidden is the stream by the mud-banks of their fallen nature. Still it glides onward, round them, if not through them ; and sometimes a beam of light falls upon it from above, as it threads its way toward the ocean of eternal love, which manifests not only its existence but its course, and that it gives back to heaven the ray it receives from heaven. Nay, by these very dark and dead seasons, the saints and servants of God are instructed. They see and feel what the flesh really is, how alienated from the life of God ; they learn in whom all their strength and sufficiency lie ; they are taught that in them, that is, in their flesh, dwelleth no good thing ; that no exertions of their own can maintain in strength and vigour the life of God; and that all they are and have, all they believe, know, feel, and enjoy, with all their ability, usefulness, gifts, and grace, flow from the pure, sovereign grace, the rich, free, undeserved, yet unceasing goodness and mercy of God. They learn in this hard school of painful experience their emptiness and nothing-

ness, and that without Christ indeed they can do nothing.
They thus become clothed with humility, that comely, becoming garb; cease from their own strength and wisdom, and
learn experimentally that Christ is, and ever must be, all in
all to them, and all in all in them.

May 8.

" *For we have not an high priest which cannot be touched
with the feeling of our infirmities; but was in all points tempted
like as we are, yet without sin.*"—HEBREWS iv. 15.

OUR gracious Lord experienced temptation in every shape
and form, for the word of truth declares that " in all points he
was tempted like as we are, yet without sin." I wish to speak
very cautiously upon this subject, for upon a point so difficult
and so mysterious there is great risk of speaking amiss. So
long as we keep strictly within the language of the Scripture
we are safe, but the moment that we draw inferences from the
word without special guidance by the Spirit of truth, we may
greatly err. You may think then, sometimes, that your
temptations are such as our gracious Lord never could have
been tempted by; but that word of the Apostle decides the
question, " in all points tempted like as we are, yet without
sin." It is a solemn mystery which I cannot explain, how
temptation in every point, shape, and form could assail the
holy soul of the immaculate Redeemer. I fully believe it. I
see the grace and wisdom of it, and my faith acquiesces in it
as most blessed truth. But I cannot understand it. I know
also and believe from the testimony of the word and that of
my own conscience, that whatever temptations he was assailed
with, not one of them could or did sully, stain, or spot his
holy humanity. *That* was absolutely and perfectly a pure,
unfallen, immortal nature, able to die by a voluntary act, but
having in itself no seeds of sickness, mortality, or death. And
yet I read that, though thus possessed of a holy, pure, and

spotless humanity, in everlasting union with his own eternal
Deity, in all points he was tempted like as we are.   I cannot
explain the mystery—I do not wish to do so.   I receive it as
a mystery, in the same way as I receive that great mystery of
godliness, "God manifested in the flesh."   But still I bless
God that he was tempted in all points like as we are ; for it
makes him such a sympathising High Priest with his poor,
exercised, tried, tempted family here below.   I have sometimes compared the temptations which beat upon the soul of
the Lord to the waves of the sea that dash themselves against
a pure, white marble rock.   The rock may feel the shock of
the wave ; but it is neither moved by it nor sullied.   It still
stands unmoved, immovable in all its original firmness ; it still
shines in all the brightness of the pure, glittering marble when
the waves recede and the sun breaks forth on its face.   So
none of the temptations with which the Lord was assailed
moved the Rock of ages, or sullied the purity, holiness, and
perfection of the spotless Lamb of God.

May 9.

*" And they shall call his name Emmanuel, which being inter-
preted is, God with us."*—Matthew i. 23.

We must never, even in thought, separate the human
nature of our adorable Redeemer from his divine.   Even
when his sacred body lay in the grave, and was thus for a
small space of time severed from his pure and holy soul by
death and the tomb, there was no separation of the two
natures, for his human soul, after he had once become incarnate in the womb of the Virgin, never was parted from his
Deity, but went into paradise in indissoluble union with it.
It is a fundamental article of our most holy faith that the
human nature of the Lord Jesus Christ had no existence
independent of his divine.   In the Virgin's womb, in the
lowly manger, in the lonely wilderness, on the holy mount of

transfiguration, in the gloomy garden of Gethsemane, in Pilate's judgment hall, on the cross, and in the tomb, Jesus was still Immanuel, God with us. And so ineffably close and intimate is the conjunction of the human nature with the divine, that the actings of each nature, though separable, cannot and must not be separated from each other. Thus, the human hands of Jesus broke the seven loaves and the fishes ; but it was God-man who multiplied them so as to feed therewith four thousand men, besides women and children. The human feet of Jesus walked on the sea of Galilee ; but it was the Son of God who came on the waves to the ship. The human lips of Jesus uttered those words which are " spirit and life " (John vi. 63), but it was the Son of the living God who spake them (John vi. 69). The human hands and feet of Jesus were nailed to the cross; but the blood shed by them was indeed divine, for all the virtue and validity of Deity were stamped upon it (Acts xx. 28).

May 10.

" And now, Lord, what wait I for ? my hope is in thee."— PSALM xxxix. 7.

TRUE religion is a very simple thing. Simplicity is stamped upon all the works of God, and especially upon the work of grace. The more genuine, therefore, our religion is, the more simple it will be. To be simple is to be child-like, and to be child-like is to have that mind and spirit without which no man can enter into the kingdom of heaven. Can we, then, with this child-like simplicity, walk step by step here with David, and follow him throughout? Can we put our seal to these things, and say, " Lord, what wait I for ? " Is your religion brought into this narrow point? " Truly, my soul waiteth upon God; from him cometh my salvation." " My soul, wait thou only upon God; for my expectation is from him." Such a frame of soul is indeed from the hand of

God, for no man ever did, or could bring himself into it. And if we can enter into one part of these heavenly breathings, we shall be able also to enter into the others, and say, " My hope is in thee." Feeling the weight and burden of sin, we shall be constrained to cry, " Deliver me from all my transgressions ; " and feeling our own weakness, and the evil of our hearts, we shall add, " Make me not the reproach of the foolish." If, then, we can sincerely, before God, employ these petitions, may we not ask who produced them ? Who wrought this experience in the soul ? From whose hands did it come ? Surely, surely, the same Lord that taught David, must have taught us; the same power that wrought in him, must have wrought in us, before we could, in sweet experience, enter into this feeling language, and adopt it as our own. Here, therefore, we see a little of what true religion is ; here we see what are the genuine breathings of a child-like spirit, and what is the experience of a man of God ; and it will be our mercy if we can see in his experience a sweet counterpart of our own.

May 11.

" Herein is my Father glorified, that ye bear much fruit; so shall ye be my disciples."—JOHN xv. 8.

WHEN the Lord Jesus Christ was upon earth he was in a suffering state ; and to this suffering image must all his people be conformed. In that suffering state he brought glory to God ; and is now exalted to the right hand of the Father. So those who suffer with him will be also glorified together ; and glorious indeed will they be, for they will shine like the stars for ever and ever, resplendent in the glorified image of the Son of God. The Apostle therefore says, " When Christ who is our life shall appear, then shall ye also appear with him in glory." The Lord did not assume angelic nature. He therefore did not adorn or beautify it ; but by assuming our nature, the flesh and blood of the children into union with his own divine Person, he invested it with surpassing lustre. This is the foundation on which a re-deemed sinner brings glory to God, not in himself, but as being a member of Christ, " of his body, of his flesh, and of his bones." What a thought it is, that the lowest believer should actually bring more glory to God than the highest angel ; and that the suffering obedience of a saint should be of higher value than the burning obedience of a seraph. To bring glory to God, then, should be our highest aim and most ardent desire. How the Lord urges this upon the consciences of his true disciples, " Herein is my Father glorified, that ye bear much fruit." A little fruit brings but little glory to God. It is in proportion to the amount of rich, ripe fruit that is borne upon the branches of the vine, that the Lord is glorified.

May 12.

" *Ye are they which have continued with me in my tempta-tions.*"—Luke xxii. 28.

Satan brought all his artillery to bear upon the Son of God. He was permitted to try him to the utmost. It was the purpose of God, that his well-beloved Son should be tempted like as we are ; and if you are God's, not a single temptation has beset you which did not beset the Lord of life and glory. Are we tempted sometimes to doubt a God of providence ? The Lord Jesus was similarly tempted, when Satan said to him, " Command these stones to be made bread." Are we tempted to vain confidence and presumption ? The Lord of life and glory was similarly tempted, when the prince of darkness said to him, " If thou be the Son of God, cast thyself down from hence." Are we often tempted to disbelieve that we are the children of God, and exercised at times with distressing suspicions and fears lest we have only a profession of religion, without its experimental power in our hearts? Satan brought the same temptation against the Lord, when he said, " If thou be the Son of God ;" as Hart says, " O, what an if was there ! " Are we tempted to turn our backs upon the Lord for the sake of what the world offers? The Lord Jesus was similarly tempted when Satan said that he would give him all that he presented before his eyes when he took him upon the mountain top. Are we ever tempted to turn from the true God and worship idols? The Lord of life and glory was similarly tempted when Satan with his infernal pride and cursed impudence proposed to the Son of God to worship him. The Son of God worship Satan ! But some may say, " Was Jesus tempted like I am ? How can that be ? He was pure, spotless, and holy; but I am full of corruption from the crown of my head to the soles of my feet. The Lord of life and glory had a perfect, unfallen nature, a holy human body, and a holy human soul, taken into union with Deity ; but I have a fallen nature, defiled in body and polluted in soul. Can there be a resemblance in our temptations ? " I would ask, what is it in you that feels the burden of temptation when Satan injects his blasphemies into your mind ? Is there not a something in you which is grieved, I was going to say tortured, by these fiery darts? Is it not the new nature ? and is not that nature spotless and holy ? Is it not born of God, and therefore as holy as God is holy, and pure as God is pure ? Thus just in the same way as your pure and holy nature that is born of God is grieved and distressed by the fiery darts of Satan, so was the holy soul of the Lord Jesus ten thousand times more grieved and tortured by the temptations of Satan presented before his pure and spotless mind. The disciples did not forsake their Lord, though so sorely buffeted with these temptations ; nay more, they, according to the measure of their faith, partook of them

individually and personally, suffering as well as sympathising
with him, and wounded, though in a far less degree, by
arrows from the same bow. And thus disciples now continue with Jesus in his temptations by suffering as members
with their covenant Head, walking, most of them, in a daily
path of trouble and sorrow, daily tempted by Satan, by the
world, and by their own evil hearts; day by day tempted to
do everything from which their spiritual nature recoils; day
by day tempted to do things which are hateful in the eyes of
a pure God, and to them too when in their right mind.

May 13.

"*And I appoint unto you a kingdom, as my Father hath
appointed unto me.*"—LUKE xxii. 29.

FOR whom is this kingdom appointed? For the presumptuous, the proud, the hypocritical, and the self-righteous?
No; not for these. "I appoint unto *you*," you that "have
continued with me in my temptations;" you that are tempted
and exercised; you that walk in the paths of tribulation;
you that follow in the print of the footsteps of a suffering
Jesus; you that know the painful exercises of temptation, and
yet are strengthened with strength in your inner man, to
"resist even unto blood, striving against sin," so as not to be
carried away or overwhelmed by it. What kingdom is
this? It is the same kingdom that the Father hath given to
Jesus. "I appoint unto you a kingdom, as my Father hath
appointed unto me." Now what is the kingdom which God
the Father appointed unto his dear Son? Is it to sit upon a
throne like an earthly monarch? To wear a diadem, and
carry a sceptre? "My kingdom," said Jesus, "is not of this
world" (John xviii. 36). The kingdom of the Lord of life
and glory was to make an end of sin, to abolish death, and
"destroy him that had the power of death, that is, the devil;"

to reign spiritually in the hearts of his chosen; to be King
and Lord in Zion, and to rule over the willing affections of
his subjects; a kingdom of righteousness, and peace, and
joy in the Holy Ghost; a kingdom of grace set up by the
blessed Spirit in the heart; a spiritual kingdom which none
can see or enter into but those that are born of the Spirit.
His kingdom is a spiritual kingdom, and consists in having a
people to see him as he is, a people to glorify him, a people
to love him, and a people for him to love. A kingdom cannot be the same to sovereign and subject, when it is of
an earthly and temporal nature. Were the earthly monarch
to impart his kingdom to his subjects, it would cease to be a
kingdom, and become a republic. But not so with a spiritual
kingdom. Jesus does not diminish his own grace by impart-
ing it to his people, nor lessen his own joy by shedding
it abroad in their hearts, nor sully his own glory by communicating of it to them. The sun has lost no light nor
warmth by the countless millions of rays that have issued
from it since it was first created. Nor does the glorious Sun
of righteousness lose the fulness that is in him by communicating of his grace and glory. In him dwelleth all the fulness
of the Godhead bodily, unexhausted and inexhaustible. Then
this kingdom which he appoints to his tried and tempted
disciples is the kingdom of grace in the heart; the kingdom
of God in the soul; the presence of Jesus within; the manifestation of that kingdom which is spoken of in Daniel ii. 44,
as set up on the ruins of all the other kingdoms, when it has
broken them in pieces.

May 14.

" Lord, lift thou up the light of thy countenance upon us."—
Psalm iv. 6.

The cry of the Church has always been, " Lord, lift thou
up the light of thy countenance upon us." You may often

feel as if immersed in the very shadow of death, and say with
Heman, "I am counted with them that go down into the
pit; I am as a man that hath no strength" (Psalm lxxxviii.
4); but the very feelings of death, the chill at your heart, and
the cold sweat upon your brow, make you long for the
appearance of him who is the Resurrection and the Life;
and who can in one moment whisper, "Fear not; I am alive
for evermore, and have the keys of hell and of death." You
may be pressed down at times with the power of unbelief,
and think and say there never was a heart like yours, so
unable to believe, so doubting at every step; but this deep
conviction of your wretched unbelief, which is the Spirit's
work to shew (John xvi. 9), only makes you long for that
living faith of which Christ himself is not only the Object,
but the Author and Finisher. You may be sunk at times in
despondency, as to both your present and future state; but
that makes you the more desire to have a good hope through
grace, as an anchor of the soul, both sure and steadfast.
You may feel at times the guilt, and not only the guilt, but
the dreadful power and prevalence of sin; but that only
makes you long the more earnestly for manifestations of
pardon and peace, and that no sin may have dominion over
you. "The mouth of the Lord hath spoken it," that sooner
or later you shall have every needful blessing. The valley
you now feel to be in shall be exalted; the mountain and hill
shall be made low; the crooked shall be made straight, and
the rough places plain, and your eye shall see the glory
of the Lord; Christ shall be made precious to your heart;
he will come sooner or later into your soul; and then when
he comes he will manifest himself as your Lord and your
God. And so you keep hanging, and hoping, and looking
up until he appears; for your heart is still ever saying,

"None but Jesus,
Can do helpless sinners good."

May 15.

*" And also I have withholden the rain from you, when there
were yet three months to the harvest: and I caused it to rain
upon one city, and caused it not to rain upon another city: one
piece was rained upon, and the piece whereupon it rained not
withered."*—Amos iv. 7.

How powerless we are as regards the rain that falls from
the sky! Who can go forth when the sun is shining in its
brightness and bid the rain to fall? Or when rain is falling,
who can go forth and restrain the bottles of heaven? He
who gives us rain from heaven and fruitful seasons, filling our
hearts with food and gladness, also turns a fruitful land into
barrenness for the wickedness of them that dwell therein.
Equally sovereign is the blessing that God gives to the
preached gospel. He holds the blessing in his own hand;
it is his to give, and his to withhold. If he bless, it is because
he has promised it; but when, where, and to whom it shall
come, is at his own sovereign disposal. Yet what do we
naturally desire when the earth is parched up for want of
rain? Knowing that there is rain stored up in the clouds
above, and that when it does come it will produce beneficial
effects, desires, if not prayers, go up that it may fall. In fact,
the earth itself, parched and dried up by heat, the very ground
itself, by the fissures and clefts which are made in the soil by
a burning sun, silently, mutely, but still imploringly calls
upon the rain to fall. Every crack you see in July is a silent
mouth asking the rain to come down. The withered herbage,
the cattle lowing in the field, the dried-up ponds and brooks,
are all imploring, though not a word is uttered, that rain
may fall. So in grace. The parched, withered, dried-up
feelings of the soul are all so many mute mouths imploring
God's blessing to come down. Nay, the very hardness,

barrenness, and sterility felt in our heart when the blessing of
God does not rest upon the word, are so many mute appeals
to the God of all grace that his blessing would attend the
word to our conscience. I say this because you may think
sometimes that you are not praying for the blessing of God to
rest upon the word, because you may not be using vocal
prayer, or are not favoured with a spirit of grace and supplications. God sees your wants, and to those wants he has
a kind regard. The babe need not, and indeed cannot ask
in so many words for food. The cry of hunger is enough.
Or even if too weak to cry, the mother knows the child
is hungry by its restless movements; and she is as pleased
to give the nutritious food as the babe is to receive it. So
you must not always measure the strength of your prayers
by the mere vocal utterance you may give to them. The
heart-searching God reads your wants, knows your desolate
case, and sees your barren condition. As in the kingdom
of his providence he views from his holy throne the parched
ground, and sends down showers because he sees its need;
so in the kingdom of his grace he looks upon the parched
condition of his people, and gives the spiritual rain because
he knows they need it.

May 16.

"*In whom all the building fitly framed together groweth
unto an holy temple in the Lord.*"—EPHESIANS ii. 21.

THE body of Christ is at present scattered, and, if I may so
speak, fragmentary. Of the members of his mystical body
some are now before the throne, "spirits of just men made
perfect." Others are still in the wilderness; others are yet
in the world, dead in trespasses and sins, uncalled by grace,
destitute of the Spirit; others at present are unborn, still
hidden in the womb of time. But earth is the stage whereon

all the members are from time to time brought into a vital, manifestive union with their living Head.

When I was a boy at school, in London, Waterloo Bridge was building; and I and my playmates used to go sometimes to what was then called "The Stone Field," on the other side of the water, where the stones that now make up Waterloo Bridge were being squared and chiselled. Every vestige of that field, I have no doubt, is gone, and the place covered with buildings; but there stands Waterloo Bridge; and those stones that I used to play upon as a boy now form a part of that beautiful structure which Canova, the great Italian sculptor, said it was worth coming to London only to see. Take the idea into spiritual things. The body of Christ is compared in Scripture to a building. "And are built upon the foundation of the apostles and prophets, Jesus Christ himself being the chief corner stone; in whom all the building fitly framed together groweth unto an holy temple in the Lord." Of this building believers are "living stones;" and many of them are at present in "the Stone Field," where they are being hammered and hacked, squared and chiselled by the hand of the great Architect. During this state, like the stones of Solomon's temple, which were hewn and squared at a distance, that "neither hammer nor axe, nor any tool of iron might be heard in the house while it was in building," so are these living stones prepared for their future glory. The mallet and the chisel are at work upon them now day by day, that in due time they may fill their designed position in the spiritual building. I remember well that all the stones which were strewn over the field were marked and numbered; and these figures no doubt denoted their intended position. Every stone so marked was in due time individually transferred to, and now occupies, the exact position that the architect designed for it. So every living stone was marked and numbered in eternity, is hewed and squared in time, and will, in future glory, be placed by the hand of the divine Architect in that place of the spiritual building originally designed for it.

May 17.

" *The statutes of the Lord are right, rejoicing the heart: the commandment of the Lord is pure, enlightening the eyes.*"— PSALM xix. 8.

As without a revelation of the doctrine of salvation we should not know how a sinner could be saved, and thus could not glorify God by our faith; so without a revelation of the precept we should not know how to serve God, and thus could not glorify him by our obedience. Look at this point, believing child of God. You long to glorify God in your body and in your spirit, which are his (1 Cor. vi. 20). You desire, whether you eat or drink, or whatsoever you do, to do all to the glory of God (1 Cor. x. 31). There are times and seasons with you when you sigh and mourn over your barren, unprofitable heart and life, and earnestly long to think and speak and act to his honour and glory who has done so much for you in providence and grace. At least, if you have no such desires you are no Christian, and are at the best but a poor, worldly, dead professor. When, then, and how far do you live to God's glory? Only then, and only so far as your life, and walk, and conduct harmonise with, and are guided by the precepts of the word. For see the con-nection. We can only glorify God outwardly by doing his will; we can only know that will, as regards our practical obedience to it, by the express revelation which he has given of it. Where is that revelation? In his word, and chiefly in the preceptive part of it. It is this which makes it " a lamp unto our feet, and a light unto our path." David therefore cried: " Order my steps in thy word;" " Make me to go in the path of thy commandments;" "O that my ways were directed to keep thy statutes!" as feeling that it was only by walking *in* the word and *by* the word that he could please God and live to his praise. We find thousands in this land who, as they think, are doing God service by plans and schemes of their own devising, priding themselves on their good works. But we may say of all these their duties and doings what Augustine said of the ancient Roman virtues, that they are but *splendida peccata* ("splendid sins"), or, to use the language of the 13th Article of the Church of England, entitled, Works before Justification, "for that they are not done as God hath willed and commanded them to be done, we doubt not but they have the nature of sin."

May 18.

" Hereby know we that we dwell in him, and he in us, because he hath given us of his Spirit."—1 JOHN iv. 13.

A right knowledge and living experience of the Person, graces and operations of the Holy Ghost upon the soul, is a very essential thing. Man is so deeply sunk, so utterly fallen, so unable to bring himself back, that he needs this holy Teacher to lead him into a saving, experimental knowledge of the truth of God; for we know nothing but by his teaching, have nothing but by his giving, and are nothing but by his making. The more clearly, then, that we are led to see, and the more deeply we are taught to feel what we are as fallen sons and daughters of Adam, the more shall we feel our need of, and the more shall we value when realised, his blessed operations upon the heart and conscience. Now, in the case of Aaron, (viewed not only as a type of Christ, but as personally ministering at the altar of the tabernacle, and thus consecrated to the office of high priesthood,) it was not sufficient that he was washed, nor that he was clothed; he must be also anointed by the holy anointing oil before he could stand in the sanctuary of God. So it is with a son of the Most High, one of "the kings and priests" that form "the royal priesthood;" it is not sufficient for him to be washed in the blood of the Lamb, and clothed in his justifying righteousness; he must be consecrated to God's service by the holy anointing; in other words, be sanctified, regenerated and renewed in the spirit of his mind, that, by being made a partaker of the divine nature (2 Peter i. 4), he may enter into a spiritual experience of the truth of God here, and enjoy the eternal pleasures which are at God's right hand hereafter. From the very nature of the fall, it is impossible for a dead soul to believe in God, know God, or love God; it must be quickened into spiritual life before it can savingly know the only true God, and Jesus Christ whom he has sent. And thus there lies at the very threshold, in the very heart and core of the case, the absolute necessity of the regenerating operations of God the Holy Ghost upon the soul. The very completeness and depth of the fall render the regenerating work of the Holy Ghost as necessary, as indispensable as the redeeming work of the Son of God. The Apostle therefore puts them together. "But ye are washed, but ye are sanctified, but ye are justified in the name of the Lord Jesus, and by the Spirit of our God." If, therefore, the soul is to enter into eternal glory, it must be prepared for glory by being made a partaker of grace. It must, in this present life, this time state, be made meet to be a partaker of the inheritance of the saints in light, be capacitated whilst here below for the eternal fruition of the Triune God, by receiving a new and heavenly nature begotten of the Holy Ghost, which as a pure spirit (for "that which is born of the Spirit is spirit") is capable of seeing, enjoying, and eternally delighting in the open vision of the Deity as manifested in the glorious Person of the God-man.

May 19.

" And I will betroth thee unto me for ever ; yea, I will betroth thee unto me in righteousness, and in judgment, and in lovingkindness, and in mercies."—HOSEA ii. 19.

COMMUNION with Christ begins below, in our time state. It is *here* that the mystery of the marriage union is first made known; here the espousals entered into; here the first kiss of betrothed love given. The celebration of the marriage is to come; but the original betrothal in heaven and the spiritual espousals on earth make Christ and the Church eternally one. As then the husband, when he becomes united to his wife in marriage ties, engages thereby to love her, cherish her, feed her, clothe her, count her interests his interests, her honour his honour, and her happiness his happiness, so the blessed Jesus, when in the councils of eternity, he betrothed the Church to himself, undertook to be to her and do for her everything that should be for her happiness and honour, perfection and glory. His own words are, "I will betroth thee unto me for ever; yea, I will betroth thee unto me in righteousness, and in judgment, and in lovingkindness, and in mercies. I will even betroth thee unto me in faithfulness; and thou shalt know the Lord." And again, " For thy Maker is thine husband; the Lord of hosts is his name ; and thy Redeemer the Holy One of Israel; the God of the whole earth shall he be called." "For as a young man marrieth a virgin, so shall thy sons marry thee ; and as the bridegroom rejoiceth over the bride, so shall thy God rejoice over thee." There must be union before communion, marriage before possession, membership before abiding in Christ and he in us, a being in the vine before a branch issuing from the stem. It is the Spirit that quickeneth us to feel our need of him ; to seek all our supplies in him and from him ; to believe in him unto everlasting life, and thus live a life of faith upon him. By his secret teachings, inward touches, gracious smiles, soft whispers, sweet promises, and more especially by manifestations of his glorious Person, finished work, atoning blood, justifying righteousness, agonising sufferings and dying love, he draws the heart up to himself. He thus wins our affections, and setting himself before our eyes as "the chiefest among ten thousand and altogether lovely," draws out that love and affection towards himself which puts the world under our feet. All religion flows from his Spirit and grace, presence and power. He is our sun, and without him all is darkness; he is our life, and without him all is death; he is the beginner and finisher of our faith, the substance of our hope, and the object of our love.

May 20.

"For God, who commanded the light to shine out of darkness, hath shined in our hearts, to give the light of the knowledge of the glory of God in the face of Jesus Christ."—2 CORINTHIANS iv. 6.

WHEN a man is walking in the darkness and death of unregeneracy, he has no true light. He may indeed have a false light, as the light of presumption, delusion, or vain-confidence; but all such borrowed light is worse than darkness; as the Lord says, "If the light that is in thee be darkness, how great is that darkness!"

The only saving light is the light of God shining into the soul, giving us to see and know "the only true God, and Jesus Christ whom he hath sent." A man may have the clearest light in his judgment, and yet never have the penetrating light of the Spirit producing conviction in his soul; he may have the soundest knowledge of the doctrines of grace, and see the harmonious scheme of salvation; and yet never have seen a holy God by divine teaching, nor have

ever felt the spirituality of God's righteous law condemning
him as a transgressor. But "the light of life," as the Lord
calls it, is sure to guide its possessor aright. If we have it
not, we shall be sure to go astray; we shall be entangled in
some error, plunge into some heresy, imbibe some doctrine
of devils, drink into some awful delusion, or fall into some
dreadful sin, and "concerning faith make shipwreck." A
false light is something like the lights which pirates hold up
to entrap ships to their destruction; or like the fires, which
the "wreckers," those dreadful characters in Cornwall, used
to kindle on their iron-bound coast, in order that the mariner
might mistake them for some friendly light-house, and run
his vessel on the rocks, where those heartless wretches
plundered it. A false light can but wreck us on the rocks of
presumption or despair. But the light of divine life in the
soul is accompanied with all the graces of the Spirit. It is
the light of the glory of God, the light of Jesus' countenance,
and the light of the Spirit's teaching, and therefore an infallible guide and guard; as the Apostle says, "Ye have an
unction from the Holy One, and know all things." And this
infallible pilot will guide the soul to whom it is given safe
into the harbour of endless rest and peace.

May 21.

*"Who his own self bare our sins in his own body on the
tree."*—1 PETER ii. 24.

WE beg of the Lord, sometimes, to give us a broken heart,
a contrite spirit, a tender conscience, and a humble mind;
but it is only a view by faith of what the gracious Redeemer
endured upon the cross, when he bare our sins in his own
body with all their weight and pressure, and with all the anger
of God due to them that can really melt a hard, and break a
stony heart. No sight, short of this, can make sin felt to be
hateful; bring tears of godly sorrow out of the eyes, sobs of

true repentance out of the breast, and the deepest, humblest confessions before God what dreadful sinners and base backsliders we have been before the eyes of his infinite Purity, Majesty, and Holiness. Oh, what hope is there for our guilty souls; what refuge from the wrath of God so justly our due; what shelter from the curse of a fiery law, except it be in the cross of Jesus? O for a view of him revealed to the eyes of our enlightened understanding, as bearing our sins in his own body on the tree. O to see by the eye of faith, all those dreadful sins which have caused us so much inward grief and trouble, all those fearful backslidings and sad entanglements on which we can but reflect with shame and grief; O to see all we have said and thought and done, which conscience testifies against, and all those innumerable evils that we have never seen or conscience has forgotten; to view them by the eye of faith taken off our guilty head and put upon the head of the Lord the Lamb. Where, oh, where, can we get relief from any other source or by any other way? There is no relief anywhere else. Where can you find pardon sealed upon your breast, forgiveness manifested to your soul, or any expectation of winning heaven and escaping hell, except in the cross, and some testimony in your own bosom of your interest in that precious blood and righteousness, and the knowledge for yourself that the dear Redeemer bare your sins in his body on the tree? I know, indeed, full well, that it requires special faith, a faith of God's own giving and raising up to believe this, an especial manifestation of salvation by the blood of the Lamb to the soul; a blessed bringing in of the power of Christ crucified to the heart. But I believe I do but speak the inmost conviction of every heart touched by the finger of God when I say, that until this is in some measure done, there is no solid relief; no true peace with God; no firm, abiding foundation on which we can stand, as if for eternity; nothing strong enough to banish the fear of death and open the gates of heaven.

May 22.

" I have stuck unto thy testimonies : O Lord, put me not to shame."—PSALM cxix. 31.

IN whatever state or stage of experience you are, it will be your wisdom and your mercy to stick to God's testimony. Has the Lord just begun a work of grace in your heart? Is he shewing to you what you are by nature, and bringing before your eyes the sins of your youth, and plunging you in deep convictions? It will be your wisdom, and it will be your mercy, to stick to that testimony; not to be driven from your standing into despair, nor pushed forward into fleshly confidence ; but to stick to that testimony which God himself has implanted. Has God made you to sigh and cry from the depths of a broken heart—to fall down before his truth? Stick to that testimony; he will not put you to shame. Again, if the Lord has done a little more for you, shewn you the least glimpse of mercy and favour, and given you some little testimony of your interest in the blood of the Lamb, it will be your wisdom, and it will be your mercy, to stick to that testimony too. You will find those who would push you presumptuously forward; you will find those who would drive you despairingly backward; you will find those who would pull you down into those doubts and fears that their own minds are exercised with, and you will find those who would draw you aside into the vain confidence in which they themselves are standing. It will be your wisdom and mercy to abide by the testimony which God himself has revealed ; and he can work in your soul that faith whereby you can and will stick to his testimony.

But some may say, " How do I know that I am sticking to God's testimonies?" I would ask, what are the feelings of your hearts towards them? Is there godly fear? Is there holy reverence ? Is there trembling awe? Is there any exercise of soul? any pouring out of the heart before God ? any realising of his presence? any trembling lest you should offend him? any desire after him? any solemn feelings whereby your soul is exercised upon his perfections? Then there is reason to believe there is some testimony of God in your conscience, and that you are sticking to it. But if your religion be such as leads to vain confidence, to self-righteousness, to presumption, to false security, and to a careless, light, trifling spirit, depend upon it you are not sticking to God's testimony, or else you have no testimony from God to stick unto. But if the Lord is bringing into your soul some sense of his displeasure; if you have trifled with him, and brought guilt into your soul and trouble into your mind, it will be your wisdom, and it will be your mercy to do, as the Lord speaks in Leviticus xxvi. 41, " accept the punishment of your iniquity ;" to put your mouth in the dust, and confess that you are vile ; not to turn aside to presumptuous confidence as though you would blunt the edge of God's sword in your soul, but to receive it in your heart, embrace it in your conscience, and to cleave to it as the testimony of God himself. "I have stuck unto thy testi- monies." To cleave to everything which God makes known in the conscience, be it judgment, be it mercy, be it a smile, be it a frown, be it a testimony for, be it a testimony against, whatever it be that comes with power, and is brought to the soul by the application of the Spirit—to cleave to it, keeps the soul in a safe and blessed spot.

May 23.

" *That he would grant unto us, that we being delivered out of the hand of our enemies might serve him without fear, in holi- ness and righteousness before him, all the days of our life."*— LUKE i. 74, 75.

THE grand point in all true religion is to be brought by

the blessed Spirit into that happy spot where we can serve
the living God free from that guilt, bondage, darkness, doubt,
and fear which often possess our mind, and are the worst
enemies of our soul's peace.   But though they are such
enemies to all true peace and happiness, yet are they mercifully overruled for our spiritual good, to convince us from
whence our help must come, to strip us thoroughly of all
creature help and hope, and bring us to the spot where the
Lord meets the soul in mercy, sheds abroad his love, and
brings near a precious Christ.   We have no reason to thank
bondage, guilt and the law, still less sin and Satan, for any
work they have done which God has overruled for our good.
And yet without some experience of these dead works and
the bondage and guilt produced by them, we could not know
what it was to have our conscience purged by the blood of
sprinkling to serve the living God.   There are reasons, therefore, and wise reasons on the part of God, why his children
should be thus vexed and plagued.   It is true it is not the
revealed will of God that his children should spend so many
of their days in darkness, doubt, and fear.   He has given us
a glorious gospel ; he has set before us in Jesus everything
for our comfort and relief ; he has promised to send his Holy
Spirit to testify of Christ, and has filled his word with
promises and invitations suited to every case.   And yet his
secret will and purpose are that we should be thus exercised
and tried, and walk in this path of darkness and desolation,
that we might value more the precious liberty of the gospel,
know more of what Christ is, and what he has done to save
us from the depths of the fall, be more deeply indebted to the
riches of free and sovereign grace, and come more personally
into the blessedness of gospel mercies as made known to
our soul by a divine power.

May 24.

"*Surely, shall one say, in the Lord have I righteousness and strength.*"—Isaiah xlv. 24.

Have you yet learnt that you are a sinner in the sight of God? Have you ever felt the length, breadth, and spirituality of his holy law? Do you feel in your very soul that without Christ's righteousness being imputed to you, and his blood being sprinkled upon your conscience, you must die in your sins and never reach the heavenly shore? Has this ever been, or is it still a matter of anxious solicitude to you? Has it ever caused sighs and groans to come out of your heart? Has the spirit of prayer ever been given, to make you plead with the Lord for the forgiveness of your sins, through the merits of a crucified Saviour? And have you any hope but in his blood, righteousness, and finished work? Now if the Lord has been pleased to exercise your soul in this way, if he has not yet granted the longing desire of your heart, he certainly will in due time reveal his dear Son in you as the God-man who has saved you from death and hell; he will apply his atoning blood to your conscience, bring near his glorious righteousness, shed abroad his dying love, give and strengthen faith, and draw it forth into a blessed assurance of your interest in the Son of his love. Or if your manifestations should not be very bright and conspicuous, he will give you a good hope through grace, as an anchor of the soul both sure and steadfast; and will draw up your affections to that blessed Lord who sits at the right hand of the Father in power, majesty, and glory. And as he does this, he enables the believer thus favoured and blessed to take these words into his lips, "*In the Lord have I righteousness.*" He cannot say it before. He may know that there is no righteousness but in the Lord; he may have utterly renounced his own; he may have sunk very deep into

guilt and bondage; but until the Lord the Spirit is pleased
to liberate him, he cannot come forth into liberty; until he
has the witness of the Spirit he cannot cry, "Abba, Father."
But when the Lord is pleased to bring near his righteousness,
to reveal his dying love, and to shed it abroad in his heart by
divine power, then he can say, "In the Lord have I righteousness." And when he has this, he wants no other; it is
complete, which no other can be. It is acceptable to God;
it is available in the courts of heaven; it will bear him up
through all the storms of time; it will smooth a dying pillow,
and land him safely in a glorious eternity.

May 25.

*"Awake, O north wind; and come thou south; blow upon
my garden, that the spices thereof may flow out. Let my beloved come into his garden, and eat his pleasant fruits."*—Song
Solomon iv. 16.

We are, most of us, so fettered down by the chains of
time and sense, the cares of life and daily business, the
weakness of our earthly frame, the distracting claims of a
family, and the miserable carnality and sensuality of our
fallen nature, that we live at best a poor, dragging, dying life.
We can take no pleasure in the world, nor mix with a good
conscience in its pursuits and amusements; we are many of
us poor, moping, dejected creatures, from a variety of trials
and afflictions; we have a daily cross and the continual plague
of an evil heart; get little consolation from the family of
God or the outward means of grace; know enough of ourselves to know that in self there is neither help nor hope, and
never expect a smoother path, a better, wiser, holier heart, or
to be able to do to-morrow what we cannot do to-day. As
then the weary man seeks rest, the hungry food, the thirsty
drink, and the sick health, so do we stretch forth our hearts

and arms that we may embrace the Lord Jesus Christ, and
sensibly realise union and communion with him. From him
come both prayer and answer, both hunger and food, both
desire and the tree of life. He discovers the evil and misery
of sin that we may seek pardon in his bleeding wounds and
pierced side; makes known to us our nakedness and shame,
and, as such, our exposure to God's wrath, that we may hide
ourselves under his justifying robe ; puts gall and wormwood
into the world's choicest draughts, that we may have no sweetness but in and from him ; keeps us long fasting to endear a
crumb, and long waiting to make a word precious. He
wants the whole heart, and will take no less ; and as this we
cannot give, he takes it to himself by ravishing it with one of
his eyes, with one chain of his neck. If we love him, it is
because he first loved us ; and if we seek communion with
him, it is because he will manifest himself to us as he doth
not unto the world.

Would we see what the Holy Ghost has revealed of the
nature of this communion, we shall find it most clearly and
experimentally unfolded in the Song of Solomon. From the
first verse of that book, " Let him kiss me with the kisses of
his mouth," to the last expressed desire of the loving bride,
" Make haste, my beloved, and be thou like to a roe or to
a young hart upon the mountains of spices," all is a " song
of loves," all a divine revelation of the communion that
is carried on upon earth between Christ and the Church.
She " comes up from the wilderness leaning upon her beloved," whilst " his left hand is under her head, and his right
hand doth embrace her." She says, " Look not upon me,
because I am black;" but he answers, " Thou art all fair,
my love ; there is no spot in thee." At one moment she says,
" By night, on my bed, I sought him whom my soul loveth ;
I sought him, but I found him not ; " and then again she
cries, " It was but a little that I passed from them, but I

found him whom my soul loveth. I held him, and would not
let him go, until I had brought him into my mother's house,
and into the chamber of her that conceived me." Comings
and goings ; sighs and songs; vain excuses and cutting self-
reflections; complaints of self, and praises of him ; the breathings of love, and the flames of jealousy; the tender affections
of a virgin heart, and the condescending embraces of a royal
spouse ;—such is the experience of the Church in seeking or
enjoying communion with Christ as described in this divine
book.

May 26.

" Sanctify them through thy truth : thy word is truth." —
John xvii. 17.

When the gospel comes "not in word only, but also in
power," it comes "in the Holy Ghost," that is, in and with
the teaching and testimony of the Holy Ghost. It is this
coming "in the Holy Ghost" which gives truth in its power
such a sanctifying influence on the heart. But you will ask,
perhaps, What is a sanctifying influence? It is the communication of holy feelings, heavenly desires, and gracious
affections; in a word, it is the breathing into the soul of that
sweet spirituality of mind which is life and peace. If we are
among the people of God, he chose us in Christ "before
the foundation of the world, that we should be holy and
without blame before him in love." If he chasten us in this
time-state, it is "for our profit, that we might be partakers of
his holiness " (Heb. xii. 10). It is this holiness of heart, this
heavenly-mindedness which I mean when I speak of the
sanctifying influence of truth in its power. Now did truth
ever come into your soul with any measure of this sanctifying
influence ? Did you ever long to get away from the chapel,
go home to your room, fall upon your knees, and have
blessed fellowship with the Father and his Son Jesus Christ?

And were you ever so favoured when you did get home? Or sometimes when alone, in reading, or meditation, or secret prayer, did the word of God ever come into your soul with that sweet unction, savour, and dew that it seemed to make the very room in which you were holy ground? I remember when God was pleased to reveal his dear Son to my soul in my sick room many years ago, I was afraid almost to go out of my room lest I should lose the sweet, holy feelings and blessed spirituality of mind which I then and there enjoyed. Depend upon it, there is a holiness of heart and affection, an inward holiness, without which no man shall see the Lord; and depend upon it, whenever truth comes into a believer's soul, it comes with that sanctifying influence, which not only gives him a meetness for, but is a blessed foretaste of the inheritance of the saints in light.

May 27.

"Husbands, love your wives, even as Christ also loved the Church, and gave himself for it; that he might sanctify and cleanse it with the washing of water by the word."—EPHESIANS v. 25, 26.

VIEW the Church without the sanctifying operations and influences of regenerating grace. She is far from Christ; she has no desire towards him, no manifest union, no communion with him; no faith in his blood, no hope in his mercy, no love to his name. Were she left always thus, where would be her meetness for heaven? But when the word of truth comes with power, and is accompanied by the influences of the Holy Ghost to the heart, then there is not only a cleansing of the conscience from the guilt and filth of sin, but the communication of a new heart and a new spirit. How plainly is this spoken of by the prophet Ezekiel, where, after the promise, "From all your filthiness and from all your

idols will I cleanse you," it is added, "A new heart also will
I give you, and a new spirit will I put within you." We
have not only therefore to be washed from our sins in the
blood of the Lamb, not only to be pardoned and forgiven
and thus have a title to heaven, but we want a meetness for
heaven; we want a new heart and a new spirit given to us,
whereby we may taste, handle, feel, and enjoy the love of
Christ as shed abroad in the heart, and experience the
flowings forth of love to him in return. As then the blood
cleanses, so the Spirit sanctifies. John therefore says, "This
is he that came by water and blood, even Jesus Christ; not
by water only, but by water and blood" (1 John v. 6). The
blood is the blood of the atonement; the water is the sanctifying influences of the Holy Ghost.

Observe the order in which these blessings come. First,
is the love of Christ in eternity; secondly, the gift of himself
in time; thirdly, the cleansing by blood; fourthly, the sanctifying by the Spirit. Now look at these things for yourselves.
Are your sins pardoned? Have you any evidence that you
are washed in the blood of the Lamb? Do you believe that
you are going to heaven? What does your belief of this, or
your hope in it, rest upon? Where are your evidences?
Surely not from merely seeing these truths in the Scripture
as the bare revelation of God, or believing them from my
statements. Such a faith and such a hope, if you have no
better, will prove delusive, and will leave you in the hands of
him who is a consuming fire. If your hope of eternal life is
well grounded, it is because the word of life has come into
your soul, and you have been not only cleansed by the application of the blood of sprinkling to your conscience, but
sanctified and renewed by the power of the word, through the
Holy Spirit, upon your heart.

May 28.

" That he might present it to himself a glorious Church, not having spot, or wrinkle, or any such thing ; but that it should be holy and without blemish."—Ephesians v. 27.

Neither others nor we ourselves now see what the Church one day will be, and what she ever was in the eyes of Jesus. He could look through all this time-state, through all the sins and sorrows of this intermediate period, and fix his eye upon the bridal day, the day when before assembled angels, in the courts of heaven, in the realms of eternal bliss, he should present her to himself a glorious Church, not having spot or wrinkle or any such thing, but holy, and without blemish. O what a day will that be, when the Son of God shall openly wed his espoused bride; when there shall be heard in heaven, "as the voice of many waters, and as the voice of mighty thunderings, saying, Alleluia : for the Lord God omnipotent reigneth ! Let us be glad and rejoice, and give honour to him : for the marriage of the Lamb is come, and his wife hath made herself ready" (Rev. xix. 7). How cleansed, how sanctified, how washed, how clothed must the Church be in that day when the very eyes of omniscience, which can read the slightest departure, even a wrinkle, from infinite purity, will find in her neither spot nor blemish, so that God himself in all the blaze of his holiness may say of the Church, "I have viewed her with an omniscient eye ; I have looked at every member of the mystical body of my dear Son ; I have examined each with all the eyes of Godhead; but there is no spot, there is no wrinkle, no blemish in any one of them; all are complete in him; all stand accepted in the Beloved."

But you may ask, and this is an inquiry well worth pressing upon your conscience, " How am I to know that I shall stand at that day without spot or wrinkle ?" To answer that inquiry, what do you know, I ask, of the cleansing, sanctifying influences of regenerating grace, of the word of truth laying hold of your conscience, of the word of power coming into your heart, of the blood of Christ being applied, and the love of God shed abroad in your heart by the Holy Ghost? If not now, yet before you are called away from these lower scenes, you are blessed with a living faith in the Son of God, with the application of his love and blood to your conscience, when time ends with you, it will open to you a glorious eternity, and for ever delivered from all your present sins and sorrows, fears and anxieties, you will be presented at the great day amongst that glorious Church, which has neither spot nor wrinkle nor any such thing. But if you live and die without any interest in these heavenly blessings, should I be faithful to my commission and to my conscience, if I were to say it will be all well with you?—that you have only on your deathbed to send for a minister to pray by your bedside, give you the sacrament, and speak a few comfortable words, and it will be all right with your soul? Should I be faithful to my commission to encourage such a delusion as this, a delusion by which thousands are continually deceived? I dare not do it. Yea, I would lift up my voice and cry aloud, " There is no salvation past, present, or future, but what flows through the precious blood of the Lamb, and is made experimentally known to the soul by the power of the Holy Ghost."

May 29.

" Holding faith, and a good conscience; which some having put away concerning faith have made shipwreck."—1 TIMOTHY i. 19.

WE find that, in the Apostle's time, there were characters who held faith, or rather what they called faith, and put away " good conscience." He mentions by name, "Hymeneus and Alexander, whom he had delivered unto Satan," that is, excommunicated them out of the Church, as heretics and blasphemers. But if to have put good conscience away, stamps a man as unfit for the visible Church of God, it behoves us to search whether we have this weapon at our side, and in our hand. What does the Apostle, then, mean by "a good conscience?" I believe he means a conscience alive in God's fear, a spiritual conscience, a tender conscience, what he calls, in another part, "a pure conscience;" "holding faith in a pure conscience," that is, purified from ignorance, from guilt, from the power of sin, "a conscience void of offence toward God and men." Wherever, then, there is living faith in the soul, there will be united with it "a good conscience." The Lord never sends forth a soldier to fight his battles with the weapon of faith only; he puts faith in one hand and "a good conscience" in the other. And he that goes forth with what he thinks to be faith, and casts aside "a good conscience," will manifest himself to be one of those characters, who, "concerning faith make shipwreck."

But why is it called "a good conscience?" Because it comes down from God, who is the Author of all good, the Giver of "every good gift, and every perfect gift." There is none good but he, and there is nothing good but what he himself implants and communicates. This weapon of a good conscience, that the Lord arms his soldiers with, works with faith, as well as proves the sincerity of faith, and tests its genuineness and reality. Faith, without a good conscience, is dead. It bears upon it the mark of nature, and however high it may rise in confidence, or however it may seem to abound in good works, it is not the faith of God's elect, of which the end is the salvation of the soul. But it may be asked, How does a good conscience work with faith? What is the connection between these two weapons, and how do they mutually support and strengthen each other? In this way. What faith believes, good conscience feels; what faith receives, good conscience holds; what faith embraces, good conscience rivets fast; when faith is weak, good conscience is feeble; and when faith is strong, good conscience is active. They grow and they wane together, and like two stems from one root together do they flourish and fade. He then alone wars the good warfare, who goes forth with faith in the one hand, and " good conscience " in the other; faith strengthening conscience, and conscience strengthening faith; each doing their separate office, but still tending to one end; each accomplishing the work which the Lord has appointed, and yet each fighting the Lord's battles, and bringing the soldier safe and victorious over his enemy.

May 30.

"But my God shall supply all your need according to his riches in glory by Christ Jesus."—Philippians iv. 19.

Oh! if there were no Christ Jesus, there could be no " supply." Howling in hell would our miserable souls be, unless there were a Mediator at the right hand of the Father; a blessed Jesus, full of love, pity, and power, co-equal and co-eternal in his divine nature with the Father and the Holy Ghost, and yet the God-Man, in whom " it hath pleased the Father that all fulness should dwell." If there were not such a blessed Mediator at the right hand of God, not one drop of spiritual comfort, not one particle of hope, not one grace or fruit of the Spirit to distinguish us from the damned in hell, would ever be our lot or portion. Oh! we should never forget the channel through which these mercies come; we should never, for one moment, think that they could come through any other Person or in any other way, than through God's only begotten Son, now in our nature, at his right hand, as our Advocate, Mediator, and Intercessor with the Father.

And this supply is " according to the riches of his glory; " which is, I believe, a Hebrew idiom, signifying *his glorious riches*—riches so great, so unlimited, so unfathomable, raising up the soul to such a height of glory, that they may well be called " glorious." And these "*in* Christ Jesus;" stored up in him, locked up in him, and supplied freely out of him, just according to the wants and exercises of God's people.

May 31.

"*For the flesh lusteth against the Spirit, and the Spirit against the flesh: and these are contrary the one to the other: so that ye cannot do the things that ye would.*"—GALATIANS v. 17.

THE Holy Spirit is especially tender of his own work upon the soul. He originally formed it; it is his own spiritual offspring; and as a mother watches over her babe, so the blessed Spirit watches over the spirit of his own creating. It is the counterpart of himself, for it is the spirit that he has raised up in the soul by his own almighty power. He, therefore, acts upon it, breathes into it fresh life and power, and communicates grace out of the inexhaustible fulness of the Son of God, thus enabling the spirit to breathe and act, struggle and fight against the flesh, so that the latter cannot have all its own way, but must submit and yield. For the spirit can fight as well as the flesh ; can act as well as the flesh; and can desire good as well as the flesh can desire evil. What a mercy for us it is that there are those heavenly breathings in our soul of the spirit against the flesh, cryings out to God against it; and that the spirit within us thus takes hold of the arm of Omnipotence without us, seeks help from the Lord God Almighty, and by strength thus communicated fights against the flesh, and gains at times a most blessed victory over it. For what can the flesh do against the spirit when animated by divine power? What are sin, Satan, and the world when they have to oppose a Triune God in arms? This makes the victory sure, that our friends are stronger than our foes, and the work of God upon our soul greater than anything sin, Satan, or the world can bring against it. This made the Apostle say, after he had been describing the inward conflict, "I thank God through Jesus Christ our Lord" (Rom. vii. 25). And when he had enumerated the opposition that the Christian has to endure on every side, he cries out, as if in holy triumph, "Nay, in all these things we are more than conquerors through him that loved us" (Rom. viii. 37).

June 1.

"Who is he that condemneth? It is Christ that died, yea rather, that is risen again, who is even at the right hand of God, who also maketh intercession for us."—ROMANS viii. 34.

As the soul is led and taught by the Spirit, it follows the Lord through all the various acts and sufferings of his life. The first spot to which the Holy Ghost takes the poor sinner is *the cross of Jesus.* *That* is the first real saving view we get of the Lord of life and glory; the Holy Ghost taking the poor guilty sinner, laden with the weight of a thousand sins, to the foot of the cross, and opening his eyes to see the Son of God bleeding there as a propitiation for sin. To be brought there by the power of the Holy Ghost, and receive that blessed mystery of the bleeding, suffering, and agonising Son of God into our hearts and consciences, is the first blessed discovery that God the Spirit favours us with.

But we pass on from that to see Jesus *sleeping in the sepulchre;* for we have to die ourselves, and we want to see the Forerunner who has entered into the grave for us. We want to feel that we can lie down in the grave, and see that narrow bed in which our body will one day be stretched, in a measure perfumed by Jesus having lain there before us. And when we have travelled from the cross to the sepulchre, we then go a step farther; to *the resurrection* of the Lord of life and glory. On the third day we view him by faith, springing out of the sepulchre in which he lay entombed,

rising up in glory and power for our justification. And thus
we see in the resurrection of the Lord Jesus the hope of the
soul for a blessed immortality. But we do not tarry there;
as the Lord the Spirit gives us eyes to see, and moves our
heart to feel, we travel one step farther; this is, to *the ascension*
of the Lord of life and glory; not tarrying on earth (for
he tarried not there), but mounting up to see him sitting at
the right hand of the Father, as the Mediator between God
and man, as the divine Intercessor, as the glorious Head of
grace, as communicating out of his own fulness gifts and
graces unto poor and needy souls, who are living in daily
and hourly bankruptcy. These want to receive perpetual
supplies of life, light, and grace out of his fulness, to keep
them in the way wherein the Lord has set their feet. So that
the ascension of the Lord Jesus up on high, and his sitting at
the right hand of God, when received into the conscience
under the power of the Spirit, is not a dry doctrine, not a
dead bone of a withered skeleton; but is so connected with
all the feelings of our heart, with all our misery and ruin, with
all our wretchedness, with all our guilt, with all our daily wants,
with all our hourly necessities, that, when led by the Spirit's
teaching to look at this Mediator at the right hand of the
Father, it becomes a truth full of blessed sweetness and power
to the heaven-taught soul.

June 2.

*" All that the Father giveth me shall come to me; and him.
that cometh to me I will in no wise cast out."*—JOHN vi. 37.

Now, poor sinner, upon whose head the beams of a fiery
law are darting; now, poor sinner, distressed in thy mind,
guilty in thy conscience, plagued with a thousand temptations,
beset by innumerable doubts and fears, canst thou not look
up a little out of thy gloom and sadness, and see that the
eternal God is thy refuge? Dost thou not cleave to him with

the utmost of thy power, as being beaten out of every other? Hast thou not taken hold of his strength that thou mayest make peace with him? Art thou not looking to him? And does he not say, "Look unto me and be ye saved, all the ends of the earth?" He bids thee look at him as Moses bade the Israelites look to the brazen serpent. Poor sinner, groaning under the weight of thy transgression, he bids thee look to him. Has the blessed Lord, he into whose lips grace was poured, not said, "Him that cometh to me I will in no wise cast out?" Why should you not look? Why should you not come to him? Will he cast you out? Do you not feel the secret drawings of his grace, movements upon your heart which make you come often with strong crying and tears, with groans and sighs, earnest, vehement, and continual supplications? What are these but the inward teachings of God, as our Lord said, "It is written in the prophets, And they shall be all taught of God. Every man therefore that hath heard, and hath learned of the Father, cometh unto me." And do you not know that the Lord himself said, that no man can come to him except the Father which hath sent him draw him? These comings, therefore, of thy soul in earnest and vehement desire are, according to his own testimony, from the special teachings and gracious drawings of God in thee. Having made his dear Son to be the refuge of thy soul, he is now drawing thee unto him that thou mayest find pardon and peace in him. But perhaps you will say, "I am so sinful, so guilty, I have been such a sinner, much worse than you can form any conception of; and it is this which sinks me so low." Art thou lower than brother Jonah when he was in the whale's belly, and, in his own feelings, in the belly of hell? And yet what said he? "Yet will I look again toward thy holy temple." Canst thou not look again toward the holy temple? Is his mercy clean gone for ever? So David felt and feared, but it was not so, for "his mercy endureth for ever ;" and that is a long and strong word. Look and live, look and live!

June 3.

"*In whom also after that ye believed, ye were sealed with that holy Spirit of promise.*"—EPHESIANS i. 13.

SEALING is *subsequent* to believing: "In whom *after* ye believed, ye were sealed." In legal documents the writing always precedes the sealing. *That* is the last act, and follows even the signing, putting an attesting stamp on the whole document, from the first word to the last signature. So in grace. The Spirit begins the work. He writes the first lines of divine truth on the soul; he makes the first impression on the heart of stone, which under his operation becomes a heart of flesh; he writes every truth that he thus makes known on the fleshy tables of the heart. He thus gives faith and hope, and then he comes with his special inward witness, and seals the truth and reality of his own work, so as not only to make it plain and clear, but to ratify and confirm it beyond all doubt and fear, questioning or dispute, either by ourself or others. The work of God on the soul sometimes seems to lie as if dead and dormant; little prayer goes up, little answer comes down. Then doubts and fears arise whether the work be genuine, and much bondage and darkness sensibly gather over the mind like a dark and gloomy cloud, which much obscures the handwriting of the divine finger. Now the blessed Spirit revives his work by some application of the word with power, some softening and melting of the hard heart by his divine influence, some communication of a spirit of prayer, some discovery of the gracious Lord, some strengthening of faith, reviving of hope, and drawing forth of love. He thus puts the seal on his own work, and stamps it as genuine. Under the sweetness and blessedness of this attesting seal many a poor child of God can look back to

this and that testimony, this and that Ebenezer, this and that
hill Mizar, this and that deliverance, blessing, manifestation,
answer to prayer, special season under the word or on his
knees, which were almost lost and buried in unbelief and
confusion. But especially when he bears witness with their
spirit that they are the children of God, and shedding abroad
the love of God in their heart becomes in them the Spirit of
adoption, whereby they cry, "Abba, Father," is his sealing
manifest and complete.

June 4.

"For all have sinned, and come short of the glory of God."—
ROMANS iii. 23.

WHAT is it to "come short of the glory of God?"   It is
to act without a view to his glory.   Now everything that we
have ever done, which has not been done with a single eye to
God's glory, has the brand of sin stamped on it.   But who in
an unregenerate state, who, as the fallen son of a fallen parent,
ever had an eye to the glory of God?   Did such a thing ever
enter into man's natural heart as to speak to God's glory, act
to his glory, consult his glory, and live to his glory?   Before
ever such a thought, such a desire can cross our breast, we
must have seen Him who is invisible; we must have had a
view by faith of the glory of the Three-One God; we must
have had a single eye given us by the Holy Ghost to see that
glory outshining all creature good.   Every movement, then,
of the selfish heart, every desire to gratify, please and exalt
self, is a coming short of the glory of God.   This stamps all
natural men's religious services with the brand of sin.   It
leaves the religious in the same awful state as the irreligious;
it hews down the professing world with the same sword that
cuts down the profane world.   When men in a state of nature
are what is called "religious," is their religion's end and aim
the glory of God, the glory of free grace, the glory of the

Mediator between God and man, the glory of the Holy Ghost, the only Teacher of God's people? Take it in its best, its brightest shape, is it not another form of selfishness, to exalt their own righteousness, and climb to heaven by the ladder of their own doings? And is not this a coming short of the glory of God? But besides that, the very glory of God requires that every one accepted in his sight should be without spot, speck, stain or blemish. A pure God cannot accept, cannot look upon, cannot be pleased with impurity; and just in proportion to the infinite purity and ineffable holiness of Jehovah, must all impurity, all carnality, all unholiness, and the slightest deviation from absolute perfection be hateful and horrible in his sight.

Now this all the election of grace are brought more or less to feel. It is the solemn and indispensable preparation of the heart for mercy; it is the introduction by the hand of the Spirit into the antechamber of the King of kings. It is the bringing of the soul to that spot, that only spot, where grace is felt, received, and known. It is, therefore, utterly indispensable for the election of grace, for all the ransomed and quickened family of God, to have this felt in their conscience, that they "have sinned, and come short of the glory of God."

June 5.

"*Having therefore, brethren, boldness to enter into the holiest by the blood of Jesus."*—HEBREWS x. 19.

NOTHING will satisfy a living soul but coming "into the holiest." He wants to have communion with God, the holy, holy, holy Lord God of hosts. He is not dealing with a God distant and afar off, an idol, a God in whom he has neither faith, nor hope, nor love; who can neither see, nor hear, nor save; a God of his own conception or of some indistinct, traditional opinion; but he feels in his very conscience that he is carrying on a sacred and holy intercourse with the God of heaven and earth, the God who has made himself in some measure known to his soul as the God and Father of the Lord Jesus Christ. With him he has to do; to him he must come; and with him he must hold holy communion. Before his heart-searching eyes he feels he stands; into his ever-open ears he pours his petition; to his mercy and pity he appeals; his compassion he craves; his love he seeks; his salvation he longs for; and his presence above all things he earnestly desires. So he must come into the holiest, for there God dwells; and to come unto God is to come there. The man who thus feels and acts is an Israelite indeed in whom there is no guile; one of the true circumcision who worship God in the Spirit, rejoice in Christ Jesus, and have no confidence in the flesh. Others are satisfied with the courts of the house, with admiring the external building, or the painted windows, carved pews, and long drawn aisles; with the mere worship of God as so much lip service. But the living soul goes beyond all that into the very heart of the sanctuary itself. As the high priest on the day of atonement did not tarry amongst the people in the court, nor with the priests in the holy place, but pressed on, ever pressed on through the thick veil until he got into the holy of holies; so with the saint of God—he does not tarry in the outer court with the profane, nor in the sanctuary with the professor, so as to be satisfied with seeing God with a veil between. But he must come into that immediate presence of God, where he may see something of his grace, behold something of his glory, feel something of his mercy, and taste something of his power. And this makes him press forward into the holiest.

June 6.

"Thus saith the Lord; I remember thee, the kindness of thy youth, the love of thine espousals, when thou wentest after me in the wilderness, in a land that was not sown."—JEREMIAH ii. 2.

IF we look at salvation, we shall see that it consists of three parts; salvation past, salvation present, and salvation future. Salvation *past* consists in having our names written in the Lamb's book of life before the foundation of the world. Salvation *present* consists in the manifestation of Jesus to the soul, whereby he betroths it to himself. And salvation *future* consists in the eternal enjoyment of Christ, when the elect shall sit down to the marriage-supper of the Lamb, and be for ever with the Lord. Now, as none will ever enjoy salvation *future* who have no interest in salvation *past;* in other words, as none will ever be with Christ in eternal glory whose names were not written in the book of life from all eternity; so none will enjoy salvation *future,* who live and die without enjoying salvation *present.* In other words, none will live for ever with Christ in glory who are not betrothed to him in this life by the manifestations of himself to their soul. According to the Jewish custom, the man, at the time of betrothing, gave the bride a piece of silver before witnesses, saying to her, " Receive this piece of silver as a pledge that at such a time you shall become my spouse." And the parties then exchanged rings. This meeting of the espoused parties together, who then saw each other for the first time, is a sweet type of the first meeting of the soul with Jesus. The damsel had heard of the youth, but till then had never seen him; as seeking souls hear of Jesus by the hearing of the ear, before their eyes see him. The vail was upon her face (Gen. xxiv. 65), as the vail is upon the heart (2 Cor. iii. 15), until Jesus rends it in twain from the top to the bottom. The bridegroom gave his betrothed a piece of silver, as a pledge that all he had was hers. And thus Christ gives to the soul, whom he betroths to himself by his own manifestations, a pledge, a token, a testimony, which, in itself, is the first-fruits and assurance of eternal glory. The parties exchanged rings, as pledges of mutual affection and eternal faithfulness. And thus, when Christ reveals himself to the soul in his dying

love, mutual engagements, mutual promises, mutual assurances
and pledges of faithfulness and love pass between the soul and
him. "One shall say, I am the Lord's, and another shall call
himself by the name of Jacob, and another shall subscribe
with his hand unto the Lord." At these seasons, " in the day
of the King's espousals," the language of the soul is, "I sat
down under his shadow with great delight, and his fruit was
sweet to my taste; he brought me to the banqueting-house,
and his banner over me was love."

June 7.

*" Hear now, O Joshua the high priest, thou, and thy fellows
that sit before thee: for they are men wondered at."—*
ZECHARIAH iii. 8.

A sinner saved is a spectacle for angels to contemplate.
As the Apostle says, "We are made a spectacle unto the
world, and to angels and to men." The ancients used to say
that "a good man struggling with difficulties was a sight for
the gods to look at." We may say, with all Christian truth,
that the mysteries of redemption are "things the angels desire
to look into;" and among the mysteries of redemption, what
greater than a redeemed sinner? That a man who deserves,
by sin original and sin actual, nothing but the eternal wrath
of God, should be lifted out of perdition justly merited into
salvation to which he can have no claim, must indeed ever be
a holy wonder. And that you or I should ever have been
fixed on in the electing love of God, ever have been given to
Jesus to redeem, ever quickened by the Spirit to feel our lost,
ruined state, ever blessed with any discovery of the Lord
Jesus Christ and of his saving grace,—this is and ever must
be a matter of holy astonishment here, and will be a theme
for endless praise hereafter. To see a man altogether so
different from what he once was; once so careless, carnal,
ignorant, unconcerned; to see that man now upon his knees

begging for mercy, the tears streaming down his face, his bosom heaving with convulsive sighs, his eyes looking upward that pardon may reach him in his desperate state,— is not that a man to be looked at with wonder and admiration? To see a man preferring one smile from the face of Jesus, and one word from his peace-speaking lips to all the titles, honours, pleasures, and power that the world can bestow; why, surely if there be a wonder upon earth, that man is one. Was not this the very feeling of the disciples when Saul first "preached Christ in the synagogues, that he is the Son of God?" "All that heard him were amazed, and said, Is not this he that persecuted the Church of God?" So we look and wonder, and feel at times a holy joy that he who reigns at God's right hand is ever adding trophies to his immortal crown. And whenever we see any of those near and dear to us in the flesh; be it husband, wife, sister, brother, child, relative, or friend, touched by the finger of this all-conquering Lord, subdued by his grace, and wrought upon by his Spirit, then not only do we look upon such with holy wonder, but with the tenderest affection, mingled with the tears of thankful praise to the God of all our mercies.

June 8.

"I am God, and not man."—Hosea xi. 9.

We speak sometimes of the attributes of God, and we use the words to help our conception. But God, strictly speaking, has no attributes. His attributes are himself. We speak, for instance, of the love of God, but God is love; of the justice of God, but God is just; of the holiness of God, but God is holy; of the purity of God, but God is pure. As he is all love, so he is all justice, all purity, all holiness. Love, then, is infinite, because God is infinite; his very name, his very character, his very nature, his very essence is infinite love.

He would cease to be God if he did not love, and if that love were not as large as himself, as infinite as his own self-existent, incomprehensible essence. The love of the Son of God, as God the Son, is co-equal and co-eternal with the love of the Father ; for the holy Trinity has not three distinct loves, either in date or degree. The Father loves from all eternity; the Holy Ghost loves from all eternity. The love of the Father, of the Son, and of the Holy Ghost, as one, equal, indivisible, infinite Jehovah cannot be otherwise but One. We therefore read of "the love of God," that is the Father (2 Cor. xiii. 14) ; of "the love of the Son" (Gal. ii. 20); and of "the love of the Spirit" (Rom. xv. 30). This love being infinite, can bear with all our infirmities, with all those grievous sins that would, unless that love were boundless, have long ago broken it utterly through. This is beautifully expressed by the prophet : "How shall I give thee up, Ephraim? how shall I deliver thee, Israel? how shall I make thee as Admah? how shall I set thee as Zeboim? mine heart is turned within me, my repentings are kindled together. I will not execute the fierceness of mine anger, I will not return to destroy Ephraim: for I am God, and not man."

June 9.

"For we which have believed do enter into rest."—HEBREWS iv. 3.

To rest is to lean upon something. Is it not? So spiritually. We want to lean upon something. The Lord himself has given us this figure. "Who is this that cometh up from the wilderness, *leaning* upon her Beloved?" The figure of "a rock" on which the Church is built, " the foundation" which God has laid in Zion, points to the same idea, that of leaning or dependence. Now when the soul comes to lean upon Jesus, and depend wholly and solely on him, it enters into the sweetness of the invitation. Have we not leant upon a thousand things? And what have they proved? Broken reeds that have run into our hands, and pierced us. Our own strength and resolutions, the world and the church, sinners and saints, friends and enemies, have they not all proved, more or less, broken reeds? The more we have leant upon them, like a man leaning upon a sword, the more have they pierced our souls. The Lord himself has to wean us from the world, from friends, from enemies, from self, in order to bring us to lean upon himself; and every prop he will remove, sooner or later, that we may lean wholly and solely upon his Person, love, blood, and righteousness.

But there is another idea in the word "rest"—*termination.* When we are walking, running, or in any way moving, we are still going onwards; we have not got to the termination of our journey. But when we come to the *termination* of that we have been doing, we rest. So spiritually. As long as we are engaged in setting up our own righteousness, in labouring under the law, there is no termination of our labours. But when we come to the glorious Person of the Son of God, when we hang upon his atoning blood, dying love, and glorious righteousness, and feel them sweet, precious, and suitable, then there is rest. "We which have believed do enter into rest," says the Apostle. His legal labours are all terminated. His hopes and expectations flow unto, and centre in Jesus — there they end, there they terminate; such a termination as a river finds in the boundless ocean.

June 10.

" The fire shall try every man's work of what sort it is."— 1 Corinthians iii. 13.

The fire which is to prove every man's work of what sort it is, is not merely God's wrath as manifested at the last day;

but his fire as significative of the *fiery trial* which takes place
in this life, and which God mercifully brings upon his people
to burn up their wood, hay, and stubble.   Now it is an inestimable mercy to have all this combustible material burnt
up before we come to a death-bed.   Fiery trials, such as God
sends through afflictions, temptations, distressing feelings, and
painful soul exercises, will burn up the wood, hay, and stubble
which any of his saints may have gathered up as a superstructure.   Guilt pressing upon a man's conscience, the terrors of
the Almighty in a fiery law, his arrows deeply fixed in the
breast and drying up the spirit, fears of death, hell, and
judgment, and the terrible consequences of dying under the
wrath of God, all these are a part of the fiery trial which
burns up the wood, hay, and stubble heaped by Babel
builders on the foundation.   All sink into black ashes before
this fire, which proves what they are, and what a vain refuge
they afford in the day of trouble.

What then stands the fiery trial?   God's work upon the
soul, the faith that he implants by his own Spirit.   It may
be weak; it may be, it must be tried; it may seem at times
scarcely to exist; and yet being of God, it stands every storm,
and lives at last.   A good hope through grace, a hope of
God's own communicating and maintaining,—like a well-tried
anchor, this will stand the storm; like gold and silver, this
will bear the hottest furnace ; lose its dross, but not lose the
pure material, but be refined, purified, and manifested all the
more as genuine metal.   So, too, these " precious stones "
(1 Cor. iii. 12), these heavenly visits, sweet manifestations,
blessed promises, comforting discoveries, and gracious revelations of the Son of God, with the whispers of his dying,
bleeding love,—these heavenly jewels can never be lost and
never be burnt up.   They may be tried, and that keenly and
sharply, but being of God's gift and operation, they are
essentially indestructible.

June 11.

"But they that wait upon the Lord shall renew their strength."—Isaiah xl. 31.

How different the religion of a living soul is from the religion of a dead professor! The religion of a dead professor begins in self, and ends in self; begins in his own wisdom, and ends in his own folly; begins in his own strength, and ends in his own weakness; begins in his own righteousness, and ends in his own damnation. There is in him never any going out of soul after God, no secret dealings with the Lord, no actings of faith upon the divine perfections. But the child of God, though he is often faint, weary, and exhausted with many difficulties, burdens and sorrows; yet when the Lord does shew himself, and renews his strength, he soars aloft, and never ceases to mount up on the wings of faith and love till he penetrates into the very sanctuary of the most High. A living soul never can be satisfied except in living union and communion with the Lord of life and glory. Everything short of that leaves it empty. All the things of time and sense leave a child of God unsatisfied. Nothing but vital union and communion with the Lord of life, to feel his presence, taste his love, enjoy his favour, see his glory— nothing but this will ever satisfy the wants of ransomed and regenerated souls. This the Lord indulges his people with. *"They shall renew their strength."* They shall not be always lying groaning on the ground, not always swooning away through the wounds made by sin, not always chained down by the fetters of the world, not always hunted in their souls like a partridge upon the mountains. There shall be a renewal of their strength; and in their renewal, "they shall mount up with wings as eagles; they shall run, and not be weary; and they shall walk, and not faint."

June 12.

" I will satisfy her poor with bread."—PSALM cxxxii. 15.

WHAT a sweetness there is in the word "satisfy!" The world cannot satisfy you and me. Have we not tried, some of us perhaps for many years, to get some satisfaction from it? But can wife or husband "satisfy" us? Can children or relatives "satisfy" us? Can all the world calls good or great "satisfy" us? Can the pleasures of sin "satisfy" us? Is there not in all an aching void? Do we not reap dissatisfaction and disappointment from everything that is of the creature, and of the flesh? Do we not find that there is little else but sorrow to be reaped from everything in this world? I am sure I find, and have found for some years, that there is little else to be gathered from the world but disappointment, dissatisfaction, "vanity and vexation of spirit." The poor soul looks round upon the world and the creature, upon all the occupations, amusements and relations of life, and finds all one melancholy harvest, so that all it reaps is sorrow, perplexity, and dissatisfaction. Now when a man is brought here, to want satisfaction, something to make him happy, something to fill up the aching void, something to bind up broken bones, bleeding wounds, and leprous sores, and after he has looked at everything, at doctrines, opinions, notions, speculations, forms, rites and ceremonies in religion, at the world with all its charms, and at self with all its varied workings, and found nothing but bitterness of spirit, vexation and trouble in them all, and thus sinks down a miserable wretch, why, then when the Lord opens up to him something of the bread of life, he finds a satisfaction in *that* which he never could gain from any other quarter. And that is the reason why the Lord so afflicts his people; why some carry about with them such weak, suffering tabernacles, why some have so many family troubles, why others are so deeply steeped in poverty, why

others have such rebellious children, and why others are so
exercised with spiritual sorrows that they scarcely know what
will be the end. It is all for one purpose, to make them
miserable out of Christ, dissatisfied except with gospel food;
to render them so wretched and uncomfortable that God
alone can make them happy, and alone can speak consolation
to their troubled minds.

June 13.

"That Christ may dwell in your hearts by faith."—Ephesians iii. 17.

God bade Moses receive from the people oil for the light,
and to set up a candlestick with seven lamps, ever burning
with this oil, to illuminate the holy place. This light was
typical, no doubt, of the Holy Spirit, but as it is only by his
own gracious light that the Lord Jesus is made known, we
may still say, that as Christ dwells in the heart by faith, faith
giving him a place in the bosom, he dwells in the enlightened
understanding of his saints, in the gracious light of his own
manifestations. Have you not seen at times wondrous beauty
in the gospel? Has not a sacred light shone, from time to
time, upon the holy page, when it testified of Christ? Have
you not seen wondrous glory in a free gospel, a gospel that
saves the sinner, and yet magnifies and glorifies the justice of
God; a gospel that reconciles every apparently jarring
attribute, brings justice and mercy to kiss each other, and
makes God to be just, and yet the justifier of him which
believeth in Jesus? Now that light whereby you saw the
glory of God in the face of Jesus Christ, was gospel light;
and as Christ came into the heart in the glory of that light,
he may be said to dwell in the shining light of his own grace.

You may complain, and often bitterly complain, of the
darkness of your mind, and it may seem at times as if you
never had any true light to shine into your soul. But I would

have you carefully observe these two things; first, that the very cause of the darkness which you feel is the presence of light. The Apostle, therefore, says, "But all things that are reproved, (margin, 'discovered,') are made manifest by the light, for whatsoever doth make manifest is light" (Eph. v. 13). Apply these words to your case. Is there not something in you that discovers to you your darkness, and not only discovers, but reproves it, and makes it manifest as a thing to be condemned? This secret something is light, for " whatsoever doth make manifest is light." And as you not only see it, but feel and mourn under it, it is "the light of life" which the Lord promised those should have who follow him. But observe, secondly, that whenever a little light dawns in again upon your soul, in that light you again see the same grace and glory in Christ which you saw in him before. Now, what a proof this is that Christ dwells in the heart by faith, and that the light in which we see him, is the light wherewith he hath enlightened our understanding, and himself dwells in it.

June 14.

" Again, they are minished and brought low through oppression, affliction, and sorrow."—PSALM cvii. 39.

OPPRESSION is the exercise of strength against weakness, the triumph of power over helplessness; so that poverty literally opens the door for oppression. It was so with Hezekiah. When Hezekiah was laid on his bed of sickness, death stared him in the face, and he expected he should be cut off, and cast into perdition. This opened the door for oppression; says he, "Lord, I am *oppressed;* undertake for me." The cold damps of death stood upon his forehead, and despair pressed upon his soul. All his fleshly religion vanished in a moment; and he had but just faith and strength enough to cry out under the gripe of the oppressor's hand at his throat, "Undertake for me" (Isaiah xxxviii. 14).

Oppression then is a weight and a burden superadded to poverty. It is not the same thing as poverty, but it is an additional infliction to poverty. A man may be poor without being oppressed; but when he is poor and oppressed too, it makes the poverty tenfold greater than before. Thus the Lord, in his dealings with his people in order to bring them down, first strips them and makes them poor; and when he has made them poor, and brought them into the depths of soul-destitution, then he causes burdens to lie on them as heavy loads, as though they would sink them into a never-ending hell. But here is the mark of life; the groaning, panting, sighing, and crying of the soul under the burden. The dead in sin feel nothing; the hypocrites in Zion feel nothing; and those that are at ease in a fleshly religion feel nothing. They may have powerful temptations; they may have alarming fears of going to hell; but as to any heavings up of a quickened conscience under the weight of oppression, as to any pouring out of the heart before God, or any giving vent to the distresses of the soul in sighs and cries unto the Lord to have mercy, to speak peace, and bring in a sweet manifestation of pardon and love, and to keep at this day after day, and night after night till the Lord appears; these are exercises unknown to the dead, and peculiar to the living family. A man may "cry for sorrow of heart, and howl for vexation of spirit" (Isaiah lxv. 14), but as the prophet speaks, "they do not cry unto God *with their heart*, when they howl upon their beds" (Hosea vii. 14). But to breathe and pant after the Lord, to groan and sigh because of oppression, to wrestle with the Saviour and give him no rest until he appears in the soul—this inward work is known only to the elect, and is out of the reach of all who have a name to live while they are dead. It is the fruit of the pouring out of the spirit of grace and supplications into their soul; it is the work of the Holy Ghost in the heart, helping its infirmities, and making intercession in it with groanings which cannot be uttered.

June 15.

" A time to kill, and a time to heal."—ECCLESIASTES iii. 3.

ALL through the Christian's life there will be "a time to kill, and a time to heal." We sometimes read in books, and hear in conversation, an experience of this kind—a work of grace commencing with very powerful convictions of sin, and the soul brought almost to the very brink of hell, and then a wonderful revelation of Jesus Christ, a powerful application of his atoning blood to the conscience, and a blessed manifestation of God's love to the soul. And then what follows? If we can credit their account, and they are not deceiving us, or not deceiving themselves, or if we do not misunderstand their statements, they possess an unwavering assurance during the remainder of their sojourn upon earth. Sin and Satan never distress nor wound them; the flesh lies calm and tranquil, like the summer sea, never lashed up by angry gusts into a storm of fretfulness and rebellion; the sea birds of doubt and fear never flit with screams around them, as harbingers of a tempest, but the gale of divine favour gently fills their sail, and wafts them along till they reach the harbour of endless rest. Is this consistent with the Scriptures of truth? Does not the word of God set forth the path of a Christian as one of trial and temptation? Can a living soul pass through many scenes without ever being killed experimentally in his feelings as one of "the flock of slaughter?" Does not a chequered experience run through the whole of a Christian's life? Does the Scripture ever afford us the least warrant to believe that a man can be walking in the footsteps of a tempted, suffering Lord, who continues for months and years together at ease in Zion, without any trouble, exercise, grief, or distress in his soul? David never was there. Jeremiah never was there. Paul never was there. Heman never was there. Asaph never was there. You will find that no saints of God, whose experience is left on record in the Bible, ever were there; but their path was one of change and vicissitude; sometimes down, sometimes up, sometimes mourning, sometimes rejoicing, but never long together in one unvaried spot. The Spirit of the Lord, in carrying on this grand work in the hearts of God's people, will be continually operating in two distinct ways upon their souls. Jeremiah was a prophet of the Lord, and he was "set over the nations and over the kingdoms to root out, and to pull down, and to destroy, and to throw down"—thus ran one part of his commission: "to build and to plant"—that was the second part of his office. These two distinct operations were to run through the whole of his mission; they were "the burden of the Lord," laid upon him at his first call to the prophetical office, and they continued during the whole of his ministry, a space of more than forty years. Did he, then, merely on one occasion pull down, and on one occasion build up? Was not the whole of his ministration, as evidenced in the prophecies that are contained in the book that bears his name, a continual pulling down with one hand, and building up with the other? So is it then with the ministration of the Spirit of the Lord in a vessel of mercy. He is continually killing, continually healing, continually casting down, continually raising up, now laying the soul low in the dust of self-abasement, and now building it up sweetly in Christ.

June 16.

"*In those days, and in that time, saith the Lord, the iniquity of Israel shall be sought for, and there shall be none; and the sins of Judah, and they shall not be found: for I will pardon them whom I reserve.*"—JEREMIAH l. 20.

SOME have feared lest in the great day their sins should be

brought to light, and they put to shame by the exposure of
their crimes to open view. But that will not be the case with
the dear family of God. We read indeed that "many of
them that sleep in the dust of the earth shall awake;" and
whilst some awake "to everlasting life," others will awake
"to shame and everlasting contempt," because their sins will
be remembered and brought against them as evidences of
their just condemnation. But the wise, who "shall shine as
the brightness of the firmament," will rise to glory and honour
and immortality, and not one of their sins will be remembered,
charged, or brought against them. They will stand arrayed
in Christ's perfect righteousness and washed in his blood,
and will appear before the throne of God without spot or
blemish. We can scarcely bear the recollection of our sins
now. But what would become of us if the ghost of one un-
buried sin could flit before our eyes in the day when the
Lord maketh up his jewels? If any one sin of the Lamb's
wife could be remembered or brought against her, where
would be the voice which John heard in Revelation, as "the
voice of a great multitude, as the voice of many waters, and
as the voice of mighty thunderings, saying, Alleluia; for the
Lord God omnipotent reigneth?" Now what was this voice?
"Let us be glad and rejoice, and give honour to him; for the
marriage of the Lamb is come, and his wife hath made herself
ready. And to her was granted that she should be arrayed
in fine linen, clean and white: for the fine linen is the
righteousness of saints" (Rev. xix. 7, 8). But suppose that
any of the past transgressions of the Lamb's wife could be
brought against her on that marriage day, any one instance
of unfaithfulness to her plighted troth, would it not be suf-
ficent to prevent the marriage, mar the wedding supper, and
drive the bride away for very shame? No, there is no truth
in God's word more certain than the complete forgiveness of
sins, and the presentation of the Church to Christ at the

great day faultless before the presence of his glory, with exceeding joy.

June 17.

"And it shall come to pass in that day, that the great trumpet shall be blown, and they shall come which were ready to perish in the land of Assyria, and the outcasts in the land of Egypt, and shall worship the Lord in the holy mount at Jerusalem."—Isaiah xxvii. 13.

CALLED by the sounding of the great trumpet, the perishing and outcasts "come." And what do they when they come? Do they trifle with sin, mock God, and abuse his grace? We read not so. They *"worship the Lord in the holy mount at Jerusalem."* They worship him in spirit and in truth; they worship him in the beauty of holiness. With purified hearts, purged consciences, and spiritual affections, they fall down before him, and their souls are impressed with a sense of the greatness of his love. They had no such heavenly feelings before; they could not therefore worship the Three-One God in the holy mount nor at Jerusalem. The great trumpet had not been blown, the jubilee had not come, the chains had not been knocked off, the shackles not loosed, and the prison-gates not thrown open; they could not therefore worship God freely, fully and calmly, with liberty of access and freedom of spirit.

But *where* do they worship him? *"In the holy mount."* The holy mount we may understand to signify spiritually Mount Zion, the place where Jesus sits in glory. This is the ancient declaration of the Father, "Yet have I set my king upon my holy hill of Zion." Here Jesus ever sits with love in his heart, grace in his lips, and the gospel in his hands. He sits on a holy hill, sways a holy sceptre, and rules in the hearts of a holy people. Men talk much of holiness; and indeed they may well talk of it, for it is a most

solemn declaration, that " without holiness no man shall see
the Lord." But what sort of holiness are most men seeking
after? A holiness of the flesh, a sanctity of the creature.
They must do this and abstain from that; and if they do
this and abstain from that, then they are holy. So many
prayers must be said, so many chapters read, so many duties
done. This is a Popish holiness, the sanctified austerity of
a St. Dominic, not that holiness without which no man shall
see the Lord. That is of a very different nature—different
every way, in source, way, means, and end. The only true
holiness is that which is produced by the Spirit of God in the
soul. Other source or fountain there is none. And how
does he produce it? By the law or the gospel? By the
gospel, certainly. When the great trumpet of jubilee sounds
in the soul, when it listens to the notes, and comes obedient
to its call, it is to worship the Lord in his holy mount at
Jerusalem. True holiness is then produced in the soul, for
then there are given spiritual desires, spiritual affections,
spiritual views, spiritual feelings, and spiritual hearts. This
is the holiness which is wrought in the soul by the Spirit of
God, and without which no man shall see the Lord.

June 18.

*" But, beloved, we are persuaded better things of you, and
things that accompany salvation, though we thus speak."*—
HEBREWS vi. 9.

WHAT is *" salvation?"* In looking at salvation, we must
consider it in two points of view; salvation wrought out *for*
us, and salvation wrought out *in* us. Salvation was wrought
out *for* the Church by the finished work of the Son of God,
when he cried with expiring breath, "It is finished." The
salvation of " the remnant according to the election of grace "
was then completely accomplished, so that nothing could be

added to, or taken from it; for "by one offering he hath perfected for ever them that are sanctified;" and thus the Church stands complete in Christ, "without spot, or wrinkle, or any such thing."

But there is a salvation which is wrought out *in* the soul; the manifestation and application of that salvation which Jesus wrought out by his sufferings, blood-shedding, and death; and this we can only know experimentally so far as the blessed Spirit brings it into our hearts, and seals it there with holy unction and heavenly savour.

But all the people of God cannot feel sure they have this salvation as an experimental reality; doubts, fears, darkness, and temptations becloud their path; Satan hurls his fiery darts into their souls; and they are often unable to realise their interest in the Lord Jesus Christ and his salvation. They do not doubt that the Lord Jesus is the Saviour of those that believe; they know that there is no other refuge for their guilty souls but the blood of the Lamb. They are effectually stripped from cleaving to a covenant of works; they are not running after things that cannot profit them, nor hiding their heads in lying refuges; from all these things they are effectually cut off by a work of grace on their souls. But through the unbelief of their hearts, the deadness of their frames, the barrenness of their souls, and the various temptations they are exercised with, they fear they have not the marks of God's family, and are not able to realise their interest in the love and blood of the Lamb. The Apostle, therefore, speaks of "things that accompany salvation;" that is, certain marks and signs, certain clear and indubitable tokens of the work of grace on the soul. And, speaking to the Hebrews, he says for their comfort and encouragement, "We are persuaded," whatever be your doubts and fears, whatever the darkness of your mind, however exercised with sharp and severe temptations, "we are persuaded" you are

in possession of those " better things," of those " things that
accompany salvation;" and that this salvation is therefore
eternally yours.

June 19.

*" But as many as received him, to them gave he power to
become the sons of God, even to them that believe on his name."—*
JOHN i. 12.

WHEREVER faith is given to the soul to "receive" Christ,
there will be mingled with this faith, and blessedly accompanying it, *love* to the Lord of life and glory; and sometimes
we may know the existence of faith when we cannot see it,
by discerning the secret workings and actings of love towards
that Saviour, in whom God has enabled us to believe. There
will be, from time to time, in living souls a flowing forth of
affection towards Jesus. From time to time, he gives the
soul a glimpse of his Person; he shews himself, as the
Scripture speaks, "through the lattice;" passing perhaps
hastily by, but giving such a transient glimpse of the beauty
of his Person, the excellency of his finished work, dying love,
and atoning blood as ravishes the heart, and secretly draws
forth every affection of the soul, so that there is a following
hard after him, and a going out of the desires of the soul
towards him. Thus, sometimes as we lie upon our bed, as
we are engaged in our business, as we are occupied in our
several pursuits of life; or at other times under the word, or
reading the Scripture, the Lord is pleased secretly to work in
the heart, and there is a melting down at the feet of Jesus, or
a secret, soft, gentle going forth of love and affection towards
him, whereby the soul prefers him before thousands of gold
and silver, and desires nothing so much as the inward manifestations of his love, grace, and blood.

And thus a living soul "receives" Christ; not merely as
driven by necessity, but as also drawn by affection. He does

not receive Christ, merely as a way of escape from "the wrath to come," merely as a something to save the soul from "the worm that dieth not, and the fire that is not quenched;" but mingled with necessity, sweetly and powerfully combined with it, and intimately and intricately working with it, there is the flowing forth of genuine affection and undissembled love, that goes out to him as the only object worthy our heart's affection, our spirit's worship, and our soul's desire. And we cannot say that less than this comes up to the meaning of the Scripture expression—" to receive Christ."

June 20.

"As ye have therefore received Christ Jesus the Lord, so walk ye in him: rooted and built up in him, and stablished in the faith, as ye have been taught, abounding therein with thanksgiving."—Colossians ii. 6, 7.

It is a goodly sight to see a noble tree; and we may gather from the strength of the tree the strength of the soil, for only in deep and good soil will such trees grow. But look at the trees of righteousness, the planting of the Lord, that he may be glorified ! What depth and richness there is in the heavenly soil in which they are planted ! View the true, real, and eternal Sonship, the glorious Deity of Jesus, and view that Deity in union with his suffering humanity ! What soil is there ! What breadth to hold thousands and thousands of noble trees ! What depth for them to root in ! What fertility to clothe them with verdure and load them with fruit ! The most fertile natural soils may be exhausted, but this is inexhaustible. For can Deity be exhausted ? Is it not its very nature to be infinite ? And when we view what our most blessed Lord now is at the right hand of God, what a perfect and complete Saviour he is for the soul to lay hold of ! Again, as the more deeply and widely that a tree spreads its roots into the soil, the more nourishment does it suck up; so it is with a believing heart. The more Christ is laid hold of by faith, the more the soul roots down into him; and the firmer hold it takes of him, and the more deeply it roots into him, the stronger it stands, and the more heavenly nourishment it draws out of his fulness. This is being "rooted in Christ." A religion must always be a shallow, deceptive, and ruinous religion if it has not Christ to root in, for then it must be rooted in self. But if it is planted and rooted in Christ, then there is a sufficiency, a suitability, a glorious fulness in him in which the soul may take the deepest root, and not only for time but for eternity; for such a faith can never be confounded, such a love never perish, and such a hope be never put to shame.

June 21.

" *Thy word is a lamp unto my feet, and a light unto my path.*"—PSALM cxix. 105.

O what a change takes place in the soul's feelings toward the word of God when God is pleased to quicken it into divine life! Nor, indeed, need we wonder why there is such a marked revolution in our feelings toward it; for it is by the power of God's word upon the heart that this wondrous change is effected. "Of his own will begat he us with the word of truth" (James i. 18). Other books may instruct or amuse; they may feed the intellect, charm the imagination, and cultivate the mind. But what more can they do? I do not mean by this to despise or set aside every other book but the Bible, for without books society itself, as at present constituted, could not exist; and to burn every book would be to throw us back into the barbarism of the Middle Ages. Let, then, books have their place as regards this life; but what can they do for us as regards the life to come? What

can our renowned authors, our choice classics, our learned
historians, our great dramatists, or our eloquent poets do for
the soul in seasons of affliction and distress? How powerless
all human writings are in these circumstances. Is it not as
Hart well says,

> " What balm could wretches ever find
> In wit, to heal affliction?
> Or who can cure a troubled mind
> With all the pomp of diction?"

Now here is the blessedness of the word of God, that when
everything else fails, *that* comes to our aid under all circumstances, so that we can never sink so low as to get beyond
the reach of some promise in the word of truth. We may
come, and most probably shall come, to a spot where everything else will fail and give way but the word of God which
for ever is settled in heaven. Then the word of grace and
truth which reaches down to the lowest case, the word of
promise upon which the Lord causes the soul to hope, will
still turn towards us a friendly smile, and still encourage us
under all circumstances to call upon the name of the Lord,
and to hang upon his faithfulness who hath said, "Heaven
and earth shall pass away, but my words shall not pass away."
Thus, under circumstances the most trying to flesh and blood,
where nature stands aghast and reason fails, there the word
of God will come in as a counsellor to drop in friendly advice,
as a companion to cheer and support the mind by its tender
sympathy, and as a friend to speak to the heart with a loving,
affectionate voice. We need not wonder, then, how the word
of God has been prized in all ages by the family of God; for
it is written with such infinite wisdom, that it meets every
case, suits every circumstance, fills up every aching void, and
is adapted to every condition of life and every state both of
body and soul.

June 22.

" He led him about, he instructed him, he kept him as the apple of his eye."—DEUTERONOMY xxxii. 10.

" HE led them *about."* This was true literally. What a circuitous, tangled, backward and forward route was that of the children of Israel in the wilderness! Yet every step was under God's direction; they never moved till the cloudy pillar led the way.

But how does the Lord lead about in *grace ?* By leading his Israel into a path of which they do not see the end. One turn of the road hides the next. I have read that you may make a road with a curve at every quarter of a mile, and yet in a hundred miles the distance will not be so much as a mile more than a perfectly straight line. So in grace. The length of the road swallows up the turnings. But these turnings make the road seem more round about than it really is. All before us is hidden. For instance, when the Lord begins a work of grace, he brings convictions of sin, opens up the spirituality of the law, makes the soul feel guilty, guilty, guilty in every thought, word, and deed. But does a man in that condition know what the Lord is about? Can he clearly trace out the work of God upon his soul ? Is he able to say, " This, this *is* the work of God upon my heart ? " For the most part, he knows not what is the matter with him ; why he is so distressed ; why he can take no rest ; why the things of eternity keep rolling in upon his soul ; why he stands in continual dread of the wrath to come ; why his mind is so exercised with thoughts upon God ; why he feels condemnation, bondage, and misery. Nor even when the Lord is pleased to raise him up to some hope, to apply some sweet promise to his soul, to encourage him in various ways under the ministry of the word, can he often take the full comfort of it. He may for a time, but it is soon gone, and he can scarcely believe it to be real. Unbelief suggests that it did not come exactly in the right way, or did not last long enough, or did not go deep enough, or was not just such as he has heard others speak of; and so he is filled with doubts, fears, and anxieties whether it was really from the Lord. But when God leads him on a step further; opens up the gospel, reveals Christ, drops into his heart some sweet testimony, gives him some blessed discovery of his interest in the Lord Jesus, and seals it with a divine witness in his heart, this banishes all his doubts and fears, and fills his soul with joy and peace. Yet even after this, when the sweet feeling is gone, he may sink again very low, and may question the reality of the revelation he has enjoyed. All this is "leading about;" for one turn of the road hides the other.

June 23.

"Blessed is the man whose strength is in thee; in whose heart are the ways of them. Who passing through the valley of Baca make it a well; the rain also filleth the pools."—Psalm lxxxiv. 5, 6.

David casts a glimpse here at those pilgrims who were taking their upward journey to worship God in Zion. He marks their road, and takes occasion to spiritualize it; for he says, "In whose heart," in whose experience, in whose soul, "are the ways" of these pilgrims Zionward.

What are these "ways?" It is this, that "passing through the valley of Baca, they make it a well." This valley of Baca appears to have been a very perilous pass, through which pilgrims journeyed toward Jerusalem; and on account of the difficulties, dangers, and sufferings that they met with, it was named "the valley of Baca," or "the valley of weeping," "the vale of tears."

But the Psalmist says, "Blessed is the man in whose heart are the ways of them, who passing through the valley of Baca

make it a well." Here is the distinctive character of the true
pilgrim. Not that he is journeying merely through the
"valley of Baca;" not that his eyes are drowned in tears;
not that his heart is filled with sorrows; not that his soul is
cut with temptations; not that his mind is tried by suffering.
But this is his distinctive feature—he "makes it a well."
This the ungodly know nothing of; this the professing
world, for the most part, are entirely unacquainted with; but
this is the secret which " no fowl knoweth, and which the
vulture's eye hath not seen."

One feature of the " valley of Baca " was, that the burning
sun above, and the parched ground beneath, at the time of
year when the pilgrims travelled, made the whole valley arid
and dry. But "they made it a well." There were wells dug
in this valley of Baca for the pilgrims to slake their thirst at.
And David, looking at these wells dug for the pilgrims,
applies them spiritually to the refreshment that the Lord's
people meet with in their course Zionward. "Make it a
well;" that is, there are from time to time sweet refresh-
ments in this valley of tears; there are bubblings up of
divine consolation; there are fountains of living waters,
streams of heavenly pleasures.

I remember a friend of mine telling me, that once while
journeying through one of the deserts in Asia, he and his
companions came to a well; and their disappointment when
they found the well was dry he said no language could
depict; their grief and trouble when, after hours' travelling,
they came at night to encamp by the well, and found that
the sun had dried it up, were indeed most acute. As, therefore, none but pilgrims through the dry and parched valley
could adequately feel the sweetness of the natural well; so
none but spiritual pilgrims, afflicted, exercised, and harassed,
can appreciate the sweetness of the " pure water of life " with
which the Lord at times refreshes the soul.

June 24.

" *They go from strength to strength.*"—Psalm lxxxiv. 7.

" *They go from strength to strength.*" It is in the margin, "from company to company." I rather think, that the meaning implied is, " they go from halting place to halting place." There were certain fixed spots where the whole company rested at night; as we read, when the infant Jesus tarried at Jerusalem, his parents knew it not: they supposed that he was " in the company;" that is, had gone on with the travelling pilgrims; but when night came, and they looked for him, he was not there.

These halting places were certain spots where the caravan of the travelling pilgrims rested at night; by these successive haltings their strength was recruited, and they were enabled to bear the long journey, rising in the morning refreshed with their night's rest.

The Psalmist viewing it spiritually says, " They go from strength to strength." At each halting place they received fresh strength to pursue their journey onward. And is not this true in grace? There are halting places in the divine life, spots of rest, where the true pilgrims renew their strength. For instance, every manifestation of the Lord is a communication of divine strength, a recruiting place, where the soul renews its strength to travel onward. Every promise that comes with sweet power is another halting place where the traveller may rest. Every discovery of interest in Christ; every glimpse of the grace and glory of Jesus; every word from the Lord's lips; every smile from the Lord's face; every token for good; every thing that encourages, supports, blesses, and comforts the soul, enabling it to go onwards towards its heavenly home, is a halting place, where the pilgrim rests, and where he recruits his weary limbs. And where can we rest, except where God rests? But does not God " rest in his love?" And can we rest anywhere short of God's love shed abroad in our heart? Does not God rest in his dear Son? Did not this voice come from the excellent glory, "This is my beloved Son, in whom I am well pleased?" All the satisfaction of God centres in Jesus; all the delight of the Father rests in the Son of his love. "Behold my servant, whom I uphold; mine elect, in whom my soul delighteth!" Can we then rest anywhere but where God rests? Is it not spiritually with us as with the Israelites of old? When the cloud tarried, they tarried; when the cloud went, they went; when the cloud moved onward, they followed it; and when the cloud stopped, they halted, and rested beneath its shadow.

June 25.

"*Every one of them in Zion appeareth before God.*"—Psalm lxxxiv. 7.

As the Lord is true, no spiritual pilgrim will ever fall and die in the valley of Baca. Some may fear that through temptation their strong passions or boiling lusts will one day break out and destroy them. No, not if they are pilgrims. "Every one of them in Zion appeareth before God." Others may think they never shall have a testimony; they never shall read their name clearly in the Book of Life; the Lord will never appear in their heart or bless their soul; they never shall be able to say, "Abba, Father." If Jesus is theirs, they shall. But are they spiritual pilgrims? Do they find it a vale of tears? Are their faces Zionward? Have they come out of the world? Do they sometimes make the valley of Baca a well? And does the rain fill the pools? And have they ever had strength made perfect in weakness? Then every one of them will appear before God in Zion. Blessed end! Sweet accomplishment of the pilgrim's hopes, desires, and expectations! The crowning blessing of all that God has to

bestow! "Every one of them appeareth before God," washed
in the Saviour's blood, clothed in the Redeemer's righteousness, adorned with all the graces of the Spirit, and made meet
for the inheritance of the saints in light. No weeping then!
The valley of Baca is passed, and tears wiped from off all
faces. No thorns to lacerate the weary feet there; no prowling wild beasts to seize the unwary traveller there; no roving
banditti to surprise stragglers there; no doubts and fears
and cutting sorrows to grieve, perplex, and burden them
there. Safe in Zion, safe in the Redeemer's bosom, safe in
their Husband's arms, safe before the throne, every one of
them appeareth before God in glory.

June 26.

"Blessed are the poor in spirit."—Matthew v. 3.

Spiritual poverty is a miserable feeling of soul-emptiness
before God, an inward sinking sensation that there is nothing
in our hearts spiritually good, nothing which can deliver us
from the justly merited wrath of God, or save us from the
lowest hell. And intimately blended with the poignant feelings of guilt and condemnation, there is a spiritual consciousness that there is such a thing enjoyed by the elect as the
Spirit of adoption, that there are such sweet realities as divine
manifestations, that the blood of Jesus Christ is sprinkled by
the Holy Ghost upon the consciences of the redeemed to
cleanse them from all guilt and filth. And thus by compar-
ing its own wants with their blessings, and having an inward
light wherein the truth of God's word is seen, and an inward
life whereby it is felt, a soul wading in the depths of spiritual
poverty, is brought to feel that it must be the manifestation of
the light of God's countenance which can alone deliver;
that it must be the testimony of God spoken by his own lips
to the heart that alone can save ; and that the want of this is
the want of everything that can manifest it to be a vessel of

mercy here, and fit it for, as well as carry it into, eternal glory and bliss hereafter.

To be poor, then, is to have this wretched emptiness of spirit, this nakedness and destitution of soul before God. Nor is it, perhaps, ever more deeply felt than in the lonely watches of the night, when no eye can see, nor ear hear, but the eye and ear of Jehovah; in these solemn moments of deep recollection, when the stillness and darkness around us are but the counterpart of the stillness and darkness of the soul, he that is spiritually poor often feels how empty he is of everything heavenly and divine, a sinking wretch without a grain of godliness; and without drawing too rigid a line of exclusion, we may unhesitatingly say that he who has never thus known what it is to groan before the Lord with break-ings-forth of heart as a needy, naked wretch, he that has never felt his miserable destitution and emptiness before the eyes of a heart-searching God, has not yet experienced what it is to be spiritually poor.

June 27.

"And patience of hope."—1 Thessalonians i. 3.

What is meant by the expression "patience?" It means *endurance;* as though hope had to endure, faith to work, and love to labour. It is the "patience of hope" that proves its reality and genuineness. Hope does not go forward fighting and cutting its way. Hope is like a quiet sufferer, patiently bearing what comes upon it. Hope is manifested in endur-ing, as faith is manifested in acting. For instance : when the Lord hides his face, when testimonies sink out of sight, when signs are not seen, when Satan tempts, when the work of grace upon the soul seems to be all obscured, and in conse-quence a feeling of despondency begins to set in, then the "patience of hope" is needed to endure all things—not to give way, but to maintain its hold. It acts in the same

way, according to the beautiful figure of Paul, as the anchor
holds the ship. What is the main value, the chief requisite
in the cable that holds the anchor? Is it not *endurance?*
The cable *does* nothing; it simply endures. It does not make
a great ado in the water; its only good quality, the only quality
wanted in it, is strength to endure, not to break. When the
waves rise, the billows beat, the storm blows, and the tide
runs strongly, then the work of the cable is not to part from
the anchor, not to break, but firmly to maintain the hold it
has once taken. And thus with the anchor too. It does
nothing, and is wanted to do nothing. To hold fast is all its
work and all its excellence. Thus it is with a hope in a
sinner's breast. Has the Lord ever shewn himself gracious
unto him? Has the Lord ever made himself precious to his
soul? ever dropped a testimony into his conscience? ever
spoken with power to his heart? Has his soul ever felt the
Spirit inwardly testifying that he is one of God's people?
Then his hope is manifested by enduring patiently everything
that is brought against it to crush it, and if God did not keep,
utterly to destroy it.

June 28.

"*And he is the propitiation for our sins.*"—i John ii. 2.

What is "propitiation?" By propitiation we are to understand, a sacrifice acceptable to Jehovah; by which God, or rather
the attributes of God are propitiated; whereby God can be
favourable; whereby mercy, grace, and pardon can freely flow
forth. Now sin, and the law condemning sin, barred out, barred
back, the favour of God. They were the opposing obstacle
to the love of God. For God cannot, as God, love sin and
sinners; therefore, the sin of man, and the holy law of God,
the transcript of his infinite and eternal purity barred back,
so to speak, the favour of God. It was needful, then, that
this barrier should be removed, that a channel might be

provided, through which the grace, favour, and mercy of
God might flow: in a word, that sin might be blotted out,
and that the law might be accomplished and fulfilled in all
its strict requirements, that God "might be just," retaining
every righteous attribute, not sacrificing one of his holy
perfections—and yet, though just, perfectly just, "the justifier
of him which believeth in Jesus." But how was this to be
effected? No seraph, no bright angel could ever have
devised a way. It lay locked up in the bosom of the Three-
One God from everlasting; and that was, that the only-
begotten Son of God, who lay in the bosom of the Father
from all eternity, "the brightness of his glory, and the
express image of his Person," should become a bleeding
Lamb, "the Lamb slain from before the foundation of the
world;" that he should take into union with his own divine
Person a human nature, "the flesh and blood of the children,"
pure, spotless, and holy, and offer up that nature, that body
which God prepared for him, a holy sacrifice. When he
came into the world, the sacrifice began; and every holy
thought, every holy word, and every holy action, in suffering
and performing, that passed through the heart, dropped from
the lips, or was performed by the hands of the only-begotten
Son of God, when he was upon earth, was part of that
sacrifice. But the grand consummation of it (the offering
up of that body especially) was, when it was nailed to the
accursed tree, and blood was shed to put away sin. Now,
this is the propitiation, the redemption, the sacrifice, the way,
the only way, whereby sin is expiated; the way, the only
way, whereby sin is pardoned.

But in order that this blessed sacrifice and atoning propitiation may pass over to us; that its value, validity, efficacy,
and blessedness may be felt in our consciences, there must
be that wrought in our souls whereby it is embraced. The
only salvation for our souls is the propitiation made by Jesus

upon Calvary's tree. There is no other sacrifice for sin but that. But how is that to pass into our hearts? How is the efficacy of this atoning sacrifice to be made personally ours? It is by faith. Does not the Holy Ghost declare this by the mouth of the Apostle? He says, "Whom God hath set forth to be a propitiation *through faith in his blood.*"

Now, this is the turning point in the soul's salvation. This is the grand point to have decided in a man's conscience before God. This is the Cape to be doubled by every one that sets forth upon the sea of salvation. Before he can double this Cape, he is driven back by the storms, and tossed by the winds; and he often fears lest he should be engulphed in the billows. But when, by living faith, he is enabled to double this Cape, to see the propitiation through the blood of the Lamb, to feel his very heart and soul going out after, and leaning upon, and feeling a measure of solid rest and peace in the blood of the sacrifice offered upon Calvary—then he has doubled the Cape of Good Hope, then he has passed into the Pacific Ocean from the stormy Atlantic, and then he begins to receive into his conscience a measure of the favour and grace of the Lord God Almighty.

June 29.

"Jesus Christ himself being the chief corner stone."— EPHESIANS ii. 20.

THE meaning of this expression, which frequently occurs in the New Testament, is, we think, often misunderstood. It is taken in the first instance from the declaration concerning our Lord in the Psalms, which he in the gospels (Mark xii. 10; Luke xx. 17) specially claimed and appropriated to himself: "The stone which the builders refused is become the head-stone of the corner" (Psalm cxviii. 22). "The head of the corner," or "the chief corner stone," the meaning of both expressions being one and the same, signifies not the stone which stands at the top of the building, uniting the corners of the two walls just under the roof, but the broad foundation stone, which is firmly fixed at the very bottom; and it is called the " corner stone" or the " head" or " chief of the corner," because being laid as a huge and broad stone for a foundation of the whole building, each wall meets upon it at the corners, it equally supporting and upholding them all.   The two walls which thus meet together represent Jew and Gentile; but each of these walls equally rests upon the broad foundation stone which is common to both, and not only supports them separately, but unites them together at the corner, where each meets and rests upon it.   It is the expression " head" which has caused the misapprehension of the word " corner stone" to which we have alluded; but the word " head" in Hebrew properly signifies the first or chief; and thus as the foundation is not only the chief stone as supporting the whole, but the first which is laid, so our gracious Lord is not only chief in dignity, but was laid first in place, for the Church was chosen in him.   In all things he must have the pre-eminence.   Thus he is first in dignity, as the Son of the Father in truth and love; first in choice, God choosing the elect in him; first in suffering, for what sorrows were like his sorrows? first in resurrection, for he is " the first-fruits of them that slept; " first in power, for "all power is given unto him in heaven and in earth;" first in glory, for he is gone before to prepare a place for his people; and we may well add, he is first in their hearts and affections, for he that loveth father or mother, son or daughter, more than him is not worthy of him.

June 30.

" Perplexed, but not in despair."—2 CORINTHIANS iv. 8.

OH! what a mercy, amidst every degree of inward or outward perplexity, to be out of the reach of Giant Despair;

not to be shut up in the iron cage; not to be abandoned, as Judas or Ahithophel, to utter desperation and suicide, and, after a long life of profession, concerning faith to make awful shipwreck! Now the child of God, with all his doubts, fears, sinkings, misgivings, and trying perplexities is never really and truly in despair. He may tread so near the borders of that black country that it may almost be debateable land whether he is walking in despair or upon the borders of it; for I believe many children of God have at times come to the solemn conclusion that there is no hope for them, for they cannot see how they can be saved or have their aggravated sins pardoned. And though this be not black despair, nor such utter, irremediable desperation as seized Saul and Judas, for there still is a "Who can tell?" yet it certainly is walking very near the borders of that dark and terrible land. I cannot tell, nor do I believe any can, how low a child of God may sink, or how long he may continue under the terrors of the Almighty; but we have the warrant of God's word to believe that he is never given up to utter despair, for the Lord holds up his feet from falling into that terrible pit, and being cast into that sea to which there is neither bottom nor shore.

July 1.

"*As the hart panteth after the water brooks, so panteth my soul after thee, O God.*"—Psalm xlii. 1.

What a striking figure has David made use of in these words. Conceive a wounded stag, with the arrow in his flank or pursued by a crowd of hunters and hounds, all eager to pull him down; conceive him to have run for some space of time under a burning sun and over heaps of sand; and conceive that at a distance this poor wounded or hunted animal sees water gently flowing along. Oh, how it pants! How its heaving sides gasp, and how it longs for the cooling

stream, not only that it may drink large draughts of the
fresh waters and lave its panting flanks and weary, parched
limbs, but, by swimming across, may haply escape the dogs
and hunters at its heels. How strong, how striking the
figure. And yet strong as it is, how earnestly does David
employ it to set forth the panting of his soul after God. We
cannot, perhaps, rise up into the fulness of this figure ; we
cannot, we dare not lay our feelings stretched fully out side
by side with his, or use the same burning, vehement, ardent
expressions. But we may at least see from them what the
saints of God have experienced in times of temptation and
trial in days of old ; and we may in some measure compare
the feelings of our soul with theirs—sometimes to fill us
with shame and confusion at our short-comings, sometimes
to stimulate and encourage us so far as we experience a
degree of similar teachings ; for these things are written for
our instruction, "upon whom the ends of the world are
come." Thus in various ways and to various ends we may,
with God's help and blessing, look at and into such expressions as we find in the words of David, and in the fear of
God search our hearts to see if we can find anything there
corresponding to the work of grace that the Holy Ghost
describes as existing in his soul. Nor be utterly cast down
nor wholly discouraged if you cannot find a full or close
similarity. Can you find *any* ? If so, take encouragement,
for the Lord despises not the day of small things. It is his
own work upon the heart and his own work alone to which
he has regard, as David felt when he said, "The Lord will
perfect that which concerneth me : thy mercy, O Lord,
endureth for ever ; forsake not the works of thine own
hands" (Psalm cxxxviii. 8). And that work will ever be a
copy in full or in miniature, a complete or reduced photograph, of the work of grace described in the Scripture as
carried on by the Spirit in the hearts of God's saints of old.

July 2.

" For the Jews require a sign, and the Greeks seek after wisdom : but we preach Christ crucified, unto the Jews a stumblingblock, and unto the Greeks foolishness."—1 CORINTH-IANS i. 22, 23.

THE mystery of the cross can be received only by faith. To the Jews it was a stumblingblock, and to the Greeks foolishness, but to those who are called, both Jews and Greeks, it is the power of God and the wisdom of God. When, then, we can believe that the Son of God took part of our flesh and blood out of love and compassion for our souls ; that there being no other way which even heaven itself could devise, no other means that the wisdom of God could contrive whereby sinners could be saved, but by the death of the cross, then the mystery shines forth with unspeakable lustre and glory. The shame, the ignominy, what the Apóstle calls the "weakness" and "foolishness" of the cross disappear, swallowed up in a flood of surpassing grace; and faith views it as a glorious scheme of God's own devising, and of the Son of God's approving and accomplishing. Viewed in this light how glorious it appears, that by suffering in our nature all the penalties of our sin, Jesus should redeem us from the lowest hell and raise us up to the highest heaven. How full of unspeakable wisdom was that plan whereby he united God and man by himself becoming God-man; empowering poor worms of earth to soar above the skies and live for ever in the presence of him who is a consuming fire. How glorious is that scheme whereby reconciling aliens and enemies unto his heavenly Father, he summons them, when death cuts their mortal thread, to mount up into an eternity of bliss, there to view face to face the great and glorious I AM; to be for ever enwrapped in the blaze of Deity, and ever folded in the arms of a Triune

God. It is this blessed end, this reward of the Redeemer's
sufferings, bloodshedding and death, which lifts our view
beyond the depths of the fall and the misery of sin, as we
see and feel it in this miserable world. It is this view by
faith of the glory which shall be revealed which enables us
to see what wisdom and mercy were in the heart of God
when he permitted the Adam fall to take place. It is as if
we could see the glory of God breaking forth through it in
all the splendour of atoning blood and dying love, securing
to guilty man the joys of salvation, and bringing to God an
eternal revenue of praise.

July 3.

*" But God forbid that I should glory, save in the cross of
our Lord Jesus Christ, by whom the world is crucified unto
me, and I unto the world."*—GALATIANS vi. 14.

AN experimental knowledge of crucifixion with his crucified
Lord made Paul preach the cross, not only in its power to
save, but in its power to sanctify. But as then, so now, this
preaching of the cross, not only as the meritorious cause of
all salvation, but as the instrumental cause of all sanctification, is "to them that perish foolishness." As men have
found out some other way of salvation than by the blood
of the cross, so have they discovered some other way of
holiness than by the power of the cross; or rather have
altogether set aside obedience, fruitfulness, self-denial, mortification of the deeds of the body, crucifixion of the flesh and
of the world. Extremes are said to meet; and certainly
men of most opposite sentiments may unite in despising the
cross and counting it foolishness. The Arminian despises
it for justification, and the Antinomian for sanctification.
" Believe and be holy," is as strange a sound to the latter as
" Believe and be saved " to the former. But, " Without
holiness no man shall see the Lord," is as much written on

the portal of life as, "By grace are ye saved through faith."
Through the cross, that is, through union and communion
with him who suffered upon it, not only is there a fountain
opened for all sin, but for all uncleanness. Blood and water
gushed from the side of Jesus when pierced by the Roman
spear.

> "This fountain so dear, he'll freely impart;
> Unlock'd by the spear, it gushed from the heart,
> With blood and with water; the first to atone,
> To cleanse us the latter; the fountain's but one."

"All my springs are in thee," said the man after God's own
heart; and well may we re-echo his words. All our springs,
not only of pardon and peace, acceptance and justification,
but of happiness and holiness, of wisdom and strength, of
victory over the world, of mortification of a body of sin and
death, of every fresh revival and renewal of hope and confidence; of all prayer and praise; of every new budding
forth of the soul, as of Aaron's rod, in blossom and fruit; of
every gracious feeling, spiritual desire, warm supplication,
honest confession, melting contrition, and godly sorrow for
sin—all these springs of that life which is hid with Christ in
God are in a crucified Lord. Thus Christ crucified is, "to
them who are saved, the power of God." And as he "of
God is made unto us wisdom, righteousness, sanctification,
and redemption," at the cross alone can we be made wise
unto salvation, become righteous by a free justification,
receive of his Spirit to make us holy, and be redeemed and
delivered by blood and power from sin, Satan, death, and
hell.

July 4.

*" For the Scripture saith, Whosoever believeth on him shall
not be ashamed."*—ROMANS x. 11.

A child of God may be often deeply exercised whether

he has any faith at all; for when he reads what faith has
done and can do, and sees and feels how little it has done
for him, he is seized with doubts and fears whether he has
ever been blessed with the faith of God's elect. This makes
him often say, "Oh, do I indeed possess one grain of saving
faith?" But he does possess it: nay, it is his very faith
which makes him so anxiously ask himself the question, as
well as see and feel the nature and amount of his unbelief.
It is the very light of God shining into his soul that shews
him his sins, their nature and number; convinces him of
their guilt and enormity; lays the burden of them upon his
conscience; and discovers to him the workings of an unbelieving heart. But besides this, if he had no faith at all he
could not hear the voice of God speaking in the gospel, nor
receive it as a message of mercy; so that he has faith,
though he has not its witnessing evidence, or its abounding
comfort. This faith will save his soul; for "the gifts and
calling of God are without repentance;" that is, God never
repents of any gift that he bestows or of any calling which
he has granted. If, then, he has ever blessed you with faith,
however small that faith may be in itself or in your own view
of it, he will never take it away out of your heart, but rather
fan the smoking flax until it burst forth into a flame. He
will never forsake the work of his own hands, for he which
"hath begun a good work in you will perform it until the
day of Jesus Christ." If ever, then, if but once in your life,
you have felt the gospel to be the power of God unto salvation; if you have ever had one view of Christ by living faith;
if but once only, under the influence of his blessed Spirit on
your heart, you have laid hold of him and felt even for a few
minutes that he was yours, your soul is as safe as though it
were continually bathing in the river which maketh glad the
city of God, continually drinking of the honey and milk of
the gospel, and walking all day long in the full light of his

most gracious countenance. Not that a man should be satisfied with living at a poor, cold, dying rate; I mean not that, but merely to lay it down as a part of God's truth that as regards salvation, it is not the amount, but the reality of faith that saves the soul.

July 5.

"*It shall bring forth new fruit according to his months, because their waters they issued out of the sanctuary.*"— EZEKIEL xlvii. 12.

THERE is always something new in the things of God. Here is a passage perhaps in the word of God that we have read and read again and again without seeing or feeling anything in it; but all of a sudden there may come a blessed flash of light upon it; we now see something in it that we have never seen before, something exceedingly sweet and precious. It is now all new; it is received as new, felt as new, fed upon as new, relished as new. It seems as though we never saw anything in the passage before. So with prayer; so with hearing. You may perhaps have had your soul shut up in distress and bondage and misery for months; you could scarcely trace anything of the life of God in you. But under the preached word, it may have pleased God to drop something which has come into your heart with warmth, and life, and feeling. Oh, how new it is! It is as new as though it were never heard before; it seems as though the eyes were now first opened to see new things, and the ears were opened to hear new things, and the heart opened to receive new things. The Lord thus fulfils that blessed promise, "He that sitteth upon the throne saith, Behold, I make all things new!" "If any man be in Christ, he is a new creature; old things are passed away, behold, all things are become new."

July 6.

" Those that walk in pride he is able to abase."—DANIEL
iv. 37.

AMONGST all the evils which lie naked and open before
the eyes of Him with whom we have to do, pride seems
especially to incur his holy abhorrence; and the outward
manifestations of it have perhaps drawn down as much as,
or more than, any other sin his marked thunderbolts. Pride
cost Sennacherib his army and Herod his life; pride opened
the earth to Korah, Dathan and Abiram, and hung up
Absalom in the boughs of an oak; pride filled the breast of
Saul with murderous hatred against David, and tore ten
tribes at one stroke from the hand of Rehoboam. Pride
drove Nebuchadnezzar from the society of his fellow-men,
and made him eat grass as oxen, and his body to be wet
with the dew of heaven, till his hairs were grown as eagles'
feathers, and his nails like birds' claws. And as it has cut
off the wicked from the earth, and left them neither son nor
nephew, root nor branch, so it has made sad havoc even
among the family of God. Pride shut Aaron out of the
promised land, and made Miriam a leper white as snow;
pride, working in the heart of David, brought a pestilence
which cut off seventy thousand men; pride carried captive
to Babylon Hezekiah's treasure and descendants, and cast
Jonah into the whale's belly, and, in his feelings, into the
very belly of hell. It is the only source of contention; the
certain forerunner of a fall; the instigator of persecution; a
gin for the feet; a chain to compass the whole body; the
main element of deceitfulness, and the grave of all uprightness. The very opposite to charity, pride suffereth not long,
and is never kind; she envieth always, and ever vaunteth
herself; is continually puffed up, always behaveth herself
unseemly, ever seeketh her own, is easily provoked, per-

petually thinketh evil, rejoiceth in iniquity, but rejoiceth not in the truth; beareth nothing, believeth nothing (good in a brother), hopeth nothing, endureth nothing. Ever restless and ever miserable, tormenting herself and tormenting others, the bane of churches, the fomenter of strife, and the extinguisher of love—may it be our wisdom to see, our grace to abhor, and our victory to overcome her, and may the experience of that verse in Hart's hymn be ours:

> "Thy garden is the place
> Where pride can not intrude;
> For should it dare to enter there,
> 'Twould soon be drown'd in blood."

July 7.

"And I give unto them eternal life; and they shall never perish, neither shall any man pluck them out of my hand."— JOHN x. 28.

THE Lord says, "I give unto them (that is, my sheep) eternal life;" not, "I will give them in the life to come; but I give it unto them now." We therefore read, "He that believeth on the Son *hath* everlasting life"—has it now, as a present, felt, and enjoyed possession. This life is given manifestly when Christ reveals himself to the soul; for eternal life is then received out of his fulness as an enjoyed possession. All, then, who have truly fled for refuge, to lay hold of the hope set before them, embrace in so doing eternal life. They live, as being manifestly in Christ, for he is "our life;" and as they embrace it in him they feel its sweet movements in their breast, in the joy it communicates, in the peace it imparts, in the prospects it opens, in the doubts it removes, in the fears it disperses. Thus, in real religion, there is something, if I may so speak, tangible, something to be laid hold of; and this distinguishes a good hope through grace from every other hope which is delusive, enthusiastic, or visionary. Depend upon it, there is a reality in vital godliness, a possession for eternity, which, therefore, kills and deadens the living child of God to a perishing world, and the fading things of time and sense. Whenever we get a view of Christ, there is a view of eternal life in him; for he is the eternal Son of God, and when he makes himself known to the soul as such, he shews us that all our life is in him. The work that he accomplished is for eternity; he lives himself for ever and ever; and those whom he has redeemed by his blood, justified by his righteousness, and sanctified by his grace, will live for ever and ever in his glorious presence. It is the eternity of his love which stamps it with its main value and blessedness; for this life being eternal, secures not only perpetuity, but immutability, prevents it from any change in time as well as from any change in eternity, and secures it firm and stable to all the heirs of promise. As, then, they lay hold of eternal life in laying hold of him who is the life, and as the sweet movements of hope spring up in their breast, it opens before their eyes a vista of immortal joy.

July 8.

" I will set him on high, because he hath known my name."— PSALM xci. 14.

A man must know the Lord's name before ever he can feel any real love to him. Now this is needful, this is what the Lord does for his people, he causes them to know his name. "They shall all know me, from the least of them unto the greatest" (Jer. xxxi. 34). "They shall all;" they shall. The Lord has declared it. They shall know me. Now what is the name of the Lord? When God revealed himself unto Moses, did he not say, "I AM THAT I AM?" This was the way God taught Moses his name, and we may gather from it that whatever God is, that is his name. God is holy, God is just, God is merciful, God is a God of love. Now the sinner must know this. He must know that God is a pure and holy God, and at first when he is beginning to learn this lesson, he is completely astonished and appalled by it. It causes him to shrink away and hide himself from God. "How can I appear before God, who is of purer eyes than to behold iniquity?" he cries. And so you see it brings distress into his conscience. It is the first work of the Spirit to "convince of sin," and a sense of God's holiness is that which brings us this conviction—our sin and God's purity. How can the sinner appear before and approach to God? And while he is under the terrors of the law, he is full of distress, and at times, perhaps, wishes he had never been born, and at other times he is tempted with hard thoughts of God, reaping where he had not sown, and gathering where he had not strawed. This is how God is seen in his perverted mind. The devil is at him, and tries all he can to harden his heart against the Almighty. But the terrors of the Almighty have taken hold of him, and he tries many ways to get these arrows extracted; but all his tugging and pulling only make the wound worse. And so he goes on until he is brought to see that God is a God of mercy, and this is revealed to him in and through the Lord Jesus. This is what clears up the mystery, when he sees Christ bleeding on the cross. Here he sees God is both a just God and a Saviour. God is pure and holy, and exacts to the utmost farthing all the enormous debt he owes, and yet to the bleeding, broken heart, he, through Christ, can and does manifest his mercy.

July 9.

" The gospel of the grace of God."—ACTS xx. 24.

WHAT does the word "gospel" signify? Gospel is a good old Anglo-Saxon word, sprung from that pure Anglo-Saxon

stock which forms the bulk, as well as the most expressive
and precious portion of our noble language, of that language
of which the daily lengthening line is gone throughout all the
earth, and its words to the end of the world, our mother
tongue, in which God seems to have set a tabernacle for the
Sun of the gospel, whose going forth is from the end of the
heaven and its circuit unto the ends of it.   Its literal meaning
is either " God's word " or message, or rather, " good news,"
or " good tidings," which is more agreeable to the original.
But if it be " good news," it must be good news of something
and to somebody.   There must be some good tidings brought,
and there must be some person by whom, as good tidings, it
is received.   In order, then, that the gospel should be good
news, glad tidings, there must be a message from God to
man, God being the Speaker, and man the hearer ; he the
gracious Giver, and man the happy receiver.   But if the
gospel mean good news from heaven to earth, it can only be
worthy of the name as it proclaims grace, mercy, pardon,
deliverance, and salvation, and all as free gifts of God's un-
merited favour.   Otherwise, it would not be a gospel adapted
to our wants ; it would not be good news, glad tidings to us
poor sinners, to us law-breakers, to us guilty criminals, to us
vile transgressors, to us arraigned at the bar of infinite justice,
to us condemned to die by the unswerving demands of God's
holiness.   And as it must be a gospel adapted to us to
receive, so must it be a gospel worthy of God to give.   This
gospel then, pure, clear, and free, is good news or glad
tidings, as proclaiming pardon through the blood of Jesus
and justification by his righteousness.   It reveals an obedience
whereby the law was magnified and made honourable, and a
propitiation for sin by which it was for ever blotted out and
put away ; and thus it brings glory to God and salvation to
the soul.   It is a pure revelation of sovereign mercy, love and
grace, whereby each Person in the divine Trinity is exalted

and magnified. In it "mercy and truth meet together, righteousness and peace kiss each other." As revealed in it, "truth springs out of earth" in the hearts of contrite sinners, and "righteousness," eternally satisfied by Christ's obedience, "looks down from heaven." If you love a pure, a clear, a free gospel, "the gospel of the grace of God," you love it not only because it is so fully suitable to your wants, so thoroughly adapted to your fallen state, but because you have felt its sweetness and power; because it not only speaks of pardon, but brings pardon; not only proclaims mercy, but brings mercy; not only points out a way of salvation, but brings salvation, with all its rich attendant blessings, into your heart. It thus becomes "the power of God unto salvation to every one that believeth."

July 10.

"*I am the vine, ye are the branches : He that abideth in me, and I in him, the same bringeth forth much fruit : for without me ye can do nothing.*"—John xv. 5.

Without a union with Christ, we have no spiritual existence; and we may boldly say that we no more have a spiritual being in the mind of God independent of Christ, than the branch of a tree has an independent existence out of the stem in which it grows. But you will observe, also, in this figure of the vine and the branches, how all the fruitfulness of the branch depends upon its union with the vine. Whatever life there is in the branch, it flows out of the stem; whatever strength there is in the branch, it comes from its union with the stem ; whatever foliage, whatever fruit, all come still out of its union with the stem. And this is the case, whether the branch be great or small. From the stoutest limb of a tree to the smallest twig, all are in union with the stem and all derive life and nourishment from it. So it is in grace : not only is our very being, as sons and daughters of the Lord Almighty, connected with our union with Christ, but our well-being. All our knowledge, therefore, of heavenly mysteries, all our faith, all our hope, and all our love—in a word, all our grace, whether much or little, whether that of the babe, the child, the young man, or the father—flows out of a personal, spiritual, and experimental union with the Lord Jesus; for we are nothing but what we are in him, and we have nothing but what we possess by virtue of our union with him.

July 11.

" And our hope of you is stedfast, knowing, that as ye are partakers of the sufferings, so shall ye be also of the consolation."—2 CORINTHIANS i. 7.

THE Lord has appointed the path of sorrow for the redeemed to walk in. Why? One purpose is to wean them from the world; another purpose is to shew them the weakness of the creature; a third purpose is to make them feel the liberty and vitality of genuine godliness made manifest in their soul's experience. What am I, and what are you when we have no trials? Light, frothy, worldly-minded, carnal, frivolous. We may talk of the things of God, but they are at a distance; there are no solemn feelings, no melting sensations, no real brokenness, no genuine contrition, no weeping at the divine feet, no embracing of Christ in the arms of affection. But when affliction, be it in providence or be it in grace, brings a man down; when it empties him of all his high thoughts, lays him low in his own eyes, brings trouble into his heart, I warrant you he wants something more than outside gospel. He wants power; he wants to experience in his soul the operations of the blessed Spirit; he wants to have a precious Jesus manifesting himself to his soul in love and blood; he wants to see his lovely countenance beaming upon him in ravishing smiles; he wants to hear the sweet whispers of dying love speaking inward peace; he wants to have the blessed Lord come into his soul, manifesting himself to him as he does not manifest himself to the world.

What brings a man here? A few dry notions floating to and fro in his brain, like a few drops of oil in a pail of water? *That* will never bring the life and power of vital godliness into a man's heart. It must be by being experimentally acquainted with trouble. When he is led into the path of tribulation, he then begins to long after, and, in God's own time and way, he begins to drink into, the sweetness of vital godliness, made manifest in his heart by the power of God.

July 12.

" *Then they that were in the ship came and worshipped him, saying, Of a truth thou art the Son of God."*—MATTHEW xiv. 33.

WHAT a beauty and blessedness there is in the deity of the Lord Jesus Christ, when viewed by the spiritual eye! Our reasoning minds, it is true, may be deeply stumbled at the doctrine of an incarnate God. My own mind, I know, has sometimes been driven almost to its wits' end by this great mystery of deity and humanity combined in the Person of Christ, for it so surpasses all human comprehension, and is so removed beyond the grasp of all our reasoning faculties. It is not, indeed, contrary to reason, for there is nothing in it impossible or self-contradictory; but it is beyond and above the reach of human thought and tangible apprehension. But when we are led to consider what would be the most certain and most fearful consequences unless the Lord Jesus Christ were what he declares he is, God as well as man, we are compelled, from the very necessity of the case, to cast ourselves with all the weight of our sins and sorrows upon an incarnate God, as the shipwrecked sailor gladly casts himself upon the rock in the ocean as the only refuge from the devouring sea. When we feel what sinners we are, and have

been, look down into the depths of the fall, and see in some
feeble and faint measure what sin is in the sight of a holy and
pure God, what can save us from despair unless we see the
deity of the Lord Jesus Christ investing his work upon the
cross and his obedience with a merit that shall suffice to
justify our guilty souls, wash away our aggravated iniquities,
blot out our fearful crimes, and make us fit to appear in the
presence of a righteous God? Thus we are sometimes absolutely compelled to throw ourselves on the deity of Christ,
as ready to perish, because in such a divine Saviour, in such
precious blood we see a refuge, and we see elsewhere no
other. We then feel that if the deity of Christ be taken
away, the Church of God is lost. Where can you find
pardon? where justification? where reconciliation to God?
where atoning blood, if there is no Saviour who merited as
God and suffered as man? We might as well leap into hell
at once with all our sins upon our head, as a sailor might
spring over the prow of a burning ship into the boiling
waves, to meet death instead of waiting for it, unless we
believe by a living faith in the deity of the Son of God. But
sometimes we are sweetly led into this glorious truth, not
merely driven by sheer necessity, but blessedly drawn into
this great mystery of godliness, when Christ is revealed to
our souls by the power of God. Then, seeing light in God's
light, we view the deity of Christ investing every thought,
word, and act of his suffering humanity with unspeakable
merit. Then we see how this glorious fact of deity and
humanity in the Person of Immanuel satisfies every want,
puts away every sin, heals every wound, wipes away every
tear, and sweetly brings the soul to repose on the bosom of
God. Sometimes, therefore, from necessity, driven by storms
of guilt and waves of temptation, and sometimes sweetly
drawn by the leadings and teachings of the Holy Ghost, we
lay hold of the hope set before us in the essential deity and

suffering humanity of the Son of God, knowing that there is a refuge in him from sin, death, hell, and despair.

July 13.

" We have such an high priest, who is set on the right hand of the throne of the Majesty in the heavens; a minister of the sanctuary, and of the true tabernacle, which the Lord pitched, and not man."—HEBREWS viii. 1, 2.

OUR blessed Lord was to be " a High Priest after the order of Melchizedec." It will be remembered that Melchizedec met Abraham returning from the slaughter of the kings, and blessed him (Gen. xiv. 19). In the same way our great High Priest blesses the seed of Abraham; for "they which be of faith are blessed with faithful Abraham ;" and as believers in the Lord Jesus Christ, they walk in his steps who "believed God, and it was counted unto him for righteousness." But Melchizedec the type could only *ask* God to bless Abraham. He could not himself confer the blessing; but Jesus, the antitype, our great Melchizedec, whose priesthood is " after the power of an endless life," blesses his people, not by merely asking God to bless them, but by himself showering down blessings upon them, and by communicating to them out of his own fulness every grace which can sanctify as well as save. Even before his incarnation, when he appeared in human form, as if anticipating in appearance that flesh and blood which he should afterwards assume in reality, he had power to bless. Thus we read that when Jacob wrestled with the angel, which angel was no created angel, but the Angel of the covenant, even the Son of God himself in human shape, he said, "I will not let thee go except thou bless me." And in answer to his wrestling cry we read that "he blessed him there." Jacob knew that no created angel could bless him. He therefore said, when he had got the blessing, "I have seen God face to face, and my life is preserved." To this blessing Jacob afterwards referred when, in blessing Ephraim and Manasseh, he said, "The angel which redeemed me from all evil bless the lads." Thus, also, our gracious Lord, immediately before his ascension to heaven, as if in anticipation of the gifts and graces which he was to send down upon them when exalted to the right hand of the Father, "lifted up his hands and blessed his disciples;" and as if to shew that he would still ever continue to bless them, "he was parted from them and carried up into heaven," even "*while* he blessed them," as if he were blessing them all the way up to heaven, even before he took possession of his mediatorial throne (Luke xxiv. 50, 51).

July 14.

"*But ye, beloved, building up yourselves on your most holy faith, praying in the Holy Ghost.*"—JUDE 20.

By the words "most holy faith," we may understand chiefly the grand truths of the everlasting gospel which are revealed unto and embraced by faith. And they are called "our most holy faith," because they are imbued with all the holiness of God; and not only so, but as they are received into believing hearts, communicate sanctification, because they have a liberating, sanctifying efficacy. The words "build up" assume that there is a foundation laid. Christ is that foundation which God hath laid in Zion, a chief corner-stone, elect, precious; and where Christ is revealed to the soul by a divine power, a foundation is laid in the heart on which every subsequent truth is to be built up. The grand thing to be clear of in our own experience is, whether Christ has been laid as a foundation in our souls or not, and if he has, we have been driven from every other as finding no rest or peace but in him. If ever he has been revealed to our souls by the mighty power of God, then we have seen and felt that in him there is a foundation on which we can stand, and that for eternity. As the Son of the Father in truth and love; having come to finish the work which the Father gave him to do; having put away sin by the sacrifice of himself, and brought in an ever-lasting righteousness in which we may stand justified, there is a foundation on which a poor, guilty soul may rest. When this foundation is brought nigh, and we, by the power of God's grace, are lifted up to rest upon it, we can say,

> " How firm a foundation, ye saints of the Lord,
> Is laid for your faith in his excellent word."

" Other foundation can no man lay than that is laid, which is Jesus Christ " (1 Cor. iii. 11).

July 15.

" Keep yourselves in the love of God."—JUDE 21.

When Christ is made known to our soul by the power of God, we have views of truth in him, of happiness in him, and of deliverance. " As ye have therefore received Christ Jesus the Lord, so walk ye in him." We receive him as the Son of the Father in truth and love; we receive him as suitable to our wants and woes; we receive him as putting away sin by the sacrifice of himself, and endearing himself to our heart in the sweet manifestation of his Person, goodness, and love. Now as long as Christ and the soul are together, there is no place for error, and no place for evil. He makes the soul tender, the heart upright, the spirit broken and contrite, truth precious, error hateful, and sin loathsome and detestable. And whilst he and the soul are engaged together, error cannot approach nor evil find an entrance, so as to get any standing-ground in the heart. But error is very subtle; it addresses itself to our reasoning powers; and when we lose sight of Christ, then error very easily creeps in; or if not error, some special lust, or something ungodly, seems by degrees to obtain power and influence, and we gradually decline from the strength of faith, the confidence of hope, and the sweet affections of love, and drop, it may be, into a cold, carnal, careless, lifeless state, where we lie open to the invasion of error and the temptations of Satan as an angel of light or an angel of darkness. But now Jude comes and says, "Keep yourselves in the love of God; and I will tell you, if you will listen to me, how you shall do it. You must build up yourselves on your most holy faith." God has laid a foundation for your faith in his holy word ; he has laid Christ as a foundation in your own soul. That is a very strong foundation; it is of God's own laying. It is very solid; it will bear any weight laid upon it. And therefore you must build up yourselves upon that most holy faith if you would have a religion which stands; because if your religion, or any part of your religion, be built upon another foundation, it will not stand. But if you build up yourselves on your most holy faith, then everything you build upon it will stand, because it rests upon the foundation, and is in harmony with it.

July 16.

"Search me, O God, and know my heart: try me, and know my thoughts: and see if there be any wicked way in me, and lead me in the way everlasting."—PSALM cxxxix. 23, 24.

THE people of God cannot take their religion upon credit; they cannot be satisfied with the endorsement of this or that good man. They must have it wrought by God himself. They are often exercised as to whence their religion came. Do you not find it so, and that it costs you many exercises? If, for instance, you are cast down, you are exercised whether it spring from godly sorrow for sin. If you are comforted, you cannot take the comfort for granted ; you must have it weighed up in the gospel balance. If you meet with providential deliverances, you cannot take them as so many certain evidences that all is right with your soul. So that every step you take you have to examine, and weigh it whether it be of

God. The dead professors, the hypocrites in Zion never have their religion tried and weighed up in this way. They know nothing of these inward exercises. They take things for granted; they nestle under some good man's wing, or get their religion endorsed by some minister, and are satisfied. But the people of God must have testimonies from the Lord himself; and they will often be sharply exercised whether they have that work in their souls which will stand in the trying hour. And if in answer to their cries the Lord is pleased to shine into their souls, and raise up clear tokens that it is from heaven, it fills their hearts with gratitude, sinks the things of time and sense, and lifts up their affections to that blessed fountain whence these testimonies came down. Thus those very things which seem against them are for them, and they derive their sweetest consolations out of their heaviest afflictions. They would not change their trying path, with all its bitter things, for the smooth flowery path in which they see thousands walk, knowing that a religion without trials and temptations will only lead the soul down into a never-ending hell. Thus at times they can feel good spring out of their exercises, and would rather be all their days a tempted, tried people, and bear those things which God inflicts, than walk in a path which seemeth right in the eyes of a man, and at the end find eternal destruction. They would rather have those chastisements which prove they are children and not bastards, than walk in a flesh-pleasing way of which the end is eternal damnation.

July 17.

" Then what prayer or what supplication soever shall be made of any man, or of all thy people Israel, when every one shall know his own sore and his own grief, and shall spread forth his hands in this house."—2 CHRONICLES vi. 29.

SOLOMON comes to experience; he puts his hand upon the

right spot. It is *knowing* his "*own sore*" and his "*own grief.*" You may know another man's; that will not profit you. You may read of experience in books, love to hear experimental ministers, and will hear no others; and yet not know your "*own* sore," your "*own* grief." Like a physician who may know the symptoms of every malady, and yet not have one malady of his own; so you may hear described every symptom of every disease, and yet be untouched by one. But the man for whom Solomon's prayer is, he that knows and feels, painfully feels, his "*own* sore" and his "*own* grief," whose heart is indeed a grief to him, whose sins do indeed trouble him. How painful this sore often is! how it runs night and day! how full of ulcerous matter, and how it shrinks from the probe! Most of the Lord's family have a "sore," each some tender spot, something perhaps known to himself and to God alone, the cause of his greatest grief. It may be some secret slip he has made, some sin he has committed, some word he has spoken, or some evil thing he has done. He has been entangled, and entrapped, and cast down; and this is his grief and his sore which he feels, and that at times deeply before God. For such Solomon prays: he casts his net upon the right side of the ship; and says, "Then hear thou from heaven thy dwelling-place, and forgive, and render unto every man according unto all his ways, whose heart thou knowest; for thou only knowest the hearts of the children of men." Yes; God alone knows the heart; he knows it completely, and sees to its very bottom.

July 18.

"Likewise the Spirit also helpeth our infirmities; for we know not what we should pray for as we ought; but the Spirit itself maketh intercession for us with groanings which cannot be uttered."—ROMANS viii. 26.

"WE know not what we should pray for as we ought."

How often do we find and feel this to be our case. Darkness covers our mind; ignorance pervades our soul; unbelief
vexes our spirit; guilt troubles our conscience; a crowd of
evil imaginations, or foolish or worse than foolish wanderings
distract our thoughts; Satan hurls in thick and fast his fiery
darts; a dense cloud is spread over the mercy-seat; infidelity
whispers its vile suggestions, till, amidst all this rabble rout,
such confusion and bondage prevail that words seem idle
breath, and prayer to the God of heaven but empty mockery.
In this scene of confusion and distraction, when all seems
going to the wreck, how kind, how gracious is it in the blessed
Spirit to come, as it were, to the rescue of the poor bewildered
saint, and to teach him how to pray and what to pray for.
He is therefore said "to help our infirmities," for these evils
of which we have been speaking are not wilful, deliberate sins,
but wretched infirmities of the flesh. He helps, then, our infirmities by subduing the power and prevalence of unbelief;
by commanding in the mind a solemn calm; by rebuking
and chasing away Satan and his fiery darts; by awing the
soul with a reverential sense of the power and presence of
God; by presenting Jesus before our eyes as the Mediator at
the right hand of the Father; by raising up and drawing forth
faith upon his Person and work, blood and righteousness;
and, above all, by himself interceding for us and in us "with
groanings which cannot be uttered." When the soul is
favoured thus to pray, its petitions are a spiritual sacrifice,
and its cries enter the ears of the Lord of Sabaoth, for "He
that searcheth the hearts knoweth what is the mind of the
Spirit, because he maketh intercession for the saints according to the will of God" (Rom. viii. 27; James v. 4; 1 Peter
ii. 5).

July 19.

"Because they have no changes, therefore they fear not God."— PSALM lv. 19.

TRUE religion is certainly the most weighty, and yet the most mysterious matter that we ever have had or can have to do with in this world. And I will tell you this, that it will either comfort you, or it will distress you. It will either exercise your mind, trouble your soul, cast down your spirit, and make you truly miserable, or else be the source of your choicest comfort and your greatest happiness. From religion come our deepest sorrows and highest joys, the greatest uneasiness and the sweetest peace. There is this peculiar feature about true religion, that in the greatest prosperity it may be the cause to us of the chiefest trouble, or in the greatest adversity be to us the cause of the purest joy. What are wealth or health, rank or titles, and every comfort the world can afford to a wounded spirit? What are poverty, sickness, persecution, contempt, a garret or a prison to a soul basking in the smiles of eternal love? Religion will surely make itself felt wherever it exists, and will testify by its power to its presence. If, then, you are a partaker of true religion, be you who, where, or what you may, you cannot be at ease in Zion, for there will be ever something working up out of your own heart or arising from some other quarter to make you uneasy. Job was once at ease, but he was not suffered to die in his nest. He therefore says, "I was at ease, but he hath broken me asunder: he hath also taken me by my neck, and shaken me to pieces, and set me up for his mark." And yet with all this unexpected and apparently cruel treatment, he could still say, "Behold, my witness is in heaven, and my record is on high." And though so exercised and distressed that he had to cry out, "My bone cleaveth to my skin and to my flesh, and I am escaped with the skin of my teeth. Have pity upon me, have pity upon me, O ye my friends; for the hand of God hath touched me;" yet he could add, in all the confidence of faith, as desirous that his words might stand for ever upon record : " Oh that my words were now written ! oh that they were printed in a book ! that they were graven with an iron pen and lead in the rock for ever ! For I know that my Redeemer liveth, and that he shall stand at the latter day upon the earth : and though after my skin worms destroy this body, yet in my flesh shall I see God : whom I shall see for myself, and mine eyes shall behold, and not another ; though my reins be consumed within me."

July 20.

" Deal bountifully with thy servant, that I may live, and keep thy word."—PSALM cxix. 17.

CAN the Lord deal any way but *bountifully* with his servants ? Why has he made you his servants? Why did he strike the chains of former servitude off your hands ? Why did he bring you out of the service of sin, the world, Satan, and self ? Why did he ever make himself precious to your heart, win your affections, and enable you to give yourselves wholly unto him ? That he might cast you off ? that he might mock your calamity ? that he might trample you one day into hell ? that he might leave you to yourself, that he might suffer Satan to overcome you, permit your lusts to destroy you; or allow your sins to be tied one day, like a mill-stone, round your neck to sink you into hell ? Oh, can our heart ever indulge thoughts so derogatory to sovereign grace ? Was it not because the Lord had bounty in his heart towards you, that he first turned your heart towards himself? Was it not because the Lord had purposes of love towards you, that he first led your feet into his paths ? Was it not because God first loved you, that he gave his Son to die for you ? Now if he has taught you, led you, upheld you, kept you, all this time, is it to cast you off *now*—to let you sink at last? He cannot do so, will not do so. Those whom he loves, he loves to the end; the good work which he has begun, he will accomplish, and bring to final perfection; and therefore all the Lord's acts are acts of bounty.

July 21.

" So then it is not of him that willeth, nor of him that runneth, but of God that sheweth mercy."—ROMANS ix. 16.

HE that is not interested in the eternal election of God the Father, in the atoning blood and justifying righteousness of God the Son, in the work and witness of God the Holy Ghost, whatever be his name, sect, denomination or profession; whatever be his outward conduct, the doctrines he professes, or the creed to which he signs his name, he will die as Esau died, as Balaam died, as Saul died, as Judas and Ahithophel died. He will never see the King in his beauty; never see the land afar off; never see the new Jerusalem, nor the blood of sprinkling, " that speaketh better things than the blood of Abel." But every living soul that has been feelingly taught his lost condition, that has known something of a resting-place in Christ, that has turned his back upon the world and the professing church, and gone weeping Zionward, in whose heart God the Holy Ghost has implanted those solemn desires, and (if I may use the expression) those solemn determinations under the divine teaching, not a determination of free will, but the inward determination of grace strengthened to it by the Spirit of God, " to join himself to the Lord in a perpetual covenant never to be forgotten"— that he may live in Jesus and die in Jesus, live out of Jesus and unto Jesus, that he may feel his power, taste his love, know his blood, rejoice in his grace; every such soul shall, like Israel of old, be borne safely through this waste-howling wilderness, shall be carried through this vale of tears, and taken to enjoy eternal bliss and glory in the presence of Him whom to see as he is, constitutes the blessedness of the redeemed. Every such poor, exercised, tempted soul shall be brought into a personal enjoyment of Christ below and of Christ above, so as to enjoy a foretaste of heaven here, and hereafter to bathe in the ocean of endless bliss.

July 22.

" *Now no chastening for the present seemeth to be joyous, but grievous: nevertheless afterward it yieldeth the peaceable fruit of righteousness unto them which are exercised thereby.*"— HEBREWS xii. 11.

IT may be said of spiritual exercises as the Apostle speaks of chastening generally, of which indeed they form a component part, that " for the present they are not joyous, but grievous; but afterward they yield the peaceable fruit of righteousness unto them that are exercised thereby." *Why* the Lord suffers so many of his people to be so long and deeply tried about their interest in Christ, *why* he does not more speedily and fully manifest his pardoning love to their souls, is a mystery which we cannot fathom. But I have observed that, where the first work was not attended with deep and powerful convictions of sin, it is usually the case, as if what was wanting in depth has to be made up in length, and a slow, continuous work compensates, as it were, for a shorter and more intense one.

I consider it, however, a great mercy where there are these exercises, for I am well convinced that exercise is as much needed for the health of the soul as of the body. Without movement the air becomes pestilential, and water putrescent. Motion is the life of the natural, and equally so of the supernatural, creation; and what are exercises, doubts, and fears, accompanied as they always are by desires and prayers, but means by which the soul is kept alive and healthy? As

Hezekiah said, " O Lord, by these things men live, and in all
these things is the life of my spirit." But if you cannot see
what good exercises have done you, can you not see what evil
they have kept you from? They mainly kept you from being
entangled in a worldly system; they have preserved you from
resting in the form without the power, and kept you from that
notional dead-letter faith which has ruined so many thousands[1].
Without exercises you could do without a revealed Christ,
without manifested pardon of sin, without the love of God
being shed abroad in your heart by the Holy Ghost.

And here most are who are not exercised—resting in " a
name to live," and in the doctrine without the experience.
But, being sick, you need a physician; being guilty, you
need mercy; and being a sinner, you need salvation; and
all this, not in word and name, but in reality, and divine
revelation and application. Your exercises give you errands
to the throne of mercy, and make you see in Christ and his
precious gospel what otherwise would neither be seen nor
cared for. At the same time, it would be wrong to rest in
exercises as marks and evidences of grace. Thirst is good
as preparatory for water; hunger is good as antecedent to
food; but who can rest in thirst or hunger? Without them,
water and food are not desired; so, without exercises, Christ,
the Water and Bread of life, is not desired nor longed for.
But these exercises are meant to quicken longing desires after
Christ, and eventually make him very precious.

July 23.

" *Turn thou us unto thee, O Lord, and we shall be turned;
renew our days as of old.*"—LAMENTATIONS v. 21.

IF we do not wish to deceive ourselves, if God has made
us honest, if he has planted his fear in our hearts, if he has
begun and is carrying on a good work in us, there will be

[1] This extract was taken from a letter to a friend.

evidences of the existence of the life of God within. *Life* is the commencement of salvation as an inward reality; for whatever the eternal purposes of God are, or whatever standing the vessel of mercy has in Christ previous to effectual calling, there is no more movement in the soul Godward till life is imparted, than there is natural life and motion in a breathless corpse that lies interred in the churchyard. But wherever divine life is implanted there will be certain fruits and feelings that spring out of this life. One fruit will be complaint, and this will arise sometimes from a feeling of the burden of sin, and at others from a sense of merited chastisement from God on account of it. But wherever this complaining is spiritual, there will be accompanying it " an accepting the punishment of our iniquity," and " a putting of our mouth in the dust." Thus where there is spiritual life there will be complaint, confession, and submission ; the effect being meekness, brokenness, and humility. This breaks to pieces self-conceit and self-justification, and the result is a searching and trying our ways whether they are of God. The fruit of this search will be, for the most part, a solemn and painful conviction that the greater part have been in the flesh; or, at least, there will be many anxious suspicions which cannot be relieved except by an express testimony from the Lord himself. This produces a going out of soul unto him, the cry now being, " Let us turn again to the Lord ; " and towards him the heart turns as to the only Source and Author of every good and perfect gift. As the quickened soul knows that he is a heart-searching God, this appeal will purge away much hypocrisy and insincerity, and deepen uprightness, sincerity, and godly integrity. And the blessed fruit and end of all this sifting work will be a coming down of gracious answers, divine testimonies, smiles of the Saviour's loving countenance, soft whispers of God's eternal favour, and the blessed witness of the Spirit within.

July 24.

" But God, who is rich in mercy, for his great love where-
with he loved us, even when we were dead in sins, hath
quickened us together with Christ, (by grace ye are saved;)
and hath raised us up together."—Ephesians ii. 4, 5, 6.

Eighteen hundred years have rolled away since the body
of Christ was quickened in the sepulchre; but the virtual
effect of that quickening reached all the election of grace,
and will stretch down to the remotest period of time. Now,
by virtue of this quickening, when the Holy Spirit comes
forward for the execution of his purpose, life enters into the
soul. "You hath he quickened who were dead." With
quickening comes living sensations, such as conviction of
sin, guilt of conscience, the fear of God, the heart broken,
the spirit of prayer, repentance unto life; in a word, all the
first work of grace in the soul. As in the body of Christ,
when quickened by the Holy Ghost, there were vital movements before that body left the sepulchre, so there are vital
movements in the soul of a child of God under the quickening operations of God the Holy Ghost, before raised up and
brought forth. He is quickened into life, and under that
quickening sees, feels, trembles, cries, groans, begs, and sues
for mercy; every faculty of his renewed mind is alive and
open to the things of God. Never do we pray, read, hear,
feel so much the power of eternal things, as when the Lord
by his Spirit and grace is first pleased to quicken us into
this spiritual life. But no *resurrection* yet; the quickening
precedes.

But as, when the breath of the Holy Ghost, so to speak,
quickened the body of Christ as it lay in the sepulchre, it
was but a preparation for the raising of that dead body from
the tomb, so the quickening operations of God the Holy
Ghost in the heart of a child of God are but preparatory to

his being raised up together with Christ. Christ's body did not remain in the tomb, though it was alive in the tomb; so those whom God has quickened, and who are still lying in the tomb of sin, misery, and wretchedness, but are sighing, suing, and begging for mercy at his hands will certainly be brought out. Christ's body was not left there when it was quickened, neither will any of you that are quickened be left in your sin and misery, in your condemnation and guilt. The same divine operation that quickened you into spiritual life will bring you out of this state of concern and anxiety into the resurrection life of Christ, as was done in the case of his body, when he rose out of the tomb.

Now, when the power of God is put forth in the soul; when mercy reaches the heart; when Christ is revealed, his word applied, and it comes forth out of the dark tomb in which it has lain, like Lazarus, bound with grave-clothes, and yet alive; when the door of hope thus is set open, and the soul is raised up to believe, hope and love, then it is "*raised* up together with Christ." The resurrection of Christ was not merely the grand testimony that God put upon him as his dear Son, for he was declared to be "the Son of God with power, by the resurrection from the dead," but he was "raised also for our justification;" and we rose in him, if we believe in his name. All the elect of God rose with him; for they are "members of his body, of his flesh, and of his bones." When he died, they died; when he rose again, they rose again; and as they rose virtually in the Person of the Son of God when he rose triumphant from the tomb, so, when the Holy Ghost applies to the heart and conscience the benefits and blessings of his death and resurrection, he raises them up and brings them out of the dark sepulchre into the open light of a glorious gospel day. And this is being "raised up together with Christ."

July 25.

"And made us sit together in heavenly places in Christ Jesus."—EPHESIANS ii. 6.

JESUS did not tarry upon the earth after his resurrection; he ascended up where he was before, and took his seat at the right hand of the Majesty on high. But when he ascended up on high, all the election of grace ascended with him. He did not leave his members behind upon earth, but he took them all virtually into heaven. And this is a pledge that they will one day be with him in the realms of eternal bliss, because they have already ascended with him, as the members of his mystical body. This, in experimental manifestation, is the lifting up of the affections, the raising up of the soul to sit together with Christ in heavenly places. Sin, death, hell, and Satan, with all the misery and wretchedness we have brought upon ourselves—to have them all under our feet, as Christ now reigns, having put all enemies under his feet—to enjoy this, is to sit with Christ in heavenly places. One of the last acts that God usually does for the soul, is the lifting it up thus to sit with Christ in the anticipation of eternal glory. To see death dethroned, hell destroyed, sin abolished, and a glorious immortality reserved for the saints of God; to enjoy this in the sweet anticipation and blessed foretastes, so as to be in heaven before we get there —this is to sit down with Christ in heavenly places, by virtue of his sitting down there "at the right hand of the Majesty on high."

Now, see what benefits and blessings spring out of a union with the Son of God. Why did God quicken your soul? Because you were a member of Christ. Why were you raised up to "a good hope through grace?" Why did mercy, peace, and pardon flow into your soul? Why were you brought out of misery and death into the light of God's countenance, and had a precious Christ revealed to your heart? Because in the day, when the Son of God rose triumphant from the tomb, you, as a member of his mystical body, rose there and then with him. Why are you sometimes privileged to have your affections on things above, attain any victory over sin, death, hell, and the grave, find your enemies put under your feet, and look forward at times with a sweet anticipation of eternal joys? Because, as a member of Christ's mystical body, you have already ascended, and are already sitting at the right hand of God with Christ, who is sitting as the Head of his body there.

July 26.

"*Only let your conversation be as it becometh the gospel of Christ.*"—PHILIPPIANS i. 27.

WHAT is this conversation? The word means the whole of your walk before God and before man. It is a very comprehensive term in the original, meaning, literally, "Conduct yourselves as citizens." It therefore includes the whole of our spiritual fellowship and daily intercourse with God and man. It thus views us as citizens of no mean city; as citizens, I may indeed say, of a heavenly city, the new Jerusalem; and it bids us walk and speak, live and act, as becometh citizens of a heavenly country. This, then, is the meaning of the word "conversation" in our text, and by it we are called to walk with God as becometh the gospel. He has reconciled us to himself by the blood of his dear Son; and when we receive the atonement, or reconciliation, as the word means, then we can walk with God in peace, equity, and amity, for sin, which made the breach, is removed out of the way. So Levi, as ministering at the altar, and those near to God, walked of old. " My covenant was with him of life and peace; and I gave them to him for the fear wherewith he feared me, and was afraid before my name. The law of truth was in his mouth, and iniquity was not found in his lips: he walked with me in peace and equity, and did turn many away from iniquity" (Malachi ii. 5, 6). This is walking in the light as He is in the light, and so far as we can do this, our fellowship is with the Father (1 John i. 3-7). And our conversation with God, our walk with God, must be as becometh the gospel of Christ. If we walk at freedom with God, in sweet liberty, with holy access, pouring out our heart before him, enjoying his presence, and having some discoveries of his goodness and mercy, then our conversation with God becometh the gospel. The gospel is a message of mercy. When, then, we embrace that mercy, and feel the power of it; when that mercy reaches our heart, melts our inmost soul, dissolves our doubts and fears, and removes legality and bondage, then we walk worthy of the gospel, as walking before God in the light of his countenance through the power of the gospel. God does not send the gospel to condemn us, for "there is no condemnation to them which are in Christ Jesus, who walk not after the flesh, but after the Spirit;" and they walk after the Spirit when they have access by him through Christ unto the Father.

July 27.

" And so were the churches established in the faith, and increased in number daily."—ACTS xvi. 5.

OH what an inestimable mercy it is for a man to know the truth for himself by divine teaching and divine testimony; to have it applied to his heart by a gracious influence and a heavenly power, so as to know for himself what salvation is, whence it comes, and above all to enjoy a sweet persuasion that this salvation has reached his heart! He will then know where to go in the hour of trouble, to whom to resort when sorrow and affliction come into his house, or illness or infirmity shake his tabernacle. He will not be a stranger to the throne of grace, nor to the sweetness of the covenant ordered in all things and sure. But there will be given him from above, out of the fulness of Christ, such grace and strength as will support him in the trying hour. It is by these gracious dealings upon his soul, that a believer becomes " stablished in the faith." Nay, the very storms through which he passes will only strengthen him to take a firmer hold of Christ, and thus become more established in the faith of him. It is in these storms that he learns more of his own weakness and of Christ's strength; more of his own misery and of Christ's mercy; more of his own sinfulness and of superabounding grace; more of his own poverty and of Christ's riches; more of his own desert of hell, and more of his own title to heaven. Thus he becomes " stablished in faith," for the same blessed Spirit who began the work carries it on, goes on to fill up the original outline, and to engrave the image of Christ in deeper characters upon his heart, and to teach him more and more experimentally the truth as it is in Jesus.

July 28.

" But mine eyes are unto thee, O God the Lord: in thee is my trust; leave not my soul destitute."—PSALM cxli. 8.

THE very cry is a pledge that the Lord will not leave the soul destitute. Strange though it be to us; it is the light that shews darkness; it is life that makes us feel deadness; nay, more, it is fertility and fruitfulness that make us feel barrenness; it is riches that make us feel poverty; it is God's teaching and presence that make us feel destitution. This very mourning over our barrenness; this very feeling of our inability to do good, is a proof of the life of God in the soul, an evidence of the work of grace in the heart. " Leave not my soul destitute." This is something genuine; this is heart-work; these are the footsteps of the flock; these are the leadings and teachings of God the Spirit in the hearts of the redeemed. These things are saving; these things will lead the soul to eternal glory. And he that knows any of these things by personal experience will one day see the glory of the Lord face to face. What do we, then, know of these things? Can we lay our experience side by side with this experience of the Psalmist, and say, " Mine eyes are unto thee, O God the Lord; in thee is my trust; leave not my soul destitute?" Wherever that prayer is, it will bring an answer; and wherever that answer is, there will be matter for everlasting praise. Blessed are the souls that know these things from genuine heartfelt experience. They will shine forth as stars for ever and ever ; and when the Lord of life and glory comes a second time without sin unto salvation, then shall they also appear with him in glory.

July 29.

" Beloved, let us love one another : for love is of God; and every one that loveth is born of God, and knoweth God."— 1 JOHN iv. 7.

" Love is of God." I can have no satisfaction, real satisfaction, that I am a partaker of the Spirit and grace of Christ except I feel some measure of the love of God shed abroad in my heart. I may have hopes, expectations, and evidences, fainter or brighter; but I have no sure, clear evidence in my own soul that I have the Spirit and grace of Christ there, except I am blessed with the love of God ; for until love comes, there is fear which hath torment. And whilst we have fear which hath torment, there is no being made perfect in love. You have no clear assurance in your own breast that God has loved you with an everlasting love ; nor have you any bright testimony that the Spirit of God makes your body his temple until this love comes into your soul. But when the crowning blessing comes of the love of

God experimentally felt and enjoyed by his own shedding of it abroad in the heart, with the communication of the Spirit of adoption to cry "Abba, Father," *that* is the sealing testimony of your possession of the true spirit; for it is "a spirit of power, and of love, and of a sound mind;" and where there is this, there is also a spirit of love and affection to all the family of God.

July 30.

"*The sighing of the needy.*"—Psalm xii. 5.

The distinguishing mark and character of a needy soul is to be full of needs. Day after day he wants divine realities to be revealed to his soul, to hear the sweet voice of mercy speaking into his heart, as from the lips of God himself, that he is an accepted child, that he may bathe, as it were, in sweet manifestations of the love and mercy of God. In the supply of want he believes the marrow of all true religion and vital godliness to consist. So that he cannot take up with his present state of need for religion. If he is in doubts and fears, or is passing through heavy temptations, and is writing bitter things against himself, he cannot say "*this* is religion;" but what he wants is something different from what he feels, even the blessed testimonies and manifestations that he is one of the Lord's own dear family; and I am very well assured from soul experience, that nothing but the application of heavenly blessings to the soul can ever satisfy the man who has had life implanted in his heart by the hand of God himself.

We therefore read of this needy person that he *sighs*. "For the oppression of the poor, for the *sighing* of the needy." He is sighing after God; groaning in the depths of his soul after the lifting up of the light of God's countenance; sighing under the weight of unbelief, the burden of infidelity, the power of temptation, the wretchedness of his heart, the carnality of his mind, the barrenness of his frame, his stupidity, his brutality, filth and corruption. He is sighing to the Lord under the burden of these things lying as a load on his conscience, and begging the Lord that he would only lift up the light of his countenance, that he would only drop one sweet testimony, that he would speak but one word to his soul, to bring with it sweet deliverance, and lift him out into all the light, and life, and liberty, and peace of the glorious gospel of the blessed God.

July 31.

" Then they cried unto the Lord in their trouble, and he delivered them out of their distresses."—PSALM cvii. 6.

OH what a mercy it is that there is a God to go to! a God who hears and answers prayer! And what a blessing it is to be able to unbosom before him the burdened spirit! Observe the words: " Then they cried unto the Lord in their *trouble.*" If you have trouble it is a sufficient warrant for you to go to God with it. Do not trouble yourself with the question, whether you are elect or non-elect. God does not put it in that shape, and you need not. The answer will best shew on which side of the line you stand. Does he not say: "Call upon me in the day of trouble: I will deliver thee, and thou shalt glorify me?" If you have a day of trouble, you have here a sufficient warrant to call upon God. Write not, then, bitter things against yourself. If you are enabled to sigh and cry unto the Lord there is life in your soul. God has quickened you by his blessed Spirit if he has put a sigh and cry into your bosom. Remember the men in Ezekiel on whom the Lord put the approving seal. It was those who sighed and cried for the abominations which they saw and felt in themselves and others (Ezekiel ix. 4). If, then, the Lord has put a sigh and cry into your bosom on account of your felt inward abominations, you are one of those on whom he has set his seal. Sanctified troubles are some of our greatest blessings; and one of their blessed fruits is that they keep us from settling on our lees and being at ease in Zion. Careless, worldly-minded, proud, covetous professors, sunk in carnality and death, where is there ever a cry in their soul? They may have a formal prayer—a morning prayer, an evening prayer, a family prayer, and all as round as a ball, and as cold as Christmas. Stiff and frozen in carnality they are ice themselves, and they bring their ice with them wherever they come. But God does not suffer his people to go on in this cold, lifeless, frozen, icy way, with mere formal devotion, lip service, and prayers worn out like an old shoe with long and continual treading. He sends afflictions, trials, and troubles upon them, takes them into the wilderness, exercises them well in the path of tribulation, and supporting them under it, raises up a cry which he is sure to hear.

August 1.

" Let thy work appear unto thy servants, and thy glory unto their children."—Psalm xc. 16.

"Let thy work appear unto thy servants." Creature works we here read nothing of. They had been long ago cut to the very ground. And what had been their death-blow? What had driven the dagger into their very heart? "Days of affliction, and years of evil." These had been their destruction; creature righteousness they had stabbed to the very heart, and let out the life-blood of human merit. There is no petition, then, "Let *our* works appear!" No. These were buried in the grave of corruption; these were swallowed up and lost in "days of affliction, and years of evil." But, "Let *thy* work," the finished work of the Son of God; the obedience of Jesus to the law; the atoning blood which he shed upon Calvary's tree; the work which he

undertook, went through, and completed,—" Oh," breathes
forth the man of God in earnest cry (and our hearts if they
have been taught by the same Spirit will unite in the same
strain), "let *thy* work appear unto thy servants!" What!
can we not see that work in the word of God? is not *that*
sufficient? Can we not hear that work set forth by good
men? is not *that* sufficient? Can we not read it as opened
up by the pen of ready writers? is not *that* sufficient? Yes;
for those who have never seen "days of affliction, and
years of evil," amply sufficient; but not for God's exercised
children; they have other thoughts and other feelings upon
these matters. *They* know what darkness of mind is, the
power of unbelief, and creature helplessness; and they know
that nothing short of the light of God's countenance, the
manifestation of God's mercy, and the teaching and witness
of God the Spirit, can make the work of Jesus appear in all
its beauty, suitability, and glory; and therefore they can say,
" Let *thy* work appear unto thy servants. Give me, Lord, a
sight by living faith of the atonement of Jesus. Shew me "
(the soul would cry in the language of Moses), "shew me
thy glory; reveal in my heart the finished work of Jesus;
sprinkle my conscience with his atoning blood; discover him
to me, and thus give me a sweet manifestation of his Person,
love, blood, and complete salvation. Let it, Lord, appear
before mine eyes, and in my heart, and seal it with divine
power upon my conscience."

August 2.

" *Underneath are the everlasting arms.*"—DEUTERONOMY
xxxiii. 27.

How Moses brought before the people the eternity of
God! He will have nothing to do with time. What is
time? A fragment, merely like the foam of the sea compared with the mighty ocean. The ocean is eternity; time is

merely the foam upon the wave. "Underneath are the everlasting arms." And depend upon it, if the everlasting arms are underneath the saints of God, for it is of and to them that the words are spoken, they are there for some purpose. God puts affliction upon affliction to bring the soul down, that it may fall into and upon the everlasting arms, and find how firm and strong they are. And have you not often found it so? Do not lie against your right. How many trials in providence you have been brought through. How conspicuously the Lord has appeared in this and that instance, so that your unbelief and infidelity were, for the time at least, thoroughly silenced, and faith saw the hand of God so clearly that you felt as if you could never doubt again. Have you not had many sweet supports on your bed of languishing, many precious seasons when you could bless God for laying upon you his afflicting hand? And have you not found that strength was always given to you according to your day, that with every trial power was given you to bear it, and that out of your deepest afflictions came your greatest blessings? Why are you not in hell? Do you not deserve to be there? Why still upon praying ground, with a good hope through grace, and your soul waiting for the Lord to appear, more than those that watch for the morning? If these arms have once supported you, will they not support you again? Would they be everlasting if they could part asunder and let you fall through? Rest upon them and you will find how strong they are.

August 3.

" When Christ, who is our life, shall appear, then shall ye also appear with him in glory."—Colossians iii. 4.

If Christ be your life upon earth; if you have a living faith in his divine Majesty; if any drops of his love have ever bedewed your soul; if any sweet smile has ever com-

forted your heart, the Apostle would say to all such, " When
Christ, who is your life, shall appear with all his saints, then
shall ye also appear with him in glory." No longer pestered
by sin and Satan, no longer carrying about a weak, infirm
tabernacle, the seat of innumerable evils and maladies, but
endued with a soul pure as he is pure, and a spiritual body
capable of enjoying the bliss and blessedness of eternity,
"then shall ye appear," ye suffering saints, who have set your
affections on him whom ye have not seen, and yet in whom
ye believe, "then shall ye also appear with him in glory."
And is not this worth struggling for? Is not this a blessed
goal at the end of the race? Is not this a worthy prize to
run for? Is not this an ample reward of all your temptations,
troubles, griefs and sorrows, to believe, and not in vain, that
" when he shall appear," you " shall appear with him in
glory?" The Lord, if it be his will, lead our souls into these
divine and blessed realities! They are the substance of vital
godliness; and so far as we feel them, and live under the
sweet influences and bedewing operations of the Spirit of
grace, these things will prove all our salvation, as they must
be, if we be rightly taught, all our desire.

August 4.

" But the God of all grace, who hath called us unto his
eternal glory by Christ Jesus, after that ye have suffered a
while, make you perfect, stablish, strengthen, settle you." —
1 PETER v. 10.

THERE is no Christian perfection, no divine establishment,
no spiritual strength, no solid settlement, except by *suffering*.
But *after* the soul has suffered, *after* it has felt God's chas-
tising hand, the effect is to *perfect*, to *establish*, to *strengthen*,
and to *settle* it. By suffering, a man becomes settled into a
solemn conviction of the character of Jehovah as revealed in
the Scripture, and in a measure made experimentally manifest

in his conscience. He is settled in the belief of an " ever-lasting covenant, ordered in all things, and sure ;" in the persuasion that " all things work together for good to them that love God, and are the called according to his purpose ; " in the firm conviction that everything comes to pass accord-ing to God's eternal purpose; and are all tending to the good of the Church, and to God's eternal glory. His soul, too, is settled down into a deep persuasion of the misery, wretchedness, and emptiness of the creature ; into the con-viction that the world is but a shadow, and that the things of time and sense are but bubbles that burst the moment they are grasped; that of all things sin is most to be dreaded, and the favour of God above all things most to be coveted ; that nothing is really worth knowing except Jesus Christ and him crucified; that all things are passing away, and that he himself is rapidly hurrying down the stream of life, and into the boundless ocean of eternity. Thus he becomes *settled* in a knowledge of the truth, and his soul remains at anchor, looking to the Lord to preserve him here, and bring him in peace and safety to his eternal home.

August 5.

" And this is life eternal, that they might know thee the only true God, and Jesus Christ, whom thou hast sent."—JOHN xvii. 3.

How many are anxious to know what is the way of salva-tion, how eternal life is to be obtained, and how to "flee from the wrath to come." But the Lord Jesus has shewn in one short sentence in what eternal life consists, that it is in the knowledge of the " only true God, and of Jesus Christ, whom he has sent." He therefore that knows the Father and the Son has eternal life in his soul. The Lord Jesus, in the sixth chapter of John, quoted this amongst other passages of the Old Testament, and says, "It is written in the prophets, And they shall be all taught of God. Every man therefore that hath heard, and hath learned of the Father, cometh unto me." He lays this down, then, as one especial fruit of divine teaching, that it produces *a coming unto him*. The Spirit, who teacheth to profit, holds up before the eyes of the soul, the Person, work, blood, love, grace, and righteousness of the Lord Jesus Christ. He shews the soul that he is just such a Saviour as it needs. He opens up the dignity of his Person, and shews that he is God-man. He makes known in the conscience that he has offered up himself a sacrifice for sin; that he has shed his atoning blood so that the sin of the Church is for ever put away from the sight of a just God. He opens up before the eyes of the mind his glorious righteousness, as that in which the Father is well pleased, and in which if the soul has but an interest, it is secure from the wrath to come. He unfolds to the heart the willingness of Christ to receive every coming sinner; he shews the treasures of mercy and grace which are locked up in him; and brings down in the heart the comforting words that he spake in the days of his flesh, such as, "Come unto me, all ye that labour and are heavy laden, and I will give you rest." "Him that cometh to me I will in no wise cast out." "If any man thirst, let him come unto me, and drink."

August 6.

" He that is slow to anger is better than the mighty; and he that ruleth his spirit than he that taketh a city."—PROVERBS xvi. 32.

WHAT a foe to one's peace is one's own spirit! And what shall I call it? It is often an infernal spirit. Why? Because it bears the mark of Satan upon it. The pride of our spirit, the presumption of our spirit, the hypocrisy of our spirit, the intense selfishness of our spirit are often hidden from us. This wily devil, self, can wear such masks and assume such forms; this serpent, self, can so creep and crawl, can so twist and turn, and can disguise itself under such false appearances, that it is hidden often from ourselves. Who is the greatest enemy we have to fear? We all have our enemies. But who is our greatest enemy? He that you carry in your own bosom; your daily, hourly, and momently companion, that entwines himself in nearly every thought of your heart; that suggests well-nigh every motive; that sometimes puffs up with pride, sometimes inflames with lust, sometimes inflates with presumption, and sometimes works under feigned humility and fleshly holiness.

Now this self must be overcome; for if self overcome us eventually, we shall perish in the condemnation of self. God is determined to stain the pride of human glory. He will never let self, (which is but another word for the creature,) wear the crown of victory. It must be crucified, denied, and mortified; it must be put off, so that Jesus may be put on; that in the denying of self, Jesus may be believed in; and that in the crucifixion of self, there may be a solemn spiritual union with Him who was crucified on Calvary. Now, are we overcoming self? Are we buffeted? What says self? "Buffet again." Are we despised? What says self? "Despise again; retort angry look for angry look, and hasty word for hasty word; 'an eye for an eye, and a tooth for a tooth.'" But what says the Spirit of God in a tender conscience? "Be not overcome of evil, but overcome evil with good."

The way to overcome self is by looking out of self to Him who was crucified upon Calvary's tree; to receive his image into our heart; to be clothed with his likeness; to drink into his spirit; and "receive out of his fulness grace for grace."

August 7

" *The fear of the Lord is his treasure.*"—Isaiah xxxiii. 6.

"The fear of the Lord is his treasure." And, oh, what a treasure is this fear! Treasure in ancient times was generally hidden; it was concealed from the eye of man, hoarded up, and not brought out ostentatiously to view. Wealthy men of old hid the knowledge of their treasures, lest they should be spoiled of them by the hand of violence. So spiritually, the fear of the Lord is hidden in the heart, and lies deep in the soul; it is not spread out ostentatiously to view, but is buried out of sight in a man's conscience. But though hidden from others, and sometimes even from ourselves, this "fear of the Lord" will act as circumstances draw it forth. There may be times and seasons when we seem almost hardened and conscience-seared; sin appears to have such power over us, and evil thoughts and desires so carry us away, that we cannot trace one atom of godly fear within; and the soul cries, "What will become of me! Where am I going now! What will come next on such a wretch as I feel myself to be!" But place him in such circumstances, say, as befel Joseph, then he will find that the "fear of the Lord" is in him a fountain of life, a holy principle springing up in his soul. Thus, this fear, which is a part of the heavenly treasure, acts when most needed. And the more the life of God is felt in the soul, the more the fear of God flows forth as a fountain of life to depart from the snares of death. The more lively the grace of God is in the soul, the more lively will godly fear be in the heart; and the more the Spirit of God works with power in the conscience, the deeper will be the fear of God in the soul.

August 8.

"Jesus saith unto him, I am the way."—JOHN xiv. 6.

How is *Jesus the way?* In everything that he is to God's people he is the way. His *blood* is the way to heaven; "for the whole path," as Hart speaks, "is lined with blood." By his precious blood shed upon Calvary's tree he has put away

sin by the sacrifice of himself, and opened a way of access to
God. His *righteousness*, also, is part of the way; for only
so far as we stand clothed in his glorious righteousness have
we any access unto, any acceptance with God the Father.
And his *love* is the way; for if we walk in love, we walk in
him, for he is love. Every part of the way was devised and
is executed by the love of his tender heart.

But the way, also, is *the way of tribulation.* Was not
Jesus himself the great Sufferer? And if he be the way, the
only way, I must be conformed to his likeness in suffering.
Not to know afflictions and tribulations, is not to know
Christ. He was "a man of sorrows and acquainted with
grief!" And if so, to have no sorrow, to have no acquaintance with grief, and to know nothing of tribulation, is to
proclaim to all with a loud voice that we have no union and
communion with the Lord Jesus Christ. But we are continually turning aside "to the right hand" or "to the left."
There is that cowardice in the heart which cannot bear the
cross; there is that slipping into carnal ease and fleshly
security, so as to get away from under the painful cross of
affliction and suffering. But when we thus turn aside "to
the right hand" or "to the left," the voice the Lord sends
after us is, "This is the way"—the way of affliction; no
other; the way of tribulation, the way of trial, the way of
exercise. This is the way in which the King walked of old;
and this is the way in which all his people have walked
before him and after him; for this is the only path in which
the footsteps of the flock can be found.

August 9.

"*Unto the upright there ariseth light in the darkness.*"—
PSALM cxii. 4.

WE often get into such dark paths, that we seem altogether

out of the secret, and feel as if there were no more grace in our souls, than in one altogether dead in trespasses and sins. And whether we look back at the past, or view the present, or turn our eyes to the future, one dark cloud seems to rest upon the whole; nor can we, with all our searching, find to our satisfaction that we have one spark of true religion, or one atom of grace, or one grain of vital godliness, or any trace that the Spirit of God has touched our consciences with his finger. Now, when we are in this dark, benighted state, we want light; we want the blessed Sun of righteousness to arise; we want the south wind to blow a heavenly gale, and drive the mists away; we want the clouds to part, and the light of God's countenance to shine into our souls, so as to shew us where we are, and what we are, and make it clear, that base and vile as we are, yet that we are interested in the love of the Father, the blood of the Son, and the teachings of the Holy Ghost. And when his word begins to distil like the rain and to drop like the dew, when the Lord himself is pleased to speak home one sweet testimony, one little word, one kind intimation—what a change it makes! The clouds break away, the fog clears off, the mists dissolve, and the soul becomes sweetly persuaded of its interest in the blood and love of the Lamb.

August 10.

"And the angel answered and said unto the women, Fear not ye : for I know that ye seek Jesus, which was crucified."— MATTHEW xxviii. 5.

WHATEVER be our state and case, if it can truly be said of us what the angel said to the women at the sepulchre, "I know that ye seek Jesus, which was crucified," we have a divine warrant to believe that "he is gone before us into Galilee. There shall we see him." He is risen; he has ascended up on high, and "has received gifts for men, yea, for the rebellious also, that the Lord God might dwell among them." He is now upon the mercy-seat, and he invites and draws poor needy sinners to himself. He says, "Come unto me, all ye that are weary and heavy laden, and I will give you rest." He allows us, he invites us to pour out our heart before him, to shew before him our trouble, to spread our wants at his feet, as Hezekiah spread the letter in the temple. If we seek communion with him, we may and shall tell him how deeply we need him, that without him it is not life to live, and with him not death to die. We shall beg of him to heal our backslidings; to manifest his love and blood to our con-science; to shew us the evil of sin; to bless us with godly sorrow for our slips and falls; to keep us from evil that it may not grieve us; to lead us into his sacred truth; to pre-serve us from all error; to plant his fear deep in our heart; to apply some precious promise to our soul; to be with us in all our ways; to watch over us in all our goings out and comings in; to preserve us from pride, self-deception, and self-righteousness; to give us renewed tokens of our interest in his finished work; to subdue our iniquities; to make and keep our conscience tender; and work in us everything which is pleasing in his sight. What is communion but mutual giving and receiving, the flowing together of two hearts, the melting into one of two wills, the exchange of two loves— each party maintaining its distinct identity, yet being to the other an object of affection and delight? Have we nothing, then, to give to Christ? Yes, our sins, our sorrows, our burdens, our trials, and above all the salvation and sanctifica-tion of our souls. And what has he to give us? What? Why, everything worth having, everything worth a moment's anxious thought, everything for time and eternity.

August 11.

*" They shall come with weeping, and with supplications will
I lead them : I will cause them to walk by the rivers of waters
in a straight way, wherein they shall not stumble : for I am a
father to Israel, and Ephraim is my firstborn."*—JEREMIAH
xxxi. 9.

OH how much is needed to bring the soul to its only rest
and centre! What trials and afflictions; what furnaces,
floods, rods, and strokes, as well as smiles, promises, and
gracious drawings! What pride and self to be brought out
of! What love and blood to be brought unto! What lessons
to learn of the dreadful evil of sin! What lessons to learn
of the freeness and fulness of salvation! What sinkings
in self! What risings in Christ! What guilt and condemnation on account of sin; what self-loathing and self-
abasement; what distrust of self; what fears of falling;
what prayers and desires to be kept; what clinging to
Christ; what looking up and unto his divine Majesty, as
faith views him at the right hand of the Father; what
desires never more to sin against him, but to live, move,
and act in the holy fear of God, do we find, more or less
daily, in a living soul!

And whence springs all this inward experience but from
the fellowship and communion which there is between Christ
and the soul? "We are members," says the Apostle,
"of his body, of his flesh, and of his bones." As such
there is a mutual participation in sorrow and joy. "He
hath borne our griefs, and carried our sorrows." "He
was in all points tempted like as we are, yet without sin."
He can, therefore, "be touched with the feelings of our
infirmities," can pity and sympathise; and thus, as we may
cast upon him our sins and sorrows, when faith enables,
so can he supply, out of his own fulness, that grace and

strength which can bring us off eventually more than conquerors.

August 12.

" *For if the blood of bulls and of goats, and the ashes of an heifer sprinkling the unclean, sanctifieth to the purifying of the flesh: how much more shall the blood of Christ, who through the eternal Spirit offered himself without spot to God, purge your conscience from dead works to serve the living God.*"— HEBREWS ix. 13, 14.

WHAT a mercy it is to have a conscience in any measure purged from dead works to serve the living God; to feel any free access to his gracious Majesty, any happy liberty in walking before him, any deliverance from doubt and fear, any removal of those exercises which try the mind and often bring heavy burdens upon the soul! Still, after all our wanderings, we must ever come to the same spot; after all our departings and backslidings, still again and again we must be brought to the same place to get the guilt removed, the mercy proclaimed, and the peace revealed. For is not this the blessedness that the blood of Christ cleanseth from *all* sin? Having obtained eternal redemption for us, his blood will never lose its efficacy, but will ever purge the conscience as long as the conscience of any burdened member of his mystical body remains to be purged, till he presents all his ransomed saints faultless before the presence of his glory with exceeding joy.

August 13.

" *A new heart also will I give you, and a new spirit will I put within you: and I will take away the stony heart out of your flesh, and I will give you a heart of flesh.*"—EZEKIEL xxxvi. 26.

THIS " new spirit " is a broken spirit, a soft, tender spirit, and is therefore called " a heart of flesh," as opposed to "the heart of stone," the rocky, obdurate, unfeeling, impenitent heart of one dead in sin, or dead in a profession. And how is this soft, penitent heart communicated? "I will put my Spirit within you." The same divine truth is set forth in the gracious promise: "And I will pour upon the house of David, and upon the inhabitants of Jerusalem, the spirit of grace and of supplications; and they shall look upon me whom they have pierced, and they shall mourn for him, as one mourneth for his only son, and shall be in bitterness for him, as one that is in bitterness for his firstborn." But what is the immediate effect of the pouring out of the spirit of grace and of supplications? A looking to him whom they have pierced, a mourning for him as one mourneth for an only son, and a being in bitterness for him as one that is in bitterness for his firstborn. This is evangelical repentance, as distinguished from legal; godly sorrow working repentance to salvation not to be repented of, as distinct from the sorrow of the world which worketh death. These two kinds of repentance are to be carefully distinguished from each other, though they are often sadly confounded. Cain, Esau, Saul, Ahab, Judas, all repented; but their repentance was the remorse of natural conscience, not the godly sorrow of a broken heart and a contrite spirit. They trembled before God as an angry Judge, were not melted into contrition before him as a forgiving Father. They neither hated their sins nor forsook them, loved holiness nor sought it. Cain went out from the presence of the Lord; Esau plotted Jacob's death; Saul consulted the witch of Endor; Ahab put honest Micaiah into prison; and Judas hanged himself. How different from this forced and false repentance of a reprobate is the repentance of a child of God— that true repentance for sin, that godly sorrow, that holy mourning which flows from the Spirit's gracious operations.

This does not spring from a sense of the wrath of God in a broken law, but of his mercy in a blessed gospel; from a view by faith of the sufferings of Christ in the garden and on the cross; from a manifestation of pardoning love; and is always attended with self-loathing and self-abhorrence, with deep and unreserved confession of sin and forsaking it, with most hearty, sincere, and earnest petitions to be kept from all evil, and a holy longing to live to the praise and glory of God.

August 14.

" For thou hast magnified thy word above all thy name."— Psalm cxxxviii. 2.

This is one of those expressions in Scripture that seem so comprehensive, and yet so amazing. To my mind it is one of the most remarkable expressions in the whole book of God. " Thou hast magnified thy word above all thy name." The name of God includes all the perfections of God; everything that God is, and that God is revealed as possessing. His justice, majesty, holiness, greatness, and glory, and whatever he is in himself; that is God's name. And yet he has magnified something above all his name; his *word*, his *truth*. This may refer to the Incarnate Word, the Son of God, who is called the Word. " There are three that bear record in heaven, the Father, the Word, and the Holy Ghost, and these three are one" (1 John v. 7). " In the beginning was the Word, and the Word was with God" (John i. 1). You may take the words either as meaning that God has magnified his Word, his eternal Son above all his great name, that is, he has set Jesus on high above all the other perfections of his majesty, or take it as meaning his written word, which is contained in the sacred Scriptures. He has magnified it above all his name in the fulfilment of it; God's faithfulness being

so dear to him, that he has exalted it above all his other
perfections. He would sooner allow them all to come to
naught, than for his faithfulness to fail.   He has so magnified
his faithfulness, that his love, his mercy, his grace would
all sooner fail, than his faithfulness; the word of his mouth,
and what he has revealed in the Scriptures.   What a firm
salvation, then, is ours, which rests upon his word, when
God has magnified that word above all his name!   What
a comprehensive declaration is this!   What volumes of
blessedness and truth are contained therein!   So that, if
God has revealed his truth to your soul, and given you
faith to anchor in the word of promise, sooner than that
should fail, he would suffer the loss of all; for he has
magnified his word above all his name.

August 15.

"*The life which I now live in the flesh I live by the faith
of the Son of God.*"—GALATIANS ii. 20.

THERE is no way except by being spiritually baptized
into Christ's death and life, that we can ever get a victory
over our besetting sins.   If, on the one hand, we have
a view of a suffering Christ, and thus become baptized
into his sufferings and death, the feeling, while it lasts,
will subdue the power of sin.   Or, on the other hand, if
we get a believing view of a risen Christ, and receive
supplies of grace out of his fulness, that will lift us above
its dominion.   If sin be powerfully working in us, we
want one of these two things to subdue it; either we must
have something come down to us to give us a victory
over our sin in our strugglings against it, or we must
have something to lift us up out of sin into a purer and
better element.   When there is a view of the sufferings
and sorrows, agonies and death of the Son of God, power

comes down to the soul in its struggles against sin, and
gives it a measure of holy resistance and subduing strength
against it. So, when there is a coming in of the grace
and love of Christ, it lifts up the soul from the love and
power of sin into a purer and holier atmosphere. Sin
cannot be subdued in any other way. You must either
be baptized into Christ's sufferings and death, or you must
be baptized (and these follow each other) into Christ's
resurrection and life. A sight of him as a suffering God,
or a view of him as a risen Jesus, must be connected
with every successful attempt to get the victory over sin,
death, hell, and the grave. You may strive, vow, and
repent; and what does it all amount to? You sink deeper
and deeper into sin than before. Pride, lust, and covetousness come in like a flood, and you are swamped and
carried away almost before you are aware. But if you
get a view of a suffering Christ, or of a risen Christ; if
you get a taste of his dying love, a drop of his atoning
blood, or any manifestation of his beauty and blessedness,
there comes from this spiritual baptism into his death or
his life a subduing power; and this gives a victory over
temptation and sin which nothing else can or will give.
Yet I believe we are often many years learning this divine
secret, striving to repent and reform, and cannot; till at
last by divine teaching we come to learn a little of what
the Apostle meant when he said, " The life I now live
in the flesh, I live by the faith of the Son of God." And
when we can get into this life of faith, this hidden life,
then our affections are set on things above. There is no
use setting people to work by legal strivings; they only
plunge themselves deeper in the ditch. You must get
Christ into your soul by the power of God; and then he
will subdue, by his smiles, blood, love, and presence, every
internal foe.

August 16.

" Ye shall know the truth, and the truth shall make you free."—JOHN viii. 32.

THE truths of the gospel, though to an enlightened eye they shine as with a ray of light all through the word, yet are they, for the most part, laid up as in veins: " Surely there is a vein for the silver, and a place for gold where they fine it." " As for the earth, out of it cometh bread, and under it is turned up as it were fire. The stones of it are the place of sapphires, and it hath dust of gold " (Job xxviii. 5, 6). But where is " the place of sapphires ? " and where this " dust of gold ? " " In the path which no fowl," no unclean professor, " knoweth, and which the vulture's eye," keen though it be after this world's carrion, " hath not seen." But to a spiritual mind sweet and self-rewarding is the task, if task it can be called, of searching the word as for hid treasure. No sweeter, no better employment can engage heart and hands than, in the spirit of prayer and meditation, of separation from the world, of holy fear, of a desire to know the will of God and do it, of humility, simplicity, and godly sincerity, to seek to enter into those heavenly mysteries which are stored up in the Scriptures ; and this, not to furnish the head with notions, but to feed the soul with the bread of life. Truth, received in the love and power of it, informs and establishes the judgment, softens and melts the heart, warms and draws upward the affections, makes and keeps the conscience alive and tender, is the food of faith, the strength of hope, and the mainspring of love. To know the truth is to be " a disciple indeed," and to be made blessedly free ; free from error, and the vile heresies which everywhere abound; free from presumption and self-righteousness; free from the curse and bondage of the law and the condemnation of a guilty conscience; free from a slavish fear of the opinion of men and the contempt and scorn of the world and worldly professors; free from following a multitude to do evil; free from companionship with those who have a name to live but are dead. But free to love the Lord and his dear people; free to speak well of his name; free to glorify him with our body and soul, which are his; free to a throne of grace and to a blood-besprinkled mercy-seat; free to every good word and work; free to "whatsoever things are good, whatsoever things are honest, whatsoever things are just, whatsoever things are pure, whatsoever things are lovely, whatsoever things are of good report."

August 17.

" But now, O Lord, thou art our Father; we are the clay, and thou our Potter; and we all are the work of thy hand." — Isaiah lxiv. 8.

Until free-will, self-righteousness, creature exertions, and human merit are dried up and withered away, till they all give up the ghost, we can never come into that spot where we are the clay, and God is the Potter. Can the clay make itself into a vessel? Can it mould itself into shape and form? Can it start from its bed, and work itself up into a vessel for use or ornament? No more can we make ourselves fit for glory, or mould ourselves into vessels of honour. If the Lord do but give us the feeling in our souls, our sweetest privilege, our dearest enjoyment, is to be the clay. Free-will self-righteousness, human wisdom, and creature strength—we give them all to the pharisees; let them make the most of them. But when the Lord indulges our souls with some measure of access to himself, and brings us in all humility and brokenness to lie low before his throne, we feel that we are nothing but what he makes us, have nothing but what he

gives us, experience nothing but what he works in us, and do
nothing but what he does in and for us. To be here, and to
lie here, is to be the clay; and to find the Lord working in
us holy desires, fervent breathings, secret cries, and the actings
of faith, hope, and love; and to feel these things freely given,
graciously communicated, and divinely wrought, and to know
the Lord is doing all this for us and in us, is to find him the
Potter, and is to be brought to the sweetest, lowliest, and
happiest spot that a soul can come into.

August 18.

" But let patience have her perfect work."—James i. 4.

PATIENCE then has its work; and what is that? Twofold,
according to my explanation of the word. 1. To *endure* all
trials, live through all temptations, bear all crosses, carry all
loads, fight all battles, toil through all difficulties, and overcome all enemies. 2. To *submit* to the will of God, to own
that he is Lord and King, to have no will or way of its own,
no scheme or plan to please the flesh, avoid the cross, or
escape the rod; but to submit simply to God's righteous
dealings, both in providence and grace, believing that he
doeth all things well, that he is a Sovereign, "and worketh
all things according to the counsel of his own will."   Now
until the soul is brought to this point, the work of patience
is not perfect; it may be going on, but it is not consummated.
You may be in the furnace of temptation now, passing through
the fiery trial.   Are you rebellious or submissive? If still rebellious, you must abide in the furnace until you are brought
to submission ; and not only so, but it must be *thorough* submission, or else patience has not its *perfect* work.   The dross
and slag of rebellion must be scummed off, and the pure metal
flow down.   It is all of God's grace to feel this for a single
moment.   But are there not, and have there not been, times
and seasons, in your soul, when you could be still and know

that he is God? when you could submit to his will, believing
that he is too wise to err, too good to be unkind? When this
submission is felt, patience has its perfect work. Look at
Jesus, our great example: see him in the gloomy garden,
with the cross in prospect before him on the coming morn.
How he could say, " Not my will, but thine be done!" There
was the perfect work of patience in the perfect soul of the
Redeemer. Now you and I must have a work in our soul
corresponding to this, or else we are not conformed to the
suffering image of our crucified Lord. Patience in us must
have its perfect work; and God will take care that it shall be
so. As in a beautiful piece of machinery, if the engineer
see a cog loose or a wheel out of gear, he must adjust the
defective part, that it may work easily and properly, and in
harmony with the whole machine; so if the God of all our
salvation see a particular grace not in operation or not properly performing its appointed work, he by his Spirit so
influences the heart that it is again brought to work as he
designed it should do. Measure your faith and patience by
this standard; but do not take in conjunction, or confound
with them the workings of your carnal mind. Here we often
mistake: we may be submissive as regards our spirit, meek
and patient, quiet and resigned, in the inward man, yet feel
many uprisings and rebellings of the flesh; and thus patience
may not seem to have her perfect work. But to look for
perfect submission in the flesh is to look for perfection in the
flesh, which was never promised and is never given. Look
to what the Spirit is working in you—not to the carnal mind,
which is not subject to the law of God, neither indeed can be,
and therefore knows neither subjection nor submission. Look
at that inward principality of which the Prince of peace is
Lord and Ruler, and see whether in the still depths of your
soul, and where he lives and reigns, there is submission to the
will of God.

August 19.

" We are troubled on every side, yet not distressed."—
2 CORINTHIANS iv. 8.

THE saint of God is "troubled on every side," because he
has on every side on which he may be troubled, a spiritual
side as well as a temporal side, a side in his soul as well as
a side in his body, a side in his supernatural as well as in his
natural life, a side in his new man of grace as well as a side
in his old man of sin. And as it is necessary for him to be
conformed to the suffering image of Christ, trouble comes
upon him on every side and from every quarter, to make him
like his blessed Lord. Nay, his troubles are multiplied in
proportion to his grace, for the more the afflictions abound
the more abundant are the consolations; and an abundance
of consolation is but an abundance of grace. Thus, the more
grace he has the greater will be his sufferings; and the more
he walks in a path agreeable to the Lord, and in conformity
to his will and word, the more will he be baptized with the
baptism of sorrow and tribulation wherewith his great Head
was baptized before him.

" Yet not distressed." The words " not distressed" literally
signify that we are not shut up in a narrow spot from which
there is no outlet whatever. It corresponds to an expression
of the Apostle's in another place where he says, " God will,
with the temptation, also make a way to escape that ye may
be able to bear it;" and tallies well with the words of David:
" Thou hast known my soul in adversities." There is the
trouble on every side. But he adds, " And hast not shut me
up into the hand of the enemy; thou hast set my feet in a
large room." " Not being shut up into the hand of the enemy"
is not being abandoned of God to the foeman's death-stroke;
and having " the feet set in a large room" is to have a place
to move about in, one which affords an escape from death

and destruction. Thus, the dying Christian has a God to go to; a Saviour into whose arms he may cast his weary soul; a blessed Spirit who from time to time relieves his doubts and fears, applies a sweet promise to his burdened spirit, gives him resignation and submission to the afflicting hand of God, and illuminates the dark valley of the shadow of death, which he has to tread, with a blessed ray of gospel light.

August 20.

" Wherefore the rather, brethren, give diligence to make your calling and election sure: for if ye do these things, ye shall never fall: for so an entrance shall be ministered unto you abundantly into the everlasting kingdom of our Lord and Saviour Jesus Christ."—2 PETER i. 10, 11.

I believe many of God's people, if not most, have much ado to " make their calling and election sure." They are not a people to take things for granted; they cannot sit at ease and say, " I have no doubt that I am a child of God;" they want something powerful, something applied, something spoken by the mouth of God himself; and short of that, they must be exercised with doubts and fears as to their state before him. Now let conscience speak; let us turn over the leaves of conscience. What says that faithful witness? Has God spoken with power to your soul? Has he pardoned your sins? Has he given you a sweet testimony of your interest in the Son of his love? Say you, " Why, I do not know that I can say all that, I do not know that God has pardoned my sins." Well, we will come a little lower then; if you cannot say that, we will take a little lower ground; can you say that you are sighing and groaning and crying at times, not always, but as the Lord works in you, for the sweet manifestations of Jesus' love to your souls? Here is a door open for you, the door of hope in the valley

of Achor. Can you come in here? Well, these are marks
of being one of God's peculiar people. But you cannot be
satisfied, short of God himself making it known to you; you
want an immediate testimony from his blessed mouth, and
nothing but that can satisfy you, and when he sheds abroad
his love in your soul, it will give you peace and comfort, and
nothing short of that can.

August 21.

"*A bruised reed shall he not break, and smoking flax shall
he not quench, till he send forth judgment unto victory.*"—
MATTHEW xii. 20.

THE gracious Man of Sorrows will never "break the
bruised reed, nor quench the smoking flax." It is true that "he
sends forth judgment," for he means to bring the soul down
into the dust; but whilst this judgment is going on, he secretly
supports; for he kills that he may make alive; he brings down
to the grave that he may bring up. But in sending forth this
"judgment," it is "unto victory." Conquest is at the end;
victory is sure. There may be a long conflict; a hard and
fearful battle, with the garments rolled in sweat and blood;
but victory is sure at last; for he will never rest till he fully
gains the day. Oh, how Satan would triumph if any saint
ever fell out of the embraces of the good Shepherd; if he could
point his derisive finger up to heaven's gate and to its risen
King, and say, "Thy blood was shed in vain for this wretch,
he is mine, he is mine!" Such a boast would fill hell with
a yell of triumph. But no, no; it never will be so; the
"blood that cleanseth from all sin" never was, never can
be shed in vain. Though the reed is "bruised," it will never
be broken; though the flax "smokes," it will never be extinguished; for he that "sends forth judgment" sends it
"unto victory." Long indeed may the battle fluctuate;
again and again may the enemy charge; again and again

may the event seem doubtful. Victory may be delayed even
unto a late hour, till evening is drawing on and the shades of
night are about to fall; but it is sure at last. And it is the
Lord that does the whole. We have no power to turn the
battle to the gate. Is there one temptation that you can
master? Is there any one sin that you can, without divine
help, crucify; one lust that you can, without special grace,
subdue? We are perfect weakness in this matter. But the
blessed Lord makes his strength perfect in this weakness.
We may and indeed must be bruised, and under painful
feelings may think no one was so hardly dealt with, and that
our case is singular. But without this we should not judge
ourselves; and " if we judge ourselves, we shall not be judged
of the Lord." If you justify yourself, the Lord will condemn
you; if you condemn yourself, the Lord will justify you.
Exalt yourself, and the Lord will humble you; humble yourself, and the Lord will exalt you.

August 22.

" O send out thy light and thy truth."—Psalm xliii. 3.

" O *send* out thy light." The Psalmist desired that light
might be sent out, that is, that there might be a communication of it. The soul walking in darkness, and enabled under
that darkness to pant and cry after light, is not satisfied with
the conviction, however deep, that with God is light. The
thirsty man is not satisfied with knowing that there is water
in the well; nor the man who has lost his way in a mine,
with knowing that there is light in the sun. One faint ray
gleaming through a chink were worth to him a thousand suns,
blazing, unseen by him, in the sky. And thus the benighted
saint cannot rest in the bare knowledge that " God is light,
and in him is no darkness at all," but his sigh and cry is that
this light may be sent out of the fulness of the Godhead into
his soul, so as to shed abroad an inward light in his heart,

whereby he may see the truth of God; whereby he may see the glory of God in the face of Jesus Christ; whereby he may see his name written in the book of life, and clearly discern his interest in the "everlasting covenant, ordered in all things, and sure;" whereby he may see Jesus, and in seeing Jesus see his own eternal union with Jesus, and in seeing his own eternal union with Jesus may enjoy sweet communion with him, so as to feel his presence in his soul, and have his glory revealed, and manifested to his heart.

But David wanted something more than light. He says, "O send out thy light and thy *truth*." What was "the truth" which he sought to know, and realise its inward power by its being sent out of the fulness of the Godhead? Doubtless, the very same truth that saints are crying to be sent out now; and this can be nothing less than "the truth as it is in Jesus;" the truth of his blood as atoning for sin, the truth of his righteousness as justifying us from all things from which we could not be justified by the law of Moses; the truth of personal and everlasting deliverance from all curse and condemnation, that truth whereby the soul is made free, according to those words, "Ye shall know the truth, and the truth shall make you free;" the truth whereby the affections are separated from the things of time and sense, and fixed on the realities of eternity; in a word, to know Jesus himself, by his own sweet revelation, for he is "the way, *the truth*, and the life," and that he may be himself enjoyed in our soul as the sum and substance of truth.

August 23.

"They shall ask the way to Zion with their faces thither-ward, saying, Come, and let us join ourselves to the Lord in a perpetual covenant that shall not be forgotten."—JEREMIAH l. 5.

"COME, *let us join ourselves* to the Lord." Does this imply any power in the creature to join himself to the Lord? No;

but it implies this—that when the Lord unites us to himself, then we unite ourselves to him; when the Lord brings the believer into a manifested union with himself, then there is a leaping forth of the soul, a going forth of the affections, a cleaving to him with purpose of heart, a believing in him with all the powers of the mind, and a solemn renunciation, a casting aside, a trampling under foot, a rejection of everything but that which stands in the power of God, as made known to the soul by the Holy Spirit.

It is not spoken in a presumptuous way: "Come, let us join ourselves to the Lord." It does not indicate any bold presumptuous *claim* upon the Lord, as if being now on the road to Zion, and being possessed of certain evidences, they could claim the inheritance, and, as it were, rush in, and lay hold of gospel blessings; but it points out the actings of living faith in the soul, which goes forth, when raised up and drawn out by the blessed Spirit. The vain confidence and rash forwardness of those who are at ease in Zion is a very different thing from the meek faith of those who are going and weeping, asking the way to Zion with their faces thitherward, whose hearts are melted by the Spirit into contrition, who renounce everything but Christ and him crucified, and desire to feel and taste the sweet manifestation of the love of a dying Lord. These, without presumption or bold familiarity, can say, "Come, let us join ourselves to the Lord," as feeling in their souls the actings of that living faith, whereby they cleave to and lean upon him, as the only prop between them and hell.

August 24.

"And he is the head of the body, the church."—COLOSSIANS i. 18.

THAT the Lord Jesus Christ should have a people, in whom he should be eternally glorified, was the original promise made

by the Father to the Son. "Ask of me, and I shall give thee
the heathen for thine inheritance, and the uttermost parts of
the earth for thy possession" (Psalm ii. 8). This was "the
joy that was set before him, for which he endured the cross,
despising the shame." This was "the purchased possession,"
"the travail of his soul," and the reward of his humiliation
and sufferings (Phil. ii. 9, 10). This people form the members
of his mystical body, all of which were written in his book,
the book of life, when as yet, as regards their actual existence,
there was none of them (Psalm cxxxix. 16). All these were
given to him in eternity, when he was constituted their covenant Head in the everlasting covenant, ordered in all things,
and sure. They thus became, in prospect of his incarnation,
"members of his body, of his flesh, and of his bones." How
touchingly did the blessed Redeemer remind his Father of
those covenant transactions, when he said in his memorable
prayer, "I pray for them: I pray not for the world, but for
them which thou hast given me; for they are thine. And all
mine are thine, and thine are mine; and I am glorified in
them." Being thus given to Christ, and constituted members
of his mystical body, they can no more perish than Christ
himself. He is their Head; and as he is possessed of all
power, full of all love, filled with all wisdom, and replete
with all mercy, grace, and truth, how can he, how will he,
suffer any of his members to fall out of his body, and be lost
to him as well as to themselves? Will any man willingly
suffer his eye, or his hand, or his foot, or even the tip of his
little finger, to be taken out or cut off? If any member of
our body perish, if *we* lose an arm or a leg, it is because we
have not power to prevent it. But all power belongs to
Christ, in heaven and in earth; and therefore no one member
of his mystical body can perish for want of power in him to
save it. But however truly blessed this doctrine is, it is only
when we are quickened and made alive unto God by a spiri-

tual birth that we savingly and experimentally know and realise it; and we are, for the most part, led into it thus. We are first made to feel our need of Christ as a Saviour from the wrath to come, from the fear of death, the curse of the law, and the accusations of a guilty conscience. When enabled, by the blessed Spirit's operations, to receive him into our heart, by faith, as the Christ of God, and to realise in some measure an interest in him, we are then taught to feel our need of continual supplies of grace and strength out of his fulness. For we have to learn something of the depths of the fall, of the evils of our heart, of the temptations of Satan, of the strength of sin, of our own weakness and worthlessness; and as every fresh discovery of our helplessness and wretchedness makes a way for looking to and hanging upon him, we become more and more dependent on him as of God made unto us wisdom, righteousness, sanctification, and redemption.

August 25.

"Jesus said unto her, I am the resurrection, and the life."— JOHN xi. 25.

How often we sink into places where we are in our feelings dead men. Has sin never slain you? Have convictions never, so to speak, knocked the life of God out of your soul? Has Satan never come with his fiery darts, with all the artillery of hell, and sought to scorch up every gracious feeling and every living desire? And have you not sunk at times in your soul into such miserable deadness of spirit, that it seemed that not only there and then you were devoid of all grace, but that it was an impossibility for grace ever again to renew and revive your soul? Here you were dead. I have often been here, which enables me to describe it to you. Yet with all this, there is a longing look, a heartfelt groan, a heaving sigh, a resisting unto blood, not an utter giving way, nor sinking down into miserable despair. God the Spirit kept alive his work upon the soul, and Christ himself as the resurrection dropped into our bosom, raised up and drew forth towards himself some fresh movements of that life which is in him. There was thus fulfilled that gracious consequence of his resurrection, "Whosoever believeth in me, though he were dead, yet shall he live." Oh, amidst all our deadness, all our gloom and desolation, all our emptiness, barrenness, and helplessness, if there be in our souls a longing look, a heart-felt cry, an earnest groan, a sincere desire toward him who is the resurrection, our prayer will ascend into his pitying, sympathising ear ; and as he is the resurrection, he will once more raise up into life and feeling our dead and drooping soul. We have no other source of life. If we were altogether and really dead, we should always continue dead unless he were the resurrection. But because he is the resurrection, he can re-animate, revive, renew, and requicken us by pouring into our hearts fresh life and feeling. It will be our mercy to be ever looking unto him, hanging upon him, believing in him, trusting to him, and giving him no rest until he appear again and again to the joy and rejoicing of our heart.

August 26.

"*He that believeth in me, though he were dead, yet shall he live.*"—JOHN xi. 25.

How can any one who is dead believe? He can, or our Lord would not have said so. I will shew you how. He is a living man as quickened into life by the power of the Spirit of God, and yet he is dead. This is the deep mystery, that though he is dead in law, dead in conscience, dead in help-lessness, yet God the Holy Ghost has breathed into him and deposited in him a seed of living faith. By this faith he cries, by this faith he sighs, and by this faith he hungers and thirsts after righteousness; yea, more, by this faith he looks

unto and believes in the Son of God. He scarcely knows
that he has faith. His faith is so weak and so small in his
own estimation, that he dare not say he has faith; and yet
he has all the fruits of faith, all the marks of faith, and all the
evidences of faith. Take as a parallel case Jonah in the
whale's belly. Had he faith or had he not faith? How low
he sank when the waves were heaped over his head, when
carried through the boundless deep in the belly of the whale.
Yet even there he could say, "I will look again toward thy
holy temple." Had he no faith? Yes, he had; and by that
faith he was saved, justified, accepted, brought out, and
delivered, and able to say, " Salvation is of the Lord." Take
Hezekiah upon his bed of sickness. Had he no faith?
How then could he turn his face to the wall and pray unto
the Lord? How could his eyes fail with looking upward,
when he said, " O Lord, I am oppressed, undertake for me?"
Take David in his mournful journey, when he went up by
the ascent of Mount Olivet, and wept as he went up bare-
foot, with his head covered, at the time of Absalom's rebellion.
Had he no faith? How then came he to pray, "O Lord,
I pray thee, turn the counsel of Ahithophel into foolishness?"
And why did the Lord answer that prayer, if it were not the
prayer of faith? In all these men of God, sunk though they
were almost to the last and lowest point, there was still the
life of faith; and by that faith they called upon God. They
looked unto him and were lightened, and their faces were
not ashamed. Here, then, is the connection between the
resurrection of the Lord Jesus Christ from the dead and the
experience of this seemingly dead soul. When Christ died,
he bare the sins of this poor dead soul in his body on the
tree, and thus atoned for them and put them away. When
Christ rose from the dead, this poor dead soul rose with him,
as a member of his mystical body. When Christ went up on
high, he ascended with him. And when Christ sat down at

the right hand of the Father, he virtually and mystically sat
down with him in heavenly bliss. Therefore, because Jesus
is the resurrection, and because as such he has an interest in
him, "he that believeth in him, though he were dead, yet shall
he live."

August 27.

*" Being made so much better than the angels, as he hath by
inheritance obtained a more excellent name than they."*—
HEBREWS i. 4.

CHRIST was *made* so much better than the angels, not as
the Son of God, because as that he *was* better than they
already, being, indeed, their Maker and Creator. Nor did
he become God's Son by being "appointed heir of all things,"
and "obtaining by inheritance a more excellent name"
than all the angelic host. If I have an only son, and he
inherits my property, his being my heir does not make him
my son, but his being my son makes him my heir. So the
blessed Jesus is God's heir. But the beauty and blessedness,
the grace and glory, the joy and consolation of his being
"the heir of all things," lie in this, that he is such *in our
nature*,—that the same blessed Immanuel who groaned and
wept, suffered and bled here below, is now at the right hand
of the Father as our High Priest, Mediator, Advocate, Representative, and Intercessor; that all power is given unto him
in heaven and earth as the God-man (Matt. xxviii. 18); and
that the Father hath "set him at his own right hand in the
heavenly places, far above all principality, and power, and
might, and dominion, and every name that is named, not only
in this world, but also in that which is to come" (Eph. i. 20,
21). But he has all this pre-eminence and glory not to *make*
him the Son of God, but because he who, as the Son of God,
"thought it not robbery to be equal with God, made himself
of no reputation, and took upon him the form of a servant,

and was made in the likeness of men : and being found in fashion as a man, he humbled himself, and became obedient unto death, even the death of the cross. Wherefore God hath highly exalted him, and given him a name which is above every name; that at the name of Jesus every knee should bow, of things in heaven, and things in earth, and things under the earth ; and that every tongue should confess that Jesus Christ is Lord, to the glory of God the Father " (Phil. ii. 6–11). The joy of heaven above, the delight of the saints here below, their only hope and help, strength and wisdom, spring from this, that the Son of God is exalted to the right hand of the Father in the very nature which he assumed in the womb of the virgin.

August 28.

" *The full soul loatheth an honeycomb ; but to the hungry soul every bitter thing is sweet.*"—PROVERBS xxvii. 7.

AFFLICTIONS, trials, and sorrows are very bitter things. And they must needs be bitter, for God never meant that they should be otherwise. When he takes the rod, it is to *make it felt;* and when he brings trouble on his children, it is that they may smart under it. Our text therefore does not, I believe, mean that the "bitter thing" is sweet when it is taken, for then it would cease to be bitter; but it is sweet on account of the blessed nourishment that is brought to the soul out of it. I remember reading, many years ago, the travels of Franklin to the North Pole ; and a very interesting book it is naturally. But there is one incident mentioned in it which just strikes my mind. In wandering over the snows of the circumpolar regions there was no food to be got for days and, I think, weeks, except a lichen or kind of moss that grew upon the rocks, and that was so exceedingly bitter, (something like "Iceland moss,") that it could only be taken with the greatest disgust; and yet upon that Franklin and his companions lived. They had no alternative; they must either eat that or die. But that bitter moss became sweet after it had passed their palates; for it had a nutriment in it which kept their bodies alive. And thus many of God's people, who have endured the most dreadful trials, have afterwards found nutriment to spring out of them. What bitter things are God's reproofs and rebukes in the conscience! And yet who would be without them? I appeal to you who fear God, whether you would deliberately choose never to experience marks of divine disapprobation, and never feel the frowns of God's anger at any time when you go wrong? I believe in my conscience that you whose hearts are tender in God's fear would say, "Lord, let me have thy frowns; for if I have not thy frowns and a conscience to feel them, what sins should I not recklessly plunge into? Where would not my wicked nature carry me, if I had not thy solemn reproofs!" These very rebukes then become sweet, not in themselves, nor at the time, but because of the solid profit that comes out of them.

August 29.

"For we are his workmanship, created in Christ Jesus unto good works, which God hath before ordained that we should walk in them."—Ephesians ii. 10.

Good works, properly so called, spring out of the inward operation of God's grace. By making the tree good he makes the fruit good (Matt. xii. 33). He works in us first the will to do that which is good, and then he gives us the power. He thus works in us both to will and to do of his good pleasure (Phil. ii. 13). Under the operations of his grace we are transformed by the renewing of our mind to prove what is that good, and acceptable, and perfect will of God (Romans xii. 2); and as this will is sought after to be known and done, good works follow as the necessary fruit. All those acts of love and affection, of kindness, sympathy, and liberality towards the Lord's people; all those instances of self-denial and willingness rather to suffer than to do wrong; all those proofs of disinterested desire to do all the good we can according to our means, position, and circumstances of life; all that striving after and maintaining integrity and uprightness of conduct in all matters of business and trust; all that strict and scrupulous adherence to our word, even to our own injury; all that Christian fulfilment of our relative duties, and the social relationships of husband and father, wife and mother, which the Scripture has enjoined —in a word, all those works which by almost unanimous consent are called "good" by men, are only really and truly good as wrought in the heart, lip, and life by the power of God.

August 30.

"And they overcame him by the blood of the Lamb, and by the word of their testimony."—REVELATION xii. 11.

IT is not "the blood of the Lamb" as revealed in the word of God, but as applied to and sprinkled on the conscience, which answers the accusations of Satan. But we may observe that there is our coming unto "the blood of sprinkling," and there is "the blood of sprinkling" coming unto us. The Apostle speaks, Hebrews xii. 22–24: *"Ye are come to* the blood of sprinkling, which speaketh better things than that of Abel." This coming *to* the blood is the first step in gaining the victory. But in Christian warfare defeat generally, if not always, precedes conquest. It is not, therefore, so easy to overcome sin, death, and hell, which are all striving against us; and usually we never look to the right quarter for help until well-nigh all hope is gone. The first gleam generally comes from a view of "the blood of the Lamb," as it were, in the distance. The lighthouse casts its glimmering rays far over the wide waste of waters, to guide into harbour the storm-tossed mariner; so, when there is a view in the soul of "the blood of the Lamb," even at a distance, it is a beacon light, which draws towards it the eyes and heart of those who are doing business "in deep waters." The light may not at first seem very bright or clear; but it is a day-star, heralding the rising of the sun. The Spirit shines on the word, and raises up faith in the soul to believe that the Lamb has been slain, that blood has been shed, that a sacrifice has been offered, and that "a new and living way" has been opened and consecrated "through the veil," the rent "flesh" of the Lord Jesus. This affords the accused soul some foothold on which it can stand and answer Satan's accusations. "True," he says, "I am a guilty wretch, a sinner, and the chief of sinners, for I have sinned against light, against convictions, against conscience, and the fear of God; my heart is altogether evil, my mind wholly corrupt, and my nature utterly depraved; I have never done any good thing; I am a wretch, and the worst of wretches, and I can never say anything too bad of myself, nor others of me; but, with all that, the Lamb of God hath shed his precious blood, and that blood 'cleanseth from all sin.'" "When the enemy comes in like a flood, the Spirit of the Lord," we read, "shall lift up a standard against him"—the blood-stained flag of the crucified Redeemer; and to come for refuge under this banner dipped in blood is to make head against Satan. Still, the victory is not fully gained. It is only when there is a coming of the blood into the heart, a sprinkling of it on the conscience, a manifestation and application of it to the soul, that Satan is effectually put to flight.

August 31.

" He giveth power to the faint."—Isaiah xl. 29.

THE Lord often gives his people power to take a longing,

languishing look at the blood and righteousness of Jesus; to come to the Lord, as "mighty to save," with the same feelings with which Esther went into the presence of the king: "I will go in, and if I perish, I perish." It is with them sometimes as with the four lepers who sat at the entering in of the gate of Samaria: "And they said one to another, Why sit we here until we die? If we say, We will enter into the city, then the famine is in the city, and we shall die there: and if we sit still here, we die also. Now therefore come, and let us fall unto the host of the Syrians: if they save us alive, we shall live; and if they kill us, we shall but die" (2 Kings vii. 3, 4). And so the Lord's people are sometimes brought to this state— "If I perish, I will perish at his footstool." If he give no answer of mercy, they will still cling to his feet, and beseech him to look upon, and save them. Now this is "power," real power. Despair would have laid hold upon their soul, if this secret power had not been given to them. Sometimes we learn this by painful experience. Our trials sometimes stun us, and then there is no power to seek or pray. But when power is given, there is a pleading with the Lord, a going out of the heart's desires after him, and a fulfilment in the soul of the experience described by the prophet, "I will wait upon the Lord, that hideth his face from the house of Jacob, and I will look for him."

God gives power also to believe; for it is the work of the blessed Spirit to raise up living faith in the heart. He gives power to hope; for it is only so far as he communicates power, that we can cast forth this anchor of the soul. He gives power to love; for it is only as he gives power, that we feel any measure of affection either to the Lord or to his people. In a word, every spiritual desire, every breath of fervent prayer, every movement of the soul heavenward, every trusting in God's name, relying on his word, and hanging upon his promises, spring out of power communicated by the Lord to the faint and feeble.

September 1.

"But now we see not yet all things put under him."— HEBREWS ii. 8.

IT is God's special prerogative to bring good out of evil, and order out of confusion. If you were to watch carefully from an astronomical observatory the movements of the planets, you would see them all in the greatest apparent disorder. Sometimes they would seem to move forward, sometimes backward, and sometimes not to move at all. These confused and contradictory movements sadly puzzled astronomers, till Sir Isaac Newton rose and explained the whole ; then all was seen to be the most beautiful harmony and order, where before there was the most puzzling confusion. But take a scriptural instance, the highest and greatest that we can give, to shew that where, to outward appearance, all is disorder, there the greatest wisdom and most determinate will reign. Look at the crucifixion of our blessed Lord. Can you not almost see the scene as painted in the word of truth ? See those scheming priests, that wild mob, those rough soldiers, that faltering Roman governor, the pale and terrified disciples, the weeping women, and, above all, the innocent Sufferer with the crown of thorns, and enduring that last scene of surpassing woe, which made the earth quake, and the sun withdraw his light. What confusion ! What disorder ! What triumphant guilt ! What oppressed and vanquished innocence ! But was it really so ? Was there no wisdom or power of God here accomplishing, even by the instrumentality of human wickedness, his own eternal purposes ? Hear his own testimony to this point : "Him, being delivered by the determinate counsel and foreknowledge of God, ye have taken, and by

wicked hands have crucified and slain" (Acts ii. 23). The
"determinate counsel and foreknowledge of God," in the
great and glorious work of redemption, was accomplished
by the wicked hands of man ; and if so, in this the worst and
wickedest of all possible cases, is not the same eternal will
also now executed in instances of a similar nature, though
to us at present less visible?

September 2.

*" Unto you that fear my name shall the Sun of righteousness
arise with healing in his wings."*—MALACHI iv. 2.

OH, what a mercy for the Church of Christ that the God
and Father of the Lord Jesus has not left her as he might
justly have left her, to perish in her sins, but has provided
for her a Saviour, and a great one, and does from time
to time encourage every poor, self-condemned sinner to
hope in his mercy ! The very things, poor, exercised soul,
that most try your mind are the very things that make
such a Saviour suitable to you. You are dark; this makes
the Sun of righteousness exactly suitable to enlighten you.
You are cold ; this makes you want the Sun to warm you.
You are cheerless and cast down ; this makes you want
the Sun to gladden you. You are barren and unfruitful,
and lament that you cannot bring forth fruit to God's glory;
you want the Sun to fertilize you. You are, at times, very
dead in your feelings, and can scarcely find any inclination
to pray, meditate, or read the Scriptures ; you want the
Sun to enliven and revive you. Are not, then, these very
trials and temptations necessary to make you feel that the
Lord Jesus is the Sun you need, the very Sun that David
(Psalm lxxxiv. 11) felt him to be? What value do those
put upon the Lord Jesus who make a fire for themselves,
and walk in the sparks of their own kindling? What is
Jesus to those who know no trouble of soul? What real

and earnest prayer or fervent desire have they after him? what ardent longing for his appearing? what breathings to see and feel his blood and righteousness? Oh! it is sharp exercises, manifold trials, and powerful temptations that make the soul really value the Lord Jesus.

September 3.

" God is faithful, by whom ye were called unto the fellowship of his Son Jesus Christ our Lord."—1 CORINTHIANS i. 9.

NOTHING distinguishes the divine religion of the saint of God, not only from the dead profanity of the openly ungodly, but from the formal lip-service of the lifeless professor, so much as communion with God.

How clearly do we see this exemplified in the saints of old. Abel sought after fellowship with God when "he brought of the firstlings of his flock, and of the fat thereof," for he looked to the atoning blood of the Lamb of God. God accepted the offering, and "testified of his gifts" by manifesting his divine approbation. Here was fellowship between Abel and God. Enoch "walked with God;" but how can two walk together except they be agreed? And if agreed, they are in fellowship and communion. Abraham was "the friend of God;" "The Lord spake to Moses face to face;" David was "the man after God's own heart;"—all which testimonies of the Holy Ghost concerning them implied that they were reconciled, brought near, and walked in holy communion with the Lord God Almighty. So all the saints of old, whose sufferings and exploits are recorded in Hebrews xi, lived a life of faith and prayer, a life of fellowship and communion with their Father and their Friend; and though "they were stoned, sawn asunder, and slain with the sword;" though "they wandered about in sheep-skins and goat-skins, being destitute, afflicted, tormented;" though "they wandered in deserts and in mountains, and in dens and caves of the earth," yet they all were sustained in their sufferings and sorrows by the Spirit and grace, the presence and power of the living God, with whom they held sweet communion; and, though tortured, would "accept no deliverance," by denying their Lord, "that they might obtain a better resurrection," and see him as he is in glory, by whose grace they were brought into fellowship with him on earth.

This same communion with himself is that which God now calls his saints unto, as we read, "God is faithful, by whom ye were called unto the fellowship of his Son Jesus Christ our Lord," for to have fellowship with his Son is to have fellowship with him. As then he called Abraham out of the land of the Chaldees, so he calls elect souls out of the world, out of darkness, sin, and death, out of formality and self-righteousness, out of a deceptive profession, to have fellowship with himself, to be blessed with manifestations of his love and mercy. To this point all his dealings with their souls tend; to bring them near to himself, all their afflictions, trials, and sorrows are sent; and in giving them tastes of holy fellowship here, he grants them foretastes and prelibations of that eternity of bliss which will be theirs when time shall be no more, in being for ever swallowed up with his presence and love.

September 4.

" God is love; and he that dwelleth in love dwelleth in God, and God in him."—1 JOHN iv. 16.

LOVE is communicative. This is a part of its very nature and essence. Its delight is to give, and especially to give itself; and all it wants or asks is a return. To love and to be beloved, to enjoy and to express that ardent and mutual affection by words and deeds,—this is love's delight, love's heaven. To love, and not be loved,—this is love's misery, love's hell. God is love. This is his very nature, an essential

attribute of his glorious being; and as he, the infinite and
eternal Jehovah, exists in a Trinity of distinct Persons, though
undivided Unity of Essence, there is a mutual, ineffable love
between Father, Son, and Holy Ghost. To this mutual, ineffable love of the three Persons in the sacred Godhead the
Scripture abundantly testifies : " The Father loveth the Son ; "
" And hast loved them as thou hast loved me ; " " This is my
beloved Son in whom I am well pleased." And as the Father
loves the Son, so does the Son love the Father : " But that
the world may know that I love the Father," are his own
blessed words. And that the Holy Ghost loves the Father
and the Son is evident not only from his divine personality in
the Godhead, but because he is essentially the very " Spirit of
love " (Romans xv. 30), and as such " sheds the love of God
abroad in the heart " of the election of grace.

Thus *man* was not needed by the holy and ever-blessed
Trinity as an object of divine love. Sufficient, eternally and
amply sufficient, to all the bliss and blessedness, perfection
and glory of Jehovah was and ever would have been the
mutual love and intercommunion of the three Persons in
the sacred Godhead. But love—the equal and undivided
love of Father, Son, and Holy Spirit—flowed out beyond its
original and essential being to man; and not merely to man
as man, that is to human nature as the body prepared for the
Son of God to assume, but to thousands and millions of the
human race, who are all loved personally and individually
with all the infinite love of God as much as if that love were
fixed on only one, and he were loved as God loves his dear
Son. " I have loved thee with an everlasting love," is spoken
to each individual of the elect as much as to the whole Church,
viewed as the mystical Bride and Spouse of the Lamb. Thus
the love of a Triune God is not only to the nature which in
due time the Son of God should assume, the flesh and blood
of the children, the seed of Abraham which he should take

on him (Hebrews ii. 14–16), and for this reason viewed by the Triune Jehovah with eyes of intense delight, but to that innumerable multitude of human beings who were to form the mystical body of Christ. Were Scripture less express, we might still believe that the nature which one of the sacred Trinity was to assume would be delighted in and loved by the holy Three-in-One. But we have the testimony of the Holy Ghost to the point, that puts it beyond all doubt or question. When, in the first creation of that nature the Holy Trinity said, "Let us make man in our image, after our likeness," and when, in pursuance of that divine council, "the Lord God formed man of the dust of the ground, and breathed into his nostrils the breath of life, and man became a living soul," God thereby uniting an immortal soul to an earthly body, this human nature was created not only in the moral image of God, but after the pattern of that body which was prepared for the Son of God by the Father.

September 5.

"*In whom are hid all the treasures of wisdom and knowledge.*"—Colossians ii. 3.

What poor, blind fools are we by nature! How insufficient is all our earthly wisdom and all our natural knowledge, to guide us into the truth! When the soul really is under divine teaching, how ignorant it feels as to every single thing it desires to know! What clouds of darkness perpetually hang over the mind! What a veil of ignorance seems continually spread over the heart! The simplest truths of God's word seem hid in the deepest obscurity, and the soul can neither see the truth, nor see nor feel its personal interest in it. Now, when a man is here, he does not go to the Lord with lying lips and a mocking tongue, and ask him to give him wisdom, merely because he has heard that other persons have asked it of God, or because he reads in the Bible that Christ is made of God "wisdom" to his people; but he goes as a poor, blind fool, as one completely ignorant, as one totally unable to understand a single spiritual truth of himself, as one thoroughly helpless to get into the marrow of vital godliness, into the mysteries of true religion, or into the very heart of Christ. For it is not a few doctrines received into the head, nor a sound creed, that can satisfy a soul convinced of its ignorance. No; nothing can satisfy him, but to have that divine illumination, whereby he "sees light in God's light;" that spiritual wisdom communicated, whereby he feels himself "made wise unto salvation;" that unctuous light shed abroad in the heart, which is the only key to gospel truth, and is its own blessed evidence, that he knows the truth by a divine application of it to his soul.

September 6.

" To see thy power and thy glory, so as I have seen thee in the sanctuary."—PSALM lxiii. 2.

EVERY place is " a sanctuary" where God manifests himself in power and glory to the soul. Moses, doubtless, had often passed by the bush which grew in Horeb; it was but a common hawthorn bush, in no way distinguished from the other bushes of the copse; but on one solemn occasion it was all "in a flame of fire," for "the angel of the Lord appeared unto him in a flame of fire" out of the midst; and though it burnt with fire, it was not consumed. God being in the bush, the ground round about was holy, and Moses was bidden to put off his shoes from off his feet. Was not this a sanctuary to Moses? It was, for a holy God was there. Thus wherever God manifests himself, *that* becomes a sanctuary to a believing soul. We want not places made holy by the ceremonies of man, but places made holy by the presence of God. Then a stable, a hovel, a hedge, any homely corner may be, and is a sanctuary, when God fills your heart with his sacred presence, and causes every holy feeling and gracious affection to spring up in your soul. If ever you have seen this in times past, you have seen God in the sanctuary; for then your heart becomes the sanctuary of God, according to his own words, "Ye are the temple of the living God; as God hath said, I will dwell in them and walk in them." Are not your very bodies the temples of the Holy Ghost? (1 Cor. vi. 19.) Does not Christ dwell in the heart by faith? And is he not formed there, the hope of glory? It is, then, not only in Christ *without*, but in Christ *within* that we see the power and glory of God. It is in this way that we become consecrated to the service and glory of God, set our affections upon heavenly things, and obtain a foretaste of eternal joy.

September 7.

" I will give thee the treasures of darkness."—Isaiah xlv. 3.

Is not this a strange expression? "Treasures of darkness!" How can there be darkness in the City of Salvation of which the Lord the Lamb is the eternal light? The expression does not mean that the treasures themselves are darkness, but that they were hidden in darkness till they were brought to light. The treasures of Belshazzar, like the Bank bullion, were buried in darkness till they were broken up and given to Cyrus. It is so in a spiritual sense. Are there not treasures in the Lord Jesus? Oh! what treasures of grace in his glorious Person! What treasures of pardon in his precious blood! What treasures of righteousness in his perfect obedience! What treasures of salvation in all that he is and has as the great High Priest over the house of God! Yet, all these treasures are "treasures of darkness," so far as they are hidden from our eyes and hearts, till we are brought by his special power into the City of Salvation. Then these treasures are not only brought to light, revealed, and made known, but the soul is at once put into possession of them.

They are not only seen, as the Bank of England clerk sees notes and sovereigns, but are by a special deed of gift from the Court of Heaven made over to him who by faith in the Lord Jesus receives him into his heart. No one has the least conception of the treasures of grace that are in the Lord Jesus till he is brought out of darkness into God's marvellous light, and knows him and the power of his resurrection by the sweet manifestations of his presence and love.

But the word *"treasures"* signifies not only something laid up and hidden from general view, but, being in the plural number, expresses an infinite, incalculable amount—an amount which can never be expended, but suffices, and suffices, and suffices again for all wants and for all believing comers. When we get a view by faith of the Person and work of the Lord Jesus and see the everflowing and overflowing fulness of his grace, and how it superabounds over all the aboundings of sin, it may well fill our minds with holy wonder and admiration. When we get a glimpse of the virtue and efficacy of his atoning blood, that precious blood which " cleanseth from all sin," and that divine righteousness which is "unto all and upon all them that believe," what treasures of mercy, pardon, and peace are seen laid up in him ! To see this by the eye of faith, and enter into its beauty and blessedness, is indeed to comprehend with all saints the length, and breadth, and depth, and height, and to know something of the love of Christ which passeth knowledge. The sun will cease to give his light, and the earth to yield her increase ; but these treasures will still be unexhausted, for they are in themselves infinite and inexhaustible.

September 8.

" Every valley shall be exalted, and every mountain and hill shall be made low: and the crooked shall be made straight, and the rough places plain."—ISAIAH xl. 4.

IF in your road heavenward, no valley ever sank before

you; if no mountain and hill ever rose up in sight; if you encountered no crooked path through the dense wood; and no rough places, with many a rolling stone and many a thorny briar in the tangled forest, it would not seem that you were treading the way which the saints of God have ever trod, nor would it appear as if you needed special help from the sanctuary, or any peculiar power to be put forth for your help and deliverance. But being in this path, and that by God's own appointment, and finding right before your eyes valleys of deep depression which you cannot raise up; mountains and hills of difficulty that you cannot lay low; crooked things which you cannot straighten; and rough places which you cannot make smooth; you are compelled, from felt necessity, to look for help from above. These perplexing difficulties, then, are the very things that make yours a case for the gospel, yours a state of mind to which salvation by grace is thoroughly adapted, yours the very condition of soul to which the revelation of the glory of God in the face of Jesus Christ is altogether suitable. So that if you could at the present moment view these trials with spiritual eyes, and feel that they were all appointed by unerring wisdom and eternal love, and were designed for the good of your soul, you would rather bless God that your pathway was so cast in providence and grace that you had now a valley, now a mountain, now a crook, and now a thorn. And even as regards the present experience of your soul, you would feel that these very difficulties in the road were all productive of so many errands to the throne—that they all called upon you, as with so many speaking voices, to beg of the Lord that he would manifest himself in love to your heart. We all want ease; we love a smooth path. We should like to be carried to heaven in a palanquin; to enjoy every comfort that earth can give or heart desire, and then, dying without a pang of body or mind, find ourselves safe in heaven. But

that is not God's way. The word of truth, the sufferings of
Christ, and the universal experience of the saints, all testify
against the path of ease; all testify for the path of trial; they
all proclaim, as with one united voice, "Wide is the gate and
broad is the way that leadeth to destruction,"—and this is the
way of ease and of that prosperity which destroys fools (Prov.
i. 32); but "strait is the gate and narrow is the way which leadeth unto life,"—and this is the path of suffering and sorrow.

September 9.

*"But this man, after he had offered one sacrifice for sins for
ever, sat down on the right hand of God."*—HEBREWS x. 12.

IT is a fundamental article of our most holy faith, that *the
man* Christ Jesus is now at God's right hand, a very man,
not a shadowy, aërial substance. "There is one God, and
one Mediator between God and men, the man Christ Jesus."
God looks at him as such with eyes of intense delight, with
ever new approbation and love; and views him as the representative of all that are interested in him; he being the Head,
the Church the members; he the Bridegroom, the Church
the bride; he the great High Priest, and the Church the
house of God. As living for her at the right hand of the
Father, he is ever presenting on her behalf the validity of
his intercession. The fact, the reality that he is there, is the
Church's joy, as it is all her hope and all her boast. "Because
I live, ye shall live also." To him, then, do we direct our
prayers; on his glorious Person we fix our believing eyes;
upon his blood we hang our hope; under his righteousness
we ever desire to shelter; to feel his presence, taste his grace,
experience his love, and know his power, is what our soul,
under divine teaching, is ever longing for. See, then, the
grounds of holy boldness for a poor sinner to enter into the
holiest. Blood has been shed, which blood has the validity
of Godhead stamped upon it. A new and living way has

been consecrated, in which a living soul may walk. A great High Priest is set over the house of God, who is ever presenting the merits of his intercession. Thus, those who feel their need of him, who cannot live and dare not die without him, whose eyes are upon him and hearts towards him, are encouraged to enter with all holy boldness into the holiest, that they may have communion with Father, Son, and Holy Ghost.

September 10.

"In all these things we are more than conquerors through him that loved us."—ROMANS viii. 37.

THOSE who know nothing of their own heart, of their own infirmities, of their own frailties, of their own inward or outward slips and backslidings, know nothing of the secret of superabounding grace, nothing of the secret of atoning blood, nothing of the secret of the Spirit's inward testimony. They cannot. Only in proportion as we are emptied of self in all its various forms, are we filled out of the fulness of Him that filleth all in all.

Now you, perhaps, (I address myself personally to some poor, tempted child of God, that in touching one, I may touch others,) are a poor, tempted creature; and your daily sorrow, your continual trouble is, that you are so soon overcome; that your temper, your lusts, your pride, your worldliness, your carnal, corrupt heart are perpetually getting the mastery. And from this you sometimes draw bitter conclusions. You say, in the depth of your heart, "Can I be a child of God, and be thus? What mark and testimony have I of being in favour with God when I am so easily, so continually overcome?" Now I want you to look to the end. What is the issue of these defeats? Remember, it is a solemn truth, and one that we learn very slowly—that we must *be* overcome in order *to* overcome. There is no setting out with a stock of strength, daily adding to it, weekly increasing it, and then gaining the victory by our own resolutions, our own innate strength. Such feigned holiness may come under a gospel garb, may wear a fair appearance; but it only more hides the rottenness of the flesh. Then, remember this—that in order to gain the victory, we must know our weakness; and we can only know our weakness by its being experimentally opened up in our consciences. We cannot learn it from others; we must learn it in our own souls; and that often in a very painful manner. But these painful sensations in a tender conscience lead a man more humbly, more feelingly, more believingly to the Lord of life and glory, to receive out of his fulness. Thus every defeat only leads to and ensures victory at the last. Says the Apostle, " In all these things we are more than conquerors." How? Through our re- solutions, through our wisdom? No; "through Him that loved us." There is no other way, then, to overcome, but by the " strength of Jesus made perfect in our weakness."

September 11.

" And my speech and my preaching was not with enticing words of man's wisdom."—1 CORINTHIANS ii. 4.

It is not the work of the Spirit to produce doubts and fears, but to overcome them. And yet we are continually subject to them. Infidel thoughts fly across the mind; doubts and questionings suggest themselves; Satan is busy in plying his arguments; a guilty conscience falls too readily under his accusations; painful recollections of past slips, falls, and back- slidings strengthen the power of unbelief, so that to come to a spot wherein there is not the least shadow of a doubt of divine realities, and, what is far more, of our own interest in them, is a rare circumstance, and only attainable at those favoured moments when the Lord is pleased to shine into the soul and settle the matter between himself and our conscience. But these very doubts, these very questionings, these cutting, killing fears, these anxious surmisings work together for good, and are mercifully overruled for our spiritual benefit. What else has brought us to this point that nothing short of demonstration will satisfy the soul really born and taught of God? It must have demonstration: nothing else will do. We cannot live and die upon uncertainties. It won't do to be always in a state that we don't know whether we are going to heaven or hell; to be tossed up and down on a sea of uncertainty, scarcely knowing who commands the ship, what is our destination, what our present course, or what will be the end of the voyage. Now all human wisdom leaves us upon this sea of uncertainty. It is useful in nature, but useless in grace. It is foolish and absurd to despise all human learning, wisdom, and knowledge. Without them we should be a horde of wild, wandering savages. But it is worse than foolish to make human wisdom our guide to eternity, and make reason the foundation of our faith or hope. What you thus believe to-day, you will disbelieve to-morrow; all the arguments that may convince your reasoning mind, all the appeals to your natural passions, which may seem for the time to soften your heart, and all the thoughts swaying to and fro which may sometimes lead you to hope you are right and sometimes make you fear you are wrong,—all these will be found insufficient when the soul comes into any time of real trial and perplexity. We want, therefore, demonstration to remove and dispel all these anxious questionings, and settle the whole matter firmly in our heart and conscience; and this nothing can give us but the Spirit by revealing Christ, taking of the things of Christ, and shewing them unto us, applying the word with power to our hearts, and bringing the sweetness, reality, and blessedness of divine things into our soul. It is only in this way that he overcomes all unbelief and infidelity, doubt and fear, and sweetly assures us that all is well between God and the soul.

September 12.

" But in demonstration of the Spirit and of power."—
I CORINTHIANS ii. 4.

In human reasoning, demonstration cannot usually be obtained except in mathematics, but not so in divine. There grace outshines and exceeds nature, for the teaching and testimony of the blessed Spirit is always demonstrative, that is, convincing beyond the possibility of doubt. It is not demonstration simply we require, not demonstration of the word, as if there were some innate proof and power in the word itself to demonstrate its own truth, though doubtless it is so when the Spirit shines upon it, but it is the "demonstration of the Spirit." This is very necessary to observe, for you will often hear the word of God spoken of, as if the Bible possessed not only demonstrative proof of its own inspiration, but was able to give that demonstration to the souls of men. But the demonstration not of the word but of the Spirit in, through, and by the word, is the thing wanted to convert sinners and satisfy saints. This is proof indeed, not cold and hard like mathematical demonstration, but warm, living, softening, and sanctifying, being the very light, life, and power of God himself in the soul. Now Paul's preaching was this demonstration of the Spirit. The Spirit of God speaking in him and by him, so demonstrated the truth of what he preached that it came, as he elsewhere speaks, "not in word only, but also in power, and in the Holy Ghost, and in much assurance" (I Thess. i. 5). There are now no Pauls; and yet, unless we have a measure of the same demonstration of the Spirit, all that is said by us in the pulpit drops to the ground; it has no real effect; there is no true or abiding fruit—no fruit unto eternal life. If there be in it some enticing words of man's wisdom, it may please the mind of those who are gratified by such arts; it may stimulate and occupy the attention for the time; but there it ceases, and all that has been heard fades away like a dream of the night; and, as regards the family of God, we may apply to all such preaching the words of the prophet: "It shall even be as when an hungry man dreameth, and, behold, he eateth; but he awaketh, and his soul is empty: or as when a thirsty man dreameth, and, behold, he drinketh; but he awaketh, and, behold, he is faint, and his soul hath appetite" (Isaiah xxix. 8). But anything which is communicated by the Holy Ghost, which is demonstrated by the Spirit to your soul, which is brought into your heart with light, life, and power, sealed and witnessed by that sacred Teacher and divine Comforter; *that* abides, you take it home with you; it comforts you, not only at the time, but when you look back to it in days to come; it is a bright spot in your soul's experience, when you can believe that then and there God was pleased to bless his word to your soul, and seal it home with a sweet influence upon your conscience. This is "demonstration of the Spirit."

And where there is this, there is "power:" for the Apostle adds, "and of power." The grand distinguishing mark of the kingdom of God is that "it is not in word, but in power." Thus power is given to believe in the Son of God, and we cannot believe truly and savingly in him till power is put forth; power to receive the Lord in all his covenant characters and gracious relationships in the gospel of his grace; power to believe that what God has done he does for ever; power to come out of every doubt and fear into the blessed light and liberty of the truth which maketh free.

September 13.

"And Enoch walked with God."—Genesis v. 24.

THE chief way whereby we walk with God is by *faith*, and not by sight. Abraham walked in this way. Unbelief severs the soul from God. There is no communion between God and an infidel. An unbelieving heart has no fellowship with the Lord Jesus Christ; but a believing heart has communion with him. It is by faith that we have fellowship with God and his dear Son; and you will find that just in proportion to the strength or weakness of your faith is your walking with God. If you have faith in blessed exercise, as you look to the atoning blood, you find that you can walk with God; you can pour out your heart before him, tell him all your concerns, spread before him the inmost movements of your mind, and look to him for peace and consolation. But when your faith is weak, when it gives way under trial, and cannot take hold of the promises, then communion is interrupted; there is no longer a walking with God. But in proportion as faith is strong, so there is a walking with God in sweet agreement; for faith keeps eyeing the atonement; faith looks not so much to sin, as to salvation from sin; at the way whereby sin is pardoned, overcome, and subdued. So it is by faith, and in proportion to our faith, that we walk together with God.

September 14.

" Blessed be the God and Father of our Lord Jesus Christ, who hath blessed us with all spiritual blessings in heavenly places in Christ."—Ephesians i. 3.

IF you are blessed with all spiritual blessings, it is only "in Christ" you are so blessed. If you were chosen before the foundation of the world, it was only "in Christ" that you were chosen. He is our covenant Head. What we are we are only in him. There is nothing in self; no fixedness there. All is fluctuating here below; all is uncertain as regards man. Certainty is with God; and the fixedness of God's purposes is our grand, our only support. Thus the doctrine of election received into the heart diffuses a sacred blessedness over the whole truth of God, for it gives stability to it. It is not a dry doctrine which men may toss about from hand to hand like a tennis ball; it is not an article of a creed written down in church articles, or a theory to be argued by divines. Nor is it a mere loose, floating idea gathered from a few dim and doubtful passages of God's word. It is no ignis fatuus, no meteor light dancing over morasses and swamps. It is a steady light set by the hand of God in the Scriptures, as he set of old lights in the firmament of the heavens to give light upon the earth. It therefore diffuses its rays over the whole of God's truth. For it is "in Christ" his people were chosen, and therefore election being in Christ, it is reflected with all the beams of the Sun of righteousness upon every gospel truth. There is not a single gospel truth, or a single spiritual blessing, which does not derive its blessedness from its connection with the Person and work of the Son of God; and what is true of all, is true of this, that the blessedness of election is because it is "in Christ."

But some may say, "These things are hard to believe." They are very hard to believe, for our unbelieving heart finds it very hard to believe anything that is for our good. We can believe Satan's lies with great readiness; we can give an open, willing ear to anything which our evil heart suggests. But to believe God's truths so as to enter into their beauty and blessedness, to feel their quickening power, and live under their cheering, invigorating influence, this is another matter. But where is the life of our religion when these things are taken away from it? Take, if you could take—God be praised it is beyond the reach of human hand !—but take away that solemn fact, that God has blessed the Church with all spiritual blessings in heavenly places in Christ Jesus, where would there be room for any blessing to rest upon our soul ? Why, any sweet promise that comes rolling into your breast, any lifting up of the light of God's countenance in seasons of darkness and adversity, any liberty in prayer, any looking up and receiving out of Christ's fulness ; all hang upon this grand point, the blessings wherewith God hath already blessed us in Christ Jesus. So that all we have to do—and it is a great thing to do—God alone can enable us to do it—is to receive what God has been pleased so mercifully to give ; and as he has blessed us with all spiritual blessings in heavenly places in Christ Jesus, to feel their power, to enjoy their sweetness, and to know for ourselves by the sealing of the Spirit that he has blessed us, even us, and that with life for evermore.

September 15.

" For the earth bringeth forth fruit of herself ; first the blade, then the ear, after that the full corn in the ear."—MARK iv. 28.

FAITH, I believe, has in it always a measure of assurance. For what is assurance? It is merely the larger growth and fuller development of faith. The nature of assurance is much misunderstood. It is often considered something distinct from faith. This is not the case. It is merely faith in a fuller, larger development. The word "assurance " in the original has a very simple, yet beautiful meaning. It means literally "a full bearing ; " and the word is applied sometimes to a large crop of corn or fruit, and sometimes to the tide coming in with a fuller wave. Now it is the same corn which grows in the fields, whether the crop be much or little ; it is the same tide that comes up the river whether in a scanty or full flow. So it is with assurance and faith : it is the same faith, only increased, enlarged, bearing more abundant fruit, or flowing in a more abundant tide. Assurance in Scripture is not confined to faith; there is " the full assurance of understanding" (Col. ii. 2), that is, a fuller measure and amount, a greater enlargement of understanding to know the truth of God. The understanding is the same; but there is a larger measure of it. So there is the full assurance of hope, that is, a hope strengthened and enlarged, bearing more fruit and flowing in a fuller tide. But it is the same hope; the same in kind, though larger in degree; a stronger anchor, and yet an anchor still (Heb. vi. 11). Similarly there is the full assurance of faith (Heb. x. 22), that is, a larger, fuller measure of faith ; a richer crop, a more abundant tide. Thus you have a measure of the assurance of faith if you have faith at all. In fact, if you have no assurance of the truth of these things, why do you follow after them ? Why do you hang upon them, why do you hope in them, and why do you seek the power and experience of them in your soul ? Have you not arrived at this point yet? "We have not followed cunningly devised fables; these things that I am following after are realities; these objects set before me are certainties." I grant that you may be much exercised about your interest in them. Still, unless you know that they are certainties, why do you believe them ? Why are you anxious to know your interest in them ? Why do you sink in doubt and fear for want of clearer evidences of an interest in them ? And why do you spring up in peace and joy the moment that a little light from them beams upon your soul, and a little sweetness out of them drops into your heart? Because you know that these things are realities. So far then you have an assurance that they are certainties, and in due time, as God is pleased, you will have the assurance in your own breast,

not only that they are certainties, but that you have them in
your own sure and certain possession.

September 16.

*"Joseph is a fruitful bough, even a fruitful bough by a
well; whose branches run over the wall: the archers have
sorely grieved him, and shot at him, and hated him: but his
bow abode in strength, and the arms of his hands were made
strong by the hands of the mighty God of Jacob."*—GENESIS
xlix. 22, 23, 24.

ONE would have thought that Joseph being a fruitful bough
could have looked with complacency, almost with holy scorn,
upon these archers who shot at him, but it was not so; *"they
sorely grieved him."* To be sold by his own brethren into
Egypt; the dreams and visions God had given him to be
derided; to be cast into prison as an ungodly man through
the very person who was tempting him to ungodliness, and
there to be neglected and forsaken; how these archers had
shot their arrows against his bosom, and sorely grieved him!
It was because he had the fear of God, because his feelings
were tender, that the arrows found a place. Had he had a
bosom of steel, had he had a heart of stone, the arrows would
have fallen off blunted and pointless; but it was because he
had tender feelings, a living conscience, warm affections,
godly fear, and a work of grace upon his soul, that he presented a tender spot for these arrows to stick in; therefore
the archers not only " hated him, but shot at him, and sorely
grieved him." But did they prove his destruction? Did any
one drain his life blood? Did he sink and die like a wounded
hart? Did he fall upon the plain and gasp out his forlorn
life? No; for *" his bow abode in strength, and the arms of
his hands were made strong by the hands of the mighty God
of Jacob."* He then had a bow; he could shoot too. And
what was his bow? and how did he direct the arrow? He

picked up the arrows that were shot at him, or rather he took them out of his own wounded bosom ; and instead of aiming these shafts against those who had so sorely grieved him, he shot upward; he launched his arrows towards the throne of the Majesty on high ; he turned their bitter shafts into prayers, supplications, and petitions. Thus the very arrows shot at him he turned into petitions wherewith to approach the throne of God. He drew his bow even up to the heaven of heavens ; and that is what you should do. Never return evil for evil; never return railing for railing. When you are shot at by the archers, do not shoot at them again. Take your arrows and bring them before the throne ; present your feelings wounded as they are, your groans and sighs, with your warm petitions, and spread them before God, who hears and answers prayer ; and you will find the benefit and blessing of it. They will beat you at shooting if you shoot at them. They can use language that you cannot. A man of birth and education, drawn into collision with a street ruffian, cannot bandy words with him ; he must pass on ; he would soon be beaten in the strife of words. So you must never shoot arrow against arrow with those archers who sorely grieve you. You have a tender conscience ; you have the fear of God; you weigh your words ; you know what will grieve your mind when it comes back upon you, and you are therefore sparing of your speech. Cease from that war ; return not a single arrow, let them shoot away, take their arrows, direct your bow upward, turn them all into prayers and supplications, and in due time sweet answers of mercy and peace will come into your bosom. Thus Joseph's bow " abode in strength," and all their arrows neither struck his bow out of his hand, nor broke it asunder. He could shoot as well as they, but not in the same way nor at the same object. We see, then, Joseph's fruitfulness; we see the source of it; we see the persecutions his soul was grieved by; and we see the final victory that he gained. God

of his infinite mercy lead our souls into the same blessed
track, apply his truth to our hearts, that our bow may abide in
strength, and that the arms of our hands may be made strong
by the hands of the mighty God of Jacob.

September 17.

*" I beseech you therefore, brethren, by the mercies of God,
that ye present your bodies a living sacrifice, holy, acceptable
unto God, which is your reasonable service."*—ROMANS xii. 1.

IF the Son of God has redeemed us by his blood, all that
we are and have belongs to him ; our body, soul, and spirit
are his.   Nothing is our own ; we are bought with a price.
In laying down his precious life for us, he has redeemed us
unto himself, that we should be his peculiar people, and not
only render to him the calves of our lips, but give him body,
soul, spirit, substance, life itself ; all that we are and have
being his by sovereign right.   He lays claim to them all, not
only as our Creator, but as our Redeemer, having bought
them by his precious blood.   When we feel his mercy warm
in our soul, can we keep body or soul back ?   Look at
Abraham.   When God called to him, and said, " Abraham ! "
what was his answer ?   " ' Here I am.'   Here is my body,
here is my soul, here is my substance, here is my wife, here
is my son ; all are at thy disposal.   What shall I do, Lord ?
Take them ; they are all thine.   Thou hast a right to them,
and thou must do with them, and thou must do with me,
what seemeth good in thy sight."   Under these feelings, then,
we should " present our bodies," not, indeed, leaving our
souls behind.   For what is the casket without the jewel ?
What is the body without the soul ?   Will God accept the
body if the soul be left behind ?   That is popery ; to give
the body, and keep back the soul.   Not so with the dear
family of God ; they present their bodies, but with their
bodies they present the soul that lodges in their body—the

house with its tenant, the jewel-case with the jewels in it. But what is it to present their bodies? They must be presented as "a living sacrifice." God accepts no dead sacrifices. You will recollect, under the Jewish law the sacrifice was to be a living animal, and that without spot or blemish. No dead lamb or kid, but a living animal, perfect in its kind, was to be the victim sacrificed. So if we are to present our bodies, there must be "a living sacrifice." It may well be asked, What have we sacrificed for the Lord's sake? Have we been called upon to sacrifice our property, prospects, idols, affections, name, fame, and worldly interests; and have we obeyed the call? Abraham did not offer Isaac until the voice of the Lord called him to make the sacrifice; but when the Lord called him to do so, Abraham at once rendered obedience to the voice. So must it be with those that walk in the steps of faithful Abraham. If they are called upon, as all are, sooner or later, to make sacrifices, those sacrifices they must make.

Now, in thus presenting our bodies "a living sacrifice," it becomes also a "*holy*" offering, because what is done in faith is accepted of God as being sanctified by his blessed Spirit. If we make a sacrifice without the blessed Spirit's operation upon our heart, it is a dead sacrifice. Men go into monasteries, deluded women enter convents, become sisters of mercy, and what not, offer their bodies a sacrifice to God, but it is not a living sacrifice, because there is no spiritual life in either offerer or offering. But when we sacrifice our warmest affections, our prospects in life, everything that flesh loves, because the gospel claims it at our hands, and we do it through the constraining love of Christ, *that* is a living sacrifice, and is "holy," because springing out of the sanctifying influences and operations of the Holy Spirit. We indeed, looking at ourselves, see nothing holy in it, for sin is mingled with all we do, but God's eye discerns the precious from the vile. He sees the purity of his own work; and he can separate what we cannot, the acting of the spirit and the working of the flesh. God looks at that which his own Spirit inspires, and his own grace produces, and he accepts that as holy.

September 18.

" And be not conformed to this world."—ROMANS xii. 2.

IN proportion as we are conformed to the spirit of this world our understanding becomes dull in the things of God, our affections · cold and torpid, and our consciences less tender and sensitive. There is an eternal opposition between God and the world lying in wickedness. In order, then, that our spiritual experience of the truth of God should maintain its ground, it must not be dulled and deadened by conformity to the world. It is like the sabre that the soldier carries into battle; it must not trail unsheathed upon the ground lest point and edge be dulled; both must be kept keen and sharp, that execution may be done upon the foe. So it is with our enlightened understanding, with our tender conscience, and our heavenly affections. If we let them fall upon the world, it is like a soldier trailing his sabre upon the pavement; every step he takes dulls both edge and point. If we are conformed to this world, we lose the sweet understanding that we had before of the precious truth of God; we lose that tender sensitiveness of conscience, whereby sin, any sin, becomes a grief and a burden to the soul. A Christian should be what was said of an ancient knight, "without fear and without reproach." The least suspicion of either would have been a blot upon Bayard's scutcheon. So the Christian's shield should be without a stain, his reputation without a blot. His character should not only be free from blemish, but even from suspicion, as untarnished as the modesty of a woman, or the honour and bravery of a man. Now, we often get into this worldly conformity, and run the risk of dulling the sword and sullying the shield, by degrees. We give way in this and in that thing. We are hedged in, it is true, by the precepts of the gospel, the alarms of a tender conscience, and many powerful restraints, so many banks and dykes to keep out the sea of the world; but, as in Holland, if one breach be made in the dyke, the sea at once rushes in, so, if one gap be made in the conscience, then the sea of worldliness rushes through the breach, and but for God's grace would soon deluge the soul. But even apart from having any peculiar temptation to make a wide breach like this, our social ties, our daily occupation, the friends and relations whom we love in the flesh, all, through their power over our natural affections, draw us aside from time to time into this worldly conformity. Here, then, is the point where we have to make our chief stand; for if we are conformed to the maxims, the principles, the customs, and the spirit of the world, we so far lose that spiritual position which is a believer's highest blessing and privilege. We descend from the mount of communion with the Lord, and fall into a cold, miserable spot, where the life of God, though not extinct, is reduced to its lowest ebb.

September 19.

"But be ye transformed by the renewing of your mind."—
ROMANS xii. 2.

As worldly conformity is subdued and departed from, there is the transforming process of which the Apostle here speaks, whereby we become renewed in the spirit of our mind. In other words, the Holy Spirit, by his work upon the soul, renews the life of God, revives faith, hope, love, prayer, praise, spirituality of mind, with every tender feeling and every godly sensation that stirs and moves in a living heart. As, then, the Spirit of God renews his work upon the heart, he brings us out of this worldly conformity. He discovers to us the evil of it ; he makes and keeps the conscience tender and sensitive ; he shews us that if we get conformed to the world we lose our evidences ; that they become dulled and obscured ; that we are soon deprived of communion with God, of comfortable access to our best, our heavenly Friend ; that our taste and appetite for spiritual things get palled ; and that our very profession itself becomes a burden. As the conscience then gets more and more awakened to see and feel these things, we become convinced that we do but reap what we have sown ; and the Spirit of God by pressing the charge more closely home, shews us, and sometimes by painful experience, such as long days of darkness, and heavy, dragging nights of desertion, the evil of worldly conformity. Now, as he thus brings us out of worldly conformity, by shewing us the evil of it, and that by this miserable cleaving to earth we rob ourselves of our happiest hours, our sweetest hopes, and our dearest enjoyments, he draws the soul nearer to Christ ; and as he keeps renewing us in the spirit of our mind, by dropping one precious truth after another into the heart, he revives faith, renews hope, communicates love, draws forth prayer, bestows spirituality of mind and affection ; and by these means a transforming process takes place, whereby the soul is brought out of worldly conformity, and is transformed into the likeness of a suffering Jesus. How we need, then, the blessed Spirit of God to be renewing us daily in the spirit of our minds, and thus transforming us into the suffering image of the sorrowing Son of God. For there is no medium between spirituality and carnality, between the image of Christ and conformity to the world. As there is no middle path between the strait road and the broad one, so there is no middle way between fruitfulness and barrenness, prayerfulness and prayerlessness, watchfulness and careless- ness, repentance and hardness, faith and unbelief, the life of a Christian and the life of a worldling.

September 20.

" That ye may prove what is that good, and acceptable, and perfect will of God."—Romans xii. 2.

The will of God is " good, perfect, and acceptable." How are we to *prove* personally and experimentally that it is all this? That good and perfect will runs counter, over and over again, to my natural inclinations, sets itself firmly against my fleshly desires. God's will calls for self-denial, but I want self-gratification; it requires obedience, but my carnal mind is the essence of disobedience; it demands many sacrifices, but my coward flesh revolts from them ; it bids me walk in the path of suffering, sorrow, and tribulation, but my fleshly mind shrinks back, and says, " No, I cannot tread in that path!" As long, then, as I am conformed to the world, I cannot see the path, for this worldly conformity has thrown a veil over my eyes ; or if I do dimly and faintly see it, I am not willing or able to walk in it, because my carnal mind rebels against all trouble or self-denial, or anything connected with the cross of Christ. But, on the other hand, if by any gracious operations of the Spirit on my heart, I am drawn out of this worldly conformity, am renewed in the spirit of my mind, and transformed into the likeness of the suffering Son of God, then " that good, and perfect, and acceptable will of God" becomes commended to my conscience.

This good, and acceptable, and perfect will is far, far out of the sight of the carnal eye, out of the sound of the worldly ear, out of the touch of the worldly hand; but is made manifest to the spiritual eye, listened to by the spiritual ear, and laid hold of by the spiritual hand. To realise this for ourselves, we shall find it good sometimes to look back and see how that divine will has, in previous instances, proved itself acceptable to our renewed mind. We can see, too, how supremely that will has reigned, and yet how supreme in all points for our good. It has ordered or overruled all circumstances and all events, amidst a complication of difficulties in providence and grace. Nothing has happened to our injury, but all things, according to the promise, have worked together for our good.

But one thing we must deeply bear in mind, that as we cannot deliver ourselves from worldly conformity, so we cannot renew ourselves in the spirit of our mind. The blessed Spirit must do both for us, and work in us to will and to do of his good pleasure. But as we are led to feel the misery of the one state, and the blessedness of the other, we shall seek after these gracious operations and divine influences ; and as the blessed Spirit from time to time brings the soul out of this worldly conformity and transforms it into the suffering image of Christ, it sees more and more the beauty and blessedness of walking in this path ; and cleaving to Christ and his cross with its tenderest affections proves for itself the goodness, acceptability, and perfection of the will of God.

September 21.

" But the anointing which ye have received of him abideth in you."—1 JOHN ii. 27.

ALL the powers of earth and hell are combined against this holy anointing, wherewith the children of God are so highly favoured. But if God has locked up in the bosom of a saint one drop of this divine unction, that one drop is proof against all the assaults of sin, all the attacks of Satan, all the enmity of self, and all the charms, pleasures, and amusements of the world. Waves and billows of affliction may roll over the soul ; but they cannot wash away this holy drop of anointing oil. Satan may shoot a thousand fiery darts to inflame all the combustible material of our carnal mind; but all his fiery darts cannot burn up that one drop of oil which God has laid up in the depths of a broken spirit. The world, with all its charms and pleasures, and its deadly opposition to the truth of God, may stir up waves of ungodliness against this holy anointing; but all the powers of earth combined can never extinguish that one drop which God has himself lodged in the depths of a believer's heart. Jonah had it locked up in the depths of his soul when he was in the whale's belly; but not all the waves and billows that went over his head, nor even the very depths of hell itself, in whose belly he felt he was, could wash away that drop of anointing oil which God had lodged in his soul. David sank deep into sin and remorse; but all his sin and misery never drank up that drop of anointing oil that God the Spirit had dropped into his heart. The prodigal son goes into a far country; but he never loses that drop of anointing oil, though he wastes his substance in riotous living. Heman complains out of the depths of his affliction; but all his troubles never drank up that holy anointing oil that God had put into his soul. Hezekiah on his apparent death-bed, when he turned his face to the wall, was sorely tried, and almost in despair; yet all his affliction and despondency never drained the holy drop of anointing oil. And so it has been with thousands and tens of thousands of the dear saints of God. Not all their sorrows, I may say more, not all their sins, backslidings, slips, falls, miseries, and wretchedness, have ever, all combined, drunk up the anointing that God has bestowed upon them. If sin could have done it, we should have sinned ourselves into hell long ago; and if the world or Satan could have destroyed it or us, they would long ago have destroyed both. If our carnal mind could have done it, it would have swept us away into floods of destruction. But the anointing abideth sure, and cannot be destroyed; and where once lodged in the soul, it is secure against all the assaults of earth, sin, and hell. The saints of God feel that it abides; for it springs up at times in prayer and desires after the living God; and it breaks forth

into faith, hope, and love. Thus it not only abides as a divine
reality, but as a living principle, springing up into eternal life.
Were it not so, there would be no revivals, no fresh communications, no renewed testimonies, no breakings forth, no
tender meltings, no breathings out of desire for the Lord's
presence, no mourning over his absence. But the anointing
abideth, and this preserves the soul from death, and keeps it
alive in famine.

September 22.

*" Father, I will that they also, whom thou hast given me, be
with me where I am; that they may behold my glory, which
thou hast given me: for thou lovedst me before the foundation of
the world."* —JOHN xvii. 24.

How great, how elevated above all utterance or all conception of men or angels, must the glory of Christ be as the
Son of the Father in truth and love! And not only is the
Lord Jesus Christ glorious in his essential Deity as the Son
of God, but glorious also in his holy, spotless humanity
which he assumed in the womb of the Virgin Mary. For
this, though the flesh and blood of the children, was "that
holy thing which was begotten of the Holy Ghost," and was
taken into union with his eternal Deity, that he might be
"Immanuel, God with us." The purity, holiness and innocence, the spotless beauty and complete perfection of this
human nature, make it in itself exceedingly glorious; but its
great glory is the union that it possesses and enjoys with the
divine nature of the Son of God. The pure humanity of
Jesus veils his Deity, and yet the Deity shines through it,
filling it with unutterable brightness, and irradiating it with
inconceivable glory. There is no confusion or blending of
the two natures, for humanity cannot become Deity, nor can
Deity become humanity; each nature remains distinct; and
each nature has its own peculiar glory. But there is a glory

also in the union of both natures in the Person of the God-man. That such wisdom should have b en displayed, such grace manifested, such love revealed, and that the union of the two natures in the Person of the Son of God should not only have, so to speak, formerly originated, but should still unceasingly uphold, and eternally maintain salvation with all its present fruits of grace, and all its future fruits of glory, makes the union of the two natures unspeakably glorious. And when we consider further that through this union of humanity with Deity, the Church is brought into the most intimate nearness and closest relationship with the Father and the Holy Ghost, what a glory is seen to illuminate the Person of the God-man, who as God is one with God, and as man is one with man, and thus unites man to God, and God to man; thus bringing about the fulfilment of those wonderful words, " That they all may be one; as thou, Father, art in me, and I in thee, that they also may be one in us." And again, " I in them, and thou in me, that they may be made perfect in one." Thus there is the glory of Christ as God, the glory of Christ as man, and the glory of Christ as God-man. And this threefold glory of Christ corresponds in a measure with what he was before he came into the world, with what he was whilst in the world, and with what he now is as having gone to the Father, according to his own words (John xvi. 28). Before he came into the world his chief glory was that belonging to him as the Son of God; whilst in the world his chief glory was in being the Son of man; and now that he is gone back to heaven his chief glory is that of his being God and man in one glorious Person.

This latter glory of Christ, which is, in an especial sense, his mediatorial glory, is seen by faith here, and will be seen in the open vision of bliss hereafter. The three disciples on the Mount of transfiguration, Stephen at the time of his martyrdom, Paul when caught up into the third heaven,

John in Patmos, had all special and supernatural manifestations of the glory of Christ; that is, surpassing what is generally given to believers. But the usual way in which we now see his glory is by the Holy Spirit " glorifying him by receiving of what is his, and shewing it to the soul." This divine and blessed Teacher testifies of him ; takes away the veil of ignorance and unbelief which hides him from view ; shines with a holy and sacred light on the Scriptures that speak of him; and raising up faith to believe in his name sets him before the eyes of the enlightened understanding, so that he is looked unto and upon; and though not seen with the bodily eye, is loved, believed, and rejoiced in with joy unspeakable and full of glory. Thus seen by the eye of faith, all that he is and has, all that he says and does is made precious and glorious. His miracles of mercy, whilst here below; his words so full of grace, wisdom, and truth; his going about doing good; his sweet example of patience, meekness, and submission; his sufferings and sorrows in the garden and on the cross; his spotless holiness and purity, yet tender compassion to poor lost sinners; his atoning blood and justifying obedience; his dying love, so strong and firm, yet so tried by earth, heaven, and hell; his lowly, yet honourable burial; his glorious resurrection, as the first-begotten of the dead, by which he was declared to be the Son of God with power; his ascension to the right hand of the Father, where he reigns and rules, all power being given unto him in heaven and earth, and yet intercedes for his people as the great High Priest over the house of God. What beauty and glory shine forth in all these divine realities, when faith can view them in union with the work and Person of Immanuel !

September 23.

" That he might make thee know that man doth not live by bread only, but by every word that proceedeth out of the mouth of the Lord doth man live."—DEUTERONOMY viii. 3.

THIS is the grand lesson which we have to learn in our wilderness journey—" that man doth not live by bread only," that is, by those providential supplies which relieve our natural wants. Thanks be to God for any bread that he gives us in his kind and bountiful providence. An honest living is a great mercy. To be enabled by the labour of our hands or by the labour of our brain to maintain our families and bring them up in a degree of comfort, if not abundance, is a great blessing. But God has determined that his people shall not live by bread only. They shall be separated from the mass of men who live in this carnal way only; who have no care beyond earthly possessions, and the sum of whose thoughts and desires is, what they shall eat, and what they shall drink, and wherewithal they shall be clothed; who never look beyond the purse, the business, the daily occupation, the safe return, the profitable investment, and how to provide for themselves and their families. God has planted in the breast of his people a higher life, a nobler principle, a more blessed appetite than to live upon bread only. We bless him for his providence, but we love him for his grace. We thank him for daily food and raiment, but these mercies are but for time, perishing in their very use, and he has provided us with that which is for eternity. What then does he mean the soul to live upon? "Upon every word that proceedeth out of his mouth." But where do we find these words that proceed out of the mouth of God? In the Scriptures, which is the food of the Church, and especially in Scripture as applied to the heart, in the words that God is pleased to drop into the soul by a divine power, which we receive from his gracious mouth, and lay hold of with a believing hand. That is the food and nutriment of our soul; the truth of God applied to our heart and made life and spirit to our souls by his own teaching and testimony. And see how large and ample the supply is. Look through the whole compass of God's revealed word, and see in it what a store there is of provision laid up for the Church of God. How this should both stimulate and encourage us to search the Scriptures as for hid treasure, to read them constantly, to meditate upon them, to seek to enter into the mind of God as revealed in them, and thus to find them to be the food of our soul. If we were fully persuaded that every word of the Scripture came out of God's mouth, and was meant to feed our soul, how much more we should prize it, read, and study it.

September 24.

" His going forth is prepared as the morning."—HOSEA vi. 3.

IT is to the living soul walking in darkness, and unable to find God, that this text speaks: "His going forth is prepared as the morning." There is an appointed time for the Lord to go forth; and this is sweetly compared to the rising of the sun. Does not "the dayspring know his place?" (Job xxxviii. 12.) Does not the sun rise every day according to the minute before appointed? Is he ever before his time, or ever after his time? Did the free will of the creature ever hurry or retard his rising for a single second? Thus it is with the going forth of the Lord for the salvation of his people, the going forth of the Lord in the revelation of his presence and his power, the going forth of the Lord from the place where he has for a while hidden himself, to come down with light and life into the soul. All his glorious goings forth are as much prepared, and the moment is as much appointed, as the time is fixed every morning for the sun to rise.

But what is the state of things naturally before the sun rises? Does not midnight precede the dawn, does not darkness come before light? And when it is midnight naturally, can we bid the sun arise and disperse the darkness? Is there not, as the Psalmist says, a waiting for the morning, naturally? "My soul waiteth for the Lord, more than they that watch for the morning." Is not the invalid tossing on his restless couch, waiting for the morning? Is not the shipwrecked mariner driven on the rocks, waiting anxiously for the morning, to know what is his prospect of safety, what friendly sail may be in sight? Is not the man benighted on the downs waiting for the morning, that the sun may arise, and he find his way homeward? But with all their waiting they cannot bid the sun arise; they must wait till the appointed time. So the going forth of the Sun of righteousness, the appearance of Christ in the heart, the sweet revelation of the Son of God, the lifting up of the light of his blessed countenance, is "prepared as the morning"—as fixed, as appointed in the mind of God as the morning to come in its season; but no more to be hurried than the sun is to be hurried up the sky. Aye, and it is as much an impossibility for us to bring the Lord into our souls before the appointed time, or keep him there when he is come, as for us to play the part of Joshua, and say, "Sun, stand thou still upon Gibeon, and thou, moon, in the valley of Ajalon."

But "his going forth is prepared as the morning," and when he goes forth, he goes forth "conquering and to conquer," mounted on the white horse spoken of in Revelation. He goes forth to conquer our enemies, to overcome our temptations, to lay our souls at his footstool, to arise like the sun in his strength, and to come into the heart with healing in his wings.

September 25.

" Likewise reckon ye also yourselves to be dead indeed unto sin, but alive unto God through Jesus Christ our Lord."—
ROMANS vi. 11.

How many poor souls are struggling against the power of sin, and yet never get any victory over it! How many are daily led captive by the lusts of the flesh, the love of the world, and the pride of life, and never get any victory over them! How many fight and grapple with tears, vows, and strong resolutions against the besetting sins of temper, levity, or covetousness, who are still entangled and overcome by them again and again! Now, why is this? Because they know not the secret of spiritual strength against, and spiritual victory over them. It is only by virtue of a living union with the Lord Jesus Christ, drinking into his sufferings and death, and receiving out of his fulness, that we can gain any victory over the world, sin, death, or hell. Let me bring this down a little to your own experience. Say your soul has been, on one particular occasion, very sweetly favoured ; a melting sense of the Saviour's precious love and blood has come into your heart, and you could then believe, with a faith of God's own giving, that he was eternally yours ; and through this faith, as an open channel of divine communication, his merits and mediation, blood, righteousness, and dying love came sweetly streaming into your soul. What was the effect ? To lead you to sin, to presumption, to licentiousness ? Nay, just the contrary. To a holy obedience in heart, lip, and life. Sin is never really or effectually subdued in any other way. Saul struck down at the gates of Damascus, and turned from persecution to praying, is a scriptural instance of the death of sin by the power of Christ. It is not, then, by legal strivings and earnest resolutions, vows, and tears, which are but monkery at best, (a milder form of the hair shirt, the bleeding scourge, and the damp cloister,) the vain struggle of religious flesh to subdue sinful flesh, that can overcome sin; but it is by a believing acquaintance with, and a spiritual entrance into the sufferings and sorrows of the Son of God, having a living faith in him, and receiving out of his fulness supplies of grace and strength —strength made perfect in our weakness. In this sense the Apostle says to the Colossians, "For ye are *dead;*" not merely by the law having condemned and slain you, as to all legal hopes, but by virtue of a participation in the death of the Lord Jesus Christ, by virtue of a living union with the suffering Son of God. "Sin shall not have dominion over you; for ye are not under the law," where sin reigns with increased dominion, "but under grace," which subdues sin by pardoning it. If you read Romans vi. with an enlightened eye, you will see how the Apostle traces out the death of the believer unto the power and prevalence of sin, by virtue of a spiritual baptism into the death and resurrection of the Lord Jesus.

September 26.

"*No good thing will he withhold from them that walk uprightly.*"—Psalm lxxxiv. 11.

There are those who walk uprightly, very uprightly, in the fear of God, and yet have little comfortable or abiding evidence that they are at present partakers of God's grace, or will be hereafter sharers of Christ's glory. But this one evidence they certainly do possess, though they can take no present comfort from it, that they walk uprightly before God and man. Let no one, however deeply experienced or highly favoured, despise this evidence of grace in others; and you who walk uprightly from a living principle of godly fear have here a marked testimony from the Lord himself that he has a special regard for you.

But what is it to "walk uprightly?" Oh! here is the grand difficulty in religion. We may talk; we may preach; we may hear; we may seem to believe; but it is when we come to *act*, to walk, and carry out into daily and hourly practice what we profess, that the main difficulty is felt and found. "The soul of religion," says Bunyan, "is the practic part;" and it is when we come to this "practic part" that the daily, hourly cross commences. The walk, the conversation, the daily, hourly conduct is, after all, the main difficulty, as it is the all-important fruit of a Christian profession. To walk day after day, under all circumstances, and amidst all the varied temptations that beset us, uprightly, tenderly, and sincerely in the fear of God; to feel continually that heart, lip, and life are all open before his all-penetrating eye; to do the things which he approves, and to flee from the things which he abhors—oh! this in religion is the steep hill which it is such a struggle to climb! We can talk fast enough; but oh! to walk in the straight and narrow path; to be a Christian outwardly as well as inwardly, before God and man, before the Church and the world; and in all points to speak and act with undeviating consistency with our profession—this is what nature never has done, and what nature never can do. In thus *acting*, as much as in believing, do we need God's power and grace to work in, and be made manifest in us.

September 27.

"Being justified freely by his grace through the redemption that is in Christ Jesus: whom God hath set forth to be a propitiation through faith in his blood."—ROMANS iii. 24, 25.

BEFORE we can have faith in Christ's atoning blood, we must see the glory of the Person of the Lord of life. "We beheld his glory," said John, speaking of himself and the other favoured disciples, "we beheld his glory, the glory as

of the only-begotten of the Father, full of grace and truth."
May I ask you a question, you who profess to know these
things? Were your eyes ever anointed to behold the glory
of Jesus? Did faith ever contemplate, did hope ever anchor
in, did love ever flow forth to the glorious Person of Immanuel? Was he ever precious to your souls? ever "altogether lovely" in your eyes? so that you could say, "Whom
have I in heaven but thee? and there is none upon earth
I desire beside thee?" Now, if you have seen his Person by
the eye of faith, you have had faith flowing out of your soul
to his atoning blood; for his atoning blood derives all its
value, all its validity, and all its efficacy from its being the
blood of that glorious Person. Upon that atoning blood we
then view infinite dignity stamped. We then view it as the
blood of the Person of Him who was God-man; and we then
see the dignity, immensity, and glory of the Godhead of Jesus,
stamped upon the sufferings and blood that flowed from his
pure manhood. When we see *that* by the eye of faith, what
a rich stream does it become ! What a fountain opened for
sin and uncleanness ! What value is stamped upon it to purge
and cleanse a guilty conscience !

Now, when this is known and felt, the soul is justified.
Justification passes over from the mind of God into the
bosom of the sinner. He never really was, in the mind of
God, in an unjustified state; but he was in his own conscience, and he was as touching the law, and he was as
regards his standing as a sinner before the eyes of a holy
Jehovah. But the moment he is enabled, by living faith, to
touch and take hold of the atoning blood of the Lamb of
God, justification passes over into his soul, and he becomes
freely justified, pardoned and accepted, through the blood of
sprinkling upon his conscience; and he stands before God
whiter and brighter than snow, for "the blood of Jesus Christ
cleanseth from all sin."

September 28.

" Say to them that are of a fearful heart, Be strong, fear not."—ISAIAH XXXV. 4.

"FEAR not." "Ah! but Lord," the soul says, "I do fear. I fear myself more than anybody. I fear my base, wicked heart, my strong lusts and passions, and my numerous inward enemies, the snares of Satan, and the temptations of the world. Thou sayest, 'Fear not.' But I do fear. I cannot help but fear." Still the Lord says, "Fear not." Let us see if we cannot find something to explain this a little more clearly. There is a crowd yonder, and a weak woman in company with her husband. He says to her all trembling and fearing to pass through the crush, "Fear not; take hold of my arm, cling close to me." She takes hold of his arm and fears not. So with the timid soul and its enemies. It says, "How can I press through this crowd of difficulties; how elbow my way through these opposing doubts and fears?" Its husband, the Lord, comes and says, "Fear not; take hold of my strength; cleave close to me!" The soul hears, obeys, and clings; its enemies give way; its doubts and fears part asunder, and it passes safely through. Or take another familiar comparison. Here is a child trembling before a large mastiff; but the father says, "Fear not, he will not hurt you, only keep close to me." "Deliver my soul," cried David, "from the sword; my darling from the power of the dog." Who is that dog but Satan, that huge mastiff, whose jaws are reeking with blood? If the Lord say, "Fear not," why need we fear him? He is a chained enemy. But how the timid soul needs these divine "Fear nots!" For without him, it is all weakness; with him, all strength; without him, all trembling; with him, all boldness. "Where the word of a king is there is power;" and this makes the Lord's "Fear nots" so efficacious. As Augustine used to say, "Give what thou commandest, and command what thou wilt." The burden still remains, but strength is given to bear it; the trials are not lessened, but power to endure them is increased; the evils of the heart are not removed, but grace is communicated to subdue them.

September 29.

" Behold, your God will come with vengeance, even God with a recompence; he will come and save you."—ISAIAH XXXV. 4.

" BEHOLD, your God will come." The Lord then is not yet come; but he says he will come, and the promise of his coming takes away the fear. He says, *"Behold."* Even that little word contains something in it noteworthy. The Lord is in the distance; his chariot is making ready; for " he maketh the clouds his chariot, and walketh upon the wings of the wind." As the Lord said to his disciples, " Lift up your heads, for your redemption draweth nigh," so by the word, " Behold," the Lord would take the eyes of his people from being ever bent on the ground or ever looking at their own miserable hearts and the difficulties and dangers of the way. " Look up," he would say, " look up; your God is coming to save you." I like to dwell on every crumb as it were of our text. The jots and tittles of God's word, like diamond dust, are to be gathered up and treasured. In Scripture there is much in a little; not like our sermons, where there is often little in much. The word of God is full to overflowing with the very essence of truth; more concentrated and fragrant than the otto of roses. Look at the next drop. Is it not the very quintessence of blessedness? *" Your* God." What, is he your God? *That* is the very dropping of everlasting love. In that one word is concentrated the essence of every blessing of the new covenant. And if God is your God, your doubts, fears, and misgivings do not break that sacred covenant tie. You are a husband, and your partner is afflicted with some mental disease; and the nature of the complaint may be such

that she hardly recognises your face, altogether doubts your
affection, and does not believe you are her husband at all.
Such cases we know are frequent. But do her doubts or
denial dissolve your love, do they cancel the marriage tie?
The state of her mind, however painful, does not alter the
marriage relationship. So if the Lord's espoused ones, through
Satan's temptations, doubt their union with him, do their fears
break the wedding ring or cancel the marriage. writings? If
covenant love matched them in eternity, and covenant grace
joined their hands in time, they are still his Hephzibahs and
Beulahs, for "the Lord hateth putting away."

September 30.

*" Blessed are they which do hunger and thirst after righteous-
ness : for they shall be filled."*—MATTHEW v. 6.

HUNGER is a painful sensation. It is not merely an appetite
for food; but an appetite for food attended with pain. So
spiritually. It is not merely a desire after Christ that constitutes spiritual hunger. "The sluggard desireth, and hath
nothing." But it is a desire attended with pain; not merely
a wish for spiritual food, but also with such painful sensations,
that unless this appetite is satisfied, the soul must perish and
die. Nothing short of this constitutes spiritual hunger. There
are many who say, "I have a desire." If it be a spiritual desire, it will be granted. But spiritual desire is always attended
with painful sensations which many are completely ignorant
of who profess to have a desire. "The desire of the slothful
killeth him." Why? Because he rests satisfied with a desire,
and never takes the kingdom of heaven by violence.

The expression "thirst" conveys a still larger meaning.
Hunger is more supportable than thirst. Persons die sooner
when left without water than without food. Intense thirst is
perhaps the most painful of all bodily sensations that a human
being can know. The Spirit has therefore made use of this

figure in order to convey the intense desire of a living soul;
—that he must have Christ, or perish—must feel his blood
sprinkled upon the conscience, or die in his sins—must "know
him, and the power of his resurrection," or pass into the
gloomy chambers of eternal woe—must have the presence of
Jesus sensibly realised, and the love of God shed abroad, or
else of all men be the most miserable.

October 1.

" The lofty looks of man shall be humbled, and the haughti-
ness of men shall be bowed down, and the Lord alone shall
be exalted in that day."—ISAIAH ii. 11.

How does the Lord humble? By discovering to man
what he is ; by opening up the depth of his fall; by making
him feel what a vile and guilty wretch he is before the footstool
of mercy ; by breaking him to pieces; by slaughtering and
laying him low; by making him abhor himself in dust and
ashes. Was not that the way the Lord took with the saints
of old ? How did he humble Isaiah ? Was it not by some
discovery of his divine Majesty, to make him cry, " I am a
man of unclean lips ! " How did he humble Daniel ? Was
it not by manifesting himself in his almighty purity, and
turning his comeliness into corruption ? How did he humble
Hezekiah ? By laying him upon a sick-bed, and laying his
sins and iniquities with weight and power upon his conscience.
None of these men produced humility in themselves. How
did the Lord humble Job ? By sifting him in Satan's sieve,
and discovering as that riddle moved to and fro in Satan's
hands the pride, peevishness, and self-righteousness of his
carnal mind. There are many who cannot bear to hear the
malady touched upon. They cannot bear to hear the corruptions of the heart even hinted at. But what real humility can
a man have except through a knowledge of himself? How
can I be humbled except I feel *that* in myself which covers

me with shame and confusion of face, and makes me loathe
and abhor myself before the eyes of a heart-searching God?
Therefore the more the glorious majesty of heaven is pleased
to unfold itself in all its divine purity in my conscience, and
the deeper discovery I have of what I am as a fallen wretch,
a guilty sinner, the more will my heart be humbled, the more
shall I be lowly and abased, the more shall I loathe myself in
dust and ashes.

October 2.

*" Grace and peace be multiplied unto you through the know-
ledge of God, and of Jesus our Lord."* — 2 Peter i. 2.

If we do not know Jesus for ourselves, by some spiritual
discovery of his Person and work, what testimony have we of
an interest in his grace? Because, there is no grace except
that which flows through him, for " grace and truth came by
Jesus Christ." This is what we should ever labour after.
Our daily, hourly desire and prayer should be, to have
spiritual discoveries of Christ; to see him by the eye of
faith; to enter into his glorious Person and finished work;
to realise his presence, taste his love, and know him and the
power of his resurrection. This is what Paul so earnestly
laboured after (Phil. iii. 10); and for the excellency of this
knowledge he suffered the loss of all things, and counted
them but dung that he might win Christ. To know him as
our Surety and Sin-bearer, our Advocate and Intercessor, our
Friend, Husband, and Brother; to know our interest in him,
and our union with him; our place in his heart, our name on
his breast, our memorial on the palms of his hands—what
can surpass the blessedness of such a knowledge as this?
Through this spiritual, experimental knowledge of him, grace
flows. As a watercourse opening upon a river brings down
its irrigating stream into the parched meadow, so a knowledge
of Christ opens up a channel through which the grace that is

in him flows into the barren, parched soul. Thus, as through grace alone we know him, so every fresh communication of grace not only makes him better known, but flows in through that very knowledge.

The grace that comes through this knowledge of him brings also peace ; for he is " our peace." He has " broken down the middle wall of partition, having abolished in his flesh the enmity, even the law of commandments contained in ordinances ; for to make in himself of twain one new man, so making peace." He, therefore, came and preached peace " to those which were afar off and to them that were nigh." His blood speaks peace to a guilty conscience ; his voice says peace to the winds and waves of the surging heart ; his last legacy was, " Peace I leave with you, my peace I give unto you ; " his dying promise was, " In me ye shall have peace ; " and, as the Prince of peace at God's right hand, he is able to fill us with " all joy and peace in believing," for his kingdom is " righteousness, and peace, and joy in the Holy Ghost." And thus, through a knowledge of him as our Lord, " grace and peace " are both " multiplied."

October 3.

" Thy life will I give unto thee for a prey in all places whither thou goest."—JEREMIAH xlv. 5.

THERE is a life given to the elect when the blessed Spirit quickens their souls,—a life eternal, communicated to them out of the fulness of the Son of God. This life is a personal, individual life ; and thus there seems to be a sweetness contained in the expression, " *thy* life." " *Thy* life will I give unto thee for a prey." This life which is treasured up in the fulness of Christ is breathed into the soul in the appointed time by the Holy Ghost, is kept alive there by his almighty power, and will burn brighter and brighter in the realms of endless day. But we may observe, from the expression made use of in the text, that this life which is given to the child of God, is given to him in a peculiar way. " Thy life will I give unto thee *for a prey.*" The word " prey " points out that this life is an object of attack. We hear of " beasts of prey," and of " birds of prey," and the expression implies a carnivorous animal. Thus the words, " Thy life will I give unto thee *for a prey,*" imply that there are ravenous beasts that are continually seeking to devour this life, voracious enemies upon the watch, who are eager to prey upon this life, which God the Holy Spirit has kindled in the soul. How accurately and how experimentally do these words describe the inward kingdom of God ! Eternal life is given by God ; and kept by him when given ; preserved by his power from ever being extinguished. And yet preserved by a perpetual miracle, like a burning lamp set afloat upon the waves of the sea ; or, to use a figure that I have somewhere seen, like a lighted taper carried over a heath in the midst of a gale of wind.

Thus, " our life is given us for a prey ; " and the power, faithfulness, and wisdom of God are manifested in keeping this life unhurt amidst all its enemies. As Daniel was preserved in the den of lions ; and as the three men were preserved in the burning fiery furnace ; so the life of God is preserved in the soul, in the midst of lions, as David says, " My soul is among lions " (Ps. lvii. 4), and amidst the fires, " Glorify ye the Lord in the fires " (Isaiah xxiv. 15). So that the life of the child of God is one continual conflict between faith and unbelief, between enmity and love, between the grace of God and the rebellion of the carnal mind, between the sinkings of the drooping spirit and the liftings-up of the light of God's countenance.

October 4.

" Whither the forerunner is for us entered, even Jesus."—
HEBREWS vi. 20.

How blessedly did the Lord comfort his sorrowing disciples when he said to them, " In my Father's house are many mansions : if it were not so, I would have told you. I go to prepare a place for you." He is gone to take possession beforehand of his and their everlasting home ; for he is ascended to his Father and their Father, to his God and their God. He has, as it were, filled heaven with new beauty, new happiness, new glory. In him dwelleth all the fulness of the Godhead bodily. His glorious Person as Immanuel is become the object of heaven's praise and adoration. The elect angels, whom he has confirmed in their standing, adore him as God-man; and the spirits of just men made perfect worship him in company with the angelic host. What a view had holy John of heaven's glorious worship, when he saw the four living creatures and the four and twenty elders fall down before the Lamb; when he heard their new song and the voice of many angels round about the throne, and all saying with a loud voice, " Worthy is the Lamb that was slain to receive power, and riches, and wisdom, and strength, and honour, and glory, and blessing" (Rev. v. 12). Heaven itself is waiting for the completion of the great mystery of godliness, when the whole Church shall be assembled around the throne ; when the marriage supper of the Lamb shall come; when the headstone shall be brought forth by the hands of the spiritual Zerubbabel, with shoutings of Grace, grace unto it. Earth itself is groaning under the weight of sin and sorrow ; and the souls of those under the.altar who were slain for the word of God, and for the testimony which they held, are crying with a loud voice, " How long, O Lord, holy and true, dost thou not judge and avenge our blood on

them that dwell on the earth ?" Nay, the very signs of the
times themselves are all proclaiming as with one voice that it
cannot be long before the Lord will come a second time
without sin unto salvation.

October 5.

*" Wherefore doth a living man complain, a man for the
punishment of his sins ? "*—LAMENTATIONS iii. 39.

WE must not understand by the word " punishment," anything of a vindictive nature. God never punishes the sins of
his elect penally ; that is, not as he punishes the sins of the
reprobate. The eternal covenant forbids this. " Fury is not
in me, saith the Lord." The elect are accepted in Jesus, are
pardoned in him, are complete in him. This is their eternal
and unalterable covenant standing—the fruit and effect of
their everlasting union with the Son of God. But though
this forbids punishment in its strictly penal sense, it by no
means excludes *chastisement.* Thus we are not to understand
by the word " punishment " in the text the infliction of God's
righteous wrath, that foretaste of eternal damnation with
which, sometimes even in this life, he visits the ungodly ; but
it signifies that chastisement which is the privilege of the heir,
and distinguishes him from the bastard. It is under this
chastisement, then, that the living man is brought to complain,
and he will often see in the afflictions that befal him the rod
of the Lord as the chastisement of sin. When he thus sees
light in God's light, he may justly say, " *Wherefore* doth a
living man complain, a man for the punishment of his sins ?"
Are they not chastisements, not punishments ; the rod of a
father's correction, not the vindictive stroke of offended
justice ?

Perhaps his property is lost through unlooked-for circumstances, or the roguery of others ; and he is brought down

from comparative affluence to be a poor man. When he can see that this is a chastisement for his pride and carnality in former days, he is able to put his mouth in the dust. Or if the Lord afflict him in his body so that he shall scarcely enjoy a day's health, when he sees and feels how he abused his health and strength when he possessed them, and at the same time perceives from how many hurtful snares his bodily affliction instrumentally preserves him, he is able at times to bear it meekly and patiently. He may also have serious afflictions in his family, or find, like David, "his house not so with God" as he could wish; but when he sees that a sickly wife or disobedient children are but so many strokes of chastisement, and far lighter than his sins demand, when he sees that they come from the hand of love, and not from eternal wrath, that they are the stripes of a Father, not the vindictive strokes of an angry Judge, he feels then that love is mingled with chastisement, and his spirit is meekened, and his heart softened, and he is brought down to say, "Wherefore should a living man complain?" Now, until a man gets there he cannot but complain. Until he is brought spiritually to see that all his afflictions, griefs, and sorrows are chastisements and not punishments, and is able to receive them as the stripes of love, he must and he will complain. But, generally speaking, before the Lord lifts up the light of his countenance upon him, before he gives him a sense of peace in his conscience, he will bring him "to accept," as the Scripture speaks (Lev. xxvi. 41), "of the punishment of his iniquity." He will thus receive these strokes of chastisement with a subdued spirit; he will confess that they are justly deserved; and his obstinacy and rebelliousness being in a measure broken, he will lie as a poor and needy supplicant at the foot of the cross.

October 6.

" Persecuted, but not forsaken."—2 CORINTHIANS iv. 9.

WHATEVER injury persecutors may do or attempt to do to a Christian, they cannot rob him of his God. They may destroy his body; they cannot destroy his soul. They may wound his reputation; but they cannot wound his conscience. They may strip him of all his earthly goods; but they cannot lay their unhallowed hands upon the treasure which God has lodged in his breast. Yea, all may forsake him as they forsook his divine Master; but God has said, "I will never leave thee, nor forsake thee." Why, then, need we dread persecution for righteousness' sake? If the Lord be on our side, whom need we fear? And who can harm us if we be followers of that which is good? But bear in mind that it must be persecution for righteousness' sake. Do not call it persecution if you are buffeted for your faults. Do not think yourselves persecuted if by your inconsistencies you have brought upon yourselves the reproach of men, or the just censure of those who fear God. But if your persecutions are brought upon you from doing the will of God from the heart, you will find the approbation of God in your conscience; nay, you will find that your very persecutions will draw down more into your soul a blessed sense of the sympathy of your great High Priest, so that as your afflictions abound, so will your consolation. Sad indeed it would be for the Church of God, if, amidst her persecutions, the Lord added to the weight of her trouble by withdrawing from her the light of his countenance and the consolations of his sensible presence. But she never more sensibly reclines on his bosom than when he gives her to drink of his cup, and thus conforms her to his suffering image.

October 7.

" At that time Jesus answered and said, I thank thee, O Father, Lord of heaven and earth, because thou hast hid these things from the wise and prudent, and hast revealed them unto babes."—MATTHEW xi. 25.

WHATEVER religious knowledge, whatever carnal wisdom, or whatever worldly prudence a man may be possessed of, if he is devoid of the life of God in his soul, he is destitute of the workings of godly fear, he has no solemn awe or reverence for Jehovah, he has never seen his sins in the light of God's countenance, he has never trembled at " the wrath to come," he has never prostrated himself with a reverential spirit before the eyes of a heart-searching Jehovah, that sees into the secret recesses of his bosom. But all his knowledge, and all his wisdom, and all his prudence leave him just where they found him, unimpressed, carnal, sensual, worldly, " dead in trespasses and sins." All his wisdom never reached beyond the surface ; it never broke up the crust of unbelief, so as to enter through that seared crust into the conscience, and produce living effects in it, as made tender by the touch of God's finger. But his knowledge, his wisdom, his prudence are all floating in his judgment, and never descend into the depths of his heart. God hides then the workings of spiritual fear from those who are " wise and prudent." He does not condescend to manifest himself to them; he does not shew them light in his light ; he does not reveal himself to their consciences ; he does not come with power into their hearts ; he does not take the veil of unbelief and blindness from their carnal minds, and shew them himself ; he takes them not where he took Moses, into the clift of the rock, " where his glory passed by ;" he deals not with them as he dealt with Isaiah, when he manifested to him the glory of the Lord in the temple ; he discovers himself not to them as he did to Job, when " he abhorred himself in dust and ashes." All their knowledge of God, therefore, is an external, intellectual knowledge, a mere exercise of the faculties of the mind, without any spiritual teaching, or any special revelation of the presence, power, glory, and majesty of God to their consciences.

But the babe, the living babe in Zion has " the fear of the Lord," in his soul, " as the beginning of wisdom." And therefore, having this fountain of life within, he has it springing up in spiritual exercises. As the Apostle speaks, he " serves God acceptably with reverence and godly fear ;" he dare not rush with presumption into his holy presence. When he comes into his sanctuary a solemn dread from time to time falls upon his spirit. He has the feelings of Isaiah when he cried : " I am a man of unclean lips ; for mine eyes have seen the King, the Lord of hosts ;" the feelings of Jacob when he was afraid, and said, " How dreadful is this place !" the feelings of Moses, when he stood by the burning bush, and put his shoes from off his feet, for the spot whereon he stood was holy ground ; the feelings of the high priest in the temple, on that mysterious day of atonement, when he entered alone, " not without blood," into the sanctuary, the holy of holies, and beheld the Shechinah, the Divine presence as a cloud resting on the mercy-seat. The babe, then, has these exercises of godly fear, which carnal, unhumbled, worldly-wise professors know nothing of. And though the babe, at times, seems to have no religion which he can really call spiritual or which satisfies himself, yet he has that tenderness, awe, and reverence which the carnal professor, however high in doctrine, however soaring in vain confidence, is utterly unacquainted with.

October 8.

" Until the redemption of the purchased possession."—
EPHESIANS i. 14.

THE Church has been redeemed by price, but is not as
yet fully redeemed by power. Christ has bought with his
precious blood both the souls and bodies of his people, but
he has not yet redeemed them openly. This redemption is
still future, and will not be accomplished till the glorious
resurrection morn, when the bodies of the dead saints will
be raised, and the bodies of the living saints changed in
a moment, in the twinkling of an eye, at the last trump.
This, therefore, is " the redemption of the purchased possession ; " and this being future we have to wait for it, as the
Apostle speaks, " But if we hope for that we see not, then do
we with patience wait for it " (Romans viii. 25). Our body
is not yet redeemed from its native corruption. But, in the
resurrection morn, when the dead will be raised incorruptible,
then the redemption of the body will be complete. Then
the inheritance will be fully entered into. The risen and
glorified saints will inherit Christ, and Christ will inherit
them ; and his purchased possession will be for ever delivered from every foe and every fear, from every sin and
every sorrow, from every corruption of body or soul, and be
crowned with an exceeding and eternal weight of glory.
Unto this day of redemption the Holy Spirit seals all the
living family of God (Ephes. iv. 30), not only by assuring
them of their interest in the inheritance, and himself being
the earnest of it, but as thereby securing to them the most
certain possession of it.

October 9.

*" The heart is deceitful above all things, and desperately
wicked: who can know it ? "*—JEREMIAH xvii. 9.

THE sin of our fallen nature is a very mysterious thing.

We read of the mystery of iniquity as well as of the mystery of godliness; and the former has lengths, depths, and breadths as well as the latter; depths which no human plumbline ever fathomed, and lengths which no mortal measuring line ever yet meted out. Thus the way in which sin sometimes seems to sleep, and at other times to awake up with renewed strength, its active, irritable, impatient, restless nature, the many shapes and colours it wears, the filthy holes and puddles in which it grovels, the corners into which it creeps, its deceitfulness, hypocrisy, craft, plausibility, intense selfishness, utter recklessness, desperate madness, and insatiable greediness are secrets, painful secrets, only learnt by bitter experience. In the spiritual knowledge of these two mysteries, the mystery of sin and the mystery of salvation, all true religion consists. In the school of experience we are kept, day after day, learning and forgetting these two lessons, being never able to understand them, and yet not satisfied unless we know them, pursuing after an acquaintance with them, and finding that they still, like a rainbow, recede from us as fast as we pursue. Thus we find realised in our own souls those heavenly contradictions, those divine paradoxes, that the wiser we get, the greater fools we become (1 Cor. iii. 18); the stronger we grow, the weaker we are (2 Cor. xii. 9, 10); the more we possess, the less we have (2 Cor. vi. 10); the more completely bankrupt, the more frankly forgiven (Luke vii. 42); the more utterly lost, the more perfectly saved; and when most like a little child, the greatest in the kingdom of heaven (Matt. xviii. 4).

October 10.

"And hope maketh not ashamed; because the love of God is shed abroad in our hearts by the Holy Ghost which is given unto us."—ROMANS v. 5.

How the Scriptures speak of "a good hope through

grace;" and call it "an anchor of the soul, both sure and steadfast, and which entereth into that within the veil." What a blessed grace must that be which thus enters into the very presence of Christ! How, too, the word of God speaks of it as the twin sister with faith and love (1 Cor. xiii. 13); and declares that it "maketh not ashamed," because it springs out of the love of God shed abroad in the heart by the Holy Ghost!

Now we learn what "a good hope through grace" is, by being tossed up and down on the waves of despondency, and almost at times sinking into despair. Evidences so darkened, the heart so shut up, the mind so bewildered, sin so present, the Lord so absent, a nature so carnal, sensual, idolatrous, and adulterous—no wonder that amidst so many evils felt or feared, the soul should at times sink into despondency. But at such seasons the blessedness of "a good hope through grace" is found; and when this anchor is cast into and enters within the veil, taking hold of the blood and righteousness of the great High Priest, how strongly and securely it holds the ship, so that it shall not be utterly overwhelmed in the billows of despair!

October 11.

"The Lord hath laid on him the iniquity of us all."—ISAIAH liii. 6.

WHAT heart can conceive, what tongue express what the holy soul of Christ endured when "the Lord laid on him the iniquity of us all?" In the garden of Gethsemane, what a load of guilt, what a weight of sin, what an intolerable burden of the wrath of God did that sacred humanity endure, until the pressure of sorrow and woe forced the drops of blood to fall as sweat from his brow. The human nature in its weakness recoiled, as it were, from the cup of anguish put into his hand. His body could scarce bear the

load that pressed him down; his soul, under the waves and
billows of God's wrath, sank in deep mire where there was
no standing, and came into deep waters where the floods
overflowed him (Ps. lxix. 1, 2). And how could it be otherwise when that sacred humanity was enduring all the wrath
of God, suffering the very pangs of hell, and wading in all
the depths of guilt and terror? When the blessed Lord was
made sin (or a sin-offering) for us, he endured in his holy
soul all the pangs of distress, horror, alarm, misery, and
guilt that the elect would have felt in hell for ever; and not
only as any one of them would have felt, but as the col-
lective whole would have experienced under the outpouring
of the everlasting wrath of God. The anguish, the distress,
the darkness, the condemnation, the shame, the guilt, the
unutterable horror, that any or all of his quickened family
have ever experienced under a sense of God's wrath, the curse
of the law, and the terrors of hell, are only faint, feeble reflections of what the Lord felt in the garden and on the cross;
for there were attendant circumstances in his case which are
not, and indeed cannot be in theirs, and which made the
distress and agony of his holy soul, both in nature and
degree, such as none but he could feel or know. He as the
eternal Son of God, who had lain in his bosom before all
worlds, had known all the blessedness and happiness of the
love and favour of the Father, his own Father, shining upon
him, for he was "by him as one brought up with him, and
was daily his delight, rejoicing always before him" (Prov. viii.
30). When, then, instead of love he felt his displeasure,
instead of the beams of his favour he experienced the
frowns and terrors of his wrath, instead of the light of his
countenance he tasted the darkness and gloom of desertion,—
what heart can conceive, what tongue express the bitter
anguish which must have wrung the soul of our suffering
Surety under this agonising experience?

October 12.

" With long life will I satisfy him, and shew him my salvation."—PSALM xci. 16.

IT is not in the number of our years that we shall find preparedness for death. It is not the longer a man lives the more will he be satisfied. No such thing. Then what can the promise mean? Why, that God will satisfy his people with their length of life, whether long or short. God takes his children home at all ages, and he always satisfies them. He always brings them to see and feel that this life is empty and vain, and that it is better, far better, to live in his presence.

You may be harassed by the thoughts of death, and be in bondage through the fears of death; and you may be saying, " How will it be with me then?" I will tell you. If you are a child of God, I firmly believe you will not be removed unwillingly and reluctantly, but you will be willing in the day of the Lord's power. You will be willing to breathe out your soul into his dear hands, to whom you will commend your spirit; you will be willing to be with Christ, which is far better. You may not now be willing. If you pluck at an unripe apple, it resists the touch, but let it be fully ripe, how little, how slight a touch will cause it to drop from the tree. You shall be gathered as a shock of corn in its season. Why, a farmer will not gather in his corn until it is fully ripe; and do you think the Lord will gather his corn into his heavenly garner and it be in an unfit and unripe state? We cannot think it. Be that thought far from us, as it is far from the Lord.

" With long life will I satisfy him, and shew him my salvation." Ah! the soul will never see it unless the Lord shews it him; but the Lord will shew it him. He says he will. " I will shew him my salvation." What can he want more? All that he may want, all that he may need in

his journey through this wilderness is there. Is there not
a sufficiency? Is there not that which he feels is enough?
If these promises be mine, be yours, and if they be fulfilled
to you and to me, what can we possibly want more?

October 13.

*"But the Comforter, which is the Holy Ghost, whom the
Father will send in my name, he shall teach you all things."* —
JOHN xiv. 26.

IF the Lord has given to any of you eyes to see and hearts
to receive this divine Comforter, praise, bless, and adore your
God and Father, and most merciful Benefactor, for his distinguishing grace in giving you to know him as *your*
Comforter; and if he has ever dropped into your soul any
of his sweet teachings, bless him that you have received
him also as the Spirit of truth into your conscience. What
but sovereign grace, rich, free and superabounding, has made
the difference between you and the world who cannot receive
him? But for his divine operations upon your soul, you
would still be of the world, hardening your heart against
everything good and godlike, walking on in the pride and
ignorance of unbelief and self-righteousness, until you sank
down into the chambers of death. Oh, it is a mercy if but one
drop of heavenly consolation has ever been distilled into your
soul, if ever you have felt or found any relief in your sorrows
and distresses from the work and witness of the Holy Ghost;
if you have ever gathered any solid comfort from any promise
applied with power, from any text dropped into your heart
with a sealing testimony, from any manifestation of the love
and blood of Christ, or from any communication of liberty,
joy, or peace such as are produced by the operation and
influence of the Spirit of God. It may have been but little,
nor did it last long; but it has given you a taste of its
blessedness, and made you long for another sip, another

crumb, another visit. But look to it well and examine carefully whether it be real, and whether, weighed in the balance of the sanctuary, you have good ground for believing that what you received with such comfort to your soul was distilled into your heart by the Comforter, and that the truth which you have felt and believed, as well as professed, has been opened up to your conscience by the Spirit of truth.

October 14.

"And be found in him, not having mine own righteousness, which is of the law, but that which is through the faith of Christ, the righteousness which is of God by faith." — PHILIPPIANS iii. 9.

HERE are the two righteousnesses clearly laid down, in one or other of which we must all stand before God—the righteousness which is of the law, and the righteousness which is of God by faith in Christ. But bear this in mind, that a righteousness to be available before God must be a perfect righteousness. This righteousness no man ever did or could produce by his own obedience to the law, for no man ever yet loved God "with all his heart and soul and mind and strength, and his neighbour as himself;" and if a man do not thus love God and thus love his neighbour, he is accursed and condemned already by that righteous law which curseth " every one who continueth not in all things which are written in the book of the law to do them." Now the Apostle felt that as this righteousness could not be yielded by himself as a fallen sinner, he must necessarily fall under the condemnation and curse attached to that holy law. Trembling, therefore, in his conscience, as feeling that the wrath of God was revealed against him, and all unjustified sinners in a broken law, and knowing that he must sink for ever under the terrible indignation of the Almighty, if he had no covering for his needy, naked soul but his own righteousness, he fled

out of it to find justification and acceptance, mercy and peace
in the righteousness of Christ. Thenceforth he " was determined to know nothing, save Jesus Christ and him crucified,"
and Jesus became to him his " all in all." When once he had
been favoured with a view of the righteousness of the Son of
God, he wanted no other for time or eternity. He saw by
faith the words and works of the God-man, and he beheld
Deity stamped upon every thought, word, and action of that
pure humanity with which it was in union, and thus investing
them with a merit beyond all conception or expression of
men or angels. He saw him by faith bearing his sins in his
own body on the tree, and by his active and passive obedience working out a righteousness acceptable to God, and
such as he and all the redeemed could stand in before the
great white throne without spot or blemish. As a traveller
overtaken by a violent thunderstorm gladly flies to a house
by the wayside wherein he may find shelter from the lightning-
stroke and the sweeping rain; or as a ship threatened with a
hurricane bends every sail to reach in time the harbour of
refuge, so does the soul terrified by the thunders and lightnings of God's righteous law, seek for shelter in the wounded
side of Jesus, and hide itself beneath his justifying obedience.
This righteousness is here called "the righteousness of God;"
for God the Father contrived it, God the Son performed it,
and God the Holy Ghost applies it; and it is said to be " by
faith " and " through the faith of Christ " because faith views
it, believes in it, receives it, and gives the soul a manifested
interest in it.

October 15.

*" My doctrine shall drop as the rain, my speech shall distil
as the dew, as the small rain upon the tender herb, and as the
showers upon the grass."*—DEUTERONOMY xxxii. 2.

WE have in our text a regular scale : the dew, the small

rain, the rain, and the showers. And this graduated scale of heavenly moisture shews that there are degrees of spiritual blessing. We must not expect all to be blessed to the same extent, nor all to receive the same measure. Yet all are of the same nature. Examine "the dew," it is water; "the small rain," it is water; "the rain," it is water; "the showers," they are still water. You cannot find any difference between the water of the dew, of the small rain, of the rain, and of the showers: they are all alike pure water, distilled from the alembic of the sky. So it is with the blessing of God upon the soul. It may fall upon one as the dew, upon another as the small rain, upon a third as the rain, on a fourth as the showers; yet all are equally and alike spiritual and divine. It is the same God that gives; through the same Jesus it comes; by the same Spirit it is communicated. All produce more or less the same effect—to soften, to moisten, to fertilise, and to revive; and all descend from the heaven of Christ's gospel; all fall from the same firmament of grace, mercy, and truth, love, blood, and salvation. The doctrine, therefore, that testifies of Jesus, and the speech that proclaims him to be a Rock, and his work to be perfect, and no other teaching, "drops as the rain and distils as the dew." There is a power in truth, when God is pleased to apply it to the heart; and whether it come in large or in small measure, whether it be in dew or shower, it is equally a proof of his mercy and love, and equally a proof that his power attends his own divine truth to our soul.

October 16.

"Your life is hid with Christ in God."—COLOSSIANS iii. 3.

THERE is nothing so deep, nothing so hidden, as the life of God in the soul. It seems to be enshrined in the lowest depths of a man's heart. It does not float upon the surface, like a cork upon the water, but sinks deep, very deep, into the very bottom of the soul. Therefore is it hidden from the eyes of a profane world; hidden from the professing world; and what is more, sometimes hidden from the subject of it himself. A child of God often cannot see his own faith, nor can he discern the life that is bubbling and streaming up in his own bosom. It is not a lake, spread abroad in the meridian sunshine to attract every eye; nor is it a brook that flows babbling on over the clear pebbles; but it is a well. " The water that I shall give him shall be in him a *well* of water, springing up into everlasting life." Therefore it is hidden from view. The best part of our religion is that which is least seen. The secret cries, groans, tears, confessions, supplications, and breathings after God do not for the most part come abroad; the despondency, heart sickness, trials, perplexities, and powerful temptations with which many a dear saint of God is exercised do not come to view. No ; nor his fears, sinkings, guilt, misery, and self-condemnation. Yes, the best part of his religion is hidden from view, for the weightiest ever sinks the deepest. And as it is with the dealings of his soul with God, so it is with the dealings of God with his soul, making and keeping his conscience tender, reviving the fear of God, drawing the heart upward into prayer and meditation, watering his spirit and bedewing it with the secret dew and rain of his grace. Thus, the best part, because the spiritual part of a man's religion, is hidden from the eyes of all, except as the fruits thereof are manifest. Take your stand upon yon hill, and see that thread of verdure spreading itself through the barren plain. Whence comes that green strip which you see? Coming down to examine it, you find a little brooklet threading its way through the barren plain. It is this brooklet that, watering the roots of the grass, gives it that verdure ; yet the brooklet itself is hidden till the eye is brought close to it. So it is with the life of God in the soul. We see the effects the verdure produced by the brooklet; but the brooklet itself, the life and grace of God in the innermost soul is hidden, "hid with Christ in God." And if not merely hidden, but hidden with Christ in God, what a sacred, what a holy, what a truly divine life it must be! If this be spiritual religion, that it dwells with Christ himself in the bosom of God, what a divine thing, what a heavenly possession! how full of eternal blessedness must the religion of a child of God be! It is locked up in two distinct places, yet united with each other by virtue of the humanity of Christ, and the faith that embraces it. If I may use the expression, one end is in the bosom of God, and the other in the believer's breast! Compare man's paltry, beggarly religion with this supernatural life of God in the soul, Christ himself formed in the heart the hope of glory. Words would fail to express the eternal distinction between them.

But the word "hidden" will carry another idea, *out of reach*, treasured up, therefore safe. What would have become long ago of the life of God in the soul, if it could have been robbed, trodden out, or lost? But this it never can be, for it is locked up in the Person of the Son of God. It is, therefore, out of the reach of Satan, sin, death, and hell; safe in Christ's keeping, locked up in his eternal bosom. Were it otherwise, where should you and I long ago have been? Where would our religion have gone to, unless we had reason to believe that it had been kindled by the power of God, and was maintained by the same power which first gave it birth? This is the grand consolation of a child of God—to believe that he has the life of God in his soul; and to feel, day by day, that he who gave that life maintains it in firm and living exercise.

October 17.

" *Grace unto you, and peace, be multiplied.*"—1 PETER i. 2.

WHEN we see and feel how we need grace every moment of our lives, we at once perceive a beauty in the blessing thus asked for in an abundant, overflowing measure. We cannot walk the length of the street without sin. Our carnal minds, our vain imaginations, are all on the look out for evil. Sin presents itself at every avenue, and lurks like the Arab in the wilderness, or the prowling night thief for every opportunity of open or secret plunder. In fact, in ourselves, in our fallen nature, except as restrained and influenced by grace, we sin with well-nigh every breath that we draw. We need, therefore, grace upon grace, or, in the words of the text, grace to be "multiplied" in proportion to our sins. Shall I say in proportion? Nay, if sin abounds, as to our shame and sorrow we know it does, we want grace to much more abound. When the neep tide of sin flows in with the mud and mire, we want the spring tide of grace to flow higher still, to carry out the slime and filth into the depths of the ocean, so that when sought for they may no more be found. Thus we want grace, free grace; grace to-day, grace to-morrow, grace this moment, grace the next, grace all the day long; healing, reviving, restoring, saving, sanctifying; and all this multiplied by all our wants and woes, sins, slips and falls, unceasing and aggravated backslidings. We want grace to believe, grace to hope, grace to love, grace to fight, and grace to conquer; grace to stand, grace to live, and grace to die. Every moment of our lives we need keeping, supporting, holding, and withholding grace; for, as a good man has said, "If the Lord leave us for one moment, he leaves us that one moment too long."

But to "grace" the Apostle adds "*peace.*" Sin breaks our peace, and sets our souls at a distance from God; trials, too, and temptations, sins and sorrows, occur every day to mar our rest; so we want peace to be multiplied as well as grace. Peace like a river, of which the stream is ever flowing; peace like the sea, of which the tides, if they do ebb, yet rise higher than they fall. We want peace, too, to establish our hearts in the truth, and in the love of it, so as to prevent our being carried about with every wind of doctrine. We are often entangled in the wily snares of Satan, and we want peace to be restored to our soul. When it is thus sadly broken, and sin has filled us with guilt and terror, we want peace to come and heal all those wounds, and establish our souls firmly in the gospel of peace. And when we shall be called upon to enter the dark valley of the shadow of death, how then we shall need "peace to be multiplied," that we may fear no evil, but find the comforting staff and supporting rod. Thus we never can have too much grace or too much peace. The more we know of sin the more shall we want grace, and the more we know of sorrow the more we shall want peace.

October 18.

"Jesus answered and said unto them, This is the work of God, that ye believe on him whom he hath sent."—JOHN vi. 29.

OH! how many a living saint is there who wants to believe in Jesus, who longs to trust in his holy name; and yet he cannot, so plagued, so pestered is he by the risings of inward unbelief. He knows that he does not yet so believe in him as to obtain deliverance; for he has an inward testimony in his conscience, that if he believed in the Lord Jesus by the power of the Holy Ghost, it would bring the love of God into his heart, extract the sting of death, and fill him with joy and peace. But as long as he feels condemned by the law and his own guilty conscience, he has an inward testimony that he has not as yet that living faith in Christ which, he is persuaded, would save and deliver him from all his guilty fears and dismal apprehensions. Therefore he labours after this special, this peculiar faith in the Lord Jesus, that he may attain unto it, or rather that God would, of his infinite mercy, bestow it upon him. Here, then, is the main labour of faith, to believe in Jesus Christ so as to obtain pardon, peace, and deliverance. Many a poor soul is labouring hard at this work, yet with a deep and increasing conviction that it is a work which he cannot perform except by the immediate power of God. So powerful an antagonist is unbelief, that, with all his attempts, he feels that he cannot subdue it, nor raise up one grain of that true faith whereby Christ is experimentally brought into the heart. But this very struggle plainly shews that there is life within, a work of God on his soul; for, from the movements of his grace, and the opposition of his carnal mind to them, all this conflict proceeds. When, then, in due time, the blessed Spirit brings Christ near to his eyes and heart, reveals him within, takes of his atoning blood, and sprinkles it on his conscience, brings forth his righteousness and puts it upon him, and sheds abroad the love of God, then he raises up that special faith in the Lord Jesus, whereby the soul hangs, and if I may use the expression, hooks itself upon his Person, as God-man, upon his blood as cleansing from all sin, upon his righteousness as perfectly justifying, upon his grace as superabounding over all the aboundings of evil, and upon his dying love as a balmy cordial against all the woes and sorrows by which it is distressed. This is believing in the Son of God; believing in Jesus Christ to the salvation of the soul.

October 19.

" Hast thou not procured this unto thyself, in that thou hast forsaken the Lord thy God, when he led thee by the way?"— JEREMIAH ii. 17.

No man knows better, I believe, than myself, that we cannot

do anything of a spiritual nature to bring us near to God, but I am equally sure that we can do many things that set us very far from him. Let all the shame and guilt be ours; all the grace and glory are God's. Every drop of felt mercy, every ray of gracious hope, every sweet application of truth to the heart, every sense of interest, every blessed testimony, every sweet indulgence, every heavenly smile, every tender desire, and every spiritual feeling, all, all are of God. If ever my heart is softened, my spirit blessed, my soul watered, if Christ is ever felt to be precious, it is all of his grace; it is all given freely, sovereignly, without money and without price. But can it be denied—I for one cannot deny it—that by our carnality, inconsistency, worldly-mindedness, negligence, ingratitude, and forsaking and forgetting the God of our mercies, we are continually bringing leanness and barrenness, deadness and darkness into our own souls? Thus we are forced to plead " Guilty, guilty!" to put our mouth in the dust, acknowledge ourselves to be vile, and confess ourselves indeed " of sinners chief, and of saints less than the least." Yet thus does God, in his mysterious dealings, open up a way for his sovereign grace and mercy to visit the soul. The more we feel ourselves condemned, cut off, gashed, and wounded by a sense of sin and folly, backslidings and wanderings from God, the lower we shall lie, the more we shall put our mouth in the dust, the more freely we shall confess our baseness before him. And if the Lord should be pleased, in these solemn moments, to open our poor blind eyes to see something of the precious blood of the Lamb, to apply some sweet promise to the soul, or to bring to the heart a sense of his goodness and mercy, how sweet and suitable is that grace, as coming over all the mountains and hills of our sin and shame. Thus is the goodness of God, as it were, reflected on and by our baseness and vileness, as we see the sun sometimes shining on and reflected by a black cloud. The black cloud of our vileness but serves to heighten the glory of the rays of free grace and the bright beams of the Sun of righteousness.

October 20.

" Thou therefore endure hardness, as a good soldier of Jesus Christ."—2 TIMOTHY ii. 3.

How is the Christian soldier made? By going to chapel, by reading the Bible, by singing hymns, by talking about religion? Just as much as the veteran warrior is made at Aldershot or Southsea. He must go into the battle and fight hand to hand with Satan and the flesh; he must endure cruel wounds given by both outward and inward foes; he must lie upon the cold ground of desolation and desertion; he must rush up the breach when called to storm the castles of sin and evil, and never " yield or quit the field," but press on determined to win the day or die. In these battles of the Lord, in due time he learns how to handle his weapons, how to call upon God in supplication and prayer, to trust in Jesus Christ with all his heart, to beat back Satan, to crucify self, and live a life of faith in the Son of God. Religion is not a matter of theory or of doctrine : it is to be in the thick of the battle, fighting with the enemy hand to hand, foot to foot, shoulder to shoulder. This actual, not sham, warfare makes the Christian soldier hardy, strengthens the muscles of his arm, gives him skill to wield his weapons, and power sometimes to put his enemies to flight. Thus it " works endurance," makes him a veteran, so that he is no longer a raw recruit, but one able to fight the Lord's battles and " to endure hardness, as a good soldier of Jesus Christ." What then have been your best friends? Your trials. Where have you learnt your best lessons? In the school of temptation. What has made you look to Jesus? A sense of your sin and misery. Why have you hung upon the word of promise? Because you had nothing else to hang upon.

Thus, could you look at the results, you would see this, that trials and temptations produced upon your spirit these two effects; that they tried your faith, and that sometimes to the uttermost, so that in the trial it seemed as if all your faith were gone; and yet they have wrought patience, they have made you endure. Why have you not long ago given up all religion? Have your trials made you disposed to give it up? They have made you hold all the faster by it. Have your temptations induced you to let it go as a matter of little consequence? Why, you never had more real religion than when you were tried whether you had any; and never held faith with a tighter grasp than when Satan was pulling it all away. The strongest believers are not the men of doctrine, but the men of experience; not the boasters, but the fighters; not the parade officers in all the millinery of spotless regimentals, but the tattered, soiled, wounded, half-dead soldiers that give and take no quarter from sin or Satan.

October 21.

"*Behold, I will bring evil upon all flesh, saith the Lord.*"— JEREMIAH xlv. 5.

THE Lord may be said spiritually to "bring evil upon all flesh," when he lays trouble and calamity upon the flesh, and upon all that the flesh loves. The blow falls upon the fruits of the flesh, when it cuts down fleshly religion, and roots up false hopes, vain confidence, and self-dependence. The effect of these strokes is to lay the soul poor and needy at the footstool of mercy; and as the Holy Ghost enlightens the eyes to see, quickens the soul to feel, and raises up power to ask, there is now a seeking after real things—substance as opposed to shadows. Thus pardon, mercy, the testimony of God in the soul, the lifting up of the light of his countenance, the sprinkling of the blood of Jesus upon the conscience, with all the other spiritual blessings revealed in the gospel, are sought after, valued, and prized. It is not enough now that they are heard from a minister, assented to in the judgment, or received on the testimony of others. They are only now so far enjoyed as they are tasted, felt, and handled in the depths of the heart. I believe I can say for myself until evil came upon me in this way, chiefly through a long illness, (though if I have life now, I had it before that visitation), yet until trouble came, and I was brought low in body and soul, I was never seeking as I have done since, the visitations and manifestations of the Lord's favour. Deceived by Satan and my own heart, I was seeking rather to make myself wise in the letter, than to feel the power of vital godliness in my soul. But ever since then, amidst many discouragements, and with many alternations and changes, I have felt led, as I never knew before, or at least not from the same pressing sense of need, to seek after the visitations and manifestations of the Lord's favour; the dew of his Spirit, the application of his atoning blood, and the inward testimonies of his love and grace. Nor can I rest for salvation upon anything else. I am not, therefore, speaking at a peradventure; I know the ground, for I have travelled it; I have lined it with laborious footsteps; and therefore having tracked it out, I speak in my measure, that which I know, and testify that which I feel.

When the Lord, then, thus brings evil upon our flesh, it is not to sweep away any *real* religion that we may possess. It is to sweep away our *false* religion. This winnowing fan is to fan away the chaff, and leave the pure grain. This keen knife of the heavenly Anatomist is only to cut away the diseased excrescences, and unhealthy tumours, and leave the sound parts uninjured. When the Lord brings distress into the soul, it is not to destroy any one grace that has been communicated by the blessed Spirit, but to fulfil that word, " Every plant which my heavenly Father hath not planted

shall be rooted up." He puts his "vessels of gold and silver"
into the furnace to take away their dross, that they may be
" sanctified, and meet for the Master's use." For he has
chosen his Zion in the furnace of affliction ; and he " sits as
a refiner and purifier of silver, that he may purify the sons of
Levi, and purge them as gold and silver, that they may offer
unto the Lord an offering in righteousness " (Mal. iii. 3).

October 22.

*" And the Word was made flesh, and dwelt among us, (and
we beheld his glory, the glory as of the only begotten of the
Father,) full of grace and truth."*—JOHN i. 14.

THE glory of Christ, in his suffering manhood, was veiled
from the eyes of all but those who were taught by the
blessed Spirit and enlightened to see it. And what glory is
still to be seen by believing eyes in an incarnate God! The
grandeur of Deity, tempered by the weakness of humanity,
and yet shining through it, as the noonday sun shines through
the clouds, which so far veil his rays that though they permit him to be seen they do not dazzle nor blind the eye!
The Son of God in the babe of Bethlehem; the " only
begotten of the Father," sweating great drops of blood in
the Garden, and hanging upon the cross at Calvary; yet in
his lowest state, when covered to man's eye with ignominy
and shame, glory streaming from every pore of his sacred
body, majesty and beauty shining forth from every lineament
of his marred countenance, and love and mercy character-
izing every word issuing from his languid lips ! None will
ever see the glory of a risen, ascended, and glorified Christ in
the open bliss of heaven who do not first see him on earth
in his humiliation as a suffering Christ; and indeed it is his
suffering glory which is now so blessed and so suitable to a
guilty sinner. To see this suffering glory of the Son of God

revealed to his soul by a divine power, made over to him as his salvation, and containing in it the essence of all his present and future happiness; this is the glory that a redeemed and regenerated saint longs to see and feel. What glory can the world give compared with the glory of the marred countenance of the suffering Son of God? By the side of his cross all earthly glory pales, withers, and dies; for death puts an end to everything naturally bright and glorious. Well has God spoken of the end of all human glory: "Therefore hell hath enlarged herself, and opened her mouth without measure; and their glory, and their multitude, and their pomp, and he that rejoiceth shall descend into it" (Isaiah v. 14). But that glory which begins with the cross ends with the crown; for "if we suffer with him, we shall also be glorified together." To see this glory of a suffering Christ by the eye of faith; to feel the heart deeply penetrated and inwardly possessed by it; to have it for our daily bread and our daily drink; to come as led by the Spirit to this ever-spread table of the flesh of Christ, this ever-flowing fountain of his atoning blood, and hear the Lord himself saying, "'Eat, O friends; drink, yea, drink abundantly, O beloved.' Here is food to feed your immortal soul; here are streams of pardon and peace; here the rivers of eternal life: 'Let him that is athirst come; and whosoever will, let him take the water of life freely;'" to see, to enjoy, to feel, and experience this in his own dry, thirsty and weary bosom, this is to see the glory of God, as revealed in the Person, work, blood, obedience, and love of his dear Son.

October 23.

"Even to him shall men come."—ISAIAH xlv. 24.

THE Lord has given an absolute promise that "In the Lord shall all the seed of Israel be justified, and shall glory."

And no less absolute is the addition, and as it were divine corollary to that promise, " To him shall men come." And who gives them will and power to come? The Father himself, according to the Lord's own words, "No man can come to me except the Father which hath sent me draw him." But will the Father draw all the chosen vessels of mercy to Jesus? Surely he will; for the Lord adds, " It is written in the prophets, And they shall be all taught of God. Every man therefore that hath heard, and hath learned of the Father, cometh unto me " (John vi. 45).

Every act of faith whereby you look to Jesus is a coming. Every beam and ray of hope in his blood and righteousness is a coming. Every sigh, groan, or tear; every contrite feeling, every breathing desire of a broken heart, all are a coming. So that though you may not be able to realise as fully as you could wish an interest in the former part of the promise, " Surely, shall one say, in the Lord have I righteousness and strength;" yet there is wrought in your soul by a divine power that secret coming whereby you have a manifested interest in the second part of it, " Even to him shall men come." We cannot come until we are drawn. " Draw me," says the bride, " we will run after thee " (Song Sol. i. 4). " The Lord hath appeared of old unto me, saying, Yea, I have loved thee with an everlasting love, therefore with lovingkindness have I drawn thee." When we are drawn, then we come, and cannot but come. It is good to come. Even those who have received must be ever coming. We get nothing but by coming. Our daily life, as one of faith and hope, is a life of coming. Our continual prayer is a continual coming. For the language of the Church still is, " And the Spirit and the bride say, Come. And let him that is athirst come. And whosoever will, let him take the water of life freely." Thus must we be ever coming that we may be ever receiving; and so everything that makes us come has in it a real or an implied blessing. Nor will you come in vain, be you who or what you may. "For him that cometh to me," the blessed Lord himself has said, "I will in no wise cast out."

October 24.

"For I say unto you, That except your righteousness shall exceed the righteousness of the scribes and Pharisees, ye shall in no case enter into the kingdom of heaven."—MATTHEW v. 20.

THERE are three kinds of righteousness, or at least three kinds of righteousness which bear that name. There is *inherent* righteousness, of which we have none. There is *imputed* righteousness, which is all our justification. And there is *imparted* righteousness, when God the Spirit makes us new creatures, and raises up in the heart that " new man, which after God " (that is, " after the image of God ") " is created in righteousness and true holiness." When the Lord, therefore, said, "Except your righteousness shall exceed the righteousness of the scribes and Pharisees, ye shall in no case enter into the kingdom of heaven," he did not mean only an *external* righteousness wrought out by his obedience to the law *for* them, but an *internal* righteousness wrought out by the Holy Spirit *in* them. Thus we read of the inward as well as the outward apparel of the Church, " The King's daughter is all glorious *within; her clothing* is of wrought gold." Two kinds of righteousness belong to the Queen ; her imputed righteousness is her *outward* robe, " the *clothing* of wrought gold ; " but imparted righteousness is her *inward* adorning, which makes her " all-glorious *within."* This inward glory is the new man in the heart, with all his gifts and graces, what Peter calls " the divine nature," " Christ in the heart, the hope of glory."

October 25.

"And we know that the Son of God is come, and hath given us an understanding, that we may know him that is true, and we are in him that is true, even in his Son Jesus Christ. This is the true God, and eternal life."—1 JOHN v. 20.

WHEN the Lord Jesus is pleased in some solemn hour to reveal himself to our soul, when he graciously condescends to take the veil from off our heart that we may behold his glory, the glory as of the only begotten of the Father, full of grace and truth, when he kindly favours us with some manifestation and discovery of himself as the Son of God, the brightness of the Father's glory and the express image of his Person, then we know that the Son of God is come. How do you know that the sun rose this morning? By the light which rose with it. So we may say, spiritually, "How do you know that the Son of God is come?" By the Sun of righteousness arising upon you with healing in his wings and the shining light which he diffuses in your heart. So the Lord speaks to Zion: "Arise, shine, for thy light is come, and the glory of the Lord is risen upon thee." That is the way in which the darkness is dispersed; for he adds, "Behold, the darkness shall cover the earth, and gross darkness the people; but the Lord shall rise upon thee, and his glory shall be seen upon thee." Did not our blessed Lord say, "I am come a light into the world, that whosoever believeth on me should not abide in darkness?" And has he not promised, "He that followeth me shall not walk in darkness, but shall have the light of life?" Now as God is light, when he is pleased to shine into the soul, we walk in the light as he is in the light, and then we have fellowship with one another, and the blood of Jesus Christ cleanseth us from all sin. This is the best, this is the surest, this is the safest way to know that the Son of God is come.

We know also that the Son of God is come by his presence; by his power put forth on our behalf; by the answers
which he gives to prayer; by the way in which he appears in
dark and gloomy hours, making crooked things straight and
rough places plain, discovering himself to us as the Way, the
Truth, and the Life, shewing unto us that in him there is rest
and peace, solid, abiding happiness, and in no other. He
thus draws and fixes our eyes upon himself, where he sits at
the right hand of the Father in the fulness of his grace, glory,
and majesty. Thus we know that the Son of God is come.
Every prayer, every petition, every sigh and cry, every longing
look that you cast up to him, and every word of his grace,
every sweet promise, every glimpse or glance of the King in
his beauty, which you receive out of his fulness, are all so
many testimonies that the Son of God is come, and that
you know that he is come.

October 26.

*" These wait all upon thee; that thou mayest give them their
meat in due season."*—Psalm civ. 27.

The " meat" which God's children long after, is to have
" the truth as it is in Jesus," in its various branches, revealed
with power to their heart. Not merely to see a certain truth
in God's word; that is like a hungry beggar looking at
savoury provision through a window, from which he is barred
out; such a sight whets his appetite rather than satisfies it.
The meat that God's people are longing after, and the only
thing which can assuage their spiritual hunger, is " the truth
as it is in Jesus" manifested, revealed, discovered, and applied
with power to their souls; dew, unction, savour, sweetness,
life, light, liberty accompanying the word, so that truth falls
as heavenly manna into their hearts. It is not sufficient that
the Holy Ghost should create the appetite, but he must over-

shadow the soul with his divine influences, breathe abroad a
heavenly savour, and fill it with some sensations of his presence, with some meltings of heart at the feet of Christ, with
some drawing forth of affection to God; and thus communicate an inward reception of the truth, and an enjoyment of
its sweetness and savour.

"Thou *givest* them." It is not to be taken out of the
Bible, because it may be read; not to be caught up, as the
minister throws it forth, because it may be heard; not to be
got out of books; but to be bestowed by the holy hand of
Jehovah himself, and received in the posture of a penitent,
in the attitude of a suppliant, a sinner prostrate at the foot of
the cross, without anything in self but wounds, condemnation,
and guilt.

But there is a due season: "Thou givest them their meat
in *due season*." There are many living souls, who are hun-
gering after divine blessings, but the "due season" has not
come. "The times and the seasons the Father hath put in
his own power." You are not yet fit for it; the Lord has to
bring you lower; you will have to travel through darker
paths, to pass through sorer exercises. There is a "due
season" for the manifestation of gospel blessings; there is a
fitting time, which the Searcher of hearts knows. And that
Searcher of hearts knows that many of the true Church of
God are at this present time in that state, that he will not
manifest to them his greatest and richest blessings. There
is a "due season," in which they are revealed and manifested
to the soul; and that season will be as suitable to all its
wants, as it will be most glorious to God. That "due
season" will most probably be when the soul will least
expect to receive it. The promise having been so long
delayed, it seems as though it would never come; the
blessing having been so long withheld, it appears as though
the Lord would never bestow it; having denied his counte-

nance so long, it seems as though he had drawn a black cloud over the throne, and through that cloud the rays of the sun would never shine. But it is a "due season;" it will surely come; "though the vision tarry, wait for it, because it will surely come, it will not tarry." There is a "set time to favour Zion," and when that set time arrives, the Lord will build up Zion and appear in his glory, for " he will regard the prayer of the destitute, and not despise their prayer."

October 27.

" Whether Paul, or Apollos, or Cephas, or the world, or life, or death, or things present, or things to come; all are yours."—
1 Corinthians iii. 22.

"Life," says the Apostle, is "yours." But how can this be? In two ways. Life present and life future, both are the Christian's, according to the words, "Godliness is profitable unto all things, having promise of the life that now is, and of that which is to come." But life present is natural and spiritual. In three senses, therefore, is life the portion of Christ's people ; life natural, life spiritual, life eternal. Life natural is theirs, for they alone can truly enjoy it. What is natural life if it hang by a thread over an awful eternity? How soon spent and gone, and how soon death and judgment close the scene. But the Christian's very natural life is his season for faith and prayer, the seedtime of an immortal harvest. Most men are life's slave, but he is life's master ; to most, life is but an opportunity of evil, but to him an opportunity of good. Spiritual life is peculiarly his, for he alone possesses it. Natural men share with him natural life ; but he alone enjoys spiritual life. This life is his because Christ is his. Christ is his life, and because Christ lives, he lives also. And then there is life eternal, which commencing now in life spiritual is transplanted above to bloom in immortality.

And then, more wondrous still, "*death*," that last enemy, that king of terrors, who makes the strongest tremble, and the stoutest heart quake; that, too, is yours, if ye are Christ's. Death is not your enemy if you are Christ's, but your friend. He may indeed in the dim and distant prospect seem to come in the guise of an enemy; you may dread the thought of his approach, and may even sink down with fear how it may be with you in that solemn hour. But if you are Christ's, death is yours as well as life, for he has abolished death, and hath brought life and immortality to light. Death then cannot harm you, because Christ died for you. Death will merely cause your poor body to drop into the ground, whilst it will open to your soul the everlasting doors through which the King of glory, the Lord mighty in battle, entered as your forerunner when he went to prepare a place for you.

October 28.

"*And ye are Christ's; and Christ is God's.*"—1 CORIN-THIANS iii. 23.

"CHRIST is God's." These are remarkable words, and need to be carefully and reverently opened up. The fulness of the mystery is beyond our grasp. Still, we may attempt to look at it in faith and godly fear. How, then, is Christ God's? First, he is God's Son—not a Son by covenant or by office; in other words, not a nominal, but a true and proper Son—a Son by nature, by his eternal mode of sub-sistence as a Person in the Godhead. "This is my beloved Son" was twice proclaimed by God the Father with an audible voice from heaven. Second, but he is also God's servant. "Behold my servant whom I uphold" (Isaiah xlii. 1). "It is a light thing that thou shouldest be my servant to raise up the tribes of Jacob" (Isaiah xlix. 6), and this he was as Messiah. But because he is by office God's servant, he is not less by nature God's Son. Here, however, he is spoken of as the

God-man Mediator, the Son of the Father in truth and love, the great High Priest over the house of God; and especially what he is as viewed in union with the Church, the Bridegroom with the bride, the Vine with the branches, the Shepherd with the sheep, the living foundation with the living stones built into and upon it. Christ, therefore, in our text is said to be God's not only as the only-begotten Son of God, but as " the Head of the body, the Church" (Col. i. 18); for, says the Apostle, " We are members of his body, of his flesh, and of his bones" (Ephes. v. 30). Christ, then, is God's, with all those that belong to him—he as much as they, they as much as he. Look, then, at these glorious truths. " Ye are Christ's " because by donation, purchase, and possession ye are members of his body. " Christ is God's " as Son, as servant, as Mediator, as Head of the Church. Then ye too are God's, because ye are Christ's; for the members are one with their covenant Head.

October 29.

" *They that be whole need not a physician, but they that are sick.*"—MATTHEW ix. 12.

A physician is useless without a case; and the deeper the case, the wiser and better physician we need. Thus a guilty conscience is a case for atoning blood, a wounded spirit for healing balm, a filthy garment for a justifying robe, a drowning wretch for an Almighty hand, a criminal on the gallows for a full pardon, an incurable disease for a heavenly physician, and a sinner sinking into hell for a Saviour stooping down from heaven. A man with a real case must have a real salvation. He is no longer to be cheated, deluded, and tricked with pretences, as a nervous patient is sometimes cured with bread pills; but he must have a real remedy as having a real disease. Christ in the Bible, Christ sitting as an unknown Saviour in the heavens, Christ afar off, unmanifested and unrevealed, is no Christ to him. "Near, near; let him come near; in my heart, in my soul, revealed in me, manifested unto me, formed within me—this, this is the Christ I want. O for one drop of his atoning blood, one smile of his blessed countenance, one testimony of his love, one gleam of his justifying righteousness!" And thus when this divine Redeemer appears in his garments stained with blood, the sinking soul hails his approach, the fowls of the mountains take flight, the beasts of the earth slink off to their dens, the dreary stump pushes forth its shoots, and the voice sounds forth from the inmost depths of the soul, "This is our God; we have waited for him, and he will save us. This is the Lord, we have waited for him; we will be glad and rejoice in his salvation."

October 30.

"*My people are bent to backsliding from me.*"—Hosea xi. 7.

What an awful error it is to deny backsliding! What ignorance it manifests of a man's own heart! How it stamps a man as a perverter of truth, and one that trifles with sin and the displeasure of the Most High! Who that knows himself and the idolatry of his fallen nature, dares deny that he backslides perpetually in heart, lip, or life? Can any of us deny that we have backslidden from our first love? backslidden from simplicity and godly sincerity, backslidden from reverence and godly fear, backslidden from spirituality and heavenly-mindedness, backslidden from the breathings of affection and pouring forth of the heart into the bosom of the Lord? And if we have not been suffered to backslide into open sin, if the Lord has kept us, and not suffered us to be cast down into the mire, yet have we not committed that twofold evil which the Lord charges upon his people: "They have forsaken me, the fountain of living waters, and hewed

them out cisterns, broken cisterns, that can hold no water"
(Jeremiah ii. 13)?

And what do we reap from backsliding? do we reap
pleasure, comfort, or peace? do we reap the smiles of God,
or the solemn testimony of the Spirit in the conscience? No.
If conscience speaks in your bosom, what does it say? That
every departure from the Lord has brought grief and trouble;
that so far from justifying yourself in your sin, you have been
ready almost to weep tears of blood, that you have so wickedly
departed from the Lord. It has been our mercy that the
Lord has not given us up to hardness of heart and searedness
of conscience, that we have not been allowed to say with
Israel of old, "I am innocent, I have not sinned" (Jer. ii.
35); but that he has "led us with weeping and with supplications." Have not some of us (I am sure I have for one)
been obliged "to go and weep," and tell the Lord a piteous
tale of backsliding; how we have departed from his fear, and
sinned basely against him; how unwilling we have been to
take his yoke upon us, and walk in his precepts? Have we
not been forced to tell him that we have been disobedient and
stubborn, filthy and vile, and has he not, in some faint
measure, led us "to turn our faces Zionward," to turn our
back upon all false ministers, upon all idol shepherds, upon
all the strength and wisdom and righteousness and will of the
creature, and given to us some simplicity, uprightness, and
integrity of heart and conscience, whereby we have turned our
face Zionward, looking for a blessing to come out of Zion,
looking for grace, looking for glory? "I will make thee
sick in smiting thee," says the Lord (Micah vi. 13), alluding
to the feeling of sickness produced by a wound, ("I am made
sick," 1 Kings xxii. 34, *margin*.) And have not these wounds
in our conscience made us, in our measure, sick of the world,
sick of the professing church, sick of hypocrites, sick of white-
washed Pharisees, sick of carnal professors, sick of our back-

slidings, sick of all but the word of God revealed with power, sick of all but the blood and love of the Redeemer, of all teachings but the teachings of the Holy Ghost, of all company but the company of the children of God? Can you say thus much? that you have turned your back upon everything but Christ, and him crucified? that you have turned away from all doctrines but those which centre in the blood of the Lamb? that you have turned away from universal charity and general philanthropy, as substituted for the power of vital godliness, (though you would desire to love and serve your fellow men as men,) and that your spiritual affections are toward God and his people? And has there been in your soul any such feeling as Ruth had when she said, "Thy people shall be my people, and thy God my God?" Any sweet response in your bosom to the voice of the Lord, "My son, give me thine heart?" "Take it, Lord, with all that I have and am!" Any casting yourself at the foot of the cross, and there entreating the Lord of life and glory to speak peace to your soul?

October 31.

"By grace ye are saved."—Ephesians ii. 5.

Oh! the volumes of blessed truth that are couched in these few words; thrown in out of the Apostle's full heart as if to give a moment's vent to his love of salvation by grace! Mercy, love, and grace are all in the bosom of God toward his saints; and yet they differ from each other. But how? *Mercy* regards the criminal; *love* regards the object; *grace*, perhaps, is a blending of the two,—the union of mercy and love. God loves the holy unfallen angels; *there* is an object of love in which there is no mixture of mercy; for having never sinned, mercy they do not need. Again, God shewed no mercy to the fallen angels; there we have justice and wrath, without mercy; but in the case of the saints of God, the election of grace, we have not only mercy and love, but we have the conjoint attribute, that uniting mercy and love in one stream flows onward to the Church, as the river of the water of life; the pure crystal river of grace. Grace means, as you well know, the pure favour of God, and, as such, is sovereign, distinguishing, free, and superabounding. Every attribute of Jehovah is distinct, and yet so blended that the whole shine forth in one glorious effulgence. The rays of the sun united form one complete body of pure, bright light; but the prism or the rainbow separates these rays into distinct colours. So the attributes of God are not confused though blended, and all shine forth in one pure bright glory. But this is the peculiar character of *grace*, that any intermixture of worth or worthiness in the object would destroy it. For if the gospel require merit, we are damned by it as inevitably as by the law. This Luther felt when, racked and torn by the words " the righteousness of God without the law is manifested," he cried out in the agony of his soul, " What! am I damned not only by the law, but damned by the gospel also ! "

This pure, free, unadulterated grace is the joy of every soul that is able to receive it; for it comes as a blessed cordial when sinking and swooning under a sight and sense of the deserved wrath of God. When, then, the pure gospel of the grace of God comes as a cordial from the Most High, it lifts up his drooping head, revives his sinking soul, and pours oil and wine into his bleeding wounds. By this grace we are justified, pardoned, accepted, sanctified, and saved with an everlasting salvation. Oh! glad tidings to perishing sinners! Oh! blessed news to those who are sinking under a sense of guilt and misery, in whom the law of God is discharging its awful curse ! When we get a view by faith, and a sweet taste of the pure grace of God, what a balm, what a cordial, what a sweet reviving draught it is. It is this which makes us prize so highly, and exalt so gladly the free grace of God; because it is so pure, so free, and so superabounding over all the aboundings of sin, guilt, filth, and folly. It never can be laid down too clearly, it never can be too much insisted on that "by grace," and grace alone, "ye are saved." If free grace has reached your soul, it has saved your soul; if free grace has come into your heart, it has blessed you with an everlasting salvation, and you will live to prove it, when your happy soul joins the throng of the blessed. If anything can lift up a drooping sinner, restore a backslider, break a hard, or soften a stony heart; draw forth songs of praise, and tears of contrition; produce repentance and godly sorrow for sin; a humble mind and a tender conscience; it is a sweet experience of the superabounding grace of God. Can we then exalt it too much? Can we prize it too highly? Can we cleave to it too closely? No; in proportion as we feel our ruin and misery, we shall cleave to it with every desire of our soul; for it is all our salvation, as it is all our desire.

November 1.

"*The entrance of thy words giveth light.*"— PSALM cxix. 130.

THE blessed Spirit is pleased sometimes to give some testimony concerning Jesus, to open up some passage of Scripture which speaks of Jesus, to cast a divine light before the astonished eyes, and to throw some of the blessed beams of gospel truth into our souls, whereby we see Jesus. We are brought sometimes in soul feeling to the desires of those Greeks who came up to worship at the feast, and went to Philip, saying, "Sir, we would see Jesus;" and from some apprehension of his beauty and loveliness, we pour out our soul before God, and say, "We would see Jesus." We want to feel his love, to have our eyes anointed to behold his glory, to look upon him as crucified for us and bearing our sins in his own body on the tree, that we may have a sweet and blessed fellowship with him as our suffering Surety, and thus, by faith, enter into the length and breadth and depth and height of that love of his "that passeth knowledge." Wherever there is a work of grace upon the soul, there will be this pining after Christ. The soul that is really taught of God can never rest satisfied short of Jesus. "There remaineth a rest to the people of God," and they can never be satisfied short of that rest, which consists in an experimental knowledge of the Son of God, as revealed by the Holy Ghost to their souls. But before the enjoyment of this spiritual rest, there is often long delay; clouds of darkness for months and years together often envelope the mercy-seat; the cross of Christ cannot be seen; the Holy Ghost does not fulfil his covenanted office in taking of the things of Christ, and shewing them to the soul; and in the absence of these heavenly manifestations, we cannot realise our interest in the things of salvation, nor can we feel our hearts sweetly composed and settled down in the blessed assurance, that when this life shall come to a close, we shall inhabit mansions prepared for us before the foundation of the world. When "with clouds he covereth the light, and commandeth it not to shine by the cloud that cometh betwixt," there are many doubts and fears, suspicions, surmises, and jealousies whether we are not deceived and deluded altogether. At such seasons, everything seems to be against us, and to stamp us as being nothing but nominal professors.

It is in such dark and gloomy seasons as these that "the entrance of God's words giveth light." For instance, some such promise as this is made sweet to the soul: "Come unto me, all ye that labour and are heavy laden, and I will give you rest." As that promise is brought home with power to the heart, and is shed abroad with some sweetness in the soul, it draws forth and strengthens faith, and the toiling pilgrim comes to the Lord, feeling himself "weary and heavy laden," and as he comes, he is indulged sometimes with a few sweet moments of rest. He is enabled to look out of fallen self, with all its miseries, and to look upon Jesus in his grace and beauty. He is favoured to cast himself simply, as he is, upon Jesus, and some sense of his atoning blood, dying love, and complete propitiation for sin is opened up to his heart. Faith springs up to lay hold of and embrace it, and he begins to taste the savour and sweetness and healing efficacy of a Saviour's blood and love. Thus "the entrance of God's words giveth light," and he feels by the divine coming in of what God has externally revealed, that inward light is shed abroad in the recesses of his soul, and he can, in some measure, realise the power of the cross of Jesus in his heart.

November 2.

"And such were some of you : but ye are washed, but ye are sanctified, but ye are justified in the name of the Lord Jesus, and by the Spirit of our God."—1 CORINTHIANS vi. 11.

JUSTIFICATION and sanctification are distinct blessings. The first springs out of, and is connected with, the finished work of the Son of God; the other springs out of, and is connected with, the work of the Holy Ghost on the soul. Sin has defiled our persons externally, as well as polluted our souls internally. We cannot, therefore, stand before God unless washed in the blood of the Lamb, and clothed in his spotless righteousness. This righteousness forms our *title* to heaven, as holiness constitutes our *meetness*. The former is our wedding robe, the latter our spiritual qualification. The hymn well draws this distinction :

> "'Tis he adorn'd my naked soul,
> And made salvation mine ;
> Upon a poor, polluted worm
> He makes his graces shine.

And, lest the shadow of a spot
 Should on my soul be found,
He took the robe the Saviour wrought,
 And cast it all around.

The Spirit wrought my faith, and love,
 And hope, and every grace;
But Jesus spent his life to work
 The robe of righteousness."

Without these two qualifications, what entrance could there be into heaven, or what happiness there, could entrance be gained? For consider not only the infinite purity and holiness of God, but the blazing splendour of his immediate presence, the piercing ray of his deep-searching eye. Who or what can live in his presence but what is absolutely perfect without and within? But this the Church could not be, unless she were washed in the blood and clothed in the righteousness of God's dear Son, and perfectly sanctified by the operations and indwelling of his Spirit. We therefore read: "Husbands, love your wives, even as Christ also loved the Church, and gave himself for it; that he might sanctify and cleanse it with the washing of water by the word, that he might present it to himself a glorious Church, not having spot, or wrinkle, or any such thing; but that it should be holy and without blemish" (Ephesians v. 25-27).

November 3.

"It is good that a man should both hope and quietly wait for the salvation of the Lord."—LAMENTATIONS iii. 26.

THE Lord does not bring his poor and needy children to a throne of grace, and send them away immediately they have come. But his purpose is, to shew them deeply what they are, to make them value his favours, to sink them lower and lower in self, that they may rise higher and higher in Christ, to " teach them to profit" (as the Scripture speaks),

to write his laws upon their hearts in lines of the Spirit's
drawing, in deep lines, "graven with an iron pen and lead
in the rock for ever;" not characters traced out in the sand,
to be washed out by the rising tide, or effaced by the wind,
but in characters as permanent as the soul itself. The work
of the Spirit in the hearts of the redeemed is radical work,
work that goes to the very bottom; nothing flimsy, nothing
superficial, nothing which can be effaced and obliterated
springs from him, but that which shall have an abiding effect,
that which shall last for eternity. The Lord is fitting his
people for eternity, and therefore his work in them is
thorough work; it goes right through them; it leaves nothing
covered up and masked over, but turns all up from the very
bottom, "discovering the foundation unto the neck" (Hab.
iii. 13), and doing in a man spiritually what the Lord threatened to do in Jerusalem literally, " I will wipe Jerusalem as a
man wipeth a dish, wiping it, and *turning it upside down*"
(2 Kings xxi. 13). Therefore he does not answer the prayers
of his children immediately when they come to his throne of
mercy and grace, but rather he deepens those convictions
that he has implanted; he makes the burdens heavier that
he has put upon their back; he hides himself instead of
discovering himself, and draws back further instead of
coming nearer. Now this is intended to make them wait
with greater earnestness, with more unreserved simplicity,
with more absolute dependence upon him and him alone
to communicate the blessing, with greater separation of
heart from all the strength of the creature, with a firmer
resolution in the soul to cast away all its own righteousness,
and to hang solely and wholly upon the Spirit's teachings,
and Jesus' sweet revelation of himself.

November 4.

"Love is of God."—1 JOHN iv. 7.

LOVE is a gift which the risen Mediator has received that he may freely communicate it out of his fulness to his people. And we must be brought to feel that it is a gift. Could we produce or keep it alive in our own hearts, we should burn incense to our own skill or our own care. Some perhaps will scarcely believe that a child of God can feel enmity against Christ; but his carnal mind is unmitigated enmity against him. And oh, what a cutting feeling it is for a follower of the Lamb to have a principle in him which hates Christ; hates, bitterly hates his Person, hates his holiness and purity; which could join in the cry, " Crucify him, crucify him," and push and strike him with the Roman soldiers and the Jewish rabble. Unless painful experience convinced us that there was such a dreadful principle within, we could not believe that there was this devilish enmity in our heart against him whom our souls desire to love and adore. But what know we about love, if we have not all this enmity, carnality, and coldness to try it? When we have been exercised with all these wretched feelings, and the Lord begins to drop into our hearts a little mercy and grace, and to draw forth our affections unto him, we then begin to feel what a sweet thing love is. Love is the sweetest balm man can taste in this life. It is so naturally. There is a sweetness in love. When we love our wives, our children, our friends, there is a sweetness and tenderness in the very feeling, that is—as moralists say of virtue—its own reward. Coldness, dislike, envy, prejudice, jealousy, suspicion, peevishness, quarrelling—these sparks of hell burn and torture every spot on which they fall. And so, if ever there is a hell in a man's bosom, it is when full of hatred against God and his people. But if ever we feel a foretaste of heaven, it is when the Lord kindles some meltings of love, some drawings of affection toward Jesus and to them that are his. Then enmity and prejudice flee away; and we feel as if we could take all the people of God into our bosom, and say, "Thy people shall be my people, and thy God my God."

November 5.

"A time to weep, and a time to laugh." — ECCLESIASTES iii. 4.

DOES a man only weep once in his life? Does not the time of weeping run, more or less, through a Christian's life? Does not mourning run parallel with his existence in this tabernacle of clay? for "man is born to trouble as the sparks fly upwards." Then "a time to kill, and a time to heal; a time to break down, and a time to build up" must run parallel with a Christian's life, just as much as "a time to weep, and a time to laugh; a time to mourn, and a time to dance." Living souls will know many times to weep; they will have often to sigh and cry over their base hearts; to mourn with tears of godly sorrow their backslidings from God; to weep over their broken idols, faded hopes, and marred prospects; to weep at having so grieved the Spirit of God by their disobedience, carnality, and worldliness; to be melted into contrition at the feet of a dying Lord, so as in some measure to be led into the path in which Jesus walked as "a man of sorrows, and acquainted with grief." They will have to bewail the falling off of those friends whom once they looked upon as bidding fairer for the kingdom of God than themselves; to weep at the cruel arrows of calumny which are shot against them by professors; to mourn over the low state of Zion, how few there are who really serve the Lord acceptably with reverence and godly fear, and adorn the doctrine in all things. But above all things will, they have to weep over the inward idolatries of their filthy nature;

to weep that they ever should have treated with such insult that God whom they desire to love and adore; that they should so neglect and turn their backs upon that Saviour who crowns them with lovingkindness and tender mercies; and that they bear so little in mind the instruction that has been communicated to them by the Holy Spirit. There is many a weeping time for God's children; and if there be one frame of mind in soul experience more to be coveted than another, it is to be weeping at Jesus' feet. We have two sweet instances of the Lord's manifesting himself to those who were weeping—one to "the woman which was a sinner," who stood behind him, and washed his feet with her tears; the other was to Mary Magdalene, who "stood without at the sepulchre weeping." Oh, how different is the weeping, chastened spirit of a living soul from the hardened, seared presumption of a proud professor! How different are the feelings of a broken-hearted child of God from the lightness, the frivolity, the emptiness, and the worldliness of hundreds who stand in a profession of religion! How different is a mourning saint, weeping in his solitary corner over his base backslidings, from a reckless professor who justifies himself in every action, who thinks sin a light thing, and who, however inconsistently he acts, never feels conscience wounded thereby! "Blessed are they that mourn, for they shall be comforted."

November 6.

"The spirit indeed is willing, but the flesh is weak."— MATTHEW xxvi. 41.

WHY is flesh so weak? Because it is fallen, because it is sinful, because it has an alliance with the temptation which is presented to it. It is weak against temptation for the same reason that a man who loves strong drink is weak against the offered dram. If we had no inward lusting after evil, no pride, no rebelliousness, no fallen nature, no carnal mind, no vile affections, nothing in us earthly, sensual, or devilish, need we fear temptation? No; for then we should be proof against it; it would be like dipping a match in water. Here our weakness lies. If we could always resist we should conquer, but resist we cannot, except by the special power of God. This is a lesson we all need to learn. The weakness of the flesh manifests itself continually in compliance, in non-resistance, in giving way, in yielding, often almost without a struggle, nay, sometimes in acting a worse and more wicked part still. How striking are the words of Hart!

> "That mariner's mad part I played
> Who sees, yet strikes the shelf."

Is there any one that knows and fears God who can say he has never played that mad part; never seen the rock ahead, and yet run upon it; never mourned, sighed, cried, groaned and repented, and yet been again overcome; never seen the evil of the snare, never felt the wire round his neck, and yet been entangled, I was going to say strangled? It is through these things that we learn the weakness of the flesh; weak to believe, weak to hope, weak to love, weak to fight, weak to resist, weak to overcome, weak to watch, weak to pray, weak to stand, weak to everything good; strong to everything evil. The flesh indeed is weak. What are all resolutions, all promises, all desires, all endeavours, all strugglings, all strivings, except the soul is held up by the mighty power of God?

And yet "*the spirit is willing.*" Here the child of God is distinguished from those who are given up as a prey to temptation. He has a willing spirit, which they have not. But how is the spirit willing? It is made "willing in the day of God's power." It is a new spirit, a free spirit, a holy spirit, a gracious spirit, and therefore a willing spirit. But what is it willing to do? Willing to obey, to watch, to pray, to be conformed to the will of God, to crucify the lusts and affections, to put off the old man and to put on the new. And how does it shew its willingness? By the very struggles it maintains against the flesh ; flesh and spirit pulling contrary ways; the spirit all willingness, the flesh all weakness ; flesh twining around spirit, spirit struggling under the firm and strong embrace of flesh. Hence the conflict; the spirit willing to read God's word, to pray and seek God's face, and pour out the heart before him ; the flesh weak, and finding prayer a burden. The spirit willing to make sacrifices, endure persecutions, bear afflictions, carry the cross, suffer with Jesus, resist even unto blood striving against sin; the flesh weak, dragging the spirit down with it, unable to stand a single moment, complying with every suggestion to evil, listening to every insinuation of Satan breathed into the ear, hearkening to the tempter, and almost as bad as he. This then, the willingness of the spirit and the weakness of the flesh, is the reason why there should be watchfulness and prayer. If there were no willing spirit, there would be no need of watchfulness; it would be useless ; nor of prayer, for it would not ascend with acceptance into the ears of the Lord of Sabaoth. If there were nothing but flesh, the believer would be all weakness; possessing spirit, there is in him some willingness, and this God looks at.

November 7.

" My people hath been lost sheep."—JEREMIAH l. 6.

WHEN God the Holy Ghost takes a soul in hand, just as the fingers of a man's hand wrote a sentence of condemnation upon the wall of the palace of the king of Babylon, so does the blessed Spirit write the word "lost" upon the conscience of every vessel of mercy ; and when he has written this word with power on their consciences, they carry it about with them branded as it were in letters of fire, in such a manner that the impression is never to be erased, until it is blotted out by the atoning blood of the Mediator.

And thus in the teachings of the Holy Ghost in the consciences of God's family, "lost, lost, lost" is written on their heart; "lost, lost, lost" is the cry of their lips; "lost, lost, lost" is the deep feeling of their soul. And none was ever found who had not the feeling *lost*, written more or less deeply upon his heart. None was ever gathered into the arms of the heavenly Shepherd; sought out upon the mountains and the hills, laid upon his shoulders, and brought home with rejoicing; none was ever brought into a spiritual acquaintance with Jesus, so as to enjoy communion with him, who had not sighed and groaned and cried under a sense of his lost state, as a guilty sinner before God.

Now when the soul has been taught by the Holy Ghost, to feel as well as to see and know itself to be without strength to deliver itself from the wrath to come, and is in consequence sunk down into despondency and dismay, then is the time when the Holy Ghost usually gives it some discovery of the mercy of God in the face of Jesus Christ. We find this sweetly set forth in that remarkable chapter, Ezekiel xvi. ' The vessel of mercy is there delineated under the figure of a new-born babe, abandoned by its mother, and "cast out in the open field, to the loathing of its person in the day that it was born." As unpitied, as abandoned, as polluted, as helpless, as perishing, as wretched an outcast is the quickened soul. But it is not left to perish. "When I passed by thee," says the loving Redeemer, "and looked upon thee, behold, thy time was the time of love; and I spread my skirt over thee" (the sign of espousal, Ruth iii. 9), "and covered thy nakedness: yea, I sware unto thee, and entered into a covenant with thee, saith the Lord God, and thou becamest mine."

November 8.

" But we have this treasure in earthen vessels."—2 CORIN-
THIANS iv. 7.

GOLD and silver, those precious metals, take no injury,
receive no spot of corruption from the vessel in which they
are contained; let them be buried in the damp earth, no
tarnish or rust forms upon them. So spiritually, the grace of
God in the heart, surrounded as it is with corruption, is not
tarnished by it, the heavenly treasure is not contaminated,
though lodged in an earthen vessel. Christ in the heart is
not defiled by the inward workings of depravity, and by the
base thoughts that strive perpetually against his grace, any
more than the gold of the Bank of England is defiled by the
dark and damp cellars in which it is stowed. And what a
mercy it is, that our corruptions cannot tarnish the grace of
God; that our unbelief cannot mix with, and adulterate the
faith of God's elect; that our despondency cannot spoil and
ruin a gospel hope; that our deadness, darkness, coldness, and
rebellion cannot mingle with and defile the love of God in the
soul! This heavenly treasure remains still as unpolluted and
pure as when God first put it there; being a part of "the divine
nature," it remains uncontaminated by the filth and corruption that surround it. Is not this a mercy for God's tried
people, that spiritual knowledge, living faith, gospel hope,
heavenly love, and the fruits and graces of God's Spirit in the
soul can never be defiled; but, like the streams of a fountain,
are ever gushing forth in pure water? What a blessing it is,
that the pure grace of God in a man's heart cannot be contaminated by the filthy streams that are dashing from a vile
nature against it, like the torrents of water from a fire-engine
against a burning house, but remains as pure as when God
the Spirit first breathed it into the soul.

November 9.

" And he said, I will not let thee go, except thou bless me."—
GENESIS xxxii. 26.

WHAT a strange intermixture there is in a believing heart
of everything to cast down and yet of everything to encourage !
How there is everything on the one side to perplex, to confuse,
and put the soul to its wits' end, and yet how on the other
there is everything to hold up its head, strengthen its faith,
support its hope, and encourage it to hold on to the last gasp !
Now this is that very trial of faith which is more precious than
of gold that perisheth, for faith is not a dead, sluggish grace, and
is never more active than when it is being tried as with fire.
You cannot give up from what you have felt and experienced,
for that is the grand evidence, the persuasion that you have the
life of God in your soul, and compared with that how worthless and valueless all other things seem to be in your eyes,
because to give that up is to give up all your hope.   Here,
then, is the grand mystery, to hang and hold on, to hold out,
and not suffer oneself to be cast away, but the more the Lord
would seem to put us away, the more to cling to him.   Was
not this the faith of the Syro-Phenician woman, who, so to
speak, would not take " No " for an answer? or, like the
faith of Ruth, " Entreat me not to leave thee?" or, like the
faith of Hannah, when " she was in bitterness of soul, and
prayed unto the Lord and wept sore?"   Does not this faith
resemble that of Heman's, when he cried out, "Wilt thou shew
wonders to the dead?   Shall the dead arise and praise thee?"
and that of Asaph, when his feet were almost gone, and his
steps had well-nigh slipped?   Thus the more the Lord seems
to put us away, the more we cling to him.   The viler we are,
the more we need his grace; and the very magnitude of our
sins only makes us hang more upon his atoning blood and

cling more closely to his word and promises as suitable to our case. Nor will anything induce us to give up our hope or relinquish our hold of his mercy.

November 10.

" In the light of the king's countenance is life; and his favour is as a cloud of the latter rain."—PROVERBS xvi. 15.

WHAT is religion without a living faith in, and a living love to the Lord Jesus Christ? How dull and dragging, how dry and heavy, what a burden to the mind, and a weariness to the flesh, is a round of forms where the heart is not engaged and the affections not drawn forth! Reading, hearing, praying, meditation, conversation with the saints of God, what cold, what heartless work where Jesus is not! But let him appear, let his presence and grace be felt, and his blessed Spirit move upon the heart, then there is a holy sweetness, a sacred blessedness in the worship of God and in communion with the Lord Jesus that makes, whilst it lasts, a little heaven on earth. It is this inward sense of the blessedness of his presence and the misery of his absence, the heaven of his smile and the hell of his frown, that makes the sheep of Christ seek communion with him. He has won their heart to himself by discovering to them his beauty and his love, and they having once seen the glory of his Person, heard the sweetness of his voice, and tasted the grace of his lips, follow him whithersoever he goeth, seeking to know him and the power of his resurrection, and counting all things dung and loss that they may win him, and have some manifestation of his love. What is to support the soul under those trials and temptations that at times press it so sore, relieve those cruel doubts which so disquiet, take away those fears of death which so alarm, subdue that rebelliousness which so condemns, wean from the world which so allures, and make it look beyond life and time, the cares of the passing hour, and the events of the fleeting day, to a solemn and blessed eternity, but those visitations of the blessed Lord to the soul which give it communion with himself? Thus were the saints of God led and taught in days of old, as the Holy Ghost has recorded their experience in the word of truth. Remembering the past, one says, "Thy visitation hath preserved my spirit." Longing for a renewal, another cries, "O when wilt thou come unto me?" and under the enjoyment of his presence the Church speaks, "He brought me to the banqueting house, and his banner over me was love."

November 11.

" But if ye be led of the Spirit, ye are not under the law."— GALATIANS v. 18.

IF we are led of the Spirit by walking in him; if he be our Guide and Teacher; if he be continually operating upon our heart, and bringing near the influences of his grace; if he be in us and with us, guiding us into all truth, making and keeping us believing, loving, prayerful, tender, watchful, humble, contrite, and sincere; if we are thus led by the Spirit, we are not then under the law. Now whilst the conflict is going on in your bosom, you are often in your feelings under the law. The law's curse is ringing in your ears, the law's condemnation piercing your conscience. The flesh in some unguarded moment, it may be, prevails: you are entangled in some evil; you slip and fall into something which brings guilt upon your conscience. Now the law thunders; inward condemnation re-echoes its peals; and the soul falls into bondage, doubt, and fear. But if you are led by the Spirit; if that blessed Guide is pleased to lead you out of yourself into Christ's blood and righteousness; if you are experimentally favoured with his blessed teachings and sweet influences, bringing with them light, life, liberty, and love, the law has no more curse for you; it cannot condemn you to hell, nor

send your soul to lie for ever under the curse of God. For
being led by the Spirit you are delivered from the curse of the
law into the blessing of the gospel; from the bondage of
the law into the liberty of truth; from law charges into gospel
mercies; from the accusations of a guilty conscience into the
witness of a good, because a purged and sprinkled conscience,
and to sum it all up in one sentence, are thus translated from
the power of darkness into the kingdom of God's dear Son.
Oh the blessedness of walking in the Spirit, and being led
by the Spirit!

November 12.

*" He will subdue our iniquities; and thou wilt cast all their
sins into the depths of the sea."*—MICAH vii. 19.

SIN subdued is the next greatest blessing to sin pardoned;
and wherever God does pardon sin he subdues sin; for the
same grace which saves sanctifies; the same grace which
casts sin behind God's back, puts its foot upon the corruptions
of the believer, and prevents iniquity from having dominion
over him. The Scripture is very plain and express upon this
point. "Sin shall not have dominion over you." Why?
"Because ye are not under the law," which gives sin its
strength and power, "but under grace," which is able to
subdue its dominion. Nor do I believe that any child of God
can ever rest satisfied except by the subduing of his sins as
well as the pardoning of them. To have his unbelief, infidelity,
worldly-mindedness, pride, and covetousness subdued by the
grace of God, its power taken out of it, its dominion dethroned,
its authority destroyed, and its strength weakened and dimi-
nished, that he may not be under the dominion of any lust,
or carried away by the strength of any secret or open sin, but
may walk before God in the light of his countenance, as
desirous to know his will and do it,—this is the desire and
breathing of every one that knows sin in its guilt, filth, and

power. How gracious, then, is the promise, how sweet the favour, that the Lord has promised to subdue our iniquities by the same grace as that whereby he pardons them; that, as we receive the blood of Christ to sprinkle the conscience, so we receive the grace of Christ to sanctify and renew the soul, and the strength of Christ to overcome all our inward and outward foes.

November 13.

"And deliver them who through fear of death were all their lifetime subject to bondage."—HEBREWS ii. 15.

IT is no evidence against you if you are subject to bondage; it is no mark against you if you cannot look death in the face without doubt or fear. Is it not " the children" who feel the bondage? And did not the Lord come to deliver them from it? Are you then not a child because you fear death? If you had no sense of sin, no tenderness of conscience, you would be as careless about death as most other people are. Thus your very bondage, your very fears, if they make you sigh and cry for deliverance, are marks of life. And the day will surely come when the Lord will remove these chilling fears and put an end to these killing doubts. As you draw near to the brink of Jordan, the Lord will be with you to deliver you, who, through fear of death, are now subject to bondage; he will extract its sting, and rob the grave of its victory, enabling you to shout " Salvation!" through his blood, even at the moment when nature sinks lowest and the last enemy appears nearest in view. Oh, what a blessed Jesus we have; what a heavenly Friend; what a divine Mediator between a holy God and our guilty souls! What love he displayed in taking our flesh and blood; what kind condescension, what wondrous depths of unspeakable grace! He loved us sufficiently to lay down his life for us. Did he not for our sakes endure the agony of the cross, the hidings of God's face, the burden of sin, the pangs of hell? And if he has done all this for us on earth, will he leave his work undone in heaven? Has he quickened you into life, made you feel your sin, taught you to seek for mercy, raised up a good hope in your heart, applied a promise to your soul, given you a testimony? He may have done all this, and yet at times your conscience may be held down in bondage and imprisonment. But it is only to make further way for his grace; to open up more and more of his willingness and ability to save to the uttermost all that come unto God by him. It is only to make himself in the end more precious to you; to shew you more of his finished work, more of his dying love and atoning blood, and more of what he is able to do in delivering you from all your fears. Thus, as the Adam fall was overruled by the wisdom of God to make manifest the riches of his eternal love, mercy, and grace, so your very doubts, fears, and bondage will be blessedly overruled to give you further discoveries of Christ, to wean you more from an arm of flesh, and to make you know more experimentally what the Lord Jesus Christ is to those who seek his face and hang upon and trust him and him alone.

A man who believes that he may live and die, and that safely, without an experimental knowledge of Christ, will never seek his face, never call upon his name, never long for the manifestations of his love. But he who feels that he can neither live nor die without him, who knows that he has a soul that only Christ can save, who has sins which only Christ's blood can pardon, iniquities that only Christ's right-eousness can cover, will be often crying to the Lord to visit his soul with his salvation, and will find no rest till Christ appears; but when Christ appears to the joy of his soul, will bless and praise him with joyful lips. And oh, what a glorious trophy will that man be of Christ's eternal victory over sin and Satan, when he will reign with him and with his assembled saints in one immortal day !

November 14.

"Having a good conscience."—1 PETER iii. 16.

WE cannot often see our faith, but we can sometimes see our conscience. We cannot always rejoice in the Lord, but we can see whether we fear his great name. We cannot always triumph over our enemies, but we can sometimes observe whether there is a sentinel upon the look out. Thus, if you want to know whether you have faith, look at faith's companion, see what faith is attended by; and if you find not "a good conscience," write death upon your religion. Throw away your sword; it is useless; it is of human manufacture; it will break in pieces when you have to encounter your enemy, the king of terrors; God's lightning will shiver it then. But if the Lord has given you "a good conscience," a tender conscience, a pure conscience, he will strengthen your arm to fight the good fight of faith. You will often think your sword is so short, and your arm so weak that you cannot fight the Lord's battles. But if he has given you "a good conscience," a conscience tender in his fear, he has put into your hands the sword of faith, and he will one day manifest it clearly, that he has himself equipped you with it, by giving you victory over all your foes. Oh, may the Lord raise up in our hearts some sweet testimony that we have "a good conscience," and then we shall have this blessed consolation, that concerning faith we shall not make shipwreck.

November 15.

"My Father, which gave them me, is greater than all; and no man is able to pluck them out of my Father's hand."— JOHN x. 29.

IN that most sublime and touching prayer which the Lord

Jesus Christ, as the great High Priest over the house of God, offered up to his heavenly Father before he shed his precious blood on the cross, there is one petition, or rather an expression of his holy will, which is full of unspeakable blessedness. " Father, I will that they also, whom thou hast given me, be with me where I am; that they may behold my glory, which thou hast given me; for thou lovedst me before the foundation of the world." The change from petitioning as a Priest to willing as a King is very remarkable, and casts a gracious light on the nature of Christ's mediatorial intercession at the right hand of God. On the footing of his covenant engagements, atoning sacrifice, and finished work, as well as from the perfect equality of his divine nature with that of the Father and of the Holy Ghost, he utters the expression of that sovereign will which was and is identically the same with the eternal will and fixed decrees of his heavenly Father. And oh, how full and comprehensive, how gracious and condescending is the will of Christ as thus expressed! How it embraces in its firm and sovereign grasp all the members of his mystical body, all the sheep of his pasture and the flock of his hand, all that the Father gave him to be eternally his own! Yes; all the countless millions who before the foundation of the world were given him as his joy and crown, as his eternal inheritance, as the delight of his heart, and the promised reward of his incarnation, sufferings, and death, were included in this expression of his holy and unchanging will. Whatever be their state and condition here below, whatever sins and sorrows they may have to sigh and groan under, whatever opposition they may encounter from earth or hell, this will of Christ holds them up so that they cannot fall out of his hand, or be deprived of their glorious inheritance.

November 16.

" Be careful for nothing; but in everything by prayer and supplication with thanksgiving let your requests be made known unto God."—PHILIPPIANS iv. 6.

WHAT a word this is! " Everything!" You are privileged, saint of God, to go to the throne of God with everything. What, with every little occurrence? Yes. What, with things that people call trifles? Yes. With your daily concerns? Yes. If you feel that there is a God who can hear you, it is your privilege to go to him in *everything.* All things are comprehended; nothing is excluded. In everything, and that by prayer and supplication. Sometimes we pray, some-times we supplicate. Prayer is something more gentle than supplication, less earnest, less fervent, less powerful; yet not less effectual. I have sometimes compared prayer and sup-plication to two things in nature. The one to a river—a stream, such as we see in our low country that flows with gentle course to the sea; the other to the torrents found in mountainous countries, that leap from precipice to precipice. The one is the calm prayer of the soul, the other the fervent cry, the earnest supplication, the breathed agony of the spirit rushing along into the bosom of God with many a broken sigh and many an earnest groan. Here the two seem contrasted. There is prayer, calm and gentle, the simple pouring out of the soul into the bosom of God; and then there is supplica-tion, which is earnest, and calls upon the Lord as though the soul must be heard. We see it in the blessed Jesus himself. We read on one occasion that he went into a mountain the whole night to pray. Now we have no reason to believe he prayed on that occasion in the same way that he prayed in the garden and upon the cross. In the one case he had sweet union and communion with his Father ; in the other he cried with groans and tears and was heard. The one was prayer; the other supplication. When your soul is calmed by the presence of God, and you feel the breath of prayer to enter your bosom, then you can pray to the Lord with sweetness and with spirit. But there are times and seasons when the soul, under the attacks of Satan and a terrible sense of guilt and shame, is obliged to cry as one that must be heard, and that is supplication. But there is another thing which is to be mingled with it, and a thing much omitted, and that is thanksgiving. These are the three constituents of a spiritual service, prayer, supplication, and thanksgiving.

November 17.

" Simon Peter, a servant and an apostle of Jesus Christ, to them that have obtained like precious faith with us."— 2 PETER i. 1.

WHAT a thought it is, that if you and I possess one grain of living faith, the same precious grace is in our hearts that was in the hearts of all the saints of God, from Abel the proto-martyr, in all the saints of the Old Testament, in all the prophets, and martyrs, and servants and apostles of God, and will subsist in the bosom of every saint down to the remotest period of time. There is but " one faith," as there is " one God, one Lord, and one baptism;" and it is by the possession of this " like precious faith" that all the family of God are knit together into one glorious body, of which the Lord Jesus Christ is the risen Head. You, in yourself, may be very poor and needy, for faith gives us to feel our poverty and need; you may think and feel yourself unworthy of the least notice of God's favouring eye; but if the blessed Spirit has raised up one grain of living faith in your soul, you stand on the same holy platform with saints, apostles, prophets, and martyrs, and you are as much " accepted in the Beloved," as much loved of God, and as much a member of the mystical body of Christ, as though you were the Apostle Peter, Paul, Enoch, Abel, Isaiah, or any of the prophets.

November 18.

"After the similitude of Melchisedec there ariseth another priest, who is made, not after the law of a carnal commandment, but after the power of an endless life."—HEBREWS vii. 15, 16.

WE may say of the life which the Lord Jesus lives in the courts of heavenly bliss that it is a threefold life. There is, first, his *eternal* life, by which I mean the eternal life of God in his divine nature. This he lives in himself; for " as the Father hath life in himself; so hath he given to the Son to have life in himself" (John v. 26). He is hereby " Alpha and Omega, the first and the last, the beginning and the end." And this life is the foundation of all his acts of mediation, as being God over all, blessed for ever.

But there is a life which he lives for himself, viz. a life of inconceivable glory in his *human nature.* This is the life which he laid down that he might take it again. This life is the cause of, and is attended with all that ineffable glory which he now enjoys in heaven. This life he lives for himself, his reward, and the glory and honour with which he is crowned; as the Psalmist says, " Thou settest a crown of pure gold on his head. He asked life of thee, and thou gavest it him, even length of days for ever and ever" (Psalm xxi. 3, 4).

But there is another life which he lives : a *mediatorial life,* a life for us. Thus we read, that " he was made a priest after the power of an endless life;" and he says of himself, " I am he that liveth, and was dead ; and, behold, I am alive for evermore, Amen; and have the keys of hell and of death" (Rev. i. 18). Now this life does not differ essentially from

the second life, of which I have spoken, the life of glory in
the human nature; but it differs in this point, that when the
work of mediation is accomplished, he will cease to live a
mediatorial life; for he will then "deliver up the kingdom to
God, even the Father, when he shall have put down all rule
and all authority and power" (1 Cor. xv. 24).

November 19.

"*But we had the sentence of death in ourselves, that we
should not trust in ourselves, but in God which raiseth the
dead.*"— 2 CORINTHIANS i. 9.

WHAT is life naturally and what is death naturally? Is not
that life in which there is breath, energy, movement, activity?
And what is death but the utter cessation of all this moving
activity and vital energy? To die is to lose life, and by
losing life to lose all the movements of life. Thus, when the
Lord takes, as it were, out of our heart and hands everything
in which we once had life, in which we lived and moved and
seemed to have our earthly, natural, and enjoyed being, and
condemns it by his holy word, so as to record therein, and in
our conscience as an echo to his voice, a continual sentence
of death against it, he delivers us over unto death. And you
will observe that none but the living family of God are so
delivered: "For *we which live* are alway delivered unto death
for Jesus' sake;" and observe also that the reason for this
mysterious dispensation is to bring to light the hidden life
of Jesus within, for the Apostle adds, "that the life also of
Jesus might be made manifest in our mortal flesh." And
observe also the connection which this sentence of death has
with the death of Christ: "Always bearing about in the body
the dying of the Lord Jesus." We must suffer with Jesus if
we are to be glorified with him; must die with him if we are
to live with him. His death is the exemplar, the model and
the means of our own; and as he had the sentence of death

in himself upon the cross, so must we be crucified with him, that we may be conformed to his suffering, dying image. Thus not only is there a death by, under, and unto the law, so as to kill the soul to all creature hope and help, to all vain confidence, and all self-righteousness; but in the continual teachings and dealings of God upon the heart, and especially in times and by means of heavy affliction, painful trial, and powerful temptation, does the Lord by his Spirit and grace execute a sentence of death in all those to whom he is giving to drink of Christ's cup and to be baptized with Christ's baptism.

November 20.

"For thy Maker is thine husband; the Lord of hosts is his name; and thy Redeemer the Holy One of Israel; The God of the whole earth shall he be called."—ISAIAH liv. 5.

As in the marriage union man and wife become one flesh, and, God having joined them together, no man may put them asunder, so when the Lord Jesus Christ, in "the everlasting covenant, ordered in all things and sure," betrothed the Church unto himself, they became before the face of heaven one in indissoluble ties. As he undertook in "the fulness of time" to be "made of a woman," she became one with him in body by virtue of a common nature; and becomes one with him in spirit when, as each individual member comes forth into a time state, the blessed Spirit unites it to him by regenerating grace. Such is the testimony of the word of truth. "We are members of his body, of his flesh, and of his bones;" "He that is joined to the Lord is one spirit." Her union, therefore, with his flesh ensures to her body conformity in the resurrection morn to the glorified body of Jesus; and her union with his spirit ensures to her soul an eternity of bliss in the perfection of knowledge, holiness, and love. Thus the union of the Church with Christ commenced in the councils of eternal wisdom and love, is made known upon earth by regenerating grace, and is perfected in heaven in the fulness of glory.

The Church, it is true, fell in Adam from that state of innocence and purity in which she was originally created. But how the Adam fall, in all its miserable consequences, instead of cancelling the bond and disannulling the everlasting covenant, only served more fully and gloriously to reveal and make known the love of Christ to his chosen bride in all its breadth and length and depth and height! She fell, it is true, into unspeakable, unfathomable depths of sin and misery, guilt and crime; but she never fell out of his heart or out of his arms. Yet what without the fall would have been known of dying love or of the mystery of the cross! Where would have been the song of the redeemed, " Unto him that loved us, and washed us from our sins in his own blood?" Where the victory over death and hell, or the triumphs of super-abounding grace over the aboundings of sin, guilt, and despair? Where would have been the "leading captivity captive," the "spoiling principalities and powers, and making a shew of them openly, triumphing over them in himself?" What would have been known of that most precious attribute of God, *mercy?* What of his forbearance and long-suffering; what of his pitiful compassion to the poor, lost children of men? As then the Church's head and husband could not and would not dissolve the union, break the covenant, or alter the thing that had gone out of his lips, and yet could not take her openly unto himself in all her filth, and guilt, and shame, he had to redeem her with his own heart's blood, with agonies and sufferings such as earth or heaven never before witnessed, with those dolorous cries under the hidings of his Father's face, which made the earth to quake, the rocks to rend, and the sun to withdraw its light. But his love was strong as death, and he endured the cross, despising the shame, bearing her sins in his own body on the tree, and thus suffering the penalty due to her crimes, reconciled her unto God " in the body of his flesh, through death, to present her holy, and unblameable, and unreproveable in his sight." Having thus reconciled her unto God, as she comes forth from the womb of time, he visits member after member of his mystical body with his regenerating grace, that " he may sanctify and cleanse it with the washing of water by the word," and thus eventually " present it to himself a glorious Church, not having spot, or wrinkle, or any such thing."

November 21.

" Make me not the reproach of the foolish."—PSALM xxxix. 8.

WHO are these " foolish?" I think the best answer to this question is given by our Lord himself, in the parable of the wise and foolish virgins. " The foolish " were those who had oil in their lamps, but none in their vessels. By "the foolish" in the text, therefore, we may understand those who have the light of knowledge in their heads, and the lamp of profession in their hands, but no oil of grace in their hearts. They are " foolish," because they know neither God nor themselves, neither sin nor salvation, neither the depth of the fall nor the greatness of the remedy. They are " foolish," as regards themselves, in thinking that light and knowledge will save them, without life and grace; and they are " foolish," as regards others, for want of an experimental acquaintance with the heart. They know nothing, therefore, of the temptations of a child of God; how he is beset on every hand; how Satan is ever thrusting at or enticing him; how his own heart is continually prompting him to evil; and how snares are in every direction laid for his feet. " The foolish " know nothing of these trials; they are Pharisees, who " make clean the outside of the cup and platter," who whitewash and adorn the sepulchre without, whilst within it is " full of dead men's bones and all uncleanness." David knew well, and every child of God knows well, that if he were allowed to slip, if he were suffered to say or do anything unbecoming, these would be the very first to make him an open reproach. "The foolish" can, and will, make no allowances for the least slip of tongue or foot, for they themselves are ignorant of the weakness of the flesh, the subtlety of Satan, the strength of sin, and the power of temptation. Were he to stumble and fall, "the foolish" would be sure to point the finger of scorn at him. In breathing forth, then, this petition, we may well suppose him to say, "Lord, whatever temptations I may be called upon to endure, whatever snares of Satan or lusts of the flesh may beset my path behind and before, O keep me, keep me that I may not be 'the reproach of the foolish;' that they may have nothing to take hold of, to make me a bye-word, and through me to reproach thy name, cause, and truth."

November 22.

"But we trusted that it had been he which should have redeemed Israel."—LUKE xxiv. 21.

WHAT a trial to their faith must the death of Jesus have been to his disciples and believing followers! When their Lord and Master died, their hopes, for the time at least, seem almost to have died with him. And indeed to the eye of sense, truth, holiness, innocence, all fell crushed by the arm of violence as Jesus hung on the cross. To the spectator there, all his miracles of love and mercy, his words of grace and truth, his holy, spotless life, his claims to be the Son of God, the promised Messiah, the Redeemer of Israel, with every promise and every prophecy concerning him were all extinguished when, amidst the triumph of his foes, in pain, shame, and ignominy, he yielded up his breath. We *now* see that, by his blood-shedding and death, the blessed Lord wrought out redemption, finished the work which the Father gave him to do, put away sin by the sacrifice of himself, reconciled the Church unto God, triumphed over death and hell, vanquished Satan, magnified the law and made it honourable, exalted justice, brought in mercy, harmonised every apparently jarring attribute, glorified his heavenly Father, and saved millions with an everlasting salvation. But should we have seen this as we see it now, had we stood at the cross with weeping Mary and broken-hearted John, heard the railing taunts of the scribes and Pharisees, the rude laughter of the Roman soldiery, and the mocking cries of the Jewish mob, viewed the darkened sky above, and felt the solid earth beneath rocking under our feet? Where would our faith have been then? What but a miracle of almighty grace and power could have sustained it amidst such clouds of darkness, such strength of sense, such a crowd of conflicting passions, such opposition of unbelief?

So it ever has been, so it ever will be in this time state. Truth, uprightness, godliness, the cause of God as distinct from, as opposed to error and evil, have always suffered crucifixion, not only in the Person, but in the example of a crucified Jesus. It is an ungodly world; Satan, not Jesus, is its god and prince; and therefore, not truth but falsehood, not good but evil, not love but enmity, not sincerity and uprightness but craft and deceptiveness, not righteousness and holiness but sin and godlessness prevail and triumph as they did at the cross. This tries faith; but its relief and remedy are to look up, amidst these clouds, to the cross, and see on it the suffering Son of God. Then we see that the triumphing of the wicked is but for a moment; that though truth is now suffering, it is suffering with Christ; and that as he died and rose again, so it will have a glorious resurrection, and an eternal triumph.

November 23.

" Who against hope believed in hope."—ROMANS iv. 18.

HOPE is a fruit of the Spirit; and the absence of hope, the thorough, complete absence of hope, stamps death upon that nominal branch, in which the absence of all hope is found. But some will say, " Are not the children of God often plunged into despair?" No; not into despair. They are often very near it, they are on the borders of it; they go to the very brink of it; the gusts from that pestiferous land may so blow their blasts upon them, that in their feelings they shall be in despair; yet no living soul ever set his foot beyond the brink, no child of God ever stepped beyond the border, so as to get into the regions of despair. If he got there, he would no longer be in "the land of the living;" if ever he set his foot over the border that separates the land of hope from the land of despair, he would be no longer calling upon the Lord to save his soul from the lowest hell, but he would be at once overwhelmed by those torrents, which would sweep him away into endless perdition. Hell is the place of despair, and the conscience of the reprobate, before he is cast into those devouring flames; and therefore, unless you know what the very feelings of the damned in hell are (which you can never be certain you do, however you may think you know them), or unless you have gone into the very feelings of despair in the conscience of the reprobate before hell opens its jaws to receive him for ever, however near you have been to the borders of that dreadful land, you never can say your foot has crossed the threshold. No; there is a "Who can tell?" a secret support of "the everlasting arms;" there is a band, a tie, wreathed round the soul by the God of all grace; there is a golden chain let down by God himself from the everlasting throne of mercy and truth, which keeps the soul from ever being drawn into that whirlpool, going down those tremendous cataracts, and being swallowed up in the boiling abyss below. There is an invisible arm that preserves the soul from being swept away by the water-floods; and this secret help is manifested by a lifting up of the heart oftentimes in prayer, and the relief sometimes experienced in pouring forth the soul in fervent cries, upholding all who feel it from being overwhelmed in the torrent of despair, when the sluices of God's wrath seem pulled up to hurry it into eternal misery. And therefore there is no child of God that has been quickened by the Spirit, but has some degree of hope, which keeps him from making shipwreck altogether. So that we do not go too far in saying that the absence of hope altogether stamps death upon a man.

November 24.

"But we are not of them who draw back unto perdition; but of them that believe to the saving of the soul."—Hebrews x. 39.

The Scriptures have brought certain marks not only to test, but also to comfort God's people. But in order to keep them tremblingly alive to the fear of being deceived; in order to set up an effectual beacon lest their vessel should run upon the rocks, the blessed Spirit has revealed such passages as we find in the sixth and tenth chapters of the Hebrews. They seem set up by the Spirit of God as a light-house at the entrance of a harbour. Is it not so naturally? Some shoal or sand-bank often lies near the entrance of a port, which the mariner has to guard against. How is he guarded? A light-house is erected on or near the spot, which warns him of the shoal. Now I look on the sixth and tenth chapters of the Epistle to the Hebrews as two light-houses standing near the entrance of the harbour of eternal safety. And their language is, "Beware of this shoal! Take care of that sand-bank! There are gifts without grace; there is profession without possession; there is form without power; there is a name to live whilst the soul is dead." The shoal naturally often lies at the very entrance of a harbour: and as the ship makes for the port, the sand-bank lies in her very course; but when the harbour is neared, the friendly beacon not only warns her of the shoal, but also points out the safe passage into the haven. And so spiritually, from these two chapters many of God's people have seen what shoals lie in the way, and have, perhaps, before they were warned off, come near enough to see the shipwrecked vessels. The gallant barks that sailed from the same port with themselves they have seen wrecked on the rocks, the freight lost, and the dead bodies and broken frag-ments floating on the waves. But these never looked for the light-house, nor saw the bank; they were intoxicated, or fast asleep; they were sure of going to heaven; and on they went, reckless and thoughtless, till the vessel struck on the shoal, and every hand on board perished. These awful warnings and solemn admonitions seem to me so written that they may scrape, so to speak, as nearly as possible the quick of a man's flesh. And they appear couched in language of purposed ambiguity that they may be trying passages; nay, the very beauty and efficacy of them, and the real good to be wrought by them, is in their ambiguity, so that the people of God may take a more solemn warning by them, and may cry unto the Lord more earnestly that they may not be deceived. Then it is not the poor, desponding children of God who are tried by these passages, that have reason to fear them; their being thus tried shews that their conscience is tender in God's fear, and that they are " the earth which drinketh in the rain that cometh oft upon it, and bringing forth herbs meet for them by whom it is dressed, receiveth blessing from God;" and that they are not that " which beareth thorns and briers, which is rejected, and is nigh unto cursing, whose end is to be burned." And thus, these very fears and suspicions, by which many of God's people are exercised, causing strong cries unto the Lord, that he would teach, guide, and lead them, are so many blessed marks that they are not graceless persons, but partakers of the grace of God, and at the same time prove, "that he which hath begun a good work in them" will carry it on, and "will perform it until the day of Jesus Christ," and bring them into the eternal enjoyment of God, that they may see him for themselves, and not another.

November 25.

" There is a path which no fowl knoweth, and which the vulture's eye hath not seen."—JOB xxviii. 7.

GROWTH in grace is not progressive sanctification and fleshly holiness on the one hand, nor a false and delusive establishment on the other. The narrow path lies between these two extremes. On the one side is Seneh, and on the other side is Bozez (1 Sam. xiv. 4), Pharisaic holiness and Antinomian security; and between these two sharp rocks lies the "path which no fowl knoweth, and which the vulture's eye hath not seen." From dashing on either of these rocks a living man is kept only by the mysterious dealings of God with his spirit, and the internal exercises through which he continually passes. A constant acquaintance with his own vileness preserves him from a self-righteous holiness in the flesh; a daily cross and a rankling thorn keep him from careless presumption. His path is indeed a mysterious one, full of harmonious contradictions and heavenly paradoxes. He is never easy when at ease, nor without a burden when he has none. He is never satisfied without doing something, and yet is never satisfied with anything that he does. He is never so strong as when he sits still, never so fruitful as when he does nothing, and never so active as when he makes the least haste. All outstrip him in the race, yet he alone gains the goal, and wins the prize. All are sure of heaven but himself, yet he enters into the kingdom, whilst they are thrust out. He wins pardon through guilt, hope through despair, deliverance through temptation, comfort through affliction, and a robe of righteousness through filthy rags. Though a worm and no man, he overcomes Omnipotence itself through violence; and though less than vanity and nothing, he takes heaven itself by force. Thus amidst the strange contradictions which meet in a believing heart, he is never so prayerful as when he says nothing; never so wise as when he is the greatest fool; never so much alone as when most in company; and never so much under the power of an inward religion as when most separated from an outward one.

November 26.

"For other foundation can no man lay than that is laid, which is Jesus Christ."—1 CORINTHIANS iii. 11.

WE are very eager to put our hands to work. Like Uzzah, we must needs prop up the ark when we see it stumbling; when faith totters, we must come to bear a helping hand. But this is prejudicial to the work of God upon the soul. If the whole is to be a spiritual building; if we are "living stones" built upon a living Head, every stone in that spiritual temple must be laid by God the Spirit. And if so, everything of nature, of creature, of self, must be effectually laid low, that Christ may be all—that Christ, and Christ alone, may be formed in our heart, the hope of glory. How many trials some of you have passed through! how many sharp and cutting exercises! how many harassing temptations! how many sinkings of heart! how many fiery darts from hell! how many doubts and fears! how much hard bondage! how many galling chains! how often has the very iron entered into your soul! Why? That you may be prevented from adding one stone by your own hands to the spiritual building. The Apostle tells us that "Other foundation can no man lay than that is laid," even Jesus Christ. He then speaks of those who build "wood, hay, and stubble," as well as of those who used "gold, silver, and precious stones;" and that the "wood, hay, and stubble" must be burned with fire. It is after the Lord has laid a foundation in the sinner's conscience, brought him near to himself, made Jesus precious to his soul, raised up hope and love in his heart, that he is so apt to take materials God never recognises, "wood, hay, straw, stubble," and rear thereby a flimsy superstructure of his own. But this gives way in the trying hour : it cannot stand one gust of temptation. One spark of the wrath to come, one discovery of God's dread majesty, will burn up this "wood, hay, and stubble" like straw in the oven. The Lord's people, therefore, have to pass through troubles, trials, exercises, and temptations, doubts and fears, and all that harassing path that they usually walk in, that they may be prevented from erecting a superstructure of nature upon the foundation of grace—" wood, hay, and stubble " upon the glorious mystery of an incarnate God.

November 27.

" And if Christ be in you, the body is dead because of sin ; but the Spirit is life because of righteousness."—ROMANS viii. 10.

WE want two things in lively operation ; a spiritual death and a spiritual life. We want death put upon the flesh, upon sin, upon everything which is ungodly, that it may not reign or rule; and we want also the communication and maintenance of a divine life which shall act Godward, exist and co-exist in the same breast, and be in activity at the same

moment. Here is sin striving for the mastery; but here also
is a view of the cross of Christ; here is a testimony of bleeding, dying love. This puts a death upon sin. But as death
is put upon sin and the lust is mortified, crucified, resisted, or
subdued, there springs up a life of faith and prayer, of hope
and love, of repentance and godly sorrow for sin, of humility
and spirituality, of a desire to live to God's praise and walk
in his fear. The cross gives both. From the cross comes
death unto sin; from the cross comes life unto righteousness.
From the cross springs the healing of every bleeding wound,
and from the cross springs every motive to a godly life. Thus,
in God's mysterious wisdom, there is a way whereby sin can
be pardoned, the law magnified, justice exalted, the sinner
saved, sin subdued, righteousness given, and the soul made
to walk in the ways of peace and holiness. Oh, what depths
of wisdom, mercy, and grace are here! Look where you will,
try every mode, if you are sincere about your soul's salvation,
if the Lord the Spirit has planted the fear of God in your
heart, you will find no other way but this. There is no other
way that leads to holiness here and heaven hereafter; no other
way whereby sin can be pardoned and the soul sanctified. It
is this view of salvation from sin not only in its guilt but also
in its power, this deliverance from the curse of the law and
well-spring of all holy, acceptable obedience, which has in all
ages so endeared the cross to the souls of God's family, and
made all of them more or less to be of Paul's mind, when he
declared that he was determined to know nothing save Jesus
Christ and him crucified.

November 28.

*" But thou, O Lord, art a shield for me; my glory, and the
lifter up of mine head."*— PSALM iii. 3.

IF your soul has ever been favoured with a taste of mercy,
with a sip of the brook by the way; if ever your conscience

has felt the application of atoning blood, or the love of God has ever been shed abroad in your heart by the Holy Ghost, when the law comes to curse you, endeavour always to bear in mind that the Lord Jesus Christ stands as the shield between you and its curse. The law has therefore nothing to do with you that believe, it has cursed Jesus Christ for you; as the Apostle declares, " He was made a curse for us;" and again, " Who his own self bare our sins in his own body on the tree," &c. Therefore the law has nothing to do with you who believe in Christ Jesus. He has intercepted the curse for you, and, by receiving it into his own body and soul, bore it harmless away from you. It is a blessed act of faith when you can thus take Christ in your arms and hold him up as a shield between the law and your conscience. And this the Apostle seems to hint at in a measure when he says, "Above all, taking the shield of faith, wherewith ye shall be able to quench all the fiery darts of the wicked;" for many of these fiery darts are taken from the law. It is indeed a great and special act of faith thus to take Jesus Christ in the arms, and holding him up in the face of the law, to be able to say, " Law, thou hast nothing to do with me; Jesus has fulfilled all thy righteous demands, and endured all thy tremendous curses. He is my shield, to protect me from thy condemning sentence; and all thy curses are harmless; they all fall short of me, because they all fell wholly upon him." I say this is a special act of faith, because we cannot do it except as divinely enabled. Otherwise, it would be but an act of presumption. I may add, also, that it is a very rare thing to be enabled so to take Christ and hold him up as a shield against the curses of the law ; but when done under the influences and operations of the blessed Spirit, it is an act of faith which God approves of and honours. Nor is there any other shield to intercept its tremendous curse.

November 29.

" This charge I commit unto thee, son Timothy, according to the prophecies which went before on thee, that thou by them mightest war a good warfare; holding faith, and a good conscience; which some having put away concerning faith have made shipwreck."—1 TIMOTHY i. 18, 19.

THIS "good warfare" is carried on against three principal enemies—the flesh, the world, and the devil; and each of these enemies so closely allied to ourselves, and each so powerful and so hostile, that they must surely overcome us, unless we are "strengthened with might in the inner man." There is the flesh, with all its baits, charms, and subtle attractions, continually laying its gins and traps for our feet, perpetually ensnaring us in some evil word or some evil work, and we in ourselves utterly defenceless against it. Said I defenceless? Yea, eager to run into it, like the silly bird that sees the grains of corn spread in the trap, but thinks not, when it flutters around it, that the brick will fall and confine it a prisoner. So we, allured by a few grains of corn spread before our eyes, often see not the snare, until we are fast entangled therein. Faith then is that eye of the soul which sees the concealed hook; by faith we call upon the Lord to deliver us from snatching at the bait; and by faith, as a spiritual weapon, we cut at times the snare asunder. Oh, how defenceless are we, when the temptations and allurements of the flesh plead for indulgence, unless faith is in exercise, unless faith realises the hatred of God against sin, and brings into our consciences a sense of God's heart-searching eye, and his wrath against all transgression! But where the Lord has put this weapon of faith into the hand of his soldier, he will often strengthen his arm to wield it in these seasons of extremity, even though that weapon should cut and wound self. How Joseph was enabled to resist the snares spread for his feet,

by calling to mind the presence of the Lord! How he was
strengthened to break asunder that bond which was fast
twining round his heart, when faith sprang up in his soul,
and he said, "How can I do this great wickedness, and sin
against God?" How the three children who were about to
be cast into the burning, fiery furnace, unless they would
worship the golden image that Nebuchadnezzar had set up,
overcame that dreadful temptation to renounce their God and
prove apostates, by living faith! Oh, what a weapon faith is,
when the Lord does but give us power to wield it! How, as
Hart says, it

> "Cuts the way through hosts of devils,
> While they fall before the word."

But when sin, temptation, and unbelief beat this weapon out
of our hands, when it lies seemingly shivered at our feet, and
we cannot get another such sword from God's armoury,
how we stand naked and defenceless before our enemies!
Therefore what need we have not merely of this heavenly
grace in our souls, but to hold it fast and not let it go,
lest the enchantress should catch our feet in her wiles and
snares.

So, again, when Satan comes in with his fierce temptations
and fiery darts, what but faith can enable the soul to stand
up against them, as the Apostle says, "Above all, taking the
shield of faith, wherewith ye shall be able to quench all the
fiery darts of the wicked." Nothing but faith in God, in his
power and presence; nothing but faith in Jesus, in his blood
and his righteousness; nothing but faith in the holy Ghost,
as lifting up a standard in the heart by means of his divine
operations; nothing but faith in a triune God can enable the
soul to battle against Satan's assaults. Therefore see how
indispensable faith is to fight a good fight, yea, so indispensable
that a good fight is called emphatically "the fight of faith:"
"fight the good fight of faith," implying that true faith will

enable a man to come off more than conqueror through every battle and to survive every conflict.

November 30.

" I will overturn, overturn, overturn it : and it shall be no more, until he come whose right it is; and I will give it him." — EZEKIEL xxi. 27.

THERE is one then to come, " whose right it is ;" there is a King who has a right to the throne, and to the allegiance of his subjects; a right to all that they are and to all that they have. But whence has he gained this right? " Until he come whose *right* it is." It is his right then, first, by original *donation* and *gift*, the Father having given to the Son all the elect. " Here am I," says Jesus, " and the children that thou *hast given me.*" "All that the *Father giveth* me shall come to me." Then, so far as we are his, Jesus has a right to our persons ; and in having a right to our persons, he has, by the same original donation of God the Father, a right to our hearts and affections. But he has another right, and that is by *purchase* and *redemption*, he having redeemed his people with his own blood, having laid down his life for them, and thus bought and purchased them, and so established a right to them by the full and complete price which he himself paid down upon the cross for them. This twofold right he exercises every time that he lays a solemn claim to any one of the people whom he has purchased. And this claim he lays when the blessed Spirit comes into the soul to arrest and apprehend a vessel of mercy, and bring it to his feet, that he may be enthroned as King and Lord in its affections. For be it remembered, that the possession of the heart with all its affections is his right; and " his glory he will not give to another ;" his property he will not allow to pass into other hands; he is not satisfied with merely having a right to the persons of his dear people, he must have their hearts; and in exercising his right to their affections, he will reign and rule supreme, allowing no rival, admitting no co-operation with self in any shape or form, but he himself to be established as King and Lord there. Then where is the soul before he comes into it in power, in sweetness, in beauty, in preciousness? What and where is it? A heap of ruins. And no man ever knew much of the preciousness of Christ, whose soul was not a heap of ruins, and in whom self had not been overturned and cast to the ground. Nay; no man ever ardently panted that the Lord of life and glory should visit his heart with his salvation, should come in the power of his resurrection, in the glory of his righteousness, in the preciousness of his presence; no man ever spiritually desired, sighed, cried, groaned, sued, and begged for the manifestation of Christ to his soul, who was not a ruined wretch before God, and in whom self had not been overturned so as to be a desolate heap, so overthrown that all the power of man could not put any one stone in its place, or rebuild the former edifice.

December 1.

" According as he hath chosen us in him before the foundation of the world, that we should be holy and without blame before him in love: having predestinated us unto the adoption of children by Jesus Christ to himself, according to the good pleasure of his will."—EPHESIANS i. 4, 5.

IT is a very solemn but a very true assertion, that no man can quicken his own soul; and it is an equally solemn, we might almost say, a tremendous truth, that the gospel only comes in power to those whom God has chosen unto eternal life. Indeed the one flows from the other; for if no man can quicken his own soul, it necessarily follows it must be of sovereign grace that it is quickened at all. Once allow the fall, and acknowledge that a man is by nature so thoroughly

dead in trespasses and sins that he cannot raise himself up
out of this state to newness of life, and the doctrine of election
necessarily follows. A living soul may reason thus : "Am I
quickened? Yes. Did I quicken myself ? No. I could
not; for I was dead in sin. Did God then quicken me?
Who but he could have given life to my dead soul? But
why did he quicken me, when dead in sins? Because he
loved me, and chose me in Christ to be an heir of his eternal
glory."   Whether, however, you can speak thus or not, there
is no doubt that the Lord has a people who are dear to him,
and to whom he makes himself dear. These, though despised
of, or unnoticed by men, are the elect of God; and if you be
a vessel of mercy whom he has thus chosen to eternal life,
the gospel either has already come, or, in his own time and
way, will be made to come with power to your heart and
conscience.

December 2.

*" That he might be just, and the justifier of him which
believeth in Jesus."*—ROMANS iii. 26.

EVERY created thing, every finite intelligence, must sooner
be annihilated, than Jehovah can sacrifice, or suffer the
slightest tarnish to come over any one of his eternal attributes.
Yet God can be just, infinitely just, scrupulously just, un-
changeably just,—and yet, preserving his attribute of justice
unchanging and unchangeable, he can still be " the justifier
of him which believeth in Jesus." The way by which this
was effected will take a countless eternity to understand, and
a boundless eternity to admire and adore.

But what is meant by the expression, "the justifier?"
"The justifier" means, that God can count man as righteous,
can freely pardon his sins, can graciously accept his person,
can impute to him righteousness without works, and can
bring him to the eternal enjoyment of himself.   And who is

the character that he thus brings to himself by justifying him? "He which believeth in Jesus." What simplicity, and yet what sweetness and suitability is there in the gospel plan! Say it ran thus, "That he might be just, and yet the justifier of *him that worketh*, that pleaseth God by his own perform-ances, that produceth a righteousness satisfactory to the eyes of infinite purity." Who then could be saved? Would there be a single soul in heaven? No; such a word as that would trample down the whole human race into hell. But when it runs thus, "That this is the mind and purpose of God, that this is his eternal counsel, which cannot pass away; that he is 'the justifier of him which believeth in Jesus,'—the poor, the needy, the exercised, the tempted, the distressed, and the perplexed, that believe in Jesus, that look to Jesus, that lean upon Jesus, and rest in his Person, blood, righteousness, and love for all things; that these are justified, that these are pardoned, that these are accepted, that these are graciously received, and saved with an everlasting salvation,"—how sweet, how suitable, does the gospel that declares this be-come to the living, believing soul!

December 3.

" If we confess our sins, he is faithful and just to forgive us our sins, and to cleanse us from all unrighteousness."— 1 JOHN i. 9.

"HE is faithful and *just.*" Oh, what a word is that! There is scarcely to my mind such a word in the Bible as that; so great, so glorious, so comforting: "He is faithful and *just.*" "Just?" say you, "why I know that God's mercy and God's grace can pardon sinners; but how can God be just, and pardon transgressors? Does not God's justice demand the punishment of sin? Does not God's justice blaze forth in eternal lightnings against the soul that transgresses his holy law? How, then, can it be true, that

G g

God can be just, and yet forgive a confessing sinner?" But it is true, divinely true, blessedly, eternally true. And in it is locked up that grand mystery of redemption by the blood and obedience of God's co-equal Son. It is locked up in this one word—"*just.*" "But how?" it may be asked. In this way. The Lord of life and glory became a security and substitute for those whom his Father gave to him. He entered into their place and stead. He endured the punishment that was due to them. For them he fulfilled the whole law by his doings and by his sufferings. For them he bled, and for them he died. For them he rose again, and for them ascended up to the right hand of the Father. And now justice demands the sinner's pardon, and puts in its righteous plea. And see the difference. Mercy begs, justice demands: mercy says, "I ask it as a boon;" mercy, as a part of God's character, looks down with pity and compassion on the mourning criminal; but justice says, "It is his due; it is his right; it belongs to him; it is his because the Redeemer has discharged his debt, because the Surety has stood in his place, because the Saviour has obeyed that law for him which he could not obey in his own person." So that when we can receive this blessed and glorious truth, that to those who confess their sins, "God is faithful," and not merely "faithful," but also "just to forgive them their sins," how it draws out of the bosom of Jehovah a full, free, and irrevocable pardon of all transgressions, and especially of those transgressions that the sinner confesses at his footstool!

December 4.

"For I am poor and needy, and my heart is wounded within me."—Psalm cix. 22.

The needy is a character who is not merely poor, empty, and naked before God, but who is feelingly in want of spiritual blessings applied to his soul. Some persons can rest on temptations, and take temptations as evidences. Others can build on doubts and fears, and rest on doubts and fears as evidences. Some can take powerful past convictions, or present convictions, and lean on them as evidences. Others can look to a profession of religion, and take that as an evidence. But a living soul must have heavenly blessings communicated immediately to his heart and conscience from the mouth of God. He must have deliverance manifested to his soul as a reality; he must have the blood of Jesus sprinkled on his conscience with divine power, to purge it from filth and dead works; he must have his eyes anointed with eye-salve to see Jesus; yea, his soul pants to be led up into sweet communion with Jesus; he wants to be taken spiritually into fellowship with Christ, that he may see him with the eyes of his soul, that he may look upon him whom he has pierced, mourn over him, and for him, and with him, and have some sweet, spiritual, and supernatural manifestation of his dying love to his soul. A nominal Christ will never do for a needy sinner, but it must be the Christ of God made spiritually known by the power of the Holy Ghost, sweetly revealed and coming into his heart with all his blessed efficacy, and shining into his soul like the sun in his strength, beaming forth blessed rays of grace and mercy. Nothing but this will ever satisfy a soul that has life in it.

December 5.

"Whom the Lord loveth he chasteneth, and scourgeth every son whom he receiveth."—HEBREWS xii. 6.

DOES not James say, "Blessed is the man that endureth temptation?" And again, "Count it all joy when ye fall into divers temptations?" Why? Is there any joy in trials, any pleasure in sorrow? No, none. But in the deliverance from the Lord; in the power of God put forth to bring the soul out; there is joy there. And, therefore, we have to walk in a dark path to make the light dear to our eyes; we have to pass through trials to taste the sweetness of the promises when applied with power; we have to endure temptations, that we may enjoy the sweetness of deliverance. And this is the way, be sure of it, that God deals with his people. Is your conscience made honest? Does that monitor in your bosom speak the truth? Tell me what it says. Does it not say, "Few trials, few consolations; few sorrows, few joys; few difficulties, few testimonies from God; few sufferings, few discoveries of love and blood?" Does not the Apostle say, "As the sufferings of Christ abound in us, so our consolation also aboundeth by Christ?" (2 Cor. i. 5.) And does he not say, "Our hope of you is steadfast, knowing, that as ye are partakers of the sufferings, so shall ye be also of the consolation?" And does he not tell us to be mindful not to forget what the Lord says when he speaks to his people, that the lot of a child is to endure chastisement? He says, "My son, despise not thou the chastening of the Lord, nor faint when thou art rebuked of him; for whom the Lord loveth he chasteneth, and scourgeth every son whom he receiveth. If ye endure chastening, God dealeth with you as with sons; for what son is he whom the father chasteneth not? But if ye be without chastisement," (O solemn word! O how applicable to thousands!) "whereof all are partakers, then are ye bastards, and not sons."

December 6.

"O Lord of hosts, blessed is the man that trusteth in thee."—
Psalm lxxxiv. 12.

Trust in God implies total self-renunciation. The moment that I trust in myself, I cease to trust in God. The moment I take any portion of my confidence away from the Lord and put a grain of it in myself, that moment I take away *all* my trust in God. My trust in God must be all or nothing.

It must be unreserved and complete, or else it is false and delusive. Is not the Lord worthy to be trusted? And if he is worthy to be trusted at all, is he not worthy to be trusted with all? What real confidence could a man have in the wife of his bosom if he could trust her with *one* key, but not with *all?* Is *that* full confidence? So, if we can trust God for one thing and not for all, it shews that we have no real trust in him. A man has no real trust in his wife who cannot give her all the keys. A man has no real trust in God who cannot give him all his heart, and put everything into his hand; family, property, body, and soul. The province and work of true faith is to put everything into the hands of God, keeping back no part of the price. It is this secret reserve that God hates; there is hypocrisy on the very face of it. Trust in God for nothing; or trust in him for all. God will not take a divided heart. Give him all, or none. And is he not worthy of it? Has he ever disappointed you whenever you have really put your trust in him? Does he not say, "Have I been a wilderness unto Israel? a land of darkness? wherefore say my people, We are lords; we will come no more unto thee?" (Jer. ii. 31.)

But David saw how few there were that with all their hearts did trust in God. This feeling seems to have made him say, "Blessed is *the man*," that peculiar man, that rare individual, "that trusteth in thee!" The blessing of God rests upon that happy, that highly-favoured man. He is blessed for time and for eternity. He has the blessing of God even now in his soul. Oh! how rare it is for us to be in that sweet, blessed frame when we can put our trust wholly in God; trust him for life and death; trust him for all things, past, present, and to come. Yet without a measure of this faith, there is no solid peace, no real and abiding rest. And to this you must sooner or later come; for you cannot carry your own burdens without their breaking your back.

But when you can cast your burden on the Lord, then you will surely find sweet relief.

May we not, then, join heart and voice with David, " O Lord of hosts, blessed is the man that trusteth in thee?" Such a one will never be disappointed. The Lord will hear his prayer; the Lord will bless his soul; will be with him in life, support him in death, and take him to be with him in eternity.

December 7.

" He that overcometh shall inherit all things."—REVELATION xxi. 7.

" HE shall inherit all things." When? In eternity? Yes. But only in eternity? O no! In time also. There is a two-fold inheritance, though one and the same; one in time, another in eternity; one the firstfruits, the other the harvest; one the earnest, the other the full sum. There is an inheriting here below, and an inheriting above; and he that never receives any portion of his inheritance below will never receive an inheritance above. Now, just in proportion as we overcome, are we put in possession of this inheritance. What are we to inherit? Riches, glory, honour, power, praise? These are worldly things; let the world enjoy them. In inheriting "all things," we are to inherit the things of God; the favour of God, the love of God, the mercy of God, the glory of God; all that a covenant God gives in giving him-self; peace here, glory hereafter; pardon below, salvation above; the beginning of rest on earth, the fulness of rest in heaven.

Now, whilst we are overcome, there is no being put into possession of this eternal inheritance. Does sin overcome us? Do we inherit pardon in being overcome? No; we inherit shame and confusion, guilt, fear and wrath. But do you, do I, ever overcome sin by the fear of God in our soul, as

Joseph did? Do I ever overcome sin by looking to the Lord of life and glory to sprinkle his blood upon my conscience? Do I ever overcome sin by the leadings and teachings of the Spirit in my heart? No sooner do I thus overcome by the blood of the Lamb, and the word of his testimony, than I enter into the inheritance. So that there is a connection, a beautiful, an experimental connection, between overcoming here below, and inheriting here below. But in order to enter into this inheritance, we must be perpetually reminded that we have no strength of our own. And thus our slips, our falls, our backslidings, our frailties, (though we would not, dare not justify them,) are mercifully overruled amongst the " all things " that work together for our good. They teach us our weakness, and by teaching us our weakness, lead us up to Christ's strength; and by leading us up to Christ's strength, to " inherit all things;" for in inheriting him, we inherit all that he is to God's people.

December 8.

"And I will be his God, and he shall be my son."—REVELATION xxi. 7.

WHAT a promise! That the God of heaven and earth will be our God, our Father, our Benefactor, our eternal, almighty Friend! and that we, in overcoming, shall receive the adoption of sons; shall be manifested as the " sons and daughters " of the Almighty, and receive the inheritance reserved for the children of God! The promise runs in connection with "him that overcometh." If we do not overcome, the promise is not for us. The promise of sonship is connected with overcoming, in the same manner as that of " inheritance " is connected with it. Do I want to receive into my heart the Spirit of adoption? Do I want to feel the love of God the Father shed abroad in my soul? Do I want to establish a blessed title to the inheritance that he giveth to his children?

How am I to get it? How is it to be obtained? By making myself religious, becoming holy, subduing my lusts in my own strength? This sets me farther from God than I was before. This makes me a god to myself! If I be saved by my own holiness, by my own strength, by my own righteousness, I worship myself; and in worshipping myself, *I become my own god*. That is idolatry, damnable idolatry; so that he who lives and dies in the worship of self, will live and die under the wrath of God as an idolater. Then how am I to receive adoption? By overcoming, not in my own strength, but in the strength of the Lord of life and glory. If I am shut up in self, I inherit self; nothing more. If I inherit the world, I have no more than the world. If I inherit sin, I inherit death, which is the wages of sin. Nothing more. But if I overcome; if weak, helpless, and defenceless, I yield myself up to the hands of thé Lord, as clay in the hands of the Potter; not seeking my own will, but looking to the Lord to make known his will in my conscience, and to work in me that which is well-pleasing in his sight,—if I have this, I have an evidence of sonship; and where that evidence is, there will be a further evidence of it in the Spirit of adoption, enabling the soul to call God "Father." And he that calls God "Father" here below, will call God "Father" above, where he will enter into the full enjoyment of it, and bathe in the consolations of Father, Son, and Spirit to all eternity.

December 9.

" *Then shall the dust return to the earth as it was : and the spirit shall return unto God who gave it.*"—ECCLESIASTES xii. 7.

NATURE shrinks from death, even apart from that which following after death makes it to so many a king of terrors. Even where grace has set up its throne, and mercy rejoices over judgment, many unbelieving, infidel thoughts at times will cross the mind and perplex the judgment about the separation of body and soul, and the launching of the spirit into an unseen, unknown world. Faith, it is true, can subdue these perplexing thoughts, better hinted at than described, but faith needs some solid ground on which to build and rest. If, then, the soul is blessed with any assured hope or sweet persuasion of interest in the blood and obedience of the Lord Jesus Christ, so as to remove guilty fears, how strengthening to faith is a view of his death, not merely as the only sacrifice for sin, but as the exemplar, so to speak, of our own. We shall all have to die, and therefore to look by faith at the death of Jesus may be a profitable subject of meditation as a relief against the perplexing thoughts to which we have before alluded. Into his Father's hands the dying Lord commended his spirit. The Father received it, for him the Father heareth always (John xi. 42) ; and thus his spirit returned unto him who gave it. Thus, by the act of dying, the soul and body of the blessed Redeemer were, for a time, fully and actually separated—as fully and actually as ours will also be at death. But follow by faith that soul of Jesus when he breathed it forth, and view it at once and immediately entering paradise, into the blissful presence of God. What food for faith is here ! How strengthening, how encouraging to a believing heart which has often been perplexed by such thoughts as we have named, to view the soul of Jesus thus passing at once into paradise. And may we not, by faith, view the soul also of the believing malefactor, when the time of release was come, winging its flight into the same paradise whither the soul of Jesus had preceded it ? If we know anything painfully and experimentally of the assaults of unbelief, the arrows of infidelity, and the fiery darts of the wicked one, and how they are all quenched by the shield of faith, we have found that faith, in order to stand firm, must have the word of truth, a " Thus saith the Lord," upon which to rest. Let us now, then, see how this stands as connected with the death

of the blessed Lord. Fortified by his holy example, if blessed
with faith in his Person, blood, and righteousness, the dying
believer may commend his spirit into the hands of Christ as
did martyred Stephen, in the same confidence that the Lord
Jesus commended his spirit into the hands of his heavenly
Father.

December 10.

" My soul thirsteth for God, for the living God."—PSALM
xlii. 2.

Has your heart ever panted after the Lord Jesus as the
hart panteth after the water brooks? Do you ever lie in the
dust mourning over your sins against such bleeding, dying
love? Do you ever ask God to kindle in your soul an intense
desire to have Jesus as your Christ, that he may be your
delight here and your portion for ever? Surely there is that
in him which is not in anything below the skies, and which if
not found here will not be found hereafter. If you have no
love or affection for him, why is it but because he has not
endeared himself to your soul? But if he has manifested himself to you, you have seen and felt enough of his blessedness
to convince you that there is no real peace or happiness out
of him. It is true that you may have many trials and temptations to encounter; many perplexities and sorrows may be
spread in your path; but be not dismayed, for the love of
Christ, if you have ever felt that love shed abroad in your
heart, will bear you more than conqueror through them all.
The Lord make and keep us faithful to the truth as it has
been made known to our consciences; and may the goodness
and mercy of God shine into our hearts and shed abroad its
rays of light and joy in our darkest moments and under our
severest trials. And O to be found in him at the great day,
as members of his body, of his flesh, and of his bones, to be
found the Lord's " peculiar treasure " in that day when he

maketh up his jewels ! And O then where will be those who are not found in the Lord Jesus ? They will call upon the mountains and the rocks to " fall on them and hide them from the face of him that sitteth on the throne, and from the wrath of the Lamb."

December 11.

" So did not I, because of the fear of God."—NEHEMIAH V. 15.

WE can never praise God sufficiently for his restraining grace ; for what should we be without it ? What an unspeakable mercy, then, it is that you cannot be what you would be, nor act as you would act, nor speak what you would speak, nor do the things you would do, because there is in you who fear God a spiritual principle which holds you up, and keeps you back from the ways of sin and death in which the flesh would walk. How this spirit of grace and godly fear kept Joseph in the hour of temptation ! How it preserved David when he had Saul in his power as he lay asleep in the cave ! How it kept Nehemiah in the fear of God from extortion and oppression ! And how, in thousands of instances, it has preserved the feet of the saints, and kept them from doing things that would have ruined their reputation, blighted their character, brought reproach upon the cause of God, and the greatest grief and distress into their own conscience !

December 12.

"I lead in the way of righteousness, in the midst of the paths of judgment; that I may cause those that love me to inherit substance."—PROVERBS viii. 20, 21.

WHENCE springs it, that God causes his people " to inherit substance," by " leading them in the way of righteousness, in the midst of the paths of judgment?" When he leads them first into the way of righteousness by opening up his holy law, it drives away all shadows. We had been heaping together, with great toil, chaff and hay and straw and stubble ; we had been like the man spoken of in Scripture, who " dreamed, and behold ! he ate, but he awoke and his soul was empty;" so we were dreaming our life away continually with shadows, with a name to live, with a formal religion, with a mere external show of godliness, content with a few ordinances and sermons, and thinking that these would shelter us in the day of wrath. These were only shadows; of no more avail to deliver our souls from the wrath to come, than the shadowy form of a mountain in the morning sun. But when the Lord began " to lead us in the way of righteousness," these shadows vanished. Something was then wanted to conciliate the favour of God; something was needed, whereby the soul could escape those piercing eyes that looked it through and through; and the soul began to look after " substance," wanted realities, needed a voice within from the Lord himself, a testimony of his eternal favour, and a manifestation of his love. There was " substance" needed. The soul began to " hunger and thirst after righteousness," to pant and long after the manifestation of Jesus' love, and to be restless and discontented and weary of everything short of the work and witness of the Holy Ghost. When the " mouth is stopped, and the soul has become guilty before God," it wants pardon, peace, mercy, blood, and love; nothing else can satisfy it, and after this it pants with unutterable longings. And when Jesus leads his people " in the way of righteousness" by shewing to them his glorious righteousness, they begin to " inherit the substance " after which they were panting. There is no substance under the law; it is but a preparing the soul to receive substance; it is emptying the soul that it may be filled; it is stripping the soul that it may be clothed ; it is wounding the soul that it may be healed ; bringing down the soul that it may be lifted up. But when he " leads in the way of righteousness," that wonderful way whereby the soul is justified by his imputed righteousness, he causes that soul to " inherit substance," to inherit it even now upon earth, to have a taste of it, the beginnings of it, the earnest of it, and the firstfruits of it.

Oh ! what a dreamy, shadowy thing is a mere profession of religion ! And what a delusive cheat is all the pleasure to be gained by sin ! How it leaves a soul naked and bare, wounded, stripped, and guilty before God ! We have often promised ourselves pleasure in sin ; and what have we found ? The wormwood and the gall. All the anticipated pleasure vanished ; and its flight left us full of guilt and shame. But if ever God indulged our souls with sweet communion with him, if ever he brought our affections to centre in himself, if ever he melted our souls at his feet, if ever he blessed us with the communications of his eternal favour and distinguishing love, there was substance in that, there was weight, there was power, there was the foretaste and earnest of a never-ending eternity.

December 13.

" And he shewed me Joshua the high priest standing before the angel of the Lord, and Satan standing at his right hand to resist him."—ZECHARIAH iii. 1.

IT is the object of Satan to keep those secure who are safe in his hands ; nor does God see fit to disturb their quiet. But on the other hand, where Satan perceives a work of grace going on, where he sees the eyes sometimes filled with tears, where he hears the sobs heaving from the contrite heart, where he observes the knees often bent in secret prayer, where his listening ear often hears the poor penitent confess his sins, weaknesses, and backslidings before God, (for by these observations we have reason to believe Satan gains his intelligence,) wherever he sees this secret work going on in the soul, mad with wrath and filled with malice, he vents his

hellish spleen against the objects of God's love.   Sometimes
he tries to ensnare them into sin, sometimes to harass them
with temptation, sometimes to stir up their wicked heart into
desperate rebellion, sometimes to work upon their natural infidelity, and sometimes to plague them with many groundless
doubts and fears as to their reality and sincerity before a
heart-searching God.   So that whilst those who have no
work of grace upon their hearts at all are left secure, and
free from doubt and fear, those in whom God *is* at work are
exercised and troubled in their minds, and often cannot really
believe that they are the people in whom God takes delight.
The depths of human hypocrisy, the awful lengths to which
profession may go, the deceit of the carnal heart, the snares
spread for the unwary feet, the fearful danger of being
deceived at the last—these traps and pitfalls are not objects
of anxiety to those dead in sin.   As long as they can pacify
natural conscience, and do something to soothe any transient
conviction, they are glad to be deceived.   But, on the other
hand, he that has a conscience tender in God's fear knows
what an awful thing it is to be a hypocrite before God, to
have " a lie in his right hand," and be deluded by the prince
of darkness ; and therefore, until God himself with his own
blessed lips speaks with power to his conscience, and establishes him in a blessed assurance of his interest in Christ by
" shedding abroad his love in his heart," he must be tried
and exercised in his mind, he must have these various tossings
to and fro, for this simple reason—because he cannot rest
satisfied except in the personal manifestations of the mercy
of God.

December 14.

*" He that believeth on the Son of God hath the witness in
himself."*—1 JOHN v. 10.

THE grand point to have decided in a man's bosom is,

whether he is Christ's or not; and this is a problem which none but the Lord himself can solve. Blessed is he who has the witness in himself; and this he can only have by believing on the Son of God, as John speaks, " He that believeth on the Son of God hath the witness in himself." This is the internal witness of the Spirit, as the Apostle declares, " The Spirit itself beareth witness with our spirit, that we are the children of God." What witness have you ever had in your bosom that you are a child of God? Or if you have not had this special witness, what marks or evidences, what tokens for good has the Lord bestowed upon you? Can you not remember something that the Lord has done for you in times past, some promise applied, some manifestation of his presence, some look of love, some softening touch of his gracious hand, which melted you into the dust, and brought sweet peace and assurance with it? It might not last long, or be very deep, but it was an evidence when felt that you belonged to Christ. You remember the time and the circumstances, the darkness, distress and bondage before, and the deliverance into sweet liberty then enjoyed; but still you are dissatisfied. You want the Lord once more to appear; you want another smile, another word, another look, another promise, another testimony, and without it your soul often sinks down into doubt and fear. Now this is the path in which most of God's saints walk; I will not say all, because some are more favoured with an abiding testimony, though even they have great sinkings and heavy trials. But with most it is a very chequered, in and out path. Thus, sometimes they are indulged with a smile, and then such darkness of mind falls upon them that they can scarcely see a single evidence. Then the sun shines again; but darkness once more covers the scene, and down they sink again into doubt, guilt, and fear. Then the Lord appears again, and then they love, and hope, and rejoice again; and so they go on, the scene ever changing, like an April day.

Still on they go until they come at last to the closing scene, when the Lord usually appears, scatters all their doubts and fears and darkness, and gives them a blessed dismissal into his own bosom of eternal rest and peace.

December 15.

" For our light affliction, which is but for a moment, worketh for us a far more exceeding and eternal weight of glory." — 2 CORINTHIANS iv. 17.

THE Hebrew word " glory " literally signifies " weight; " and the Apostle seems to have some allusion to that circumstance by connecting, as he does, the two words together. There is indeed a natural connection between what is weighty and what is solid and substantial. He would thus represent future glory as something solid, lasting, and durable, and therefore utterly distinct from the light, vain trifles of time, and even the passing afflictions of the day or hour. But he seems chiefly to be alluding to the exceeding greatness of that glory which is to be revealed as compared with our present faculties of body and mind and all our present conceptions. It is as though he should say, " In our present imperfect state, with our limited faculties of mind, and our weak, frail tabernacle, we could not bear the weight of that immortal glory which is prepared for the saints in the realms of bliss." " Eye hath not seen, nor ear heard, neither have entered into the heart of man, the things which God hath prepared for them that love him." Heaven, with its opening bliss, would crush our present body and soul at once into the dust. " No man," said God to Moses, " can see me and live." When John in Patmos had a view of the glory of his risen Lord, though he had lain in his bosom at the last supper, yet he fell at his feet as dead. Therefore, we must have our soul purified from all stain of sin and expanded to the utmost of its immortal powers, and our body glorified and conformed to the body of the Lord Jesus Christ, that soul and body may alike be able to bear the weight of eternal glory with which they are to be clothed. As the Apostle speaks, "Not for that we would be unclothed, but clothed upon, that mortality might be swallowed up of life."

But there is something in the word "*glory*" that I must not pass by. The Lord, in that touching chapter, John xvii, thus prays, or rather thus expresses his heavenly will, "Father, I will that they also, whom thou hast given me, be with me where I am; that they may behold my glory, which thou hast given me." This is the "weight of glory" that the Apostle speaks of, not merely freedom from sin and sorrow, not merely seeing Christ as he is, but beholding and enjoying that unutterable glory which the Father gave him, which is all the glory of Godhead as revealed in, and shining through his human nature. The fulness and perfection of this glory is reserved for the saints of God to enjoy when they shall see him as he is, and know even also as they are known. We see a gleam of it when Christ is revealed to the soul; when the heavens are opened to faith; when his beauty and blessedness are manifested to our heart by the power of God. But the "exceeding and eternal weight of glory" can never be fully comprehended in this present life.

December 16.

"*Not unto us, O Lord, not unto us, but unto thy name give glory, for thy mercy, and for thy truth's sake.*"—PSALM cxv. 1.

MANY of God's dear children cannot get much beyond gentle intimations of his mercy, passing touches of his gracious hand, and softenings of heart under a sense of undeserved goodness and love; yet they feel sensibly relieved by what their faith thus lays hold of and brings in, and give glory to God. Sometimes again, as they hear the preached word and get a blessing under it, or some precious promise comes home to their soul with divine power, or they are favoured in secret prayer, and light and life break in upon their mind, they see such a glory in what is thus made known to them that they glorify God for what they see and feel. But more especially when the way of salvation is opened up to them; when Christ is revealed to their soul by the power of God; when they see that wondrous plan unfolded, how God can be just, and yet the justifier of him who believeth in Jesus; then as they view in the greatness of the mystery of the Person of Christ the blessed solution of the problem which has so exercised their mind, they freely and fully give all the glory to God. "Lord," they cry, "who and what am I, that thou shouldest have had pity and compassion upon me, shouldest have touched my heart by thy grace, shouldest have planted thy fear in my breast, led me to pray and seek thy face, and listened to my feeble cries, shouldest thus have given me to hope in thy mercy, and blessed my soul with a manifestation of thy dear Son? Oh, who and what am I to be thus favoured, when thousands are left to perish in their sins? Oh, how glorious art thou! what a good God! how thy mercy melts my heart, and thy goodness softens my soul! To thy name be all the honour and praise, both now and for ever and ever." Here is giving glory to God. Thus, true faith will always give God the glory; will never take an atom of its own praise to itself, but will ascribe the whole glory to God as its sole author and finisher, until blessings here end in blessings hereafter, and streams of grace on earth issue into the boundless ocean of glory in heaven.

December 17.

"Set your affection on things above, not on things on the earth."—COLOSSIANS iii. 2.

How are we to set our affection on things above? Can we do this great work of ourselves? No; it is only the Lord himself manifesting his beauty and blessedness to our soul, and letting down the golden cord of his love into our breast, that draws up our affections, and fixes them where he sits at God's right hand. In order to do this, he captivates the heart by some look of love, some word of his grace, some sweet promise, or some divine truth spiritually applied. When he thus captivates the soul, and draws it up, then the affections flow unto him as the source and fountain of all blessings. We are not flogged into loving him, but drawn by love into love. Love cannot be bought or sold; it is an inward affection that flows naturally and necessarily towards its object and all connected with it; and thus, as love flows out to Jesus, the affections instinctively and necessarily set themselves "on things above, and not on things on the earth."

But what are these "things above?" They are all things stored up in Christ, that breathe of Christ, and come out of Christ. Pardon, peace, righteousness, love, "joy unspeakable and full of glory," with strength against sin, victory over death and hell; power against besetting lusts and temptations; in a word, every blessing wherewith God hath blessed his people "in heavenly places in Christ;" these are the "things above," that the soul has to set its affections upon. But we must have some view by faith of the Person of Christ, the eternal Son of the eternal Father; he must be revealed to our soul by the power of God before we can see his beauty and blessedness, and so fall in love with him as "the chiefest among ten thousand and altogether lovely." Then everything that speaks of Christ, savours of Christ, and breathes of Christ, becomes inexpressibly sweet and precious.

This is "the golden oil" that flows into the heart; this is "the sweet-smelling myrrh which drops upon the handles of the lock;" this is "the aloes and cassia out of the ivory palaces;" this is "the love which many waters cannot quench, nor the floods drown;" and by an experience of this

the affections become set on things above. And in no other
way can they be lifted up from earth to heaven. We cannot
control our affections; they will run out of their own accord. If
then our affections be earthly, they will run towards the earth;
if they be carnal and sensual, they will flow toward carnal and
sensual objects. But when the Lord Jesus Christ, by some
manifestation of his glory and blessedness, or the Holy Ghost,
by taking of the things of Christ and revealing them to the
soul, sets him before our eyes as the only object worthy of and
claiming every affection of our heart, then the affections flow
out, I was going to say naturally, but most certainly spiritually
towards him; and when this is the case, the affections are
set on things above.

December 18.

" God is the Lord, which hath shewed us light."—PSALM
cxviii. 27.

THE Psalmist was clearly possessed of light, for he says,
" God is the Lord, which hath shewed us light." He was
evidently, then, possessed of light; and this light was in him
as " the light of life." This light had shone into his heart;
the rays and beams of divine truth had penetrated into his
conscience. He carried about with him a light which had
come from God; in this light he saw light, and in this light
he discerned everything which the light manifested. Thus
by this internal light he knew what was good and what was
evil, what was sweet and what was bitter, what was true and
what was false, what was spiritual and what was natural. He
did not say, This light came from creature exertion, this light
was the produce of my own wisdom, this light was nature
transmuted by some action of my own will, and thus gradually
rose into existence from long and assiduous cultivation. But
he ascribes the whole of that light which he possessed unto
God the Lord, as the sole Author and the only Giver of it.

Now, if God the Lord has ever shewed you and me the same light which he shewed his servant of old, we carry about with us more or less a solemn conviction that we have received this light from him. There will, indeed, be many clouds of darkness to cover it; there will often be doubts and fears, hovering like mists and fogs over our souls, whether the light which we have received be from God or not. But in solemn moments when the Lord is pleased a little to revive his work, at times and seasons when he condescends to draw forth the affections of our hearts unto himself, to bring us into his presence, to hide us in some measure in the hollow of his hand, and give us access unto himself; at such moments and seasons we carry about with us, in spite of all our unbelief, in spite of all the suggestions of the enemy, in spite of all doubts, fears, and suspicions that rise from the depths of the carnal mind, in spite of all these counter-workings and underminings, we carry about with us at these times a solemn conviction that we have light, and that this light we have received from God. And why so? Because we can look back to a time when we walked in no such light, when we felt no such light, when everything spiritual and heavenly was dark to us, and we were dark to them.

December 19.

"God is our refuge and strength, a very present help in trouble."—PSALM xlvi. 1.

THE Christian who has ever known what it is to worship God in spirit and in truth has a God to help him in his direst extremities; for as long as the spirit of prayer abides in his bosom—and that spirit once given is never taken away—he can at times and seasons pour out his heart before God, and find help and strength in him. This, then, is one of his blessed resources, that he has a God to go to, the Lord of Sabaoth, into whose ears his cries may enter. But besides this, all the promises are on his side, which are yea and amen in Christ Jesus. Nor is he without sword or shield, or the whole armour of God. Nor is he without faith and hope, or secret supplies of strength made perfect in weakness. Nor is he without a knowledge of the truth, nor destitute of evidences of an interest in it. Thus, let a Christian be involved in the greatest perplexity, there is still the voice of prayer in his bosom, and still the goings up and actings of a living faith upon the Son of God who has been manifested to his soul, still the firm anchorings of hope within the veil. He is not like a sailor cast upon a wide ocean without rudder, chart, or compass. He knows what to do; he knows what course to steer; he knows the land to which his eyes are ever directed. Let him sink into the greatest perplexity, he still knows there is at the right hand of the Father a Jesus, upon whom help is laid as one that is mighty. Still, still the solemn fact is recorded deep in his mind, an ineffaceable impression has been left upon his soul from former discoveries of the King in his beauty, that this Jesus is able to save to the uttermost all that come unto God by him. Thus he is not left without resource, help, or hope.

December 20.

" The love of Christ, which passeth knowledge."—EPHESIANS iii. 19.

THAT eminent saint, the Apostle Paul, who had been in the third heaven, and there saw glorious sights, and heard unspeakable words, though he exhausted human language to set forth the surpassing excellency of the love of Christ, comes at last to this point: " It passeth knowledge." Indeed it must pass knowledge. Is it not infinite? What measure, then, can be assigned to the love of Christ? If Christ be God, and as such the equal of the Father, his love is as infinite as Deity. Our love is the love of the creature ; the love of God is as great as Deity, as infinite as the self-existent I Am; it must needs therefore pass knowledge. You may wonder sometimes— and it is a wonder that will fill heaven itself with anthems of eternal praise—how such a glorious Jesus as this can ever look down from heaven upon such crawling reptiles, on such worms of earth,—what is more, upon such sinners who have provoked him over and over again by their misdeeds. Yes, that this exalted Christ, in the height of his glory, can look down from heaven his dwelling-place on such poor, miserable, wretched creatures as we, this is the mystery that fills angels with astonishment. But it is the glory of Christ thus to love; it is his special glory to take his saints to heaven, that they might be witnesses of his glory and partakers of it. Therefore, it is not because we are such crawling reptiles, that we are such un-deserving creatures, that we are so utterly unworthy of the least notice from him, we are to put away all this matchless love from us, and say, "Can Christ love one like me? Can the glorious Son of God from heaven his dwelling-place cast an eye of pity and compassion, love and tenderness upon one like me, who can scarcely at times bear with myself; who see and feel myself one of the vilest of the vile, and the worst of the worst? Oh, what must I be in the sight of the glorious Son of God?" And yet, he says, "I have loved thee with an everlasting love." This love has breadths, and lengths, and depths, and heights unknown. Its breadth exceeds all human span; its length outvies all creature line; its depth surpasses all finite measure-ment; and its height excels even angelic computation.

Now this is the very reason why this love is so adapted to us. We want a love like this; a love to spread itself over us, to come down to our lowest depths; a love that can land us safe in heaven. A love short of this would be no love at all. We should exhaust it by our sins if this love were not what it is here represented. Long ago we should have out-sinned this love, and drained it dry by our ingratitude, rebellion,

and misdoing.   But because it is what it is, love so wondrous,
so deep, so long, so broad, so high; it is because it is what it
is that it is so suitable to every want and woe.

December 21.

" Yea, though I walk through the valley of the shadow of
death, I will fear no evil: for thou art with me; thy rod and
thy staff they comfort me." —Psalm xxiii. 4.

Death, the gaunt king of terrors; Death, who with his
scythe in his resistless hand, mows down whole millions of
the human race; Death, who awaits his victims at every
corner; Death, that must soon lay you and me low in the
grave,—casts a shadow wherever he comes. He visits the
sick room, and casts a shadow there; he hangs over the
cradle, and his shadow falls on the infant's face; he comes in
the Indian letter from abroad, or with the black seal and
mourning envelope put into our hand at home; and these
tidings or these tokens cast a deep shadow over our hearts.
Indeed, where is the place where death does not cast his
shadow? where the house where this shade has never fallen?
In fact, he never comes without it. He is "the last enemy;"
he is the final fulfilment of the original curse. And though
death, to a saint of God, is stripped of its terrors, robbed of
its sting, and disarmed of its victory; though, to the expiring
believer it is but a portal of life into the mansions of eternal
bliss, yet, say what we may, the portal casts a shadow. Even
David, though full of sweet confidence that "the Lord was
his shepherd," at the very time when "his cup ran over"
with the Lord's goodness and love, calls it "the valley of the
shadow of death." "The rod and the staff" comforted him,
and he "feared no evil," but it was still "a valley," overhung
by frowning mountains and dark, overarching woods, and
"the shadow of death" was spread upon it from the entrance
to the end. And yet it is but a "shadow." To the graceless,

the Christless, the impenitent, the unbelieving, it is a substance, for the wrath of God, which burns to the lowest hell, awaits them at the end of the valley, to plunge them into the lake that burneth with fire and brimstone. But to those who die in the Lord, in the sweet enjoyment of peace through his blood, it is but a passing shadow. For them the substance died when Jesus died. It was buried in his tomb, but did not rise with him, for he destroyed it when he "abolished death and brought life and immortality to light."

December 22.

"That ye may be perfect and entire, wanting nothing."— JAMES i. 4.

THE word "perfect" in the Scripture does not mean, as applied to a saint of God, anything approaching to the usual idea of perfection, as implying spotless, sinless holiness, but one who is matured and ripened in the life of God, no longer a child but a grown man. As a tree grown to its full stature is said to have attained perfection; so when the Lord the Spirit has brought forth the work of patience in your soul, as far as regards that work you are perfect, for it is God's work in you; and so far you are "entire," that is, possessing all which that grace gives, and "wanting nothing" which that grace can communicate. To submit wholly to the will of God, and be lost and swallowed up in conformity to it, is the height of Christian perfection here below; and he that has that wants nothing, for he has all things in Christ. What, then, is the greatest height of grace to which the soul can arrive? Where did grace shine forth so conspicuously as in the Lord Jesus Christ? and where did grace manifest itself more than in the gloomy garden and on the suffering cross? Was not the human nature of Jesus more manifestly filled with the Spirit, and did not every grace shine forth in him more conspicuously in Gethsemane and on Calvary than when enraptured upon the Mount of Transfiguration? So there is more manifested grace in the heart of a saint of God who, under trial and temptation, can say, " Thy will be done," and submit himself to the chastening rod of his heavenly Father, than when he is basking in the full beams of the Sun of righteousness. How often we are mistaken in this matter; longing for enjoyment, instead of seeing that true grace makes us submit to the will of God, whether in the valley or upon the mount!

December 23.

" And let the beauty of the Lord our God be upon us: and establish thou the work of our hands upon us; yea, the work of our hands establish thou it."—Psalm xc. 17.

What is this beauty? "The beauty of the Lord our God." It is, therefore, the beauty of the God-man; the comeliness, the holiness, the perfection, and glory that ever dwell in the Son of God. Now "days of affliction, and years of evil" have marred all creature comeliness. There was a time, perhaps, when we could take some pleasure and delight in what we were, or what we vainly fancied we should be. Our own righteousness had a beauty and comeliness to us; and our religion was amiable and pleasing in our own sight. But what has become of it? Marred, marred; effectually marred. By what? "Days of affliction, and years of evil." These have effectually ruined, defaced, and polluted all creature comeliness. In a word, we were once deeply in love with self; but self has been shewn to us such a hideous monster, in so vile and despicable a light, that we have fallen out of love with him altogether; and we have seen, at times, such beauty, glory, loveliness, and suitability in the Son of God, that as we have fallen out of love with self, we have fallen in love with him. Thus as all our own beauty and our own comeliness have been marred and defaced, the beauty and comeliness of the Lord have risen in due proportion. So that this has become the desire of our soul, " ' Let the beauty of the Lord our God be upon us.' Let us stand accepted in it; let it be put upon us by the imputation of God himself; let us be clothed with it manifestly before the eyes of a heart-searching Jehovah. Let the beauty of Jesus' atoning blood, the beauty of his perfect righteousness, the beauty of his dying love, the beauty and holiness of his glorious Person be upon us, covering all our filth, guilt and shame, spreading itself over all our nakedness, sin and pollution, that when God looks upon us, he may not see us as we are, marred, defaced, and full of wounds and bruises and putrifying sores ; but may see us standing accepted in the Beloved, with ' the beauty of the Lord our God' upon us." Oh, what a matchless robe is this! It outshines angels': for it is the righteousness of God's only-begotten Son! And if we stand with " the beauty of the Lord our God" upon us, we can bid defiance to all law-charges, to all the accusations of a guilty conscience, and to all the darts from hell.

December 24.

" *Not by works of righteousness which we have done, but according to his mercy he saved us.*"—TITUS iii. 5.

To view mercy in its real character, we must *go to Calvary.* It is not sufficient to contrast the purity of God with the impurity of man. That indeed affords us some view of what mercy must be to reach the depths of the fall; a sideface of that precious attribute. But to see its full face shining upon the redeemed, we must go by faith, under the secret teachings and leadings of the Holy Ghost, to see " Immanuel, God with us," grovelling in Gethsemane's garden. We must view him naked upon the cross, groaning, bleeding, agonizing, dying. We must view Godhead and manhood united together in the Person of a suffering Jesus ; and the power of the

Godhead bearing up the suffering manhood. We must view that wondrous spectacle of love and blood, and feel our eyes flowing down in streams of sorrow, humility, and contrition at the sight, in order to enter a little into the depths of the tender mercy of God. Nothing but this can really break the sinner's heart.

> "Law and terrors do but harden,
>   All the while they work alone;
> But a sense of blood-bought pardon
>   Soon dissolves a heart of stone."

Law terrors, death and judgment, infinite purity, and eternal vengeance will not soften or break a sinner's heart. But if he is led to view a suffering Immanuel, and a sweet testimony is raised up in his conscience that those sufferings were for him—this, and this only will break his heart all to pieces. Thus, only by bringing a sweet sense of love and blood into his heart does the blessed Spirit shew a sinner some of the depths of the tender mercy of God.

December 25.

" Who, being in the form of God, thought it not robbery to be equal with God: but made himself of no reputation, and took upon him the form of a servant, and was made in the likeness of men."—PHILIPPIANS ii. 6, 7.

THE humanity of our blessed Lord was actual flesh and blood from the moment of its conception, a perfect human body, to which was united a perfect human soul ; both without sin, or else he could not be the Lamb without blemish ; both without sin, or his pure humanity would not have been that "holy thing" born of the Virgin, which should be called the Son of God. Thus he came forth as the Lamb of God, without spot or blemish. Well indeed might the Apostle say, "Great is the mystery of godliness." Here as in a glass we see the wonderful love of Jesus, that he who is the Son of God, co-equal and co-eternal with the Father and the Holy Ghost, a sharer of the Father's essence, of the Father's glory, should stoop so low to lift us up so high; that he should condescend to unite to his glorious Person our nature, flesh and blood; to wear a human body like our own; to feel as we do, to speak as we do, to walk as we do, to eat and drink and hunger and thirst and weep and sigh and mourn as we do; yet all the while be the Son of God, and should have a divine nature in as close union with human nature as our soul has with our bodily frame. We cannot tell how our soul is in union with our body. We know it is so, but how we cannot tell. We only know the fact, but we cannot explain the mode. So we cannot tell how Christ's divine nature is in union with his human nature; we know it is so by the testimony of God, by the express revelation of his word. That revelation to a believer answers all inquiry. But if any man say to me, "Can you explain the mystery of the two natures in Christ?" I ask in my turn, "Can you explain the mystery of your own existence? Can you explain to me how you are able to lift up your own hand, see with your own eye, hear with your own ear, move with your own foot? No man has ever yet been able to explain this apparently simple thing; a feat which every child can perform, but a fact which no philosopher can understand. Can you tell me how mind can act upon matter? how you wish to do a thing with your mind, and can do it instantaneously with your body? When, then, you can explain your own existence and unravel the mystery of your soul acting in union with your body, then I will allow that you may unravel the mystery of the union of Deity and humanity in the Person of the Son of God, as he lived upon earth, and as he now lives in heaven." Beautiful upon this mystery are the words of Hart:

> "How it was done we can't discuss;
> But this we know, 'twas done for us."

Happy those who can use these words without a wavering tongue!

December 26.

"Faith is the substance of things hoped for, the evidence of things not seen."—HEBREWS xi. 1.

WHAT an eminent grace is the grace of faith! I call it, sometimes, the Queen of graces; for faith seems to lead the van, though hope and love follow almost side by side. But still, faith, as the Queen, seems to go in the foremost rank, and to claim the most eminent place. Now, what is faith? That is a question of questions, for on it hangs heaven or hell. God himself has given us a clear definition of it, where he says, "faith is the *substance* of things hoped for." In other words, faith in the soul gives a realisation to the things in which we are brought to hope, takes what to most men are airy shadows, mere words and names, and gives them a substantial existence, a firm abiding place in the heart and conscience. The Apostle calls it also *" the evidence of things not seen."* That is, faith, by believing the testimony of God, is to us an internal eye, whereby we see those things, which to the natural eye are invisible. Thus adopting the Apostle's definition, we may call faith the eye of the soul, as we read, " By faith he endured, seeing him who is invisible." For it is only by faith that we see either God, or the precious things of God. It is only by faith that we feel their power. It is only by faith that we know they have a real subsistence, or that we ourselves have a substantial interest in them. But this faith is the special gift of God. It is not the exercise of any intellectual faculty. It is not the result of reasoning or argument. Nor does it spring from any historical proof. It is a special gift of God, a grace of the Spirit raised up by the power of God in the soul, and acting upon the truth of God as the blessed Spirit draws it forth. Jesus is the Author;

Jesus is the finisher of it; and we have no more, and I believe no less faith, than he himself, by his almighty power, is pleased to grant and to sustain.

But, looking at faith and some of its properties, we may branch out a little in describing how faith acts. There is an expression of the Apostle's that casts a sweet light upon the work of faith, where he says, "Unto us was the gospel preached, as well as unto them; but the word preached did not profit them, not being mixed with faith in them that heard it." Here he brings forward a special operation of faith, in that it mixes with the word of truth. And it does it thus. God the Holy Ghost applies God's word to the conscience. He thus raises up the grace of faith; this grace of faith embraces God's testimony, and so intermingles itself with this testimony that it enters into it, appropriates it, and gives it a substantial realisation and personal indwelling. See how this was done in the instance of Abram. God comes to him in the night visions, and says to him, "Fear not, I am thy shield and exceeding great reward." But Abram, in a fit of unbelief, says, "What wilt thou give me, seeing I go childless, and the steward of my house is this Eliezer of Damascus?" The Lord then takes him abroad into the air, shews him the stars of the sky, and tells him, "So shall thy seed be." Now here was the testimony of God in a certain promise to Abram's conscience; upon this, faith immediately sprang up in his soul; for we read, "Abram believed God, and it was counted unto him for righteousness." When God spake to his soul, Abram believed it by the operation of God's Spirit on his heart. So it is with every child of God. He believes what God speaks to him, he inwardly, spiritually credits it, because he feels what God the Spirit applies to his soul with power; for the same Spirit that applies God's word to his heart raises up the faith in his soul that mixes with the word applied, and thus gives the word a substantial realisation, a firm abiding place in his conscience.

December 27.

" *They shall mount up with wings as eagles.*"—Isaiah xl. 31.

It is said of the eagle, that he mounts up towards the sun; and that of all birds, he is the only one which can gaze upon the sun with unshrinking eye. So with faith in the soul. The Lord's people alone can look by faith upon the " Sun of righteousness," gaze upon a glorious Immanuel at the right hand of the Father, and see a precious Jesus ever interceding for them, and drawing them near to his bosom. And when this blessed Jesus communicates a measure of his love and blood to their consciences, and raises up and draws forth faith in his name, then the soul begins to mount up with these wings like eagles, soaring higher and higher, till it comes into the presence of God; mounting up in higher and higher circles of spiritual flight, till it penetrates into the very sanctuary of Jehovah.

Now, has not your soul thus soared sometimes as upon eagle's wings? Have there not been those communications of divine life and light, those mountains of faith, those anchorings of hope, those goings forth of love, whereby your soul was enabled to mount up and find delight in Jesus, and felt his name, love, and blood precious? Have you not mounted up too, not only in the exercise of living faith and hope, but also of heavenly affection? Sometimes we are so fastened down to this earth, this vale of tears, this waste-howling wilderness; so chained down to it, that we are like a bird with a broken wing, and cannot mount. We are swallowed up in the world, forgetting God and godliness. But are there not times and seasons when the soul is delivered from these chains and fetters, when earthly cares drop off from the mind, when our wings are new moulted, and fresh pinions as it were given, when the world and its temptations, sin and its snares are left behind, and there is a sweet mounting up in the feelings of heavenly affection? This is to "mount up with wings as eagles," and the soaring soul never ceases to mount till it comes into the very presence of the Three-One God of Israel.

December 28.

"And now, brethren, I commend you to God, and to the word of his grace, which is able to build you up, and to give you an inheritance among all them which are sanctified."— ACTS xx. 32.

NOT only did Paul " commend" the church at Ephesus " to God," but he commended them also in an especial manner " to the word of his grace." There is a difference between " grace" and " the word of his grace." Nothing but grace can save the soul; nothing but superabounding grace can blot out and hide from the view of justice our aggravated iniquities. But " the *word* of his grace" is that word which brings this grace into the heart, which communicates life and power to the soul, which the Spirit by his inward teaching and testimony seals on the conscience, and by which he reveals and sheds abroad that favour of which he testifies. This is what the Lord's people want. It is " the word of grace" that reaches their soul. It is not reading of grace in God's word that brings peace into their hearts; it is " the word of his grace," when he is pleased to speak that word with a divine power to their souls, that brings salvation with it.

Now, the Lord's people are continually in those trying states and circumstances, out of which nothing can deliver them but " the word of God's grace." If the soul have to pass through severe trials, it is not hearing of grace that can deliver it out of them. If it be beset with powerful temptations, it is not reading about grace that can break them to pieces. But "the word of his grace," when the Lord himself is pleased to speak with his own blessed lips, and apply some promise with his own divine power, supports under trial, delivers from temptation, breaks snares to pieces, makes crooked things straight and rough places plain, brings the prisoner out of the prison-house, and takes off the yoke by reason of the anointing.

December 29.

"For the preaching of the cross is to them that perish foolishness; but unto us which are saved it is the power of God." — I CORINTHIANS i. 18.

HAS the gospel ever come to you in power? If it has, it has done something for you. Has it ever, then, dispelled your many doubts and fears? Has it ever made Jesus precious to your soul; ever brought with it light, life, liberty, and love; ever given you access to the bosom of God; ever communicated that spirit of holy boldness and filial confidence, whereby, as a successful wrestler, you were enabled to prevail with God, and get a blessing out of his hands and heart? But it is useless to talk of power when nothing is done. A manufacturer says to an engineer, "I want you to construct me an engine of a hundred horse power." But if the engineer make the engine, and upon trial it be found only of ninety, and the work require a hundred horse power, the engine is so far useless. Now, what would his employer say to him but, "What a mistake you have made! I ordered an engine of a hundred horse power, and this is only ninety. It will not do the work I want. Take it away." So in grace. We want a power that can move certain weights; the weight of sin, for instance, from off a guilty conscience; killing fears of death and hell; the burden of unbelief; the heavy load of carnality; many grievous temptations that make the soul cry,

"Lord, I am oppressed, undertake for me." What heavy weights are there to be lifted off; what huge stones to be rolled away from the sepulchre; the world to be overcome; lusts and passions to be crucified; the old man of sin mortified; Satan to be defeated and put to flight! But besides all these weights to be removed, and enemies to be overcome, there is the soul to be saved, heaven to be brought near, hell put out of sight, the law to be for ever silenced, death to be robbed of its sting, and the grave of its victory, and an eternal course of glory to be won. Oh, what a mighty work has to be done in us and for us—a work which no man ever has done or can do for himself!

December 30.

"A living stone, disallowed indeed of men, but chosen of God, and precious."—I PETER ii. 4.

THOUGH "disallowed of men," the Lord Jesus Christ is "chosen of God;" and God, I speak it with reverence, cannot make an unwise choice. To think *that*, would be to attribute folly to the Most High. He is "chosen of God," because he alone was fitted for the work. It would have crushed an archangel to bear what Jesus bore. No bright angel, nor glorious seraph, no created being, however exalted, could have borne the load of sin; and therefore none but God's own Son, not by office, but by eternal generation, the Son of the Father in truth and love, could bear the weight of imputed sin and guilt. As Hart says,

> "Such loads of guilt were on Him put,
> He could but just sustain the weight."

But he was "chosen of God" that he might be Zion's Representative, Zion's Sinbearer, and Zion's glorious Head; that there might be a foundation for the Church to rest upon with all her miseries, all her sins, all her sorrows, all her base backslidings and idolatries, all her weight of woe and depths of guilt. It need be a *strong* foundation to bear this Church, so loaded with degradation, ignominy, and shame ! God's own Son, and none else in heaven or in earth, could bear all this. "Look unto me, and be ye saved, for I am God, and *there is none else.*"

He was "chosen of God" in eternity, in the divine councils, that he might be a Mediator. He was "chosen" to become man; chosen to become the Rock of Ages, Zion's resting-place, harbour, anchorage, and home. Jesus was ever, therefore, and ever will be, unspeakably "precious" to the Father's heart. Man despises him, but God honours him; man disallows him, but God values him as his co-equal Son. God, therefore, not only values him as his "fellow," and has chosen him to be the Mediator, but he is in his eyes unspeakably "precious;" precious in his Deity, precious in his humanity, precious in his blood, precious in his obedience, precious in his sufferings, precious in his death, precious in his resurrection, precious in his ascension to God's right hand, precious in the eyes of God as the Great High Priest over the house of God, and the only Mediator between God and man. Is he not worthy of all your trust, all your confidence, all your hope, and all your acceptance? Look where we will, he is our only hope. Look at the world, what can you reap from that but a harvest of sorrow? Look at everything men call good and great; all that man highly values, good perhaps for time, but valueless for eternity. Perhaps no one could put a higher value than I upon what man naturally regards as good and great, especially upon human learning, and attainments in knowledge and science. Yet I have seen them as compared with eternity, to be but breath and smoke—a vapour that passeth away and is no more seen. But the things of eternity, the peace of God in the heart, the work of the Spirit upon the soul, with all the blessed realities of salvation—these are not like the airy mists of time, the vapours that spring out of earth and return to earth again, but are enduring and eternal, " an inheritance incorruptible, and undefiled, and that fadeth not away."

December 31.

" My counsel shall stand, and I will do all my pleasure."— ISAIAH xlvi. 10.

THERE is one grand idea running through the whole of Scripture from Genesis to Revelation; and this one grand idea runs through every part of the sacred page, and, like a golden band, unites the whole together. What is this one grand thought? God has many thoughts as well as we, for he tells us that " the thoughts of his heart stand to all generations." But we read also in the same verse of " the counsel of the Lord, which standeth for ever;" and elsewhere of his " working all things after the counsel of his own will " (Psalm xxxiii. 11; Ephes. i. 11). Thus in the mind of God, as well as in the mode of his subsistence, there is unity and variety. There is his one thought, and his many thoughts; for though his thoughts are many, his counsel is but one; and this counsel is the exaltation and glorification of his dear Son. It may be as well briefly to trace this unity of thought and the variety of its expression. We see it, then, first expressed in the creation of the first man, when God made him " in his own image, after his own likeness." There was the expression of God's one thought; for Adam the first was a type of Adam the second, and as Christ was by lineal descent " the son of Adam," there was a foreview in the creation of the first man of the incarnation of God's dear Son, who is the brightness of his glory and the express image of his Person. Now next observe how all things were put under Adam's feet, and he thus made the visible head of creation. Read this exaltation of Adam in the light of Psalm viii, and you will see how the inspired Psalmist, as interpreted by the Apostle (Heb: ii. 7–9),

viewed Adam, in having all things put under his feet, as a
type of Jesus, whom God has crowned with glory and honour,
set him over the works of his hands, and put all things in
subjection under his feet.   Look next at the first promise
given after the fall, that the seed of the woman should bruise
the serpent's head.   There we have God's one thought again
expressed, his dominant counsel in the incarnation of his dear
Son, as the seed of the woman, to bruise Satan's head. Look
at Noah preserved in the ark with his family when the rest
of the world was swept away by the deluge, that from the
loins of Adam might come the promised seed.   Take the
case of Abraham, called by a special calling, that in him and
his seed all the nations of the earth might be blessed.   Here
we have again God's one thought.   Take, again, the whole
of the Levitical dispensation.   Every rite, every sacrifice, every
type, every ordinance, all still bear the same stamp of God's
one thought, and indeed every part of Scripture is but an ex-
position of this one thought of God's heart, of this one counsel
of his eternal will.   The word of God is a perfect mystery to
us, and we see no beauty or harmony in the various books of
either the Old Testament or the New until we see the mind
of God in it, gather up God's thoughts, and especially that
grand thought which I have spoken of as binding the whole
together, viz. the exaltation of his dear Son to his own right
hand as the promised reward of his sufferings and death, and
the glorious result of his resurrection and ascension up to the
courts of bliss.

INDEX.